HOW TO START A MAGAZINE

HOW TO START A MAGAZINE

James B. Kobak

M. Evans and Company, Inc.
New York

M. Evans and Company, Inc.
216 East 49th Street
New York, New York 10017

ISBN: 0-87131-927-6

Book design and type formatting by Bernard Schleifer

Printed in the United States of America

9 8 7 6 5 4 3 2 1

Contents

Part III: The Various Operations in Publishing a Magazine

Part IV: Making the Most of a Magazine's Strong Brand

Appendices: Facts about the Business and Sources of Information

To Hope, my bride of sixty years,
without whom nothing is possible—
and with whom nothing is impossible.

PREFACE: How This Book Is Organized

THE MAGAZINE BUSINESS is not like any other. Everything is dependent on developing a creative product that the public will want to read. The only equipment needed is some paper, a pencil, and a few computers. As one publisher put it, "My inventory goes down the elevator every night." A magazine is entirely the result of the intellectual efforts of a handful of people.

Chances are that many of you will have little familiarity with the way things are done, the organizations in the field, where to get information, or the terminology used.

If you have worked in publishing, you probably know some parts of the business, but not every aspect. And, even if you have been involved in starting a magazine before, every magazine is different and every start-up is different. While some of your experience may be helpful, you will find other aspects to be quite different.

It is impossible to detail every step someone who is starting a particular magazine must consider. I have tried to explain how the business operates and the process that should be followed. That process is the same regardless of the nature and subject matter of the magazine.

The text is divided into four parts, plus appendices:

I. BASICS ABOUT MAGAZINES: Here we examine just what a magazine is, why magazines exist, why there is a constant need for new magazines, the size of the field, the current situation of the industry and its bright future, what makes for a successful magazine, the life cycle that all magazines go through, and who actually starts most successful new magazines.

II. WHAT IS INVOLVED IN STARTING A MAGAZINE: The logical sequence of the steps involved in starting magazines is explained, starting with the key to success—the editorial content that people want—and discussing how to test the concept for a new magazine, produce a pilot issue, develop a business plan, assemble a staff, raise money, and make it work.

III. THE VARIOUS OPERATIONS IN PUBLISHING A MAGAZINE: A discussion of how the magazine business is carried on, beginning with the organization of a magazine company and its various departments—editorial, advertising, circulation, and production—how things are done in each area and how the areas interact with each other, the methods of keeping track of what's going on, and how to plan for the future.

IV. MAKING THE MOST OF THE STRONG BRAND ESTABLISHED BY A MAGAZINE: How the warmth, aura, and personality of a magazine can lead to the extension of its activities into other areas—database marketing, international, book publishing, the Internet, and custom publishing.

APPENDICES: FACTS ABOUT THE BUSINESS AND SOURCES OF INFORMATION: Including the recent history of consumer and business magazines, organizations and publications serving the industry, other sources of information, major suppliers and consultants, glossary of terms used, and postal classifications and rates.

This book is not intended to tell you all about magazine publishing and how to do it, but, hopefully, it will put you on the track to understanding how things are done—and help you avoid trying to reinvent the business—and, possibly, avoid a few missteps and heartaches.

* * *

While I am a firm believer in the equality of the sexes in business and other organizations, I deplore the results of this from a grammatical standpoint. I have reluctantly adopted the word "their" to indicate either the singular or plural, but cannot stand what the use of "he or she," "him or her," and "his or hers" does to the flow of text, so I hope the ladies will forgive me when I use only the male gender at times.

I have also broken other rules of grammar by capitalizing certain words in order to more surely identify what I refer to, such as "The System" when talking about the way single-copy sales are handled, "Business Plan" when referring to that for a new magazine, "Launch Scenario" when discussing the start-up, and probably some other such items.

You may find acronyms, abbreviations, and other simplifications often used. The principal ones are:

MPA	Magazine Publishers of America. The association of consumer magazines.
ABM	American Business Media. The association of business magazines.
DMA	Direct Marketing Association.
SRDS	Standard Rate & Data Service. A monthly in consumer and business volumes listing the major magazines striving for advertising. It gives considerable information about their circulation, advertising rates, and other data.
ABC	Audit Bureau of Circulation. One of the two principal organizations auditing circulation.
BPA	The other principal organization auditing circulation.
PIB	Publisher's Information Bureau. A subsidiary of MPA that measures the advertising space and income of the major consumer magazines.
BIN	Business Information Network. A subsidiary of ABM that measures the advertising space and income of the major business magazines.
TV	Television, including cable.
The Net or the Web	The Internet.
Postal Service	The United States Postal Service that distributes the mail in this country.
Ad Age	The magazine *Advertising Age*
PCH	Publishers Clearing House. A major direct mail subscription agent.
AFP	American Family Plan. The other major direct mail subscription agent.
Edit	editorial
Ad	advertising
Circ	circulation
Subs	subscriptions
Ad Rep	An independent advertising representative
P & L	Profit-and-loss statement
G & A	General and administrative expenses
T & E	Travel and entertainment expenses

You may also find words in the text with which you do not identify. I have tried to keep these to a minimum, but there is an extensive glossary, which I believe explains them.

INTRODUCTION: Some Immutable Laws of Magazine Publishing

1. THERE IS NO MAGAZINE BUSINESS. Every magazine is in a different business. It has different readers and different advertisers. If you hadn't noticed, *Vogue* is not very much like *Playboy*—and neither resembles *Aviation Week* or *Billboard.* Because of this, what works for one magazine rarely works for another. And advice from the publisher of one magazine may be counterproductive for another.

2. The first law of publishing—The less you give them, the more you charge. Consider the *Los Angeles Times*—it has oodles of very large pages and costs $.50 per issue. *U.S. News,* a weekly, costs $2.95. *Fortune,* a monthly, costs $4.95. But the weekly newsletter, *MIN*, which sends you just 8 to 10 pages, costs $13.90 per issue.

3. There are ways things are done in this business, as in every other, that may not be the best way—or even an intelligent way. But, when you are trying to start a magazine, you shouldn't be the one to try a completely different system. You will just add difficulties to an already very hard process. Please stay with the known methods, good or bad though they may be.

4. The reader is King, no matter what else you think. He decides everything. I probably will say that in many different ways throughout this book.

5. A magazine doesn't care how it is delivered to the reader—whether on the newsstand, through the mail, with the daily newspaper, by fax, on the Internet, or by thought transference.

6. The media loves the media. Just as magazines love to discuss what is going on in other media, so do newspapers, TV, cable, radio, the Internet, and all other media love to discuss magazines. This makes it relatively simple to develop public relations and other such programs for magazines. On the other hand, when the other media discuss a magazine's problems, it also gives the public the idea that magazine publishing is a much riskier business than it really is.

7. Testing is a way of life in the magazine business. Since magazines appeal to the public—and since they are delivering copies on an ongoing basis—it is possible to test most everything before committing to permanent ways of doing things.

Part I:
Basics about Magazines

CHAPTER I

The Wonderful World of Magazines

AT THIS MOMENT the magazine business in the United States—and throughout the world—is in close to the healthiest condition in its history. Until recently, there was just about the *most* of everything the industry has ever had:

- The most consumer magazines
- The most business magazines
- The most publishing companies
- The most advertising pages
- The most advertising dollars
- The most single-copy sales
- The most subscriptions
- The highest advertising rates
- The highest circulation prices
- The most revenue
- The most profits

This happy situation has been temporarily derailed by the Recession of 2000. History, however, has shown that the magazine industry has recovered from every previous recession to become even stronger than before.

At the time of this writing the dot.com disaster has taken place, we are in the Recession of 2000, and it is shortly after the terrorism of September 11. All this has resulted in a slow-down in the growth of the magazine field, but has not affected its basic strength. Some data which indicates this is shown in appendix A, "Recent History of Magazines."

History has shown that the magazine industry experiences a sharp decline in advertising some 6 to 12 months after the start of a recession and starts to recover 6 to 18 months after the recession ends. This would indicate that the current one started in the third quarter of 2000 and that magazines began to feel the major effects during the first quarter of 2001. The drop in advertising in this case has been particularly severe in those fields where the dot.com business was important.

The lag in advertising happens very quickly because it it so easy to cut advertising versus other costs, even though good sense dictates that this should be the last item that should be reduced. And the lag in recovery exists because it takes time to reinstate a full program.

Because of the great number and variety of magazines, as well as the ease of entering the field, there are no really good statistics about the overall size of the industry or its growth. Some of the data available is discussed in greater detail in appendix A, "Recent History of Magazines."

What is apparent from the information available, which primarily covers the largest, most meaningful, and presumably most successful magazines, is that there has been enormous and continuous growth in the industry since World War II. Here are some indications of this:

Consumer Magazines

2000	1990	1980	1970	1960	1950
Magazines listed in SRDS, including farm magazines					
2,787	2,135	1,456	1,197	759	634
Advertising measured by PIB—Includes only the major national magazines					
Magazines included					
248	167	102	89	79	84
Pages (thousands)					
287	172	115	77	75	68
Dollars (millions)					
17,665	6,758	2,846	1,169	830	430
Circulation reported by ABC—Does not include those audited by other organizations or those whose circulation is not audited					
Magazines included					
836	627	446	339	298	250
Circulation (millions)					
379	366	281	245	189	147

Business Magazines

2000	1995	1990	1980	1970	1960
Magazines listed in SRDS					
5,330	4,208	2,924	2,376	2,310	1,772
Advertising estimated by ABM Dollars (millions)					
5,503	4,077	1,495	836	535	234

Note that the above figures are incomplete, and in some cases may suffer a little from my interpretation. They only measure the most commercially viable properties. Not included are some major magazines and lots of smaller ones that do not take advertising, some that are published less frequently than quarterly, and others that companies and other organizations put out for their own use.

These figures leave us with a number of questions:

- If things are so great now, how did they get that way? Can they keep up in a future fraught with the unknown?
- Will the public decide that it just doesn't want one more magazine—or to pay one more cent for the ones it reads?
- Will advertisers find that the Internet and cable channels are better advertising vehicles than magazines? Can they afford constantly increasing rates?
- Will the public find that reading from a printed page is passe versus getting its information and entertainment from the radio, a TV tube, the computer monitor, or some hand-held device?
- Will the cost of paper, printing, and distribution make the publishing of magazines on paper uneconomic?
- Will the Postal Service make it impossible to get magazines delivered in a timely fashion and at a reasonable cost?

My answer is: For the foreseeable future, we will continue to see major growth in the magazine industry—in number of publications, in circulation, and in advertising, but that the delivery methods may change. Ideas, information, and entertainment don't care how they are delivered.

Print on Paper Will Be the Major Way People Access Their Magazines

Being able to hold material in your hand, to transport it wherever you go, to flip through for the information you want, to discard what does not interest you, to skip around through the pages, to save those parts you want to keep—the advantages of print on paper go on and on.

Habits have been established since the invention of the printing press. We have grown up learning to read from books, magazines, and newspapers. This will not change no matter what improvements the electronic media may develop.

Magazines Exist Because People Have Interests—and Want to Read about Them

As time goes on, several factors tend to expand the interests people have:

- More and better education. When you realize that some 88% of our population has completed high school and a great many go on to college, with over 28% graduating, you can see that they learn about a great many things they might never have heard about with lesser education.
- Greater affluence. With more disposable income,

the average person is able to pursue his interests, no matter how diverse, to a much greater extent.

- Growth of travel. Anyone can—and does—go anywhere now. This is a very recent phenomenon. We all now see things that we may not have even heard about before—all over the world, and possibly in outer space.
- Continued technological changes. These, in addition to changes in the ways information is delivered, require explanation and understanding by the public in general.
- Most important: the continued expansion of all kinds of media.

It started with Gutenberg and movable type. This gave us the ability to read books, broadsides, newspapers, direct mail, and, of course, magazines.

Then came the radio—and, after that, magazines' best friend—television—to broaden our horizons. You may have heard that television caused the demise of a number of major magazines and was the magazine field's biggest enemy during its great growth period from 1945 to 1970. This is an erroneous concept based on the idea that TV took a great deal of advertising from magazines. Actually, the enormous prices paid for TV time expanded advertisers' horizons about what they could spend for all kinds of advertising—and the magazine industry had one of its greatest growth periods during those same years. At the same time TV broadened peoples' interests and helped increase both the number of magazines and the amount of readership.

Since then TV has been greatly expanded through the many—and seemingly unlimited—number of cable and satellite channels. It has become the source of even more interests for the viewers, and has brought with it the need for even more magazines.

And the Internet—with all those new interests just a touch away! While it is still too early to try to completely quantify its effect on magazines, it is already obvious that it will continue to greatly enhance the industry.

This history of continued growth, of course, does not mean that any one magazine will continue to be healthy. Each has its life cycle, which, once again, depends on peoples' interests. For the industry as a whole, however, there will be a constant need for new magazines, no matter what delivery method is used.

Why the Magazine Industry Will Continue to Succeed

Technical Changes Have Continuously Improved Magazine Operations

The computer has enabled magazines to make gigantic leaps in fulfilling subscriptions, in pinpointing where circulation prospects may be, in selling subscriptions, in letting us design specific magazines for specific readers, in streamlining the single-copy sales operations—and in countless other ways.

Printing and allied operations have been revolutionized in recent years. New web presses turn out copies with superb full-color quality at speeds previously unheard of—and can now also be used for short-run magazines. Layouts, typesetting, and other editorial operations are now performed at the publishing house where they belong, instead of by outside suppliers. Means have been perfected whereby it is no longer even necessary to use film at any point in the process, let alone engravings, color separations, and other hard copy.

Paper manufacturers have been able to develop ever lighter-weight paper as well as recycled paper with fine qualities of color reproduction and opacity. Advances in binding techniques can literally enable a reader to design his own magazine. A publisher can now pick and choose the pages that are sent to each reader. Satellite printing plants have made it possible to print in several places simultaneously to get speedier delivery at less cost.

Distribution of copies has been improved as publishers have taken more and more of the cost of delivery from the Postal Service by delivering copies that are not only in ZIP code order, but actually by carrier route. (A caveat here—the very future of the Postal Service as we know it is in doubt with the growth of e-mail.)

The sale of single copies (so-called newsstand) has in recent years been taken over primarily by the retailers, where it logically belongs, in place of the very awkward and wasteful national distributor-wholesaler-retailer system that had existed for so long.

A Magazine Doesn't Care How It Is Distributed

As of this writing, magazines are printed en masse and distributed to their readers either as single copies through newsstands or through the mail and other mass distribution channels.

Efforts to develop "magazines of the Air" through radio and TV have not achieved any real success, nor have efforts to develop magazines using the Internet.

Some other delivery systems, however, may be developed in the future, perhaps using the Internet, or facsimile, or e-book methodology.

Readers Love Their Magazines

Publishers don't realize how much. When magazines go out of business, a handful of readers ask for their subscription money back, but the publisher gets many more letters telling him how much readers liked the magazine and that they hope it will be back soon.

Consider that readers actually are able to find the magazines they want on our overcrowded newsstands. They obviously know what they want to read and are willing to search for it. Adding to their fun is seeing the great variety of publications available.

Subscribers stick to their magazines, in spite of the way they are sometimes treated in the fulfillment process—the first issue coming weeks after it has been ordered, with billing and renewal series that are cold, impersonal, and full of unreadable jargon (see chapter 44, "Fulfillment: My Good Customer J002684RO6JIBD23C.")

Perhaps the best indication that readers are loyal fans is this: Magazine prices have been raised and raised in recent years with very little complaint. The public still wants its magazines.

Advertisers Love Their Magazines

Even though they may not often say it. Consider the constantly increasing flow of pages and dollars into magazines, but also how advertisers react when a magazine reduces its circulation.

I'll never forget the time *McCall's* was having trouble making profits, that was back in 1971 or so. It had circulation of some eight million then. There was no way this much circulation could be maintained without inordinate expense year after year. *McCall's* announced that the circulation would be reduced to seven million—and then held their breath to see what the advertisers would think. Simple: they said "We need you and would rather have you with seven million than not at all." Since then, of course, lots of magazines have reduced their circulations without adverse reactions from advertisers.

Advertisers also recognize that television and other video devices are far more expensive than magazine advertising. The chances are that they will remain that way, even with all those new channels. Remember, there is no "sandlot" television programming. You have to spend lots to develop the quality of programs the public is used to. The same is true of the Net.

CHAPTER 2

Just What Is a Magazine?

I KNOW WHAT a magazine is when I see one—and what is not a magazine when I see one of those, too. But in the end, trying to develop a precise definition is about as useful as arguing about what a democracy is or how many angels can dance on the head of a pin. It is not worth the trouble.

Here are some of the criteria I use:

- It is printed on paper.
- It is issued periodically—at least four times a year.
- It contains news, entertainment, and/or information that is of interest to a general audience or to an audience of people with special interests.
- It is circulated to people who are interested in the subject matter it covers.
- Its circulation may be paid or not paid.
- It may—or may not—carry advertising.
- It can be published by individuals, commercial companies, newspapers, associations and other not-for-profit organizations, or governmental or other bodies.
- It can be delivered through the mail, through the sale of single copies, through newspaper and other alternate delivery methods, by fax, on the Internet, or through other means.
- It can be in the format of a newspaper, a book, or other type of publication.
- It is larger than a pamphlet.
- It may—or may not—have the making of a profit as a goal.

What it is not:

- A comic book, although it may contain comics.
- A puzzle book, although it may contain puzzles.
- A catalog, or a magalog, although it may contain catalog-type pages.
- An almanac, although it may carry material that could be carried in an almanac.
- A directory, although it may carry material that could be carried in a directory.
- A program, unless it is issued on a periodic basis.
- An advertisement or sponsored for one organization in magazine format.
- A newsletter, although a newsletter may have some of the characteristics of a magazine, including carrying advertising.
- An internal house organ.

Types of Magazines

There are several major types of magazines:

CONSUMER MAGAZINES—Those that are published for the general public, usually for information, news, entertainment, and other such interests. There are several major types of consumer magazines:

- **General Interest**—Those which might be of interest to anyone, such as the *Reader's Digest, Entertainment Weekly, National Geographic,* and *The New Yorker.*
- **Newsweeklies**—Devoted to bringing the news to readers, such as *Time, Newsweek,* and *U.S. News & World Report.*

- **Special Interest**—The vast majority of consumer magazines, covering fields from boating to babies to sports, and almost everything else you can imagine.

- **Regional Magazines**—City magazines, alternative newsweeklies, and others devoted to activities in specific geographic areas.

BUSINESS MAGAZINES—Often called trade magazines, useful for those in business, the professions, government, or not-for-profit organizations. These are of several different types:

- **General Business**—Covering the whole economy, such as *Business Week, Fortune,* and *Industry Week.*

- **Special Business Interests**—The vast majority of business magazines, devoted to specific industries, professions, or other business sectors from automotive to legal to toys and hobbies. Within the larger special business interest fields there often are subcategories:

  - Umbrella magazines covering an entire industry, such as *Advertising Age*.
  - Splinter magazines covering parts of an industry, such as *Catalog Age* or *Brand Marketing*.
  - New product tabloids confined to news and ads about new products, such as *Industrial Equipment News*.
  - Professional journals, mostly covering areas of the medical field, but also in other disciplines such as engineering and chemistry.

FARM MAGAZINES—Historically farm magazines have been carried as a separate category because many of the largest magazines were devoted to serving farm families from both a business and a lifestyle standpoint. With the decline of the family farm, most farm magazines today would be considered in the business classification—see appendix A, "Recent History of Magazines."

OVERLAPPING MAGAZINES—The categories above are not always as distinct as they may sound. For instance, some in the general business, computer and some other areas have readers who are in both the consumer and business categories.

CHAPTER 3

Is Communication Wanted?

THIS IS OFTEN a basic problem. You have a consuming interest in a subject, but it really may not be anything that others want communication about, even if they have an interest in the same subject. If that's the case, there is no reason to publish anything.

Consider the exercycle. Millions of them have been sold (although the number in use is in question), but I doubt if their owners are panting for a magazine about them. What would you write about? How to oil them? The best TV programs to watch while riding? Where to store them when you stop using them three months after you buy them?

Or commuting. Lots of us do it. But what good would it do to try to communicate the best way of accomplishing it? Or to tell you what to read while you are on the train or subway? (There is however, a way of folding a newspaper which only experienced commuters know, which I am willing to share with you.)

While these may be extreme examples, there are an awful lot of other subjects that some people thought needed magazines, only to find to their dismay that there were just not enough other people interested in the subject—or enough to write about—to provide the basis for a magazine.

CHAPTER 4

Why a Magazine—Why Not Something Else?

For reasons that I really do not understand, it seems that, when people have something they want to communicate about, they think in terms of starting a magazine. In many cases, other forms of communications may be infinitely better.

Consider my friend Arthur Lipper, the former publisher of *Success* magazine, who wanted to start a magazine addressed to the parents of gifted and talented children. Certainly a worthy thought. But a magazine didn't seem to be the way to go about it. In the first place, there probably would never be much circulation because only a small percentage of the population has children who are really gifted or talented (although all parents believe their children fit that description). But, beyond this, there really are not many advertisers who would want to reach these parents—only book publishers, specialized schools, and the like.

The answer, of course, was to abandon the magazine idea and publish a newsletter. It has prospered and benefited the parents of these kids ever since.

By the same token, many subjects lend themselves better to books, where they can be treated at length and in depth.

And, while I don't like to admit it, there are some things that really cannot be adequately handled on the printed page, but that require living, breathing, moving examples to make their point.

Here's one example, which involved the Boy Scouts—and, in this case, did not concern a magazine.

As you probably know, the Scouts have what I consider a subversive group called the Cub Scouts. (I consider them subversive because they meet at the home of their Den Mother once a week for about four hours—and make her life miserable as they wrestle, scream, run, jump, and do just about everything else except tackle the project for the week.)

The Scouts, in their infinite wisdom, issue the Den Mother a booklet that describes the various projects (several hundred of them) that can be tackled—and gives detailed instructions of how to build kites one week, take a trip on the train the next, etc.

The one thing they never mention is how to keep order during the Den meeting.

How much better it would be to have a half-hour TV presentation once a week with suggestions about how to handle the kids while they are in your house for the afternoon. Perhaps then the boys themselves would be able to complete the projects rather than ending with the distraught Den Mother—and a reluctant Den Father who has had to finish off the project for the boys. And then maybe all the boys could become Webelos, whatever they are.

CHAPTER 5

What Is a Successful Magazine?

THROUGHOUT THIS BOOK I will be discussing the question of whether a magazine has been successful or not—in many instances I will probably discuss whether it can "work" or not. In my lexicon a magazine works when it has been profitable from a financial standpoint.

I well recognize that many publishers and companies may also have other motives for publishing magazines, often to further their causes—religious, political, personal, do good, commercial—and that they may not be interested in having financially prosperous magazines if they believe they are accomplishing their other objectives.

I, however, have what may seem to many to be a peculiar approach. If a magazine cannot produce enough income through its circulation, advertising, and other commercial sources to be able to make a profit, the chances are that it is not a good enough field or a good enough product to be published—and probably is not accomplishing the other objectives its publishers have for it either.

Financial success signifies that the magazine has established an audience that finds it interesting and useful, and that the magazine format is an effective way of communicating its particular message. This is the premise of this book.

CHAPTER 6

Magazines Are Not Just Needed—They Must Be Wanted

I HAVE THE impression that every man, woman, and child in the United States has an idea for the one magazine that is "needed" by the American public.

The word "needed" is usually used by those who want to start a magazine, because they think it is a much stronger word than "wanted." This is backward. Just because *you* think a magazine is needed has no relation to whether anyone *wants* it. If no one wants it, there won't be any magazine. It's like trying to get kids to eat tapioca pudding because they need it: all that will happen is that they will pour it into a drawer when you aren't looking, to be found many weeks later.

Who ever thought that there would be a *need* for magazines servicing such strange and diverse areas as these—yet they exist because people *wanted* them:

- *Teddy Bear & Friends*—For those who collect and make teddy bears and other stuffed animals
- *Apple Seeds*—Featuring information about health education and benefits
- *Tattoo*—Covering the world of tattooing
- *Twins*—Parenting information about multiples
- *Freeze*—For adventure skiers
- *Ferrets*—For those with these animals as pets
- *Pulp*—Covering Japanese media

Magazines do not exist in and of themselves. They exist only because people have interests and *want* communication about those interests. The number of magazines has been continuously increasing only because the number of those interests has been increasing, not because there is a *need*.

In the area of business magazines, the growth has come about because of new inventions, developments of whole new and large industries, increasing globalization of business, and new ways of doing old things. Consider that, not too many years ago, there were no such things as PCs, genetics, fiber optics, scanners in supermarkets, space exploration, the Web, and so much more.

CHAPTER 7

Magazine Publishing Is Not a Management-Intensive Business,

Including Lessons to Be Learned from the Curtis Publishing Company

MAGAZINE PUBLISHING involves three functions:

1. Developing an editorial product that will appeal to whatever public you are after—a unique and highly creative task;
2. Marketing that product to the public (commonly called circulation), also a unique and highly creative task;
3. Marketing the product through highly sophisticated selling methods to a small number of advertisers who want to reach the public that reads each specific magazine.

These three tasks call for three different kinds of creative people—all highly skilled, well trained, and very motivated. To be good at any of these jobs does not require management skills of more than an elementary degree. In the process of publishing a single magazine, there is no requirement that stresses management. Nor is there any natural upward route or training program involving management skills, except in the very largest companies.

This is as it should be. Magazine publishing is not a management-intensive business. Not only that, but overmanagement or overorganization of people in any of these three key areas tends to stifle the creativity, the motivation, and the fun of the jobs they are trying to do.

The optimum size for a magazine's staff will depend, of course, on the type of magazine. A typical monthly special-interest consumer magazine probably operates most smoothly with somewhere between 20 and 30 people. This gives a staff big enough for specialists in the various areas of publishing, but keeps it small enough so that an informal and collegial management style will be most effective.

The optimum size for other types of magazines will, of course, vary with their nature. If circulation is controlled rather than paid, the same type of circulation skills will not be needed. If it is a business magazine catering to a small, closely knit field, only a handful of highly knowledgeable people may be needed. If it is staff-written, more editorial people will be required. A news magazine, of course, will need a much larger staff.

A small, highly skilled group—all dedicated to the specific magazine itself—represents the optimum for a magazine publisher.

The Curtis Publishing Company

One of the most glorious chapters in the history of American publishing involved the Curtis Publishing Company with its stable of magazines—*Saturday Evening Post, Ladies' Home Journal, American Home, Holiday,* and *Jack & Jill.*

On the other hand, the demise of the *Post* as it had been, and the breakup of Curtis, was one of the saddest chapters because it could have been avoided.

I am not talking about personalities, although there were plenty of those as Otto Friedrich discussed in his book, *Decline and Fall,* but rather am discussing the core of the problems—a basic strategic management error that should be avoided in running a magazine business, or any other business for that matter.

I had the opportunity over a number of years to work with several companies that thought seriously about buying Curtis. This gave me a chance to review its history, operations, and potential in depth.

Vertical Integration—The Management Concept

Without going into precise historial details about why, it seemed wise to the operators of the company over the years to adopt the concept of vertical integration—meaning controlling all stages of the business from raw materials to the consumer.

The classic reasons for this theory are:

1. To ensure adequate supplies,
2. To avoid paying profits to other manufacturers and/or middlemen,
3. To ensure quality.

The problems, all of which beset Curtis, are:

1. Flexibility is lost.
2. Large investments are needed.
3. The businesses are not similar and require different management talents.
4. Management becomes too preoccupied to run the basic business well.

The Curtis Empire

In the early 1960s Curtis consisted of:

1. Five magazines,
2. A small book-publishing operation,
3. A very large printing operation near Philadelphia,
4. Two paper manufacturing plants in Pennsylvania,
5. Land with large timber reserves in Pennsylvania and Canada,
6. Computerized circulation fulfillment utilizing first-generation General Electric computers (which had been purchased rather than rented),
7. A large engraving plant,
8. A circulation company with several subsidiaries that sold Curtis magazines and those of other publishers in several ways:
   a. As a national distributor for single copies and paperback books
   b. Subscriptions through a school plan
   c. Subscriptions through a door-to-door field force
   d. Subscriptions through a catalog agency
   e. Subscriptions to Curtis magazines by direct mail and other standard methods

As you can see, just about every step was covered from the growing of trees for paper to the sale of copies to the ultimate consumer. At the high point in 1960, sales amounted to $260 million (about $1.5 billion today), all but about $20 million from the magazines.

As adjuncts to all this, the company owned substantial amounts of land and had some handsome buildings in downtown Philadelphia, plus lots of equipment. It also had a fleet of picturesque electric trucks that could be seen hauling paper, magazines, and other things around Philadelphia.

Extensive support and management capabilities were necessary. In 1960 more than 400 of its 11,000 employees were in the accounting department.

A Few Poor Decisions in Addition

Timber Reserves

Curtis owned 262,000 acres of land in Canada and Pennsylvania that were covered with timber. Unfortuately, they did not realize that it was almost entirely hardwood, which is good for making furniture, but is not suited for paper making and could not be useful in the magazine operations. (As an investment, the Canadian land, surprisingly, turned out to be valuable because of mineral deposits that were later found.)

Paper-Making Plants

All the Curtis magazines, except *Jack & Jill,* had large page sizes. When the crisis came, one way substantial sums of money could have been saved was to reduce them to standard size (as so many other magazines have done). Unfortunately, however, this would have required extensive changes to the paper-making machines at a cost of many millions of dollars. The plants, too, were old and in need of modernizing, so their sale value was minimal.

Printing Plant

While the printing facilities were relatively modern, the presses, like the paper machines, were suited only for large-size magazines. Rebuilding them would have been very expensive. From a possible sale standpoint, the plant had little value because it was useless without the assurance of the continuation of the magazines.

Engraving Facilities

The engraving plant was out of date and its products were not up to the standards of the industry. Substantial investment would have been required to bring it up to snuff. But it, too, had little value without assurance of the continuation of the magazines.

Subscription Fulfillment

The first-generation General Electric computers had been purchased some years back (from GE instead of other companies because it was their largest advertiser) and were hardly a match for the third-generation machines that were in use at the time. GE by that time had gone out of the business.

They were programmed in a language that was not good for fulfillment. Costs were very high. It was difficult to make savings without extensive reprogramming and equipment updating.

Circulation Company

Curtis Circulation was a large and highly profitable company that did a good job both for Curtis and for other publishers. It had a substantial market value and ultimately was sold (although not, in my opinion, for as much as it was worth).

The problem with the Circulation Company was its success. It was operated as an independent entity. It was in charge of the acqusition of all circulation for the Curtis magazines, but there was very little contact or planning in conjunction with the publishing operations

Circulation was often obtained without regard to the effect on the bottom line. At times the circulation effort was zigging while a magazine was zagging. (The schizophrenic problem discussed in other places in this book.)

Management Myopia

Probably even more important in the breakdown of the company was the psychological effect on the key people of running an empire.

Of the thousands on the payroll, only some 600 were directly involved with publishing. All the others were in manufacturing, circulation, data processing or support. So the top management turned more and more of its attention over the years to these operations. In effect they forgot that the whole structure was dependent on the magazines. They thought they were in the manufacturing business.

I recall during the darkest days discussing the "double-ended presses" with the president and being unable to get him to focus on anything having to do with improving the operations of the magazines.

Further, the sheer size of the operation made management difficult when troubles arrived. You just cannot make major changes quickly in a company with thousands of people. Too many departments have become dukedoms (if not kingdoms). Too many positions are entrenched. Too many changes in basic thinking are required.

Search for a Buyer

Even in the darkest days, some of us thought the company could have been preserved and could flourish again, but this time as a publishing company. Detailed plans were developed that, in addition to reorganizing, hiring some key people, and doing some other normal management steps, would have involved such things as:

- Changing the name of the company
- Moving to New York from Philadelphia
- Selling the paper, printing, and engraving plants —or giving them away

Several substantial companies whose names you would recognize investigated purchasing the company. The price, when you factored in the way the tax losses could have been used by some of them, was as low as $9 million.

In the end, however, all the potential buyers who could have restored it to its former glory bowed out. It was just too big and too complex to clean up and set right quickly. And it was too hard to find executives who were capable and also willing to tackle the challenge.

CHAPTER 8

The Life Cycle of a Magazine

JUST AS WITH PEOPLE, each magazine has a life cycle. Magazines can do nothing more than reflect the interests of people. As times change, interests change. Because of this, new magazines will always be needed—and existing ones will be serving interests people no longer have.

Stages of the Life Cycle, Like the Stages of Human Growth

I have included below a few examples of where some of the better-known magazines might be said to be in their life cycles. Some of their publishers might differ with me—and this is not meant to predict the future of any of these publications.

The stages of a magazine's life cycle parallel those of a person's:

1. Infancy—When the child is first born—full of sound and fury—but also at its most vulnerable, requiring careful feeding and nurturing. (Examples: *O, Rosie, Real Simple*)

2. Childhood—Marked by very rapid growth, but subject to major troubles if not carefully guided and controlled. (Examples: *Maxim, More, Teen People*)

3. Adolescence—Mature in many respects, still growing, almost taking care of itself, but subject to periods of exuberance and doubts. (Examples: *ESPN, Red Herring, Marie Claire, Business 2.0, Martha Stewart Living*)

4. Adulthood—At the peak of its strength, but with the seeds of eventual destruction inherent in the very nature of the product. (Examples: *Vanity Fair, Men's Health, Forbes, Golf Digest*)

5. Middle Age—The longest period—one of stability followed by gradual decline, a period which for some magazines seems to be almost forever, but for others is relatively short. (Examples: *Reader's Digest, Vogue, Playboy, Car & Driver, Time*)

6. Old Age—When it is a struggle to retain enough vigor to stay alive and alert. (Examples: *Family Circle, Good Housekeeping, Popular Mechanics, Esquire*)

7. Living Death—Magazines that should be put out of their misery, but whose owners cannot face the inevitable. (Examples—*TV Guide, Penthouse, Mad, New Choices, Sporting News*)

It may seem strange to liken a magazine's life to the same stages that people go through, but actually magazines take on many of the qualities of people. They are not sterile products such as boxes of soap flakes, but have a personality, a mystique, an existence, a warmth that transcends mere words and pictures on paper. This is why we all shed a tear or two when one does finally go through its death throes.

The length of the life cycle for most magazines is difficult to predict. A few are relatively obvious—a magazine devoted to the millenium had a built-in end. At the other extreme are some magazines that seem as if they should go on forever, such as *Parents*, *Bride's, Baby Talk.*

How can you tell where a particular magazine is in its life cycle? During the growth periods it is pretty apparent, if it hasn't stumbled in any one of a thousand possible ways. The difficult part is later—how to determine when the inevitable signs of decay have grown strong enough to indicate that the end is in sight.

Telltale Signs of the Golden Years

You can tell that people are losing interest in your particular subject through a number of rather obvious signs. You should be able to feel this without resorting to these signs, but usually you don't want to believe it is happening.

- The cost of obtaining new subscriptions is rising, for no apparent reason.
- Renewal rates start to decline.
- Newsstand vitality seems to be eroding.
- Readership scores, both editorial and advertising, start to go down.
- The number of advertisers shrinks.
- It becomes difficult to hire the people you want.

The signs are really the obvious ones you don't want to accept. For a time you might convince yourself that there is nothing wrong with the magazine itself, but just that a few mistakes have been made, or the economy is bad, or some other external and unrelated factor.

Magazine A—Revenue and Earnings Through Its Life Cycle

Figure 8.1 is a graph showing the revenue, expenses and profits in brief form throughout a magazine's forty-year life cycle. Figure 8.2 shows the specific dollar amounts of income, etc. for each year. Remember that every magazine is different. Each is in the various stages of its life cycle for different lengths of time; is of a different size (in circulation, advertising, and dollars); can change in form, frequency, and in other ways; and can be run well or badly.

Magazine A was devoted to a special interest consumer field. Its peak circulation was a little over 300,000, and it was quite prosperous for many years. The graph traces the life of Magazine A through its forty-year history. It can give an idea of what happened at various stages of that life, as well as the size of the profits that were attained.

Figure 8.1. Magazine A Revenue and Earnings During Its Life Cycle

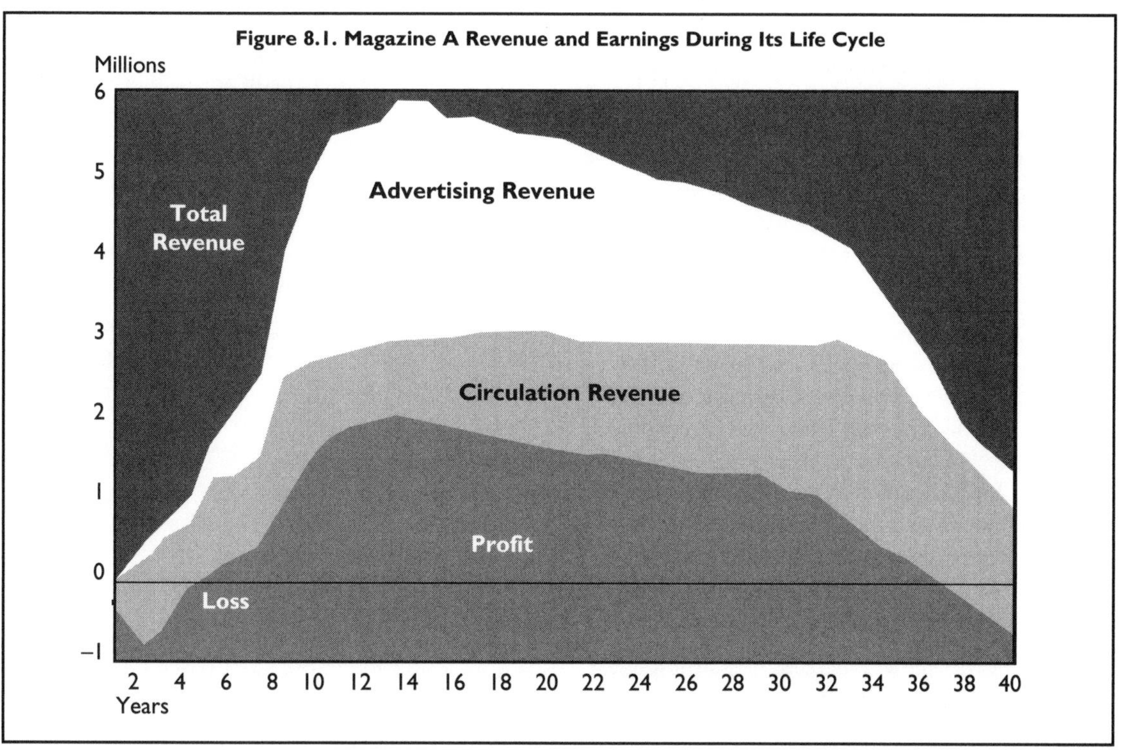

The data are, of course, hypothetical, but are not too far from the actual operations of such a magazine. Profits that can be earned from brand extensions have not been included. These can often account for as much profit as the magazine itself—note the Reader's Digest and Time book operations.

INFANCY

Year 1 shows the costs involved in planning, developing a pilot issue, testing the concept, staffing, and then doing a major mailing to acquire subscriptions—the income from which will not show in the first year and is included in Year 2.

Year 2 is the typical opening phase of a magazine's operations. A charter subscription price of $12 has been offered and every effort has been made to gain circulation early so that renewals will be available soon and advertisers will be impressed. A charter advertising rate has been used to obtain some space in the first issues, although only ten pages per issue were received.

CHILDHOOD

Year 3 continues the subscription efforts. The advertising rate has been increased to some $50 per thousand circulation and there is further advertising acceptance with 15 pages per issue.

Year 4 shows the first breakeven—and indicates that the magazine can be successful. Renewals are strong. Advertiser acceptance continues. Year 5 continues this pattern with the first profits shown.

ADOLESCENCE

Years 6, 7, and 8 indicate rapid growth of circulation and reader acceptance despite a subscription price advance to $14. Advertisers have recognized that the magazine is here to stay, unless it stumbles, and pages increase rapidly. Total revenue grows at a startling rate, and profits of $3 million are realized for the first time.

ADULTHOOD

Years 9 to 15 show Magazine A at its strongest. Circulation continues to grow despite the magazine's high price, but the publisher is wise not to push this too fast. Probes at developing circulation higher than 300,000 are done carefully and apparently do not work out well. Complete advertising acceptance has been gained with the grand figure of 1,000 pages attained in Year 13, giving profits of $7 million. Profit margins are well above 30% of revenue.

Yet even during this period of great strength, the seeds of decline can be seen. Circulation over 300,0000 does not seem to be economically feasible. After reaching the 1,000-page mark, advertising declines because of a contraction in the number of advertisers in this special interest field, a phenomenon that seems to occur in every field as it matures. The decline in the profit margin in Years 13 to 15 indicates that the magazine's operations have begun to harden and that it has accumulated some fat which is difficult to reduce.

MIDDLE AGE

Years 16 to 31 show a long period of good profits, although declining operations are evident in all aspects of the operation. Advertising pages continue to slowly decline as the number of advertisers dwindles. Circulation is still strong, but the cost of acquiring subscribers keeps increasing. The result of these two trends is a constant reduction of profits, but still a great many dollars were earned during these years.

OLD AGE

Years 32 to 37 show the inevitable. In an effort to increase profits, the publisher raises the subscription rate and allows circulation to drop even further. The advertising rate is reduced, but pages continue to decline. Finally, in Year 37, we are back to a breakeven.

LIVING DEATH

Years 38 to 40 show continued declines—and losses are suffered. The publisher carries the magazine along for three loss years based on the forlorn hope that things will turn around.

Figure 8.2. Magazine A Revenue and Earnings During Its Life Cycle

	Year	CIRCULATION Price (Average)	Amourt (Thousands)	Revenue (Thousands)	ADVERTISING Page Rate	Pages	Revenue (Thousands)	Total Revenue (Thousands)	Profit (Loss) (Thousand)	% Profit to Revenue
Infancy	1	$0	$0	$0	$0	$0	$0	$0	$-500	—
	2	12	73	880	2500	120	300	1180	-1200	—
	3	12	104	1240	5000	180	900	2140	-800	—
Childhood	4	14	114	1600	6250	240	1500	3100	0	—
	5	14	179	2500	7500	300	2250	4750	560	11.80%
Adolesence	6	14	189	2640	8500	400	3400	6040	1060	17.50%
	7	14	229	3100	9500	500	4750	7850	1570	20.00%
	8	20	250	5000	12500	600	7500	12500	3130	25.00%
Manhood	9	20	265	5300	13750	910	12513	17813	5340	30.00%
	10	20	280	5600	14000	960	13440	19040	5880	30.90%
	11	20	285	5700	14250	960	13680	19380	6570	33.90%
	12	20	290	5800	14500	970	14065	19865	6970	35.10%
	13	20	300	6000	15000	1000	15000	21000	7350	35.00%
	14	20	300	6000	15000	970	14550	20550	6960	33.90%
	15	20	305	6100	15500	870	13485	19585	6460	33.00%
Middle Age	16	20	305	6100	15500	850	13175	19275	6260	32.50%
	17	20	310	6200	15500	810	12555	18755	6020	32.10%
	18	20	310	6200	15500	790	12245	18445	5810	31.50%
	19	20	310	6200	15000	770	11550	17750	5480	30.90%
	20	20	305	6100	15000	770	11550	17650	5400	30.60%
	21	20	300	6000	15000	770	11550	17550	5300	30.20%
	22	20	300	6000	15000	740	11100	17100	5160	30.20%
	23	20	300	6000	15000	700	10500	16500	4950	30.00%
	24	20	300	6000	15000	670	10050	16050	4810	30.00%
	25	20	300	6000	15000	650	9750	15750	4680	29.70%
	26	20	300	6000	15000	630	9450	15450	4510	29.20%
	27	20	300	6000	15000	600	9000	15000	4380	29.20%
	28	20	300	6000	15000	570	8550	14550	4180	28.70%
	29	20	300	6000	15000	530	7950	13950	3950	28.30%
	30	20	300	6000	15000	500	7500	13500	3600	26.70%
	31	20	300	6000	15000	470	7050	13050	3400	26.10%
Old Age	32	24	260	6200	13500	410	5535	11735	2790	23.80%
	33	24	250	6000	12500	400	5000	11000	2200	20.00%
	34	24	225	5400	11250	360	4050	9450	1620	17.10%
	35	24	200	4800	10000	300	3000	7800	1020	13.10%
	36	24	175	4200	7500	270	2025	6225	500	8.00%
	37	24	150	3600	5000	200	1000	4600	0	—
Living Death	38	20	150	3000	5000	200	1000	4000	-540	—
	39	16	150	2400	5000	200	1000	3400	-1140	—
	40	16	110	1760	4000	150	600	2360	-1400	—
Total			9673	$191620		22290	$304068	$495688	$131390	26.50%.

During its lifetime Magazine A took in more than $190 million of circulation revenue and more than $305 million from advertisers, for a total of some $496 million. Profits over the period, even including the losses at the beginning and end of life, were about $131 million or 26.5% of revenue. It sold some 10 million years of copies, was read by uncounted millions of people, and carried more than 22,0000 advertising pages.

LESSONS TO BE LEARNED

1. Magazines all have life cycles. A magazine exists only because of the interests of people. Those interests change as time goes on, and inevitably a point is reached when the publication is no longer wanted. Before that happens, the number of advertisers in the field usually contracts as the major companies gobble up the smaller producers.

2. Magazines should aim for high profits. A creative product such as a magazine should have a chance to be highly profitable—or should not be started. By highly profitable, I mean 30% or more on sales over a long period, with a return on the capital invested of 10, 20, or many more times. (In this case, many times those figures.)

If you cannot foresee this type of operation and profits when you start, forget it. Compared with most businesses, magazine publishing should be golden—or the basic concept is flawed.

3. Careful early planning is essential. This is a long-term business. Taking more time—and spending carefully at the beginning—can make the difference between a great success and a so-so business. A handful of poor decisions at the start can reduce the chances for real success over the entire life of the magazine. I am referring to such decisions as:

- Insisting on an oversized page with all the additional costs that entails
- Insisting on paper and printing quality that is expensive, when readers may not recognize the difference.
- Using a very low circulation price in order to get readers quickly, only to find that the road to achieving prices that will bring good profits is very long and very expensive—or that they can never be reached.
- Rushing to acquire more circulation than the magazine can sustain at a reasonable cost.
- Instituting an advertising rate base that cannot be sustained naturally without great cost—a cost that is paid not just once, but that is incurred every year as nonrenewals must be replaced.

4. Magazines can be good earners for a long time. With careful planning, a magazine can be put on the road to profits for many years. Middle age is not bad, if it is recognized as being just that—and if efforts during those years are confined to maximizing profits rather than trying to become a young kid again. Our example indicated that over the history of Magazine A, an investment of $2.5 million resulted in profits over its life cycle of more than $130 million. And this was without considering the by-products that would have made the profits much higher.

5. Telltale signs of the cycle are easy to read, if you look for them. During the first few formative years, such things as reader and advertisers' acceptance at adequate prices are relatively easy to test. If the big winner is not there, better quit before the investors' funds have all been spent for what is going to be a loser—or just a borderline project.

As we reviewed Magazine A, we saw that circulation resistance, advertiser contraction, and hardening of the arteries within the company were easy to spot in its later years. Even the death throes were apparent if wishful thinking had not made us hold on too long.

Figure 8.3 is my estimate of where various magazines have been in their life cycles for some years beginning in 1972 and continuing through 2001. You will see how some of them proceed through all the stages from infancy until death. The asterisks indicate those that are no longer published. You will note that some of the infants never made it to childhood and that some did not survive after that.

Figure 8.3 Consumer Magazines—Place in Life Cycle

	1972	1976	1981	1984	1987	1990	1995	2001
INFANCY								
	*Environmental Quality	*L'Officiel	*Art Express	*Enter	Conde Nast Traveler	*Meniories	*Civilization	O (Oprah)
	*Ms	Firehouse	*Familles	Vanity Fair	Victoria	Soap Opera Update	Tmie Out NY	Rosie
	*On the Sound	*New West	*On Cable	Art & Antiques	Parenting	*Wigwag	*George	Real Simple
	*World	*Vintage	*High Technology	*The Yacht	*Walking	*Joe Franklin's Nostaigla	Jane	*Talk
CHILDHOOD								
	Washingtonian	*Book Digest	*Dial	*On Cable	*The Yacht	*Walking	Vibe	*Industry Standard
	Penthouse	*Sphere(Cuisine)	*New Shelter (Practical Homeowner)	*New Shelter	Vanity Fair	Conde Nast Traveler	Smart Money	Maxim
	*Intellectual Digest	*New Times		*Dial	Art & Antiques	Victoria		In Style
		*Family Food Garden	*Venture			Parenting		More
ADOLESCENCE								
	Rolling Stone	*Ms	Self	*High Technology	*Manhattan inc.	*The Yacht	Parenting	ESPN
	Psychology Today	*CB	*Life(Monthly)	*Venture	Elle	Vanity Fair	Victoria	Red Herring
		Money	Inc.	PC	*New Shelter	Art & Antiques	Conde Nast Traveler	Business 2.0
		Early American Life	*Omni	*American Health	*Venture			Martha Stewart
MANHOOD								
	Prevention	Rolling Stone	Smithsonian	Self	PC	Elle	Vanity Fair	Vanity Fair
	Sports Illustrated	Psychology Today	Mother Earth	*Life(Monthly)	*American Health	Architectural Digest	Elle~	Mens Health
	Playboy	Washingtonian	Soap Opera Digest	Inc.	*Byte	Deer & Deer Hunting	Architectural Digest	Golf Digest
		Penthouse		*Omni				Bride's
MIDDLE AGE								
	Boys Life	Boys Life	Bays Life	Boys Life	Boys Life	Boys Life	Boys Life	Boys Life
	Sunset	Sunset	Sunset	Sunset	Sunset	Sunset	Sunset	Sunset
	Hot Rod	Hot Rod	Hot Rod	Hot Rod	Hot Rod	Hot Rod	Hot Rod	Hot Rod
	Newsweek	Newsweek	Newsweek	Newsweek	Newsweek	Newsweek	Newsweek	Newsweek
	McCall's	McCall's	McCall's	McCall's	McCall's	McCall's	McCal!s	Prevention
	*Life(weekly)	Prevention	Prevention	Prevention	Prevention	Prevention	Prevention	Sports Illustraated
		Sports Illustrated	Sports Illustrated	Sports Illustrated	Sports Illustrated	Sports Illustrated	Sports Illustrated	Rolling Stone
		Playboy	Playboy	Playboy	Playboy	Playboy	Playboy	Washingtonian
			Rolling Stone	Rolling Stone	Rolling Stone	Rolling Stone	Rolling Stone	Smithsonian
			Psychology Today	Washingtonian	Washingtonian	Washingtonian	Washingtonian	Self
			Washingtonian	Penthouse	Penthouse	Penthouse	Smithsonian	Inc.
			Penthouse	Smithsonian	Smithsonian	Smithsonian	Soap Opera Digest	PC
				Mother Earth	Soap Opera Digest	Soap Opera Digest	Self	
				Soap Opera Digest	Self	Self	Inc.	
					*Life(monthly)	*Life(monthly)	PC	
					Inc.	Inc.		
					*Omni	*Omni		
						PC		
						*American Health		
						*Byte		
OLD AGE								
	Religious magazines	Religious magazines	Jack & Jill	Jack & Jill	Jack & Jill	Jack & Jill	Jack & Jill	Jack & Jill
	*Screen Stories	*Screen Stones	Horticulture	True Story	True Story	True Story	Penthouse	Penthouse
	True Story	True Story	*AD	*Saturday Review	*Saturday Review	*New Shelter	*Life(monthly)	McCall's (now Rosie)
			True Story	Harper's	Harper's	*Venture	*Omni	Soap Opera Digest
						Woman's Day	*American Health	True Story
						*Modem Photographer	*Byte	Woman's Day
						Mother Earth	True Story	Mother Earth
							Woman's Day	
							Mother Earth	

Business Magazines and the Life Cycle

The same stages are followed by business magazines—except that both the ups and the downs usually happen in a shorter space of time—and with more abruptness. Consider the rise and fall of computer magazines some years ago—and the current situation for publications covering the Web.

When a business magazine is started, it is usually badly wanted (and perhaps even needed) in the field it serves. During the early years of a field's development, a good business magazine can make an enormous difference in the speed of growth and prosperity of the companies in the field it covers.

As the field goes through its life cycle, so must the business magazines serving it. Most fields are marked by rapid growth, the entry of a great many suppliers, and the development of creative new techniques and inventions. These make the magazine most useful for readers and also bring about a great growth in advertising. It also usually results in the start-up of a number of magazines, some of which become highly profitable (and many that do not make it, either because they have tried for a niche in the market that does not exist, or because of tough competition).

From there, as the field matures, there is a slowdown in new ideas, new products, new applications, and new suppliers. Normally there is a contraction in the number of suppliers as mergers take place until, in most older fields, just a handful of companies dominate.

The decline in new ideas results in a lesser need for business magazines by the readers. The decline in the number of suppliers results in a smaller universe of potential advertisers. Many of the magazines serving the field go out of business or are absorbed by their competitors. A few usually survive and continue to be profitable, but at a substantially reduced scale.

I tracked a number of business magazines in three fields that are in different periods in their growth cycles. These show how things have worked out over the period from 1980 to 2001:

A Field That Is Still Growing: Travel, Business Conventions, and Meetings

This field appears to still be growing as more and more meetings and conventions are held in virtually all business fields. It is interesting that, despite the introduction of new communications devices such as the Internet and cell phones, face-to-face conventions and other affairs have flourished.

Number of magazines published:

1980	10
1990	23
2001	37

This, however, tells only part of the story. Consider these statistics:

Total number of different magazines published during the period: 69

New magazines started	59
Still published	32
Now dead	27

Only five of the original ten magazines are still being published.

A Growth Field That Has Settled Down: Radio, TV, and Video

Since 1980, changes in this field have included the expansion of cable as well as the introduction of satellite, mobile, digital, and wideband technology and other such improvements, but the peak of these changes seems to have been passed.

Number of magazines published:

1980	40
1990	68
2001	50

Total number of different magazines published during the period: 190

New magazines started	150
Still published	45
Now dead	105

Only nine of the original forty magazines are still being published

Magazines devoted to	Started	Remaining
Cable	14	4
Satellite	12	0
Mobile	6	1

A Comparatively Stable Field: Air Conditioning, Heating, Plumbing, Refrigeration, Sheet Metal, and Ventilating

Number of magazines published:

1980	23
1990	24
2001	24

Even though this was a stable field, we still see a good deal of churn as magazines have come and gone:

Total number of different magazines published during the period: 48

New magazines started	25
Still published	12
Now dead	13

Twelve of the original twenty-three magazines are still being published.

What Do These Examples Tell Us?

The conclusions from these three examples are about what you would expect:

1. A large number of new entries in the growth period, many of which died
2. The replacement of most of the original magazines with new ones in the growing fields
3. The death of a great many of the magazines started during the growth period

What you might not expect, however, is the churn that seems to take place in even the most stable fields.

CHAPTER 9

Curing the Sick Magazine

IT MAY SEEM strange to spend time discussing sick magazines in a book devoted to starting a magazine. But the more you know about what makes for profits—and losses—in the business, the better your chances of launching a successful title—and of avoiding some of the pitfalls of the business.

Signs That a Magazine Is Sick

- Losses are incurred—or profits are declining.
- You chronically do not meet your budget.
- You skipped some issues.
- It looks and feels more like a pamphlet than a magazine.
- This is the fifth year in a row that you said "Wait till next year."
- Subscribers are being carried in arrears.
- Your mother-in-law says the magazine is terrible.
- You are no longer asked to be on industry panels at conventions.
- Key employees have stopped asking if they can buy the magazine, are looking for jobs, or have become more interested in the pension plan than "a piece of the action."
- Your fiercest competitor wants to know if he can take over your subscription liability.

Little telltale signs like these tell you that something is wrong. But citing one of these difficulties is like saying "I don't feel good," or "I have a stomach ache," or "My leg hurts."

Diseases That Can Afflict Magazines

The good news is that there are only a few diseases—about 13 have been identified so far—that can afflict a magazine. One is invariably incurable, a few others are possibly fatal if not quickly corrected, and most lend themselves to cures if properly treated.

INCURABLE

1. The field being served is declining or has disappeared. Magazines exist because people have interests. When those interests change, there is no longer a need for the magazine.

POSSIBLY FATAL

2. The editorial product ceases to interest the public. Editorial content, of course, is a very fragile thing—and difficult to measure. It is very easy to blame every illness on editorial. This is usually too simplistic. There are, however, times when it becomes clear that the editorial product no longer pleases the audience—sometimes because the editorial direction has changed although the field has not, and sometimes because the direction has not changed to keep up with the times.

3. Circulation has been pushed beyond its natural level. One of the more frequent mistakes made in the magazine business is to try to make a successful magazine more successful by increasing circulation, thereby being able to increase ad rates and, therefore, profits. What happens if you push too far? You find that you must keep on buying readership—not once, but every single year because those last subscribers renew just terribly. The cost of doing this can be unbelievably high.

4. The magazine is suffering from schizophrenia. Magazines can have mental disorders—after all, people are operating them. Schizophrenia is the most common one. This happens when the editor is putting out one product while the ad and/or circulation people are promoting another. Or circulation is acquiring readers with certain characteristics, while advertising is trying to sell a different readership. This is more common in magazines than you might think and, of course, can lead to disaster. Even worse, of course, is the magazine with an unidentified editorial thrust. Then no one can sell it to either readers or advertisers.

5. Strong competition has overwhelmed the magazine. In a few cases magazines have ignored their competitors to the point where these outsiders have almost completely dominated a field both in circulation and advertising. This can reach the point where a magazine is not able to respond without inordinate expense.

Diseases That Are Curable If Treated

6. Circulation efforts are weak. There may be nothing wrong with the field—or the product. It may simply be that the best methods of acquiring and holding readers are not being followed.

7. Advertising effort is weak. It is easy to say "All we need are 10 more ad pages per issue and everything will be fine." But it usually isn't that easy to get those added pages.

8. Lack of cost control is eating up profits. On the surface, magazines do not seem to be subject to runaway costs. After all, prices for paper, printing, postage, and most everything else are relatively fixed and well known. Don't you believe it! I have seen cases where a new production director could save literally millions in the paper, printing, and distribution area. Some editors are able to pay twice as much for manuscripts and artwork as others. And some organizations simply have no idea of how to control any of their costs.

9. The reader is being given too little. This can be done in lots of ways—too few pages, too little good stuff, poor paper or printing, not enough color, rotten graphics, little substance, advertising clutter making it feel that there is no editorial, and on and on.

10. The reader is being given too much. It is also possible to give too much—so that the reader is turned off. The "too much" is usually the result of running pieces that are too long. Pages cost money—and lots of it. It is cheaper to edit better and reduce the length of articles than to pay for useless words that may turn readers off.

11. Pricing is too aggressive. Although magazines are less price sensitive than most products, there is always a point where people will not pay one penny more. This applies to both advertisers and readers. The only way to know is through testing.

12. Pricing is not aggressive enough. A more common ailment is not advancing prices fast enough. Most publishers are amazed at the amounts readers and advertisers will pay when they like a product. To price too low is committing hara-kiri. If you cannot charge enough to make good profits, you are better off admitting it and closing up, rather than suffering a long, painful, and expensive death.

13. Planning and research are poor or nonexistent. Characterizing all these diseases is a lack of thinking through what is being done and why. Unfortunately, few publishers are trained in planning techniques, and many are not even familiar with all the aspects of the business they are in—they may be good at advertising, or at editorial, or at circulation, but not know how the entire process works.

Symptoms of a Magazine's Failing Health

There are a number of major symptoms that can lead you to a diagnosis of just what the trouble is:

- Circulation Symptoms
  - Declining renewal rate
  - Declining results of new subscription promotion efforts
  - Declining single-copy sales
  - Deteriorating reader demographics
- Advertising Symptoms
  - Advertising pages declining
  - Quality of advertising declining
  - Net received per page declining
  - Cost of obtaining advertising pages increasing
- Competitive Symptoms

Competitors gaining in circulation
Competitors gaining in advertising

- Profit Symptoms
  Profits are declining or are nonexistent

Note that there are no direct symptoms of problems with the editorial content. These come out in the symptoms of weakness in circulation and advertising.

Figure 9.1 tells you how the symptoms indicate which diseases a magazine may have. The symptoms are listed across the top, and the diseases that cause them run down the side. As you can see, every disease shows a decline in profits—and the disease of Lack of Planning can affect any aspect of a magazine's operations.

Resources Needed for Diagnosing the Symptoms

Making the diagnosis is not very difficult because, even though every magazine is different, there are many common resources available for making a diagnosis. Here are the major ones:

Financial Statements

I always find that the first clues—and sometimes the only clues—to what is going on come from a review of the financial statements. If nothing else, this review will tell you the best places to do more digging.

We are talking, of course, about not just the raw financial figures but also budgets, statistics, and future projections discussed in detail in chapter 52, "Keeping Track of What's Going On."

Data and Trends about the Field Covered

Most fields are well researched, by the government, by industry associations, by business magazines, and in other ways. Your own magazine—and your competitors'—probably has already done studies for advertisers that will indicate the trends.

The Magazine Itself

Even if you are in love with your magazine and have difficulty seeing that anything is wrong, you can easily determine such things as:

- The number of editorial pages
- Amount of editorial color
- Number of different articles
- Balance of articles in each issue
- Marketability of the editorial treatment
- Length of articles
- Number of advertisements and pages by category
- Quality of advertisers

Figure 9.1. Symptoms of a Magazine's Disease

DISEASE	Circulation Symptoms				Advertising Symptoms				Competitive Symptoms		Profit Symptom…
	Declining Renewal Rate	*Declining New Subscriptions*	*Declining Single Copy*	*Deteriorating Demographics*	*Declining AdPages*	*Declining Ad Quality*	*Declining Ad Net Per Page*	*Increasing Ad Costs*	*Competitors Improving Advertising*	*Competitors Improving Circulation*	
INCURABLE											
Field Disappearing	XXX	XXX	XXX	XXX	XXX	XXX	XXX	XXX			XXX
Possbily Fatal											
Editorial No Longer of Interest	XXX	XXX	XXX	XXX	XXX	XXX	XXX	XXX	XXX	XXX	XXX
Circulation above Natural Level	XXX	XXX	XXX	XXX							XXX
Schzophrenia	XXX	XXX	XXX	XXX	XXX	XXX	XXX	XXX	XXX	XXX	XXX
Strong Competition	XXX	XXX	XXX	XXX	XXX	XXX	XXX	XXX	XXX	XXX	XXX
TREATABLE											
Weak Circulation Efforts	XXX	XXX	XXX							XXX	XXX
Weak Advertising Efforts					XXX	XXX	XXX	XXX	XXX		XXX
Lack of Cost Control											XXX
Reader Given Too Little	XXX	XXX	XXX						XXX		XXX
Reader Given Too Much											XXX
Pricing Too Aggressive	XXX	XXX	XXX		XXX			XXX			XXX
Pricing Not Aggressive Enough											XXX
Lack of Planning	XXX	XXX	XXX	XXX	XXX	XXX	XXX	XXX	XXX	XXX	XXX

Readership research

Magazines may be the most researched objects in the country. Techniques of all kinds have been developed, not only for the benefit of obtaining advertising, but also for editorial purposes. Research either has been, or can be, developed to determine:

- Who are the readers?
- What are their characteristics—demographic and psychographic?
- What do they read in the magazine?
- How often do they read it?
- Do they save it? Why?
- How many other people read it?
- What other magazines do they read?
- What would they like to see more of?

If you haven't already done this type of research, the techniques are well known. They include mailed questionnaires, focus groups, telephone interviews, and personal interviews.

Advertising records

The past records of advertising in dollars and pages—and versus competition—probably already include breakdowns by

- Advertiser
- Agency
- Product
- Size of ads
- Frequency
- Salesman
- Color, bleed, and position

Other things to look at include:

- Rate cards—and changes made in them over the years
- Promotion
- Sales techniques and aids
- Cost and profit by salesperson
- Lost advertising—and why
- Share of market in space and dollars

All this can be supplemented by further research—either your own or by an informed outsider—into advertiser and agency attitudes toward you, the magazine, the competition, the field, the promotion, and the individual salespeople.

Circulation Records

Circulation sometimes seems to have more information than one can handle—and often the data are put together in ways that don't tell you much. It is worth spending time to develop meaningful reports so that you can quickly determine trends in both subscriptions and single-copy sales over a period of years.

For subscriptions you will want information by source (and don't forget that each list in the mail is a separate source), by effort, and by time of year about the following:

- Price and offer
- Return percent
- Pay-up percent
- Conversion percent
- Renewal percent
- Revenue versus cost

For single copies you should have data on the draw, returns, and net sale by:

- Issue
- Section of the country
- Wholesaler
- City
- Chain
- Individual outlet
- Price

You will also want to have such helpful information as promotional support, the weather, and other outside events that may have affected sales.

Cost Data

Financial statements are fine as far as they go, but often you must look at the underlying material from which they were developed. This would include:

- The costs of the major items—paper, printing, and distribution
- Payments to all sorts of other suppliers—there are lots
- Travel and entertainment
- Number of employees per department
- Fringe benefits
- Everything else

INDUSTRY DATA

The associations in the field (ABM and MPA) develop cost and other data periodically that you can compare with your own data. *Folio* does salary surveys annually for various departments. And other studies are sometimes made.

COMPETITIVE INFORMATION

Information on just about everything done by your competitors is available to you. You can count advertising and editorial pages; read their circulation reports; get copies of their advertising and circulation material, which usually include results of research they have done; inspect their rate cards; and read their magazines.

If they are on the newsstand, you can usually get their sale and return percentages as fast as they can through your single-copy national distributor.

If you are smart, you will regularly develop operating statements for your competitors so that you will have some idea of how they are doing financially. This is not as hard as it may seem. After all, they face the same cost figures you do.

Check Dun & Bradstreet and other public information about them.

And, if there isn't enough public information, chances are that you, or one of your people, have friends over there. But don't forget—they know just as much about you.

Steps in Diagnosing a Magazine's Symptoms and Diseases

Figure 9.2 gives a step-by-step procedure for examining the various symptoms that can afflict a magazine—and the corrective steps you can take. As you can see, it starts, as everything else does in the magazine business, by examining the readers' reactions to the magazine.

This chart is in the form of a tree. By working from left to right you can examine each symptom in a logical order of importance and arrive at the diagnosis of what disease is afflicting your magazine—and the steps that are needed. As you can see, these steps can range from stopping publication altogether to simply imposing cost controls or increasing prices.

Figure 9.2. Diagnosing a Magazine's Diseases

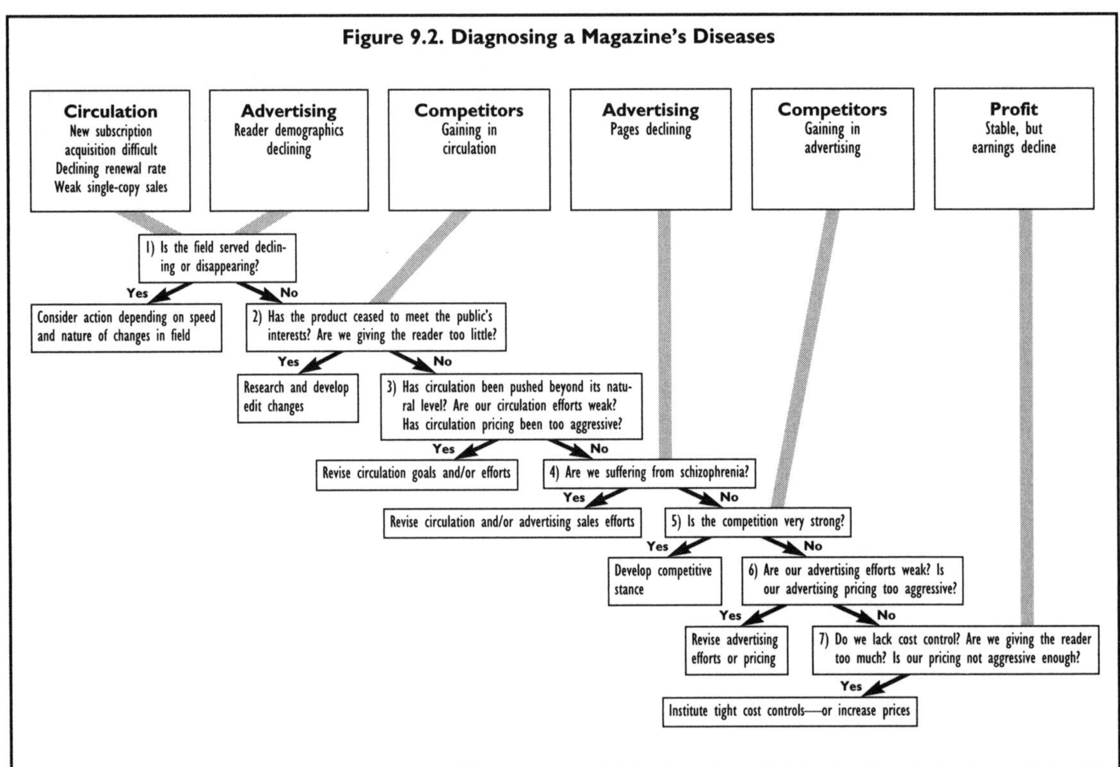

CHAPTER 10

Resurrection of a Dying—or Dead—Magazine

IN RESEARCHING THIS chapter I ran into an article by Herbert Swartz from *Folio*, February 1986, headed "Why Some Magazines Never Die." Its first paragraph rightfully belongs in the chapter on mythology.

"The concept of a phoenix-like rise in magazine publishing remains a constant. Magazines may die, but not all remain buried. Think of *The Saturday Review*, *Life* and *Look*, *The Saturday Evening Post*, *Inside Sports*, and *Media People*."

I did just that—I thought about each of those magazines. Here is what has happened to each:

- *The Saturday Review* did rise phoenixlike fifteen times, but it has been dead for a number of years, never, I believe, to rise again. Three or four of its incarnations were masterminded by Norman Cousins, who just would not give up.
- *Life* was out of business for over ten years before Time, Inc. started it once again as what was really a new magazine. Don't forget that the original *Life* when I was a kid was a humor magazine with no pictures in it at all. Once again, however, it recently has been buried.
- *Look* died and a failed attempt was made to resurrect it in about 1980.
- *The Saturday Evening Post* still lives, not at all as the wonderful magazine it was at its best, but as a health magazine published just six times a year with only some 385,000 circulation. Its death as a major magazine was the subject of the best-selling book *Decline and Fall* by Otto Friedrich.
- *Inside Sports* was started by *Newsweek* and restarted a couple of times later by others, but it never made it.
- *Media People*—died in infancy.

I also thought about *Colliers,* which was of the same stature as these others, whose death was the subject of Teddy White's best-seller, *The View from the 40th Floor.*

This dismal history does not mean that magazines cannot be resurrected when they show signs of ending their lives. To get a feel for the situation, I looked into the history of the longer-lived magazines listed in the September 2000 issue of the Consumer SRDS. Some 41 of the 2,041 consumer magazines listed were started prior to 1900, or over a hundred years ago. One hundred seventy-seven more were started prior to the end of World War II in 1945, and 410 between then and 1975. A total of 628, or 31% of all those listed, were over 25 years old.

It is probable that just about all these magazines have had several face-lifts during those many years—and undoubtedly had to change their editorial thrust more than once.

Of these older magazines, 134 are published by not-for-profit organizations that may not have had to meet the stringent requirements for being profitable in their own right. These would include *National Geographic, Audubon, Smithsonian, American Rifleman,* and many others. And of the 494 magazines over 25 years old, 125 are regional.

About 300 have circulation of less than 100,000, mostly in narrow fields where changes may be easier to keep up with—such as art and antiques, boating, crafts and hobbies, hunting and fishing, horses, and the like.

The others are in larger fields where greater changes have been taking place. Many have been able to recast themselves from time to time to keep up with current thinking:

- Business—*Business Week, Forbes, Fortune*
- General interest—*Atlantic, Harper's, Ebony, National Enquirer*
- Home—*House Beautiful, Architectural Digest, Better Homes and Gardens, Home Mechanix, Early American Homes, Unique Homes*
- Newsweeklies—*Time, Newsweek, U.S. News & World Report*
- Science—*Popular Science, Science News, Scientific American, Popular Mechanics, American Scientist, Sciences*
- Travel—*Gourmet*
- Women's—*Good Housekeeping, Ladies' Home Journal, Family Circle, Glamour, Parents, Seventeen, True Story, Woman's Day, Mademoiselle, Harper's Bazaar*

Major reconstructions that seem notable:

- *Reader's Digest,* which for many years did not take advertising, then accepted all but liquor and tobacco, later agreed to run tobacco, and finally broke down and accepted liquor.
- *McCalls,* which actually increased its page size and went in for greatly increased artwork and color for a time, later reduced its page size, and recently changed not only its nature but also its name when it became *Rosie.*
- *Town & Country*
- *New Yorker*
- *House & Garden* (actually stopped publishing for a time and changed its name temporarily to just *HG*)
- *New York Times Magazine*
- *Sporting News*
- *Travel Holiday* (actually a merger of two older titles)
- *Playboy,* which in the 1970s decided to be establishment and not follow *Penthouse, Hustler,* and their ilk, but which has now reverted back

Some launched a new magazine using an old name

- *Redbook*—which had for many years been a fiction magazine.
- *Cosmopolitan*—Helen Gurley Brown made it what it is today.
- *Vanity Fair*—Relaunched many years after the original had passed away.

More recent rejuvenations have included *Health, Prevention, Boys' Life, Harvard Business Review, Art & Antiques, Family Handyman.*

The real point is that, despite the inevitable life cycle of magazines, it is sometimes possible to resurrect a title.

That same article in *Folio* notes 12 factors that may make it easier to give new life to an old title. There may be some truth to the first two:

1. "A magazine's title is valuable." This certainly has proven true for *Life, Vanity Fair,* and a number of other magazines.
2. "Evolution is not death." This seems to have been true for many magazines listed above, as well as others.

All the other reasons cited seem to be based only on wishful thinking:

3. "Failed expectations are misleading." The history of *The Saturday Review*, *Inside Sports*, and *Families* certainly does not bear this out. If you have a concept no one wants, trying to revive it doesn't help.
4. "A business with emotions." That part is certainly true. That's why you see pictures of editors crying on the front page of newspapers when a magazine passes away. But that doesn't mean it is smart to try to restart a dying magazine.
5. "Easier than a start-up." It may have been true that it was easier for the Meredith Corporation to buy *Ladies' Home Journal* when it was in trouble a number of years ago than to start a completely new women's magazine. But remember that they knew the field well and had all the resources to salvage the magazine. Not many others do.
6. "Ego and pride." The "I can do it better" syndrome. Very rarely successful.
7. "The call of the institution." Which means that some magazines have become institutions—and therefore someone should step in to save them.

The Saturday Evening Post was one of those. Not a very good reason, in my opinion.

8. "Profits are possible." Maybe.

9. "Editorial excellence." No doubt that is needed in a resurrection—but so is it in the everyday life of every magazine.

10. "The right cocktail parties." There is no question that more than one magazine has been purchased so that the new owner could put it on his cocktail table and tell people that he owns it. But is that a good reason to try to resurrect a magazine?

11. "Faith in the new editor." Same as "I can do it better" syndrome.

12. "White knight to the rescue." Same.

Almost all the magazines that have had a long and healthy life have done it under the aegis of the company that started them, which made changes periodically as needed. Very rarely has a new owner stepped in to save a magazine, although it has happened at times as evidenced by some of the larger ones:

- *U.S. News & World Report*
- *Popular Mechanics*
- *Esquire*
- *Atlantic*

And the smaller ones, including:

- *Southwestern Art*
- *Cruising World*
- *Vogue Patterns*
- *World Press Review*
- *Practical Horseman*

CHAPTER 11

Why Some Magazines Succeed and Others Fail

BEFORE THINKING ABOUT trying to start a magazine, it is important to understand why some magazines succeed and others fail. By succeeding, I mean that they become nicely profitable—I am not talking about artistic successes that are not profitable—or those that are supported financially for other reasons.

The Key Factor: The Field the Magazine Covers

Far and away the major reason for a magazine's success is the field it covers. If the people who participate in the field feel that communication through a magazine is desirable, you can put out a perfectly awful magazine and still have it succeed. If you remember the early 1980s, when microcomputers were just getting started, there were a great many magazines devoted to them—most of which were almost unreadable. But they all sold lots of copies and carried lots of advertising. As the manufacturers dropped out of that field, so did the magazines. Today there are just a handful, but most of these are quite healthy.

In the last few years we have seen a rash of new magazines devoted to the Web that were thick with advertising and with lots of circulation. It was hard to fail for a while, but we are now watching the same magazines suffer as the field matures. The dropouts have started, and more are on the way.

Magazine Fads

What are the next fields that will develop? I don't have any idea. The public decides that—and I don't know anyone who can predict it.

One of the reasons that there are lots of failures is that like most things, magazines are subject to fads. A few years ago we had a fad of science magazines (*Science 89, Science Digest,* and *Discover*). It took several years for publishers to understand that the world is not crazy about science magazines. Now only *Discover* remains, and it doesn't look too healthy.

A few years later there was a spate of magazines devoted to the hip people in New York City. But those people didn't seem to be interested because *Spy, Egg, 7 Days,* and *Details* all passed away about the same time. (Actually, *Details* did not pass away. It is the first magazine that has had not one, but two sex changes. At first it was for men, then changed to be addressed to women, and now it is again edited for men.)

We have also seen a number of efforts to start magazines for older people. *Mature Outlook, Prime Time, Lear's, Golden Years, McCall's Silver, Vintage,* and some others tried and failed. They failed because old people don't want magazines for old people. They want to read regular magazines. The publications that *do* work in this field are devoted to local rather than national interest. (Still existing are *Modern Maturity, My Generation,* and the *AARP Bulletin,* all of which are published by AARP and distributed to its members—not exactly freestanding magazines. And the Reader's Digest Association continues to struggle with *New Choices.*)

Other fields that are receiving lots of attention these days include:

- Adventure travel
- Affluent people
- African Americans
- Brides
- The Internet
- Computer games
- Gardening
- Gay readers
- Health
- Country and log homes
- Lifestyles
- Parenthood
- Teens
- City and other regional
- Older women
- Golf

Some Fields Have Never Been Good Candidates for New Magazines

Sports

This huge field has, until recently, had just two large magazines serving it—*Sports Illustrated* (which, incidently, lists itself as a news magazine) and *Sporting News. Sport* was around for years but was never profitable and finally passed away. Several different publishers tried *Inside Sports* before it expired. *ESPN* has joined the fray in an oversize format with lots of promotion on the cable networks and so far seems to be succeeding.

You will note, however, that there are no meaningful magazines for baseball, football, basketball, hockey, or other spectator sports despite the enormous coverage on TV.

Golf magazines seem to be the ones that really flourish. Why? I guess it's because you are personally involved and do not have to be terribly proficient. The sport also leads to lots of advertising because you need a lot of equipment and destinations can be important.

Children's Magazines

Children are apparently hard to find. The magazines that have attained respectable circulations are confined to those that have easy ways of attracting readers. *Sesame Street* through the TV program, *Disney* through its many activities, *Sports Illustrated for Kids* through its parent magazine, and *Boys' Life* through the Boy Scouts.

Advertising, however, is hard to come by in these magazines because of the varying ages of the kids and their different interests. On the other hand, magazines for how to be parents are flourishing.

Serious Magazines

Those devoted to politics, world affairs, and the like often have difficulties. *New Republic, National Review, The Nation, Mother Jones* and *The World and I* all have to be subsidized. Even the likes of *Harpers* and *Atlantic* have rarely had profitable in recent years. The newest entry, *George,* came in with a great deal of sound and fury, but passed on after the tragic death of JFK Jr. Its prospects were questionable before that.

WARNING

If you have an idea for a magazine that doesn't involve some brand-new human endeavor or interest, and no magazine is successfully covering it, be very careful. Magazines have probably been tried before in your field and failed. Or, if not, there may be some other very good reason why they cannot work.

WARNING

Some fields are not as good as they look. Probably the most obvious are regional magazines. Some of these, of course, are highly profitable, such as *New York* and *Los Angeles.* But unless the region you are covering has a large population plus an unusual hold on its citizens, it is very difficult to make profits. The reason is obvious—the universe of available readers is small. This makes it expensive to get and keep readers. With low circulation, ad rates must remain low. As a result, it is very hard to make good profits. For reasons that I do not understand, some larger cities just don't seem to be able to support profitable city magazines—Des Moines, Houston, Denver, and St. Louis are examples. State magazines are pretty well confined to *Texas Monthly,* but that may be because Texas is a state of mind in addition to being a geographic area

Fields That Don't Want a Magazine

Since the field is the most important ingredient in the success of a magazine, would-be publishers must be very careful not to let wishful thinking lead them to see a field where none exists. Some examples:

- *On the Sound*—This was a magazine started by experienced magazine people to cover all the people who live on or near Long Island Sound. This includes parts of The Bronx, Connecticut, Rhode Island, Massachusetts, and all of Long Island. The only problem was that these people really have nothing in common except the weather and traffic. Most live in relatively self-contained communities and rarely stray even into the next town. In any case, no one wanted the magazine.
- *Women's Sports*—Started in 1971, this magazine was never able to attract an audience, despite the obvious increase in women's participation in sports in recent years. Perhaps this was simply because of the lack of interest in sports magazines in general, as discussed above. Conde Nast purchased the magazine and changed its name and contents to *Women's Sports and Fitness,* but this didn't work either.
- Magazines about house plants—At one time there were three, all started about the same time—*HousePlants and Porch Gardens, Plants Alive,* and *Popular Gardening Indoors*. All three got about 300,000 circulation relatively quickly. But after about three years, they all began having trouble getting new subscriptions and keeping renewals. The only explanation was that there simply was not enough subject matter to keep interest up. After you have told readers not to overwater and to talk to their plants, there really isn't much more anyone wants to know. Today there seems to be a spate of new gardening magazines, a field that has never been kind to magazines. I have to wonder whether this field has really changed.
- *TV Cable Week*—Launched by Time, Inc. to be a competitor to *TV Guide*. This was later the subject of a book—*The Fanciest Dive*—which described a typical big-company foul-up—the kind that can happen in any industry. The basic problem was that they didn't understand the cable business, so the magazine never had a chance.

Today, of course, we are seeing a decline in *TV Guide* as the television and cable world has changed.

Unfocused Editorial Content Can Kill a Magazine

Lots of magazines go into business without knowing what they are trying to write about. Sounds ludicrous, but it happens more than you can imagine. If *you* don't know what the editorial content is supposed to be, how can a reader? Some examples:

- *New Times* and *Quest*—Both these magazines were to be upbeat magazines for yuppies, but their editorial approaches had not been thought through and the contents wavered. It was as if the editors did not know what they were trying to do. This happened to be the case, and the readers found it out very quickly.
- *Spring* was a magazine for young women that would compete with the major women's magazines. Like those above, however, the editorial wavered. To straighten things out, we got the ten editors in a room together and tried to find from each what the editorial thrust of the magazine was supposed to be. Got ten different answers. Killed the magazine.
- *Vanity Fair*—As a faithful magazine maven, I subscribed quickly when I got the first mailing announcing the relaunch in 1983. A month later I got a mailing listing 200 human endeavors and interests and asking which ones I would be most interested in. It was obvious then that they had no idea of what the magazine was going to be about. The first issue was an inch thick with advertising, but the editorial rationale was not understandable. The second issue had almost no ads. Since then, of course, things have been defined, editors have been changed, and now it is one of the most coherent, popular, and successful magazines published.
- *Sports Illustrated*—When it was started, it covered almost every imaginable sport including polo, quoits throwing, lacrosse, and badminton. For the first 13 years it lost uncountable millions. Since then, of course, the magazine has featured baseball, football, basketball, and other spectator sports—and has been a big winner.
- *Human Sexuality*—This was one where the publisher of a magazine for doctors called *The Medical Aspects of Human Sexuality* had the idea that a consumer edition of the same magazine would sell. The content of the medical magazine, even though

it was for doctors, was not full of medical terms or other esoteric material. (Doctors apparently don't know any more about the subject than the rest of us.) Unfortunately, when the issues were published, they resembled *True Story* and were not at all what we had in mind. No one bought it.

WARNING

If you ever find an editor saying that "we will start the magazine and the editorial will evolve as we go along," you are in really bad trouble.

Inadequate Financing: An Excuse, Not a Reason

Too often we hear the complaint that the project would have succeeded, but "we were undercapitalized." Sure you were, but whose fault what that? Two possibilities: either you didn't plan right, or you didn't raise the amount you knew you needed. In virtually all these cases, the undercapitalization story is simply an excuse, not a reason.

WARNING

It is just too easy to get into the magazine business. All you have to do is get a printer and start publishing, using whatever resources you might be able to beg, borrow, or steal.

There is nothing sadder than to get a call from someone saying he has just put out the third issue of his magazine and now needs money (usually immediately) to continue publishing. I can't recall anyone in that position who was actually able to get more money to carry on.

If you reach that point, the only answer is to stop publishing and try to raise the money you need. There is nothing more expensive than paper, printing, and postage. Even one more issue can consume cash at an alarming rate.

When I tell people to stop publishing, the answer invariably is something like this: "But I have to keep publishing. Think of the readers who have subscribed and are breathlessly waiting for the next issue, and the advertisers who will never come back if we don't continue publishing."

The real point is that you probably don't have very many readers or advertisers. Remember two of the immutable laws of publishing: Readers love their magazines and advertisers love their magazines. They will both still be there waiting for you later when you have more capital.

Poor Execution

Yes, this actually happens at times, but not terribly often.

One magazine in the epicurean field was started by two husband-wife teams—should have been a warning. One team was to get the advertising. They were experienced as ad reps and we had the utmost confidence in them. The other team, the editors, were somewhat untried. Throw into the mix a new, inexperienced circulation director and adequate financing. The magazine was published. The editorial content was excellent. Circulation was right on track with projections. But the advertising team never got any advertising and we never did find out why. But that was the end. (Incidently, the magazine was later relaunched and is successful to this day.)

Another example is the regional magazine covering a large state, started by experienced publishing people who had all worked for a large publishing company. This was a case where everything went wrong. The editorial was awful. The design was unattractive. Then they passed up looking for advertising locally in the region and concentrated on trying to get only national advertising. This was kind of dumb because we all know that national advertisers don't go into regionals—at least not early on. And so it quickly failed.

There was a beautiful magazine in a special interest consumer field—also started by an experienced publishing group, all of whom had worked for a large publishing company. Everything went fine—good editorial, circulation on target, advertising about as expected. Just one problem: Cost control was unknown to these people. If you could buy a color separation for $200, they could find a way to spend $800. They literally spent themselves out of business.

Then there's the case of the nice high-end fashion magazine. The editorial content was good and the advertisers were happy, but a magazine of this kind necessarily has a limited potential for circulation. The publisher insisted on using only direct mail to obtain subscriptions. Any good circulation person knows that circulation is made up of a few thousand subscribers acquired from each of a whole bunch of different sources. Had an effort been made to use other sources in addition to direct mail, the magazine probably would have succeeded.

Business Magazines

The discussion about why some magazines succeed and others fail has been primarily devoted to consumer magazines because the relationship of the success of a field to the success of a magazine is not as obvious for a consumer magazine as it is for business magazines.

In chapter 8, "The Life Cycle of a Magazine," we talked about how magazines reflect each business field as it starts, matures, and later contracts, and showed examples of the situation in three different fields.

In addition to being dependent on the health of the field covered, business publishers are subject to the same mistakes as consumer publishers—believing in fads, covering fields that don't want magazines, having unfocused editorial content, starting with inadequate financing, and executing poorly.

CHAPTER 12

Start-ups: The Record for Existing Publishing Companies

THREE THINGS USED to puzzle me:

1. The vast majority of new magazines are started by people who know nothing about publishing rather than by existing publishing companies.
2. Publishing companies have been no more successful when they launch new magazines than people who have never been in the business.
3. Almost all the breakthrough new magazines have been started by people outside the business, not by publishers.

The September 2000 issue of SRDS lists 481 consumer magazines with over 100,000 circulation that were started after 1980. Sixty-eight percent were launched by other than existing publishers. Of the 154 magazines that publishers started, 84 were spin-offs of existing properties.

This is not to imply that there is anything wrong with spinning off a profitable property, but it does seem strange that only 70 brand-new successful magazines were developed within the entire industry, while outsiders provided 327.

Who Publishes the Successful New Magazines

I was surprised, too, to find that publishing companies were no more successful when they did start new magazines than were people who had never been in the business. But every study I have made showed this same result.

Because this research has been confined to SRDS, chances are that many more magazines were started by nonpublishers than that service ever listed. But the overall story is the same: Publishers don't do any better when they start a new magazine than the outsiders do, and maybe they don't do as well.

Who Dreams Up the Breakthrough Publishing Concepts

The definition of a breakthrough publishing concept may be a little debatable, but consider who started some of the magazines in new fields in relatively recent periods:

- *Time,* the first news magazine, by Harry Luce in 1923
- *Hot Rod,* the first magazine addressed to the automotive field, by Bob Petersen in 1948
- *Rolling Stone,* the first magazine for contemporary music, by Jann Wenner in 1967
- *Scientific American,* the first real science magazine, resurrected by Gerry Piel in 1950
- *PC,* the first magazine for computer users, by David Bunnell in 1981
- *Backpacker,* the first of the active-outdoor magazines, by Bill Kemsley in 1973
- *Organic Gardening,* the first magazine in that field, by J. I. Rodale in 1942
- *Essence,* the first magazine for black women, by Ed Lewis and his three partners in 1970
- *Black Enterprise,* the first black business magazine, by Earl Graves in 1970

- *Inc.,* the first magazine for small business, by Bernie Goldhirsch in 1979
- *Bride's,* the first magazine for brides, by Wells Drorbaugh in 1934
- *Institutional Investor,* the first magazine for professional investment people, by Gil Kaplan in 1967
- *Trailer Life,* the first magazine in its field, by Art Rouse in 1941
- *Playboy,* the first "men's sophisticated magazine," by Hugh Hefner in 1953
- *New York,* the first real city magazine, by Clay Felker in 1968
- *Golf Digest,* the first golf magazine, by Bill Davis in 1950
- *Mother Earth News,* by John Shuttleworth in 1970
- *Psychology Today,* by Nick Charney in 1967
- *Parents,* by George Hecht in 1926
- *Ski,* by Dave Rowan in 1935
- *Mariah,* by Larry Burke in 1976
- *Texas Monthly,* by Michael Levy in 1973
- *Utne Reader,* by Eric Utne in 1984
- *Reader's Digest,* by the Wallaces in 1922

You can go on and on!

Of course some breakthrough magazines have been started by publishers, but not very many:

- *Business Week,* the first general business magazine by McGraw-Hill, in 1929
- *Life,* the first picture magazine by Time, Inc., in 1941
- *Men's Health,* the first in that field, by Rodale Press in 1986
- *George,* the first political magazine, by Hachette Fillipachi in 1999

And probably a number of others.

Logic Says That Publishers Should Lead in Starting Magazines

It seems logical that existing publishers should be in the forefront of those who start successful properties. After all, a publishing house has many important advantages:

- Knowledge of the business
- Management skills that should ensure careful planning and monitoring of a new venture
- Marketing skills that should ensure that sales efforts are handled well, as well as an understanding of what makes readers and advertisers buy
- Supplier contacts that should ensure quality work at good prices, whether it be for printing, paper, fulfillment, artwork, photographs, manuscripts, or single-copy sales
- Creative skills that should ensure an understanding of what makes for a quality editorial product and the techniques for developing it
- Knowledge of markets and where there may be gaps that a new publication can fill
- People with ideas for new products
- Outsiders—and insiders—many of whom would prefer to work on new ideas and opportunities rather than on existing properties
- Money with which to launch new properties

If you agree with some of my basic theories about magazine publishing—that publishing properties exist as a result of people's interests and not in and of themselves; that people's interests are constantly changing; that there is a life cycle for every property (all will grow, flourish, and then die at some point); and that there is a constant opportunity for new properties—then you would expect that the operator of a publishing company would be constantly involved in breakthrough new projects as well as by-product magazines, just to keep up with the parade.

Yet an attitude exists in almost all publishing companies that Seth Baker best expressed when he was the head of ABC Publishing. He said, "Starting a new magazine is more risky that drilling for oil in Central Park."

Why Publishers Do Not Start New Magazines

I started out by saying that I used to be puzzled by this lack of interest in new properties in publishing companies. On reflection, however, it really is not very puzzling, although it may be erroneous thinking. It is not just one problem, but many (and the problems are not necessarily peculiar to publishing.) The reasons lie in the nature of organizations and the people who inhabit them, versus the nature of the people who start new things.

It's People, Not Organizations

The successful concept—big or small—must come from someone, whether he knows anything about publishing or not, who has an instinct about what the public's latest interest is and has the dedication to pursue that instinct to its conclusion.

A company, or one of its people, may have that same instinct at times, but the tendency in companies is to throw money at an idea, rather than to dedicate its best people to making a new magazine work. After all, why would you jeopardize a sure and proven winner like *Cosmo* by asking Helen Gurley Brown to go try something else?

You cannot just throw a new magazine at employees and expect them to display an entrepreneur's dedication. They may not relate to the concept—or at least not be in love with it to the extent needed to make it work.

Most companies are made up of people who work very hard at *doing* things and at keeping everything going in an orderly and organized manner. Most people don't like change. The entrepreneur threatens them because they don't know where his spirit will light or whose department he will want to improve next.

Entrepreneurs are very different. They are idea people. They want to start things and change the old. They don't enjoy life involved with keeping everything working smoothly.

The entrepreneur, on his side, does not realize that the *COMPANY* is bigger than all of us. He also does not realize that in many cases he may be wrong—or that he will probably be dismissed because he has great ideas, but cannot make them work.

Getting Agreement Is Tough

We are all individuals and each of us has his own favorite interests. Our backgrounds and experiences are quite different. You play tennis, I play golf, and we probably could never agree to start a magazine in either of these areas.

You were brought up in the idealistic sixties, I in the patriotic forties, and our ad director is a member of Generation X. We see things quite differently.

If you have ever tried to sell a magazine—or to raise money for a project—you know what I mean. I know more than 200 groups and companies who say they want to buy publishing properties, but when a specific property comes on the market, it is rare that more than three or four are interested.

Start-up Experience Is Limited

The major job in most companies is to make the most of what exists—we might call their managements "caretakers" without the negative connotations of that word. There are techniques to start-ups —and, unless you have been through a number of these, you just don't know enough about these techniques, no matter how big the company or how good you may be at your job.

I have watched large, seemingly experienced companies make the same start-up mistakes as the rankest publishing amateur: lack of a crystallized editorial product, inadequate planning, disbelief of test results, insufficient capitalization, poor staffing, refusal to read the telltale signs of an idea that won't fly, not asking for skilled outside help, and so on.

The really big and expensive mistakes in starting magazines are usually made by those who think they know the answers because they are in publishing. It turns out that these people don't realize how different starting a magazine is from running something after it is up and going.

Specialized Skills May Be Scarce

You may be great at putting out a business magazine, but know nothing of the editorial, advertising and circulation problems of a consumer magazine—and you probably don't have anyone on the staff who does. Selling advertising may seem to be a common thread, but selling business and selling consumer advertisers is very different. Different agencies, different selling techniques, different facts and research are needed.

The same is true in every other area. Direct mail subscription selling is a high art. If you are not expert at it, you must be very careful. Appealing to consumers editorially is very different from appealing to business people. What works in France or Germany may not go in the United States, and, if you think you can conquer the American single-copy situation, no matter where you are from, forget it.

Starting New Things Is Risky

Sure it is—but so is *not* starting them. Public companies are geared to think about earnings per share. On this factor hangs the price of their stock and the measure of the success of the people who run them. Managers in public companies are rarely in their jobs for more than a few years. Start-ups take time—and normally the head of a public company will have left before the benefits of a new project can be fully felt.

The problems of the public company are particularly significant in publishing. The costs of starting new magazines are not capitalized, but are considered to be almost entirely current expenses. They affect earnings per share immediately. In other businesses, where tangible assets are important, depreciation is often a creature of the future. The costs of building and equipping a manufacturing plant will not affect the bottom line for some time.

In privately owned publishing companies, which are generally smaller, the investment in start-ups that don't work can be so large as to destroy the company completely. If you are making a comfortable living and can pass along a valuable property to your heirs, why should you risk it all—or a lot of it—on starting something that could be a disaster?

Timing Problems

Even those companies that would like to invest in new ventures have timing problems. Few are large enough to set up long-range programs for launching new things. They may be investing in other expensive projects when the new venture appears. Or perhaps one of their existing properties is having a temporary downturn. And what about recurrent recessions?

Who Decides?

Lots of companies have procedures and committees organized for buying new computers. Few have similar systems for the really important, major decisions such as acquisitions, start-ups, and divestitures.

These major decisions are limited in number and depend in the end on the feelings of the boss. Very few bosses are equipped by education, training, or experience to cope with such decisions. The process is disorganized and, in most cases, poorly done

Most manufacturing concerns have organized research and development programs. Aside from Time, Inc., which for several years had a new magazine group but has now disbanded it, no one in publishing has yet approached such a concept seriously.

Few companies believe that they can contemplate a program large enough to try five projects for every one that succeeds, yet that is the only way to do such things—whether you are in publishing or some other field.

* * *

When all these difficulties are taken into consideration, it doesn't seem quite so puzzling that existing publishing companies do not start completely new projects very often. Nor is it so strange that most publishers would rather let an entrepreneur do it—and then buy him out when the property is successful.

That doesn't mean that this is the wisest course to take.

My puzzlement today has changed, I no longer wonder why publishers don't start new magazines. I wonder why so many publishers who have been loathe to try new magazine concepts have spent oodles of money experimenting with the Internet just because it is there—when they have no real idea of what will be gained from it, or, often, even how it works.

CHAPTER 13

Why and How Existing Companies Can Start Magazines

THE REASON EXISTING publishing companies should continually be involved in start-up magazine projects is very simple. It is the only way a company can keep up with the parade. Since every magazine has a life cycle, and since interests continually change, there is a constant need to rejuvenate the company by getting involved in new magazines

Most publishers buy successful properties when the entrepreneurs reach the point where they want to stop running them, either because they are tiring of it, or because they may be great as entrepreneurs, but poor as operators. Or maybe (most likely) they want to cash in while their properties have a value they never dreamed of.

Pitfalls of Expansion through Purchase

This approach to growth is simple, but is not necessarily the wisest course. While buying things, and going through the investigation and negotiating process, is stimulating, it is also hazardous, particularly if you don't do it often. More than once a company has purchased a property for a lot of money only to find one or more of these problems:

- The property was not exactly what they had expected to find, despite all the due diligence in the world.
- They did not really understand the field they were entering.
- Some of the key players they thought they were buying, including the founder, did not stay because they no longer felt the need to work hard, particularly for someone else.
- The process of investigating and negotiating the purchase took a great deal of the key operating people's time, resulting in declining results in the existing properties.
- Integrating the people and processes of the acquisition into the present organization was time-consuming, expensive, and caused considerable friction between the new and old employees, further reducing anticipated earnings. At times it couldn't be done at all.
- Rosy future projections for the purchased property seem farther away than anticipated, or possibly might never be reached.
- The price paid was more than the property was worth because there were a number of other companies bidding—and it was the only way it could have been obtained. That's the "After all, you only buy it once" syndrome.
- The synergism that was expected with the purchase did not happen. It rarely does, and the word should probably be eliminated from our vocabulary.

In other words, the purchase was not as wonderful as anticipated for one or many reasons.

Financial Results—Purchase versus Start-up

Any comparison of a purchase versus a start-up is necessarily fraught with many caveats on both sides, and the likelihood that many readers will disagree with most or all the premises. But let's give it a try.

PURCHASE

Suppose you buy a consumer magazine with circulation of about 500,000 in a good field that is still growing, but at a slow rate. It is close to its best profits (that is probably why the seller wants to sell). There are a number of competing buyers, so you pay a good, but not outrageous, price for it.

Revenue	$10.0 million
Cash profits	2.5 million
Price at 18 times earnings	45.0 million

You anticipate that you will be able to increase profits to $3 million for the ensuing five years—and possibly more in years after this. At the end of that period it should be worth the same $45 million if you had to sell it. The multiple would be lower because the field is more mature and the magazine is no longer growing as fast.

START-UP

Say you have an opportunity to start-up a property that, within five years, will be at the stage of the magazine above. You estimate that you can start it with losses of $5 million during the test period and first two years, and after that it will be at break-even and then become profitable.

Here is a year-by-year cash comparison for the first five years. Tax effects and the income that could be earned on the cash not used for the purchase or for the start-up have been omitted for simplicity, but they are more favorable for the start-up than the purchase.

	Purchase	Start-up
Purchase	$(45.0)	$—
Year	*Profit or (Loss)*	
1	3.0	$(2.0)
2	3.0	(3.0)
3	3.0	—
4	3.0	.5
5	3.0	2.0
Total	$(30.0)	$(2.5)

The value of each property is the same at the end of the period.

This precise scenario could not happen, but it gives an idea of what might happen if, instead of making the purchase, the $45 million had been used for searching out and testing a number of new magazines, and launching three or four that succeed. The company would be in a vastly superior position.

Financial people in large companies that are not in the magazine business are rarely able to relate to start-up magazines. First, they don't understand why there is no cost of goods sold and gross profit. Second they are afraid of the accountants' fiction of a large liability called deferred subscription revenue.

More than once I have seen them put the figures for starting magazines into their standard return on investment (ROI) formulas—only to come to the conclusion that the results are so close to infinity that they could not possibly be right—so there must be something wrong with the entire concept. This has killed a number of what might have been very profitable operations.

How a Publisher Can Develop an R&D Program

It would, of course, be foolish for a company just to try one new project—or even two. You cut the odds of success down too far. What is needed is an organized program so that a failure or two is just part of the game, and those risks we mentioned before are spread over a large number of opportunities.

Here are the steps in developing a program:

1. Reach the conclusion that it is a good idea and make the decision to attack such a program as intelligently and as wholeheartedly as you do everything else—not an easy decision.
2. Reorganize so that one of your best people has the authority and responsibility to make the program work.
3. Fund the enterprise adequately—or don't bother.
4. Make sure there is careful planning, good monitoring, and a specific decision-making process to determine which ventures to address.
5. Do *not* put unnecessary restrictions on the projects that can be investigated. Size does not always relate to the amount of profit that can be earned, and just because you don't relate to certain fields, don't exclude them.

6. Do it off-line. Locate the people involved away from your headquarters. Keep them out of your day-to-day decisions on other matters. Keep them off your normal committees. Ignore the reactions and comments of the line managers you see every day. They don't know anything about new projects.

7. Let the world know that you have established the R&D operation so that you will hear about a few good—and a great many bad—concepts from outsiders. Whatever you do, don't confine the ventures to those dreamed up in house.

8. When you get involved with outside entrepreneurs, be sure they are adequately rewarded for their ideas, work, and dedication. Don't be afraid to give them "a piece of the action"—and a good one at that.

9. Use all the help you can get inside your own company. Lots of people enjoy the fun of helping out with a new project. But don't be afraid to hire direct mail consultants, headhunters, marketing consultants, and others, no matter whose feelings in the company are hurt.

10. In the same vein, don't impose your own internal services on the new ventures. They might not fit—and can lead to internal warfare, which means bloodshed, plus many unnecessary expenses.

CHAPTER 14

Mythology of New Magazines

"The failure rate of new magazines is about the same as that for new restaurants."

THIS IS OFTEN said, particularly by those in the venture community. To some extent, they may be correct. I have often estimated that some 90 to 95% of the new magazines that are announced failed or were never started at all. It's just too easy to start a magazine. With an idea—and some money—anyone can print up a magazine. Unfortunately, a great many people do.

But if you do it right, with all the planning and testing that we will be discussing, I have found that the success rate (not the failure rate) is about 70%. That's pretty good for a startup in any field.

The Outstanding New Magazines of the Year

Every year various publications tell you their versions of the outstanding new magazines. It isn't quite like the Academy Awards, but sort of along the same line. The only problem is that they don't give you the criteria on which they make their selections—and you often find that the ones they pick are no longer being published—or actually never even got their first issue out. Among those which have been discussed recently have been *dads, Grok, Fuse,* and *One,* all of which you will have trouble finding.

The reason, of course, is that the publications making the picks are the victims of what the politicians call *spin*. They hear about the new magazines that have the best, or at least the most expensive, public relations programs.

In some cases I also have the feeling that they sometimes give space to the most outlandish ideas that happen to come across their desks, which can make for interesting reading, but does not help the publication much.

The Launch of a New Magazine Is a News Event

New magazines seem to interest everyone in the same way as, I suppose, new TV programs, and they bring about lots of comment. Everyone is interested in hearing about any new magazine and, regretfully, the death of any magazine, old or new.

If you are the one doing the launch, of course, you do everything you can to publicize it, with the hope that this will help ensure its success. Think of the hype that accompanied the launch of *O,* Oprah's magazine, *George* by JFK Jr., *Brill's Content, Talk,* or the *ESPN* magazine.

If there is enough of this kind of PR, it certainly can be helpful in selling some newsstand copies, if that is the kind of magazine you are publishing, and you should take advantage of it.

Samir Husni's Guide to New Consumer Magazines

Each year since 1985, Samir has issued a book listing all the new magazines that are supposed to have been started, along with pictures of the covers of many of them. These indicate that some 231 to 1,063 new magazines have been launched each year since then, with the numbers generally increasing as the years have gone by.

The book is misnamed because it really is just a list of the titles that he has found on newsstands, rather than a guide to all the new magazines.

Included in this list are special issues, which may be put out only once, such as all the one-shots covering Princess Diana in 1997. It also includes such annual publications as *Connecticut Golf 1999.* It is doubtful, too, that all the publications that announced regular 6 or 12-time publishing actually ever achieved that.

A review of the 864 titles listed by Samir Husni for 1999 indicated that only 73 were listed in SRDS. Only 353 listed a frequency of 4 times a year or more, and of these, a number seemed to be business rather than consumer magazines; 8 were custom titles issued for specific companies rather than being magazines that were trying to make it on their own; and a great many had been published long before 1997, one as long before as 1948, so they were not new at all.

In other words, this is simply a compendium of titles that have first been found on newsstands in that year, no matter their frequency, rather than a record of new magazines. If you understand the background, it still gives some indication of the amount of new magazine activity, but its real value is very limited.

It does, however, make interesting reading.

Part II: What Is Involved in Starting a Magazine

CHAPTER 15

Steps in Starting a Magazine

THERE IS NO formula for starting a new magazine, because no two magazines are in the same business. The start-up for each must be individually planned.

While there is no formula, there is a very logical procedure. If you follow it, the whole affair will be easier to accomplish, will save time and effort, and, hopefully, will increase the chances for success. At the worst, you will find early on that there is very little chance for success and you will save many hours of struggle, work, and eventual grief.

Steps in Starting a Magazine

1. Crystallize the editorial content.
2. Develop a business plan.
3. Print a pilot issue.
4. Test the reaction of potential readers and/or advertisers.
5. Hire the staff.
6. Publish.

Omitted from this list is the item that may be the most difficult and that may take longer than anything else—raising money. The search for capital goes along concurrently with the other steps, but must be carefully planned and organized. If you try to get capital before you are fully prepared, you may find that you have wasted a chance with some of your prime prospects. Raising capital will be discussed separately—see chapter 28, "Raising Money."

CHAPTER 16

Starting a Magazine Is Like Nothing You Have Ever Done Before—Even If You Have Done It Before

STARTING ANY NEW venture involves doing many things that are different from anything you have ever done before. And, to make it worse, magazine publishing is very different from almost any other business. It requires activities as diverse as:

• Developing a long-range plan covering at least five years, which details every aspect of the magazine from its start-up through its profitable operation—and perhaps even up through its eventual disposition. Doing long-range planning of any activity is difficult. Consider that you are developing the plan for an intangible product that has to appeal both to the public and to advertisers. All this is based on nothing except a concept that you have dreamed up out of whole cloth. On top of this, you must develop the plan probably knowing very little or nothing about many aspects of publishing, even if you have been working in some area of the field.

• Finding and assembling a team of people with highly developed, but diverse, skills who, hopefully, are as excited about and dedicated to the concept of the magazine as you are. This is harder than you may think because there are at least three distinctly different types of people involved in any magazine: (a) editors, who are highly talented literary types devoted to developing written material and design that will appeal to the public; (b) advertising salespeople, who are skilled in selling an intangible product at a high price, usually in a one-on-one personal situation; and (c) circulation people, who know how to sell an intangible product to the public. These are a peculiar breed whose talents combine both marketing creativity and the handling and interpretation of statistics.

• Inspiring, directing, and working with this team of very different types who may not relate to each other very well at the start. Since the people are so different, managing them can be difficult at times, particularly since you have never worked together before. It is probable that at some point the team will break up. As long as you, and they, realize that from the start, when the breakup comes, try to make it as friendly as possible.

• Contracting for services and working with suppliers including:

PRODUCTION—printers, paper manufacturers, shippers, and the Postal Service

EDITORIAL—writers, designers, artists, and photographers

ADVERTISING—salespeople, independent sales representatives, promotion designers, and producers and research companies

CIRCULATION—subscription agencies, single-copy distributors, and subscription fulfillment concerns

ADMINISTRATIVE—landlords, utilities, telephone companies, office supply concerns, insurance companies, and tax authorities

• Choosing and working with a group of outside consultants and other professionals whom you may never have worked with before. This will involve people who help in the publication of the magazine, such as designers, subscription consultants, single-copy consultants, production consultants, copywriters, promotion consultants, public relations consultants, research people, and general publishing consultants. In addition there are lawyers, accountants, tax people, bankers, financial people, and many others. If you have never worked with outsiders before, you will want to know how to get the most from them. See chapter 31, "Getting the Most from Outside Professionals."

• Getting involved in every aspect of the magazine. You will have to worry about the salespeople's commission rates, where the water cooler is placed, payment of payroll taxes, what printer to use, and everything else—when what you really want is the fun of publishing the magazine.

• Raising large and small amounts of money—partly from your friends, relatives, and neighbors, partly from wealthy individuals, venture firms, and Wall Streeters, or from other publishers. This, as will be discussed in detail later, is usually the most difficult part of the entire process. You will find that selling others on your wonderful dream takes longer, is more depressing, and is more frustrating than anything else you have ever done—this is true even if you are just selling it inside the company where you are working.

• Exhibiting the dedication that will make you quit your old job so that you can spend nights and days working on the magazine for many months or years. It usually means 18-hour days, seven days a week, for three years or so before you break down. At the same time you have to keep your family happy. One way to avoid a divorce is by getting your spouse involved in the magazine, too.

• Having the persistence and strength to be turned down often, reach the brink of disaster a few times, and to carry on anyway. But—good news—the longest time I have ever seen between development of the concept of a magazine and its first issue was only 15 years.

• Having the strength of mind and character to drop the project if you find that the world didn't really want your magazine after all.

CHAPTER 17

The Launch Scenario

THE LENGTH OF time it takes between the development of an idea for a new magazine and the publication of the first issue may seem at first to be incredibly long. For a paid circulation consumer magazine, it will be at least 21 to 30 months. A controlled circulation magazine would be somewhat shorter, 18 to 24 months. Of course, as we say about everything else in this business, this will depend on the specific project.

We are discussing something much more complex than a simple timetable. It is a complete program for getting started in a planned and intelligent manner. We will discuss each step in the launch process, as well as the reason for it, the length of time it might take, who is involved in performing it, the probable cost, and what you will have accomplished.

There can, of course, be all sorts of different types of magazines, but for the sake of simplicity we will be talking about just two types of start-ups: paid circulation consumer magazines and controlled circulation business magazines.

The scenario will be different for each magazine depending on the field covered and its size, the type of circulation and the difficulty of obtaining it, the ease of selling advertising, the economic situation at the time, and just about everything else.

> **WARNING**
> Don't set your mind on a specific date for publishing the first issue—and certainly don't ever announce one—until you have developed the launch scenario. You lose credibility quicker by missing publication dates than any other way.

Launch Scenario for a Paid Circulation Consumer Magazine

Figure 17.1 is a typical launch scenario for a paid circulation consumer magazine. Each of the headings is explained below.

- *Year and Month.* An estimate of the time it takes for each major step.
- *Step.* The major step to be performed.
- *Outsider Employed.* While the entrepreneur and his team will do most of the work, some steps involve specialized skill and experience where an outside expert will be invaluable.
- *Estimated Cost.* For the outsiders who are used, as well as the cost of the specific items that must be purchased, such as the test mailing and the printing of the pilot issue.
- *Go/No-Go Points.* These are built in to force you to reevaluate the project at every conceivable point where a decision to abort intelligently can be made. It will help your investors understand how carefully you are going through the launch process, with checks at every reasonable point to judge the feasibility of the project—and that you will not waste all their money if there is any point where the project does not seem to be feasible.

TIMING

This scenario applies only to the steps needed in launching the magazine and does not include any time needed in raising capital. That, of course,

Figure 17.1. Launch Scenario—Paid Circulation Consumer Magazine

Year and Month	Step	Outsider Employed	Estimated Cost	Go/No-Go Points
Year One				
January	Editorial planning			Financial plan not good enough
	Financial plan—First try	Consultant	$10,000	
February	Editorial planning			
March	Editorial planning			Editorial plan not good enough
April	Focus groups—First round	Market researcher	$10,000	Focus groups negative
May	Pilot issue	Magazine designer	$10,000	
June	Pilot issue	Magazine designer	$10,000	
July	Pilot issue	Magazine designer	$10,000	Unable to develop suitable pilot
August	Print pilot issue	Printer	$50,000	
	Test mailing planning	Circulation consultant	$10,000	
September	Focus groups—Second round	Market researcher	$10,000	Focus groups negative
	Test mailing planning	Circulation consultant	$10,000	
October	Test mailing planning	Circulation consultant	$10,000	
November	Test mailing planning	Circulation consultant	$10,000	
December	Test mailing dropped 100,000 pieces	Mailing house	$70,000	
Year Two				
January				
February				
March	Test mailing results	Circulation consultant	$5,000	Test mailing fails
	Financial plan—Second try		$10,000	Financial plan not good enough
April	Hire staff	Executive recruiter	$50,000	Unable to hire suitable staff
September	First issue			

could add many months (or years) to the timing.

Figure 17.1 shows the launch scenario for a national consumer magazine—a special interest title which might have as much as 500,000 circulation some day. It calls for some $285,000 in seed money. This amount does not take into account any special arrangements you might be able to make with the outside suppliers or consultants, such as giving them a small part of the ownership rather than cash, which might reduce the capital outlay. Nor does it include the cost of keeping the entrepreneur alive.

A larger circulation magazine would, of course, require more testing in the mail. A smaller, or regional title, could not afford—or need—this much and would have a smaller budget, but probably not a faster timeline.

By arbitrarily starting in the month of January in Year One, I have shown the shortest time it would take before the first issue—18 months. This time schedule makes it possible to make a test mailing in December that year, the most attractive month for magazines. If you must start at some other time, it will take considerably longer. (See chapter 22, "Testing a New Magazine through Direct Mail.").

If any of the steps takes longer than it shows here, you will also have a longer time schedule. For instance, if the test mailing results turned out to be "iffy"—or if for other reasons you wanted a confirmation mailing of the test—you should wait until the next good mailing period to do that, in June. You would probably then test at least 300,000 pieces, which might cost another $150,000. Your whole time schedule, of course, would then be moved forward by another six months or so.

Editorial Planning

That concerns the crystallization of the editorial concept and the development of the detailed issue plans which are discussed in chapter 18, "If You Can't Say It in Ten Words." You might figure three months to do this, but if it doesn't come easily, probably more.

(I have seen some cases where it took over a year—but the delay was well worth it.) The more specifically the magazine is oriented to a special market, the quicker. The more general the editorial content, the longer it usually takes. There is presumably no cost since it is done by the entrepreneur and the other members of the team who are not paid at this point.

Financial Plan—First Try

This should be done early on to be sure that the basic concept is financially feasible. This is discussed further in chapter 20, "The Business Plan." This financial plan, of course, is not the full-fledged business plan you will use in fund-raising and other activities. Costs listed here include the use of a magazine model for planning and fees for consultants.

Focus Groups—First Round

The need for testing and the function and methodology of conducting focus groups in that testing is discussed in chapter 21, "Test, Test, Test." The more general the magazine, the more focus groups will be needed because you will want to sample different types of people in different areas of the country. Figure about $2,500 for each group.

Pilot Issue

The need for this and the form it will take are discussed in chapter 19, "Print a Pilot Issue." Figure it will take some four months to do the editorial work, to have the design for the magazine created, to obtain sample advertising pages, and to have the pilot printed. If you have trouble with the editorial matter or the design, however, it could take much longer. It was assumed here that the editorial material would be created by the entrepreneur and his staff at no cost, but that a skilled magazine designer would be needed. The costs will vary depending on the nature of the magazine.

Test Mailing

The schedule here indicates that about three months are needed to develop the mailing grid, write and print the mailing pieces, order lists, and do everything else prior to making the mailing. Planning for the test should start at least three months prior to that to be sure the copy is suitable and the lists are available. The cost will depend on the nature of the magazine, the number of different tests made, and the size and complexity of the mailing.

Focus Groups—Second Round

This time the pilot issue is used in conducting this testing. This will give you a second reading about the concept—and also a reaction to the pilot issue.

Test Mailing Results

Results will be available for analysis about three months after the mailing. You will undoubtedly be watching the mail every day before that, but try to avoid reaching any conclusions too early. In some cases the responses come in very quickly and then die. In other cases they seem to dribble in forever. In addition to the natural quirks of the recipients, they may be influenced by weather conditions in various parts of the country and other extraneous and unpredictable things. The $5,000 cost listed here is for the cost of the return postage you will pay. The higher this cost gets, of course, the better the results and the happier you will be.

Financial Plan—Second Try

This will be based on the results of the mailing as well as estimates of the other costs that you will have developed during the year or so since the first try was made. Chances are that you will have made a number of other calculations during the interim, in any case.

Hiring Staff

A discussion of the staff you will need, where you can find them, and what you will have to pay them is in chapter 26, "What People Do You Need, and When." In this chart I have included the use of an executive recruiter to help hire the key players at a considerable cost. It is probable that, during the year or so while the launch process has been going on, you will have made arrangements for most, if not all, the key people you will need. In that case, you may not have to incur this cost.

You would want the staff on board at least six months prior to the publication of the first issue so that editorial operations will be proceeding smoothly by the time regular publication takes place, advertisers can be contacted early, and circulation activities can be planned far in advance. Of course, you would be foolish to hire the staff—and they would be foolish to join—before you are sure of the results from the test mailing (or the later confirmation mailing if that is required).

When Should the First Issue Be Published?

In a very few cases, there may be specific times when a magazine should appear. For instance, you might feel that a magazine on ecology would do well to come out on Earth Day to take advantage of all the publicity. This is rarely essential, even though you may think it is.

For most magazines, once you have gone through the steps above, the timing of first issue will probably be dictated by the timing that is best for selling advertising.

The vast majority of major advertisers make up their budgets for the following year in the fall. It is very hard for a new magazine to get advertising if it is not in those budgets. Logically, the best time for the first issue would be early in the following year, say March or April.

WARNING

A recession—or the threat of one—must also be considered. In either case, advertisers delay making up their budgets until they have a clearer picture of what the next year will bring. In recession times, the first quarter of the year is often very far down in advertising, much more than in later periods during the year.

This timing of the first issue would also seem to fit with the circulation efforts of the magazine, since it is probable that a major mailing would have been made during the December-January mailing period, and you would want to be sure to have readers for the first issue, which you would not have before March or April.

You might feel that you should publish one or more issues in the fall so that there is publicity for the new magazine—and advertisers could see the first issues while they are making up their budgets. This makes sense only if those issues have enough ads to make them meaningful. A thin issue may hurt more than it helps.

There is also a school that says that it doesn't make much difference when the first issue comes out because there won't be much real advertising in the first year or two anyway. If this is correct, and I doubt it, then cost factors should rule.

Launch Scenario for a Controlled Circulation Business Magazine

Many of the steps for a business magazine are the same as for a consumer magazine, but, since most business magazines are focused on relatively narrow areas of interest, the timing in certain areas may be a little shorter. For a controlled circulation magazine, there is no need to test the sale of subscriptions in the mail.

This scenario applies only to the steps needed in launching the magazine and does not include any time that might be needed in raising capital. That, of course, could add many months (or years) to the timing.

Figure 17.2 shows the launch scenario for a national business magazine—which might have as much as 50,000 circulation. It calls for some $100,000 in seed money.

This amount doesn't take into account any special arrangements you might be able to make with the outside suppliers and consultants, or specific knowledge you may have of the industry involved that might reduce the capital outlay.

On the other hand, since the entire income structure of a controlled circulation magazine depends on the sale of advertising, a longer period than for consumer magazines for selling is usually helpful.

An umbrella magazine for an industry, such as *Advertising Age,* might require more testing and editorial planning. A smaller title, or a new product tabloid, may not need this large a budget—and can be developed faster.

Editorial Planning

That is, crystallizing the editorial concept and developing the detailed issue plans, which is dis-

Figure 17.2. Launch Scenario—Controlled Circulation Business Magazine

YEAR AND MONTH	STEP	OUTSIDER EMPLOYED	ESTIMATED COST	GO/NO-GO POINTS
Year One				
January	Editorial planning			Financial plan not good enough
	Financial plan—First try	Consultant	$10,000	
February	Editorial planning			
March	Editorial planning			Editorial plan not good enough
April	Focus groups/in-depth interviews/First round	Market researcher	$10,000	
May	Focus groups/in-depth interviews/First round	Market researcher		Focus groups negative
June	Pilot issue	Magazine designer	$10,000	
July	Pilot issue	Magazine designer	$10,000	
August	Pilot issue	Magazine designer	$10,000	Unable to develop suitable pilot
September	Print pilot issue	Printer	$30,000	
	Focus groups/in-depth interviews/Second round	Market researcher	$10,000	
October	Focus groups/in-depth interviews/Second round	Market researcher	$10,000	Focus groups negative
November	Financial plan—Second try	Consultant	$10,000	Financial plan not good enough
December	Hire staff			Unable to hire suitable staff
Year Two				
May	First issue			

cussed in chapter 18, "If You Can't Say It in Ten Words." You might figure three months for the editorial plan, but if it doesn't come easily, probably longer. The more specialized the field, the quicker. An umbrella magazine for an industry might require considerably more editorial planning. A new product tabloid could be a very simple editorial project.

Financial Plan—First Try

This should be done early on to be sure that the basic concept is financially feasible. This is discussed further in chapter 20, "The Business Plan." This financial plan, of course, is not the full-fledged business plan you will use in fund-raising and other activities. Costs listed here include the use of a magazine model for planning and fees for consultants.

Focus Groups or In-Depth Interviews

Readership research may be even more vital for a business publication than for a consumer magazine. The need for testing, and the function and methodology of conducting focus groups is discussed in chapter 21, "Test, Test, Test." Here again, the more general the interest, the more focus groups are useful because you will want to sample people in different parts of the industry.

In addition to the focus groups, or in some cases, in place of them, there should be in-depth interviews with key people in the field. Since both buyers and sellers are interested in the field, the same people are frequently readers as well as advertisers. Their opinions can be vital for both readership and advertising purposes, so in-depth interviews may serve both purposes.

Pilot Issue

The need for this and the form it will take are discussed in chapter 19, "Print a Pilot Issue." Figure it will take some four months to do the editorial work, to have the design for the magazine created, to obtain sample advertising pages and to have the pilot printed, although this time may be shortened for some simpler magazines such as new product tabloids. It is assumed here that the editorial material would be created by the entrepreneur and his staff at no cost, but that a skilled magazine designer would be needed. The costs will vary depending on the nature of the magazine.

Focus Groups or In-Depth Interviews—Second Round

This time the pilot issue will be used in conducting the focus groups and the in-depth interviews. This will give a second reading—and a reaction to the pilot.

Financial Plan—Second Try

This will update the plan based on the results of the focus groups and in-depth interviews with both readers and advertisers, as well as later estimates of the other costs that you may have developed since the first try was made. Chances are that you will have made a number of other calculations during the interim, in any case.

Hiring Staff

A discussion of the staff you will need, where you can find them, and what you will have to pay them is in chapter 26, "What People Do You Need." It is probable that outside help will not be needed in finding and recruiting staff for a business magazine and that you will have made arrangements for most, if not all, of the key people you will need.

You would want them on board at least six months prior to the publication of the first issue so that editorial operations will be proceeding smoothly by the time regular publication takes place, advertisers are contacted early, and circulation activities are planned far in advance. But you would be foolish to hire them—and they would be foolish to join—before you are sure of the results of your in-depth interviews and advertiser reactions.

When Should the First Issue Be Published?

To a great extent the steps above will set the timing for publishing the first issue. But, since the magazine depends solely on advertising, you want to give yourself plenty of time to find out whether you can sell advertising to the bellwether advertisers. I suggest at least nine months. For most magazines, once you have gone through the steps above, the timing of the first issue will probably be dictated by what is best for selling advertising.

The vast majority of major advertisers make up their budgets for the following year in the fall. It is very hard for a new magazine to get advertising if it is not in those budgets. So you would logically think that the best time for the first issue would be early in the following year, say March or April.

WARNING

A recession—or the threat of one—must also be considered. In either case, advertisers delay making up their advertising budgets until they have a clearer picture of what the next year will bring. Because of this, in recession times the first quarter of the year is often very far down in advertising—much more than in later periods during the year.

Some might feel that you should publish one or more issues in the fall so that there is publicity for the new magazine—and advertisers could see the first issues while they are making up their budgets. This makes sense only if those issues have enough ads to make them meaningful. A thin issue may hurt more than it helps.

There is also a school that says that it doesn't make much difference when the first issue comes out because there won't be much advertising in the first year or two anyway. If this is correct, and I doubt it, then cost factors should rule.

WARNING

There is a temptation in the business field to want to publish the first issue at one of the major conventions or shows for the industry. This should be avoided if it reduces the time you have to sell. It also may not fit with the fall advertising budget cycle. You certainly don't want to have a thin issue just when it will get the most exposure.

CHAPTER 18

If You Can't Say It in Ten Words or Less, You Don't Know What Your Magazine Is All About

YOU HAVEN'T GOT anything until you crystallize the editorial concept. (Some people like to create a mission statement. This usually discusses circulation and advertising. I am simplistic enough—and enough editorially oriented—to believe that everything starts with pleasing the reader. Once you accomplish this, you can take up the other parts.)

The editorial concept is not a question of simply selecting a title, or a subject to be covered, but means defining just what you want to say to the readers. This is not easy. I have seen times where weeks and months were devoted to trying to crystallize just what the magazine is all about—without, in some cases, ever reaching a sound conclusion.

Many magazines have failed because the editors did not know what they were trying to do. Here are two, unfortunately typical, concepts I have seen:

> "The magazine will be bright, witty and chatty—serious without being ponderous. Graphics will be used liberally and will be designed to complement the text without being obtrusive. Headlines will be lively and catchy. We will take a stand, but not go out of our way to be controversial."

> "*Social Living* will be a handsome, high-quality monthly publication with strong editorial and outstanding graphic appeal. It will have a pronounced viewpoint aimed at the responsive audience of individuals who move in the inner core of society. *Social Living* will be informative without being tedious; provocative, but always in good taste. It will reflect the upscale, eclectic lifestyle of its readership."

What did they say?

Nothing!

Even a law review tries to do all the things they mentioned, but these examples have not really defined the editorial content, spirit, or quality of the products.

> If you can't say it in ten words or less, you don't know what your magazine is all about.

Your ten words should not include any adjectives—and certainly should not hint that it might be ponderous, tedious, or not in good taste.

Here are some good ones:

- *Time,* the weekly newsmagazine
- *Self,* the self-improvement magazine for today's complete woman
- *Guideposts,* America's source for inspiration
- *Vanity Fair* covers the whys of central characters of our time
- *Newsweek* covers the news in depth and provides follow-through.
- *Family Fun,* for families with children 3 to 12, and about the fun things they can do together (16 words—forgiven)

The ten words, of course should also be used in your business plan, in raising money, and for selling both circulation and advertising.

A Year's Issue Plans

You really won't know whether you have an editorial concept that will hold together, be interesting, and cover your subject until you have developed detailed issue plans for at least a year's worth of issues.

These plans should include for *each* item in *each* issue, including feature articles, columns, departments, editorials, cartoons, letters to the editor, and every other piece that will be carried in the magazine:

- The title
- A paragraph describing what will be in the piece and what the tone will be
- Who might write it
- Length—in pages
- Graphics that might accompany it

Note that this is not just a simple table of contents, but real plans—a much more extensive recital. As you go through this exercise, you will find that you will be moving different pieces from one issue to another so that each issue hangs together—and is still able to surprise the reader every so often.

You will probably be tempted to develop cute or provocative titles for different pieces. This is not really needed, or even helpful. What we are trying to do at this point is to get good, interesting, and balanced issues. Don't be shy about naming possible authors for different pieces. Their names are used at this point just to give an indication of the style of the piece.

This may seem to be a very difficult and time-consuming exercise. It is, but until you do it, you won't really know whether you have a magazine or not. In fact, the person who benefits most is usually the entrepreneur. When you finish, you will realize that you really will be able to put out a good magazine.

The development of issue plans for a year's issues is really the minimum required for crystallizing the concept. Depending on the skill and experience of the people involved, and the nature of the subject matter, another year or two's issues must often be done.

About now in the seminars I have conducted over the years, someone is bound to point out that his magazine is much too timely to be able to develop plans for a whole year ahead—and therefore he is unable to complete this exercise. That's a cop-out. You must do the plans the way you would today—and, if you have to make changes when you actually start publishing, so be it.

Of course, during the process it often happens that you discover that the concept does not jell, or becomes too narrowly defined, or would be too expensive to produce, or should be a newsletter or a book or something else, but not a magazine. Too bad! But better to find it out now, before you go through the rest of the process.

CHAPTER 19

Print a Pilot Issue—How Else Can You or Anyone Else Know What the Magazine Will Be Like?

WHEN YOU START a new magazine, it is vital to know just what it will look and feel like. The principal reason, however, for actually printing an issue is for yourself—so that you know you can put out a good magazine. But there are all sorts of other people you can use it with:

- Potential investors—probably the best thing you can show them
- Potential employees
- Potential suppliers

It can be the prime promotion piece when you start going after advertising. You should print thousands of copies to give to advertisers and agencies.

Why go to the expense of actually printing copies? Because people cannot visualize things, that's true even for those of us in the business.

The best way to show them what the magazine will be like is to give them a copy of it, or something close to it.

WARNING

Anything less really does not do the job. I have seen people try pasted-up dummies. They don't look like magazines—and they certainly don't feel like magazines. I have seen them try boards like the storyboards used for TV and the same problems hold true. I have seen beautiful full-color slides and computer layouts used. That doesn't do it either for most people, and particularly those not in the business.

The best pilot issue is exactly like a real issue of the magazine—with all the articles written and artwork included—plus sample advertisements of the kind that would normally run in the magazine. But writing, editing, and printing a whole issue can be very expensive and you may not have enough money to do that. So we often compromise.

Say your eventual magazine will be 96 pages plus the cover. You might print 40 pages plus the cover, with 24 containing editorial matter, and advertisements on the remaining pages. But you don't want to hand someone a 40-page magazine because it will look and feel thin and will flop when someone picks it up, like the year-end issues of *Time* and *Newsweek.* It won't pass the "heft" test. In that case, we fill it up with blank paper. Then it feels the way the real magazine will feel.

What do the 40 pages contain? A contents page (or two), two columns, and several features. If you have enough money, you will write the full text and include all the graphics of all the pieces. That would be best. If you can't afford that, make sure to include the headlines, subheads, the first two paragraphs, captions, call-outs, and blurbs—and, of course, all the graphics.

That leaves you with lots of text area to fill up. Here you want something that looks like a real magazine. Don't use anything that doesn't (such as so-called Greek type). Instead, copy real text from other magazines (such as *Time*) in your typeface so that it looks like real magazine copy.

Another way to show the breadth of the subject matter you will carry is to use cover lines from one issue, a contents page that describes another issue's contents, and actual articles from a third issue, with coming attractions for a fourth. That way you have a better chance of interesting an advertiser or an investor in one or more of the pieces shown.

The advertising pages could carry 16 pages of typical ads. We have found that publishers of new magazines have, so far at least, been able to convince advertisers and agencies to lend them the color separations for these. In fact, it serves to acquaint these people early with the eventual magazine—a sort of warm-up process.

CHAPTER 20

The Business Plan

ONCE THE EDITORIAL has been crystallized, the next step is to develop a well-thought-out, detailed business plan that describes what you plan to do, how you plan to do it, and the results to be expected.

The business plan serves a number of functions:

1. It forces you to decide on every aspect of how operations will be carried out. For instance, in the editorial area you must fix the number of editorial pages; the size of the editorial staff; what you will pay each employee; what outside editorial and/or design consultants are needed and their cost; what manuscripts, artwork, and photos have to be purchased and at what cost; how much travel will be needed—and everything else needed to create a good product.
2. It describes the project to potential investors. This is so important that the form of the plan is usually determined with them in mind.
3. It helps attract employees, consultants, and other supporters.
4. It impresses potential suppliers so that you can get help and support from the best of them.

Writing the business plan is a big, complex project. At the same time, one of its goals is to make the project and carrying it out seem simple. Because it is hard to come to grips with future plans in the abstract, it is best developed first by making detailed financial projections. In developing these projections, you necessarily must make decisions about every aspect of the business.

The Business Plan

What It Tells You

Basically, the business plan will show that you can publish a magazine profitably based on reasonable assumptions about readership response, advertising support, and normal cost factors.

In working out the plan you will often find that major changes must be made in thoughts you might previously have had in order to reach satisfactory profits. For instance, you may have to drop your grand plan for publishing weekly and compromise on six issues during the first year—with a gradual move over time to 12 issues. You might reluctantly agree that 50-pound stock reproduces color as well as is needed even though you really wanted 70-pound. You might realize that the idea would be a better newsletter than a magazine. You might decide that you don't need many ad salespeople during the first year because there won't be much advertising early on in any case.

WARNING

You may even find that you must drop your seemingly wonderful project because there just is not a good enough risk/reward ratio—and you can't develop good enough profits to justify the amount of capital needed. It's better find this out now, not after the business has started.

Style

While the business plan helps you determine whether your concept can succeed and what reasonable assumptions can make that happen, it is also key in raising money. You must keep the potential investor in mind when you write it.

Consider a typical investor's situation. He most likely gets 40 calls or business plans of one kind or another a week. He cannot possibly spend time with every entrepreneur who wants to see him—and get anything done besides. He is well aware that the entrepreneur who asks for "just 15 minutes" cannot be dislodged in less than an hour or two. So he asks you to send something. Makes sense. Send your investor a well-thought-out business plan. It may well be the only chance you will get to see him. That being the case, here are some DOs and DON'Ts:

- DO—Make sure that the basic concept comes through very clearly and concisely. As always, crystallizing the editorial concept is vital.

- DO—Make sure that the flavor of the magazine comes through in your descrption of the editorial content. .

- DO—Be very businesslike and professional. Good typing (word processing), no typos, simple cover—like a business report, not an advertising presentation. At this point you want to come across as a thoughtful business person; tomorrow you can be the colorful editor or salesperson.

- DO—Build in several Go/No-Go Points. In every project there are a number of key things that must take place or failure is inevitable. One might be good results from the first big mailing; another, the ability to get a certain number of advertising pages by a certain time. There should be evaluation dates at which these key indicators are reviewed. If certain minimums have not been achieved, then the project should be stopped so that the investors will not lose all their money.

- DON'T—Send anything over 20 pages. I have gotten documents 200 and 300 pages long at times. My immediate reaction is to want to throw them away—and I'll bet that's what lots of people do. (I have, so far, resisted that temptation and just send them back, telling the writers to get them down to 20 pages.) I finally figured out how these enormous documents came into being. They represent the thought processes of the entrepreneurs over the past three years or so of preparation. Not really very stimulating reading, to say the least.

- DON'T—Try to explain the magazine business. You are not an expert in it and will not do it very well. If you think you must tell your investor about the business, get a reprint of an article a real expert has written and include that.

- DON'T—Try to reinvent the accounting business when doing projections. Use normal accounting terminology. Follow the format the magazine industry uses in developing the figures. Type the pages with figures just the way an accounting firm would do it—no boxes around the figures, no arrows, circles, or anything else you think looks good. Throw away all your desktop publishing devices for this purpose.

- DON'T—Use any color—or bleed. This is not a slick Madison Avenue presentation. It is a business plan and should look like one.

- DON'T—Use any words over three syllables.

- DON'T—Include an executive summary. I know that this is the current fad, but if your business plan is 20 pages or less, it isn't needed. Besides, I always feel that someone is writing down to me when he includes an executive summary. If you want to stress the excitement of the concept, do it in your cover letter.

- DON'T—Mention anything about raising money. We all know that this is one of the primary purposes of the plan, but don't say anything about it. Consider this document as an internal memorandum for you and your team. There is a very good reason for this. If, after you have raised the money, one of the investors claims that your data misled him in some way, the legal consequences can be quite severe.

Before you actually ask people for money, you should have a private placement memorandum prepared by your attorney. This is a fat document that, in addition to telling about the project, tells all the reasons why no one should invest in it. This document is for your later protection, but there is no sense in spending money for it until you know that you have live investors.

What It Contains

The normal business plan for a magazine contains eight sections:

1. The Concept
2. The Editorial Content
3. The Market for Readers
4. The Market for Advertisers
5. The Competition
6. The People Involved
7. Ancillary Activities
8. Financial Projections

Let's look at each of these sections. I have included, as examples in each section, material from business plans of the following very different magazines because I believe they show various ways in which each section might be explained. I have purposely stayed away from magazines you might recognize.

The Body Surfer Person—My yet-to-be published consumer title that will soon become one of the leading consumer magazines.

Abacus—A business magazine (with consumer overtones) that was inches from publication back in the infancy of the computer field in the 1970s and whose proposed editorial content seems to be very prophetic today. The magazine was to be published by the American Federation of Information Processing Societies (AFIPS), but was not started because of some internal problems.

Elan—A lifestyle consumer magazine for career-oriented black women that published several successful issues before the company backing it went into bankruptcy (for reasons that had nothing to do with the magazine).

Stratos—A business magazine (also with consumer overtones) for companies and individuals owning private airplanes for business purposes, which has been published for several years.

THE CONCEPT

First, state the idea for the publication as simply as possible. If your ten-word concept statement is good enough, that may be all that you need. Briefly amplify the reason for the concept by giving some facts explaining the field, its size, the trends, and other data.

You might do as well, in some rare instances, just to say something like "Golf is the fastest-growing sport in America. There are two successful major magazines devoted to golf. We think there is room for a third with a different focus." Then, of course, you would have to explain the differences and why they are important.

The concept should not be more than one page.

The Body Surfer Person

We all know that body surfing is sweeping the United States as no other sport ever has—and is just as popular in other parts of the world.

The Body Surfer Person is designed for anyone who has ever body surfed—or wanted to—as well as for body surfing spectators. It is for men, women, teenagers, and children. The magazine describes the experience of body surfing for the beginner and offers tips and advice to the expert.

With handsome graphics in four color, it is also a travel guide to the best surfing beaches in the world, giving specifics about wave and wind conditions, lifeguard quality, housing facilities, etc.

In a light-hearted and sometimes tongue-in-cheek manner, it tells the reader what is going on in the body surfing world and reflects the simple but wonderful lifestyle of a holiday in the surf and sun.

abacus

abacus will record and make explicit the history, discoveries, achievements, problems, and promises of one of man's most important tools—the computer.

abacus will be authored by the men and women who are immersed in a specific computer discipline who wish to communicate the significance and impact of their work to others in the computing field and to the informed public.

abacus will act as a technical forum for the profession in communicating with other sciences and technical disciplines, and with the informed public.

abacus will act as a forum for those in the computing field to communicate innovations in computing, and the impact of computing to decision-makers in industry, business, and government.

abacus will embody the collective image of the hundreds of thousands of men and women who have made computer-related disciplines their career and profession.

abacus will make understandable the subtle

nuances of technical and scientific innovations and will objectively detail the effect of computers on all our lives.

abacus is not just another publication. It embodies the continuing responsibility of those active in computing to communicate the impact of a machine that is changing the future even as it helps to create it.

Elan

Elan is the only lifestyle magazine for the career-oriented black woman who is enjoying success and wanting more.

Elan's editorial strikes a balance between showing how to achieve success and how to enjoy its benefits. Its monthly pages cover career management, self-fulfillment, and developing one's own personal style. Features on personal finance, fashion, travel, relationships, and cultural interests round out the editorial package.

Elan appeals to the multifaceted needs of readers who are on the move; open to new ideas; and striving to reach their potential with confidence, enthusiasm, and style.

Stratos

The passengers on business aircraft are primarily corporate executives, their customers, and others who are the most influential, highest paid, and in other ways the leaders of their companies.

(Followed by details of who they are, reasons for using the aircraft, and some specific instances of use.)

There are some 11,000 turbo-powered aircraft in the United States and Canada in this fleet, with some 6,000 more primarily used internationally. Far from being the playthings of the chairmen and CEOs of major corporations, business aircraft are operated in as professional and as sophisticated a manner as the major airlines. (Followed by details about their operations.)

Stratos offers advertisers these affluent decision makers in a place specifically engineered to create a relaxed state of heightened awareness where they are isolated from the demands, distractions, and rigors of their daily routines. Advertising is attractive for three types of goods and services:

- Aviation related
- Luxury consumer
- Business related

The Editorial Content

Expand on the editorial approach of the magazine and how you will carry it out. You don't need to include the whole year's worth of editorial plans that you have prepared, but a list of typical feature articles is essential, together with a description of the regular columns. You will also want to describe the kind of graphics, color, charts, and other helps that will accompany the editorial material. If, as is true for the great majority of magazines, the advertising will also be of interest to readers, discuss that, too.

Three or four pages should cover this.

The Body Surfer Person

The editorial content of *The Body Surfer Person* will consist of a mix of feature articles and regular departments, plus an eight-page pictorial essay in full color depicting one of the finest surfing beaches in the world.

Sample feature articles are:

- Robert Redford discusses the ecological threat to our beaches. *The Body Surfer Person* interviews the superstar who is widely respected for his determination to preserve the wilderness of our planet and the overwhelming need for good body surfing beaches. Eight-page interview with photographs.

- The Seaweed Quiche—Suggested author Julia Child. There are many varieties of seaweed and almost all of them are edible. Some are tastier than others. Child leads you step-by-step through several seaweed quiche recipes and the best wines to be consumed while preparing each. Recipes list ingredients and pictures of types of seaweed and the resulting dishes. Three–four pages.

- A Photographic Portfolio. *The Body Surfer Person* takes you to the famous Palm Beach of Sydney, Australia. Twelve photos, some aerial, show you the panorama of lifeguarding drills at one of the loveliest beaches for body surfing in the world. A special feature explains about the famous shark patrols, as well as the helicopters available for safety purposes—and gives a list of the nearest hospitals. Eight pages.

• Where to Go, Where to Stay, How to Get There. By our round-the-world correspondents, this article will cover specific data about six of the world's greatest surf beaches. This month we cover Copacabana, Rio; Biarritz, France; Palm Beach, Sydney; Newport Beach, California; Curtain Bluff, Antigua; and Davis Bay, St. Croix. This is a factual section of listings including:

- Weather you can expect at different seasons of the year, including wave types and heights
- Facilities at each beach as well as needed data about wave heights, wind speeds, water temperature, undertow, lifeguard availability, etc.
- Hotels, guest houses, campsites, private homes, and villas for rent and their prices
- Information about local transportation
- Ways and costs of getting there
- Prices and availabilities

This section is perforated for easy tear-out—twelve pages.

• *Meeting a Girl at a Macho Beach*—Suggested author, Ann Landers. The best way is to politely hand her the top/bottom of her bikini after she surfaces from a wave. Ann gives tips on what to do after that—Two pages.

• *Getting on Top of the Wave* by the current surfing champion. It's all in the timing—don't flail away. Just glide in at the right time. A picture instruction guide for amateurs. Four pages.

• *Up to the Curl*—News pages prepared by the editors. Includes latest results of surfing contests, news of various associations, governmental regulations, human interest stories, and the like. Graphics as needed. Four pages.

• *Teaching Your Parents to Body Surf* (humor). Suggested author—Soupy Sales. Eventually they will thank you for opening their eyes to the Greater Life out there, but you must be prepared for resistance. Two cartoons. Two pages

In addition there will be the usual one- or two-page columns:

- Editorial
- Exercise Corner
- Crossword puzzle
- Horoscope
- Fashion (beach accessories and bathing suits)
- Health (sunburn prevention, sea urchins, etc.)
- Legal advice
- Endpaper
- Carefully placed throughout the magazine will be line drawings and cartoons in black and white.

A great deal of the advertising in the magazine will be generic to the subject, as it is in many magazines with a travel component. Because of this, much of it will be as useful and of as much interest to readers as the editorial content.

abacus

The proposed new AFIPS publication has been compared to *Scientific American. abacus* intends to describe the current state-of-the-art in the computer field in language that can be understood by those actively involved with computing; by professionals in related technical disciplines; by the informed public; and by leaders of industry and government. The articles will be written by experts, professionally edited and well-illustrated.

Each month the magazine will publish at least four full-length articles.

• In the pilot issue, *Colossus and the Ultra Secret* is the story of a previously secret computer built during World War II to break the German military ciphers generated by the Enigma machine. It reveals that Colossus, not ENIAC, was probably the world's first programmable electronic digital computer.

• *The Limits of Data Base Security* points out that even in theory there is no foolproof way to safeguard confidential information from potential abuse.

• *The Verification of Programs* describes how, by incorporating proofs of correctness into a computer program, it is conceptually possible to determine whether the program is free of errors.

• *Microcomputer Weather Networks* explores how thousands of microcomputers—linked to form a network supercomputer—could be used to improve the accuracy of weather forecasts.

abacus will also have ten departments:

• Feedback consists of letters of particular interest to readers.

• The Authors presents a short biographical note about each author and book reviewer.

- The Editorial is written and signed by a guest author who takes a stand on an issue of significance to those in the computing field and the informed public.
- Public Policy is an analysis of significant trends in the public area that affect the computer field and are affected by it.
- Bits and Bytes is a selection of short items, some newsworthy, some merely amusing or interesting.
- Personal Computing is a monthly column devoted to the interests of the growing number of individuals—many of them nonprofessionals—who have bought small computers for their homes or offices.
- Computer Games is pure fun—but the kind that deepens one's awareness of the strengths and weaknesses of programs, languages, and machines.
- Books contains in-depth reviews by experts of significant works in the computer field.
- The monthly Calendar summarizes the most important professional meetings in the months ahead.
- Readings is a bibliography of works on the subjects covered in the publication. Each work cited is accompanied by a thumbnail review indicating why the author recommends it.

The Market for Circulation

Here you marshal all the facts you can find about the proposed audience for the magazine. Include any that will demonstrate why the audience will be interested in reading the magazine, and be anxious to buy it, if it is to have paid circulation.

Don't go to the Census Bureau or other heavy statistical sources for this information if you can avoid it. Reasons: (1) for most new magazines you don't need to; (2) you probably are not a statistician and will not understand or use the information very well; and (3) your readers probably are not very good at understanding that stuff either.

Instead, take a much simpler approach. Do what I call Yellow Page research. I am not sure I can completely explain that, but if you have traveled a lot, you probably know what I mean. When I land in a strange city and want to know what is going on, I read the Yellow Pages as well as all the descriptive literature the hotel has left in the room. You can learn a lot about the place that way.

I recall visiting the capital city of one state noted for its oil production and found listed all the events for the month including "Cultural Events." The total Cultural Events consisted of three rodeos. I then knew a lot about that city.

The real point here is that magazines are the most researched products in the world. They have to be in order to attract advertising. They know more about their readers than just about any other business knows about its customers.

Take advantage of the fact that most new magazines are something like existing magazines. Because of this, original research is rarely needed. The research done by existing magazines is readily available.

Suppose you wanted to start a new city magazine for Philadelphia (and assume that there never had been one). A little research will tell you that other city magazines generally end up with circulation somewhere between that of the regional edition of *Time* and that of *Newsweek*. They also have the same demographic characteristics as these two, which, of course, advertisers are interested in.

Time's Philadelphia circulation is 152,000; *Newsweek*'s is 120,000. You could expect that a city magazine there would be about 140,000. (The actual *Philadelphia* magazine's circulation *is* about 140,000.) You can then adopt all the demographics from the research that the other two magazines have available. You can see that you can apply the same type of thinking to almost any other new magazine.

The Body Surfer Person

Since there is no magazine currently dealing (even peripherally) with the subject of body surfing, it is difficult to estimate the market for readership, so Yellow Page research may not be usable. An educated guess is that there are at least 20 million body surfers in the United States alone, with the worldwide figures at least double that.

This is based on the latest Bureau of Census report of 2000 that:

- Swimming is the largest participation sport in the country, with approximately 130 million people active in 1997. 25% of these people swam five or more times in that year.

• On a typical summer weekend, more than four million people visit ocean beaches in the New York area alone. While not all of them are ardent body surfers, at least 20 percent do surf, either on purpose or inadvertently.

• Estimates are that more than 500 million visits are made each year to the ten major beach areas in the United States (Coney Island, Jones Beach, Riis Park, Jersey Shore, Miami Beach, Ocean City, Laguna Bay, Waikiki, New Beach, and Virginia Beach). This number can easily be doubled for the great many lesser beaches, giving a total of more than 1 billion visits.

• Assuming average attendance per person to be ten visits, a total of 100 million people each year go to ocean beaches. A conservative estimate that only one in five is a body surfer yields a total of 20 million.

Another indication of the size of the market can be gleaned from an analysis of the circulations of the magazines presently serving the fringe areas of the sport: swimming, sailing, diving, canoeing, and board surfing. Interestingly, there has been a strong rise in the number of publications and the circulation of those serving the swimming area: board surfing, scuba, kayaking, and the like, while the boating population has been declining. At the same time, the circulation of magazines devoted to travel to areas with ocean beaches has been increasing while the travel field as a whole has been relatively constant. (Put lots of material about the amount of circulation, prices, and types of readers of the other magazines here in your business plan.)

Elan

The primary *Elan* market consists of 2.5 million black women between the ages of 25 and 54 with household incomes of $15,000 or more. (This was written in the 1980s before a good deal of inflation.)

Elan readers are college educated, professional, affluent, and achievement oriented.

- 69% are college educated.
- 87% are professionals or managers.
- 44% have household incomes of $25,000 or more.
- 85% reside in 35 major urban areas.

The *Elan* woman is an opinion leader and considers her work to be not just a job, which influences her selection of magazine reading. In addition to the other black consumer publications, she reads *Harper's Bazaar* for fashion, *Working Woman* and *Savvy* for career direction, *Money* for money management, *Better Homes* for home decorating, and the newsweeklies for information.

It is anticipated that a substantial secondary readership will also be developed among younger aspiring black women and men professionals.

abacus

The potential universe of readers of *abacus* includes over 100,000 members of the constituent associations of AFIPS who are in the computing field; approximately 700,000 computer professionals of whom the vast majority are not members of any professional society; and at least 500,000 management executives, government officials, and other persons who are concerned with computer applications.

The potential readership also includes many thousands of educators and students at all levels. More than 15,000 university students are already invoiced as members of AFIPS Constituent Societies.

Many AFIPS society members will be reached directly through the planned addition of a subscription check-off to their dues notice. Other members and potential readers will be reached primarily through direct mail.

A small newsstand sale is expected in selected areas. Newsstand sales are an effective way to gain regular subscriptions at low cost, establish the presence of the magazine, and make advertisers aware of it. (Following this were the names and circulations of 16 "significant magazines in the computer field," only five of which are still being published.)

Stratos

Stratos circulation will be similar to that of the in-flight magazines, supplemented by mailings. 70,000 copies will be placed on the seats of the 10,500 private aircraft by Signature Flight Support Services, which has locations at over 40 airports in the United States and Europe, doing routine ground servicing. The average plane has 6.5 seats.

30,000 copies will be mailed to lists of registered owners and corporate officers of the registered owners from lists of AMSTAT, the leading aviation list services company.

The Market for Advertising

This section should give specifics about the types of products and services that would logically be advertised to the audience. This would be broken down into two parts—those advertisers who are generic to the field, and the more general advertisers who want to reach the field because of the nature of the audience.

Explain the importance of advertising to the success of the venture. If the venture is projected to break even with circulation revenue alone, with advertising the key to big profits, say it. If the success or failure is based primarily on advertising, say that.

The same kind of Yellow Page research as you did on circulation can be done in the advertising area, using the results achieved by other magazines to prove your point. You do this by finding magazines that are somewhat like the one you are starting and try to estimate how much of this would also fit with your magazine. It is good to actually develop lists of advertisers and the products that would fit in your magazine to quantify this.

The Body Surfer Person

Advertising prospects for *The Body Surfer Person* are substantial because the audience is large and attractive to advertisers, as has been amply proven.

The magazine is aimed at an upscale, affluent, well-educated audience of leaders in the 21 to 39 age group. It is interesting that our survey showed that some 40 percent of the body surfers fit this group. Further, this elitist group, which is of greatest interest to advertisers, consider themselves "body surfers," while the other, downscale group, call the sport "riding the waves." This difference makes identification easy, and the continued efforts of the downscale group to advance to the higher class means more readers in the future.

The research shows an audience profile with these characteristics:

- Sex Male 66%
  Female 34%
- Median age 28.4
- Median household income $39,650
- Managerial and professional 67%
- Cars owned—average 2.8
- Own house 92%
- Trips for body surfing 1999 27
- Trips abroad for body surfing 6
- Highest level of education
  College 82%
  Graduate school 51%
- Active in religious or community affairs 98%

Elan

The primary aim of advertisers is to deliver selective markets with maximum efficiency and the impact to promote product trial and, ultimately, loyalty.

Over the past two decades a distinct black market has evolved, exhibiting a catch-up buying psychology. This new pattern of consumption by blacks is particularly evident in the top 60 metropolitan are as of the country that account for over 45 percent of the total $163 billion black Gross National Product. The advertiser is, therefore, concerned with the rising black affluence and particularly with the better-educated emerging blacks who spend the lion's share. More than half the total black income is in 25% of total black households, with the $15,000-plus household income segment being the fastest-growing black market segment in both number of people and average earnings.

Elan provides advertisers with a unique and effective environment to communicate with mature, sophisticated, and affluent black women bursting with buying power. The advertising potential is enormous.

The *Elan* woman:

- Travels
- Wears designer clothes
- Frequents good restaurants
- Owns a car
- Uses credit cards
- Buys premium wines and liquors
- Purchases luxury household items
- Is a heavy user of health and beauty aids

(Followed by a list of advertisers selling the items above.)

The *Elan* advertising market is in a class by itself boasting premium products for a premium audience.

Stratos

Advertising in *Stratos* is attractive for three types of goods and services:

- Aviation-related
- Luxury consumer
- Business-related

Aviation Related—Advertisers of aviation-related goods and services have long faced a difficult challenge: How to get their message to the true decision-makers in any big-ticket, aviation related purchase—in other words, how to target the guy who, though he rides in the back of the corporate aircraft, signs the check. The editorial missions of traditional business aviation publications are all targeted to the flight crew.

Professional pilots, though highly trained for a technically demanding position with lots of responsibility, are emotionally involved with their avocation.

A good analogy for the relationship between pilots and the corporate decision makers is the relationship between a chauffeur and his passenger. While the chauffeur would probably prefer to spend his day driving a Ferrari, the boss prefers the luxury of a stretch Lincoln limousine.

Luxury Consumer—No other publication has such a captive high-profile and affluent audience as *Stratos*. The editorial of the magazine adds to this with its emphasis on travel, autos, and other expensive tastes and hobbies.

Logical advertisers include luxury cars, yachts, travel, resorts, jewelry, cameras, fashion, real estate, liquor and wine, cosmetics, electronics, and the like.

Coupled with these types of advertisers are investment, insurance and other such services required by the most affluent people.

Business-Related Advertising—The passengers on business aircraft are at the highest level of their corporations—and when on planes are almost always on business trips. It is the perfect setting for selling corporate image, financial, consulting, legal, and other businesses where purchases are made at the highest levels.

COMPETITION

Discuss the specifics about the other magazines and other media serving the market. While magazines are the principal competition, data about newspapers, radio, TV, cable, the Net, and other media should be included. If information is available regarding the shortcomings of the competition, use it only if it is factual and accurate.

> **WARNING**
>
> It is very tempting to claim that there is no real competition for your new magazine. The main danger is that there probably is some competition even if peripheral—and that your potential investors will find that out. Then you are really in trouble.

Just about any magazine has competition. The trick is to turn this to your advantage. Suppose you were going to start a new women's magazine, along the lines of one of the Seven Sisters. (The Seven Sisters are the old-line major women's magazines: *Good Housekeeping*, *McCall's*, *Redbook*, *Better Homes*, *Family Circle*, *Ladies' Home Journal*, and *Woman's Day*.)

The approach you might take is that there are seven (or more now) magazines in the field with over 5 million circulation each. There obviously is room for another with a somewhat different editorial slant.

The type of information you should include about the competitors—and about your proposed magazine—is:

- Publisher
- Frequency
- When established
- Circulation
  - Subscriptions
  - Single copy
  - Other
  - Audited by
- Prices
  - One year subscription
  - Single copy
- Advertising rate—one time
  - Black and white
  - Four color
- Cost per thousand circulation
  - Black and white
  - Four color
- Advertising pages—for five years
- Advertising dollars—for five years

You will, of course, want to explain how your editorial content differs from the others—and how your audience will differ.

Elan

Elan competes in the black consumer magazine field, which includes *Essence, Ebony,* and *Black Enterprise.* The competitive environment is summarized as follows:

	Essence	***Ebony***	***Black Enterprise***
Year Established	1970	1945	1970
Frequency	Monthly	Monthly	Monthly
Circulation			
Subscription	616,335	1,515,868	214,690
Single Copy	185,337	235,387	14,055
Total Paid	801,672	1,751,255	228,745
Subscription Price	$12.00	$16.00	$15.00
Single Copy Price	$ 1.50	$ 2.00	$ 1.95
Rate base	800,000	1,700,000	230,000
Ad Rates			
Four Color	$18,320	$29,990	$11,610
Black & White	$12,210	$22,199	$ 9,080
Cost per thousand			
Four Color	$22.90	$17.64	$50.48
Black & White	$15.26	$13.06	$39.48
Advertising Pages			
1983	969	1,050	720
1985	947	1,200	763
Readership Profile			
Median Age	31.2	32.4	34.0
Household Income	$21,265	$17,654	$21,951
Percent			
College educated	43.2	32.9	56.8
Employed	69.0	9.6	87.2
Professional/ Managerial	19.7	14.6	28.6
Percent			
Male	26.2	39.7	55.2
Female	73.8	60.3	44.8
Total Audience (thousands)	2,908	7,141	1,709

Sources: SRDS and media kits

Stratos

No other magazine competes directly in delivering the level of corporate executives in an environment such as that offered by private aircraft, nor with the type of editorial content specifically tailored for these readers. Those that might be considered competitive, and the reasons why they are not, include:

- General interest business magazines—*Business Week, Fortune, Forbes, Harvard Business Review,* etc.

  Why Not? Much larger circulations among all levels of business, with editorial aimed at specific business news and solutions.

- In-Flight magazines—*Delta Sky, American Way,* etc.

  Why Not? Much larger circulation among all levels of business with editorial primarily of a general or travel nature. Demographics of a declining nature because of more leisure travelers.

- Aviation magazines—*Aviation Week, Business & Commercial Aircraft,* etc.

  Why Not? Business publications for those in the aviation field rather than the passengers.

- Magazines for the affluent—*Town & Country, Robb Report, Departures,* etc.

  Why Not? Lifestyle magazines, but not necessarily for business people in their own environment.

People Involved

Investors really invest in two things: the concept and the team of people who are going to run the magazine.

The business plan should spell out in detail who will handle editing, advertising, and circulation. Tell who will be the boss. Don't forget the importance of a good financial person—investors want to be sure this part of the operation is in good hands. Give brief biographies of the key players—maybe a paragraph on each.

In some cases the people you have assembled will not want their names to appear in any documents until they are sure that money has been raised. They simply do not want their present employers to know of their future plans until they are firm. When this happens, you must give a nonrevealing biography together with a statement such as "name to be revealed later." This really isn't good enough in the long run. If you are really getting close to assembling the capital, these people will have to be produced—in person, if not on paper. If they are the right people—and as good as you expect—their presence at meetings will do a great deal to sell the investors—possibly they will do it even better than you.

It is also good to put in the names of various consultants and other professionals who have helped with the project. This indicates that you have the good sense to get professionals to help in the areas in which you are not an expert.

To add credibility, list the names of the bank, the law firm, the accounting firm, and other groups you expect to use. You will normally have to be sure that they agree to work with you, even though there may not be anything for them to do until later. It is best to have firms that are either known as being familiar with publishing (there aren't many) or well-known names. Include the name of a person they can contact in each of these organizations.

I have limited the example here to that concerning *The Body Surfer Person* for what I believe are obvious reasons.

The team of people who will manage *The Body Surfer Person* promises to be one of the strongest groups in the magazine field. Here are the highlights of their backgrounds:

- PUBLISHER—David P. Superwave entered the publishing world in 1982 as assistant to the president of Fowles Enterprises. This followed a tour of duty in the armed services following his graduation from Harvard in 1981. In 1992 David became associate publisher of *Sea World,* rising to publisher after four years. He was instrumental in increasing the circulation from 40,000 to 100,000. *Sea World* merged with *Shellfish* in 1968 when David was made chairman of the board. He is an avid water sports enthusiast.

- EDITOR—(name withheld by request)—is a seasoned professional who has spent her entire writing and editorial career of over 25 years in special interest sports magazines. She has specialized in water sports and worked her way up to the top editor's spot. She is presently on the staff of a highly successful leading sports magazine. She is an avid participant in outdoor sports, having been at various times in her career a fresh-water fishing and canoe guide, a surfing instructor in Hawaii, and the champion long-distance swimmer of Rhode Island in 1953.

- CIRCULATION DIRECTOR—Coleman Boyd has been circulation director of *Ballyhoo* magazine for 15 years. He has competed successfully in body surfing contests worldwide.

- ADVERTISING DIRECTOR—(Name withheld by request) has been senior advertising director of an existing special interest magazine.

- CONTROLLER—Peter Rathbone is a CPA and partner in the Los Angeles office of Touche, Ernst, Waterhouse. He has worked with many clients in the magazine industry.

- ATTORNEYS—Lord, Sherman, Hughes—New York.

- ACCOUNTANTS—Haskins and Lybrand—New York.

- CIRCULATION CONSULTANTS—Walter, Eliot, Dick and Jim, Inc.

ANCILLARY PROJECTS

Because of the brand name most magazines develop with the public, a great many have been able to develop other activities making use of the cachet they have established. For instance, Time-Life Books and Reader's Digest Books and Records were developed based on the subscription lists of the magazines. In some cases the ancillaries become bigger businesses than the magazines themselves.

You should briefly describe any projects of this kind that you feel you can develop. Since they depend on having a successful magazine first, do not do any more than mention the types of things you have in mind—or you detract from the magazine, which is the base for everything. Get into details later.

FINANCIAL PLAN

It goes without saying that all investors are vitally interested in the financial aspects of anything they become involved with. Show a forecast of receipts and disbursements on the cash basis for the start-up

Figure 20.1. Cash Projections (in thousands)

	Pre Publication	Year One	Year Two	Year Three	Year Four	Year Five
Revenue						
Subscriptions	$ 39	$4,724	$5,754	$6,406	$6,554	$6,449
Newstand		373	1,334	2,213	2,882	3,173
Advertising		330	3,270	6,075	8,488	10,478
List Rental		210	415	548	592	614
Total Revenue	39	5,637	10,773	15,242	18,516	20,714
Disbursements						
Mechanical & Distribution	13	1,285	3,733	5,921	7,619	8,858
Editorial	78	419	621	662	716	765
Advertising	106	567	817	953	1,072	1,173
Circulation Promotion	80	3,725	4,225	4,583	4,729	4,755
Fulfillment	—	129	287	392	439	441
General & Administrative	156	717	824	862	891	921
Other	205	—	—	—	—	—
Total Disbursements	638	6,842	10,507	13,373	15,466	16,913
Net Cash Flow	$ (599)	$(1,205)	$ 266	$ 1,868	$ 3,050	$ 3,801
Total Cash Flow	$ (599)	$(1,804)	$(1,538)	$ 330	$ 3,380	$ 7,181

High Negative Cash Flow: $(3,136) Month Two, Year Two. This forecast is based on estimates and assumptions contained on this and other pages. No opinion is expressed as to the future accuracy of these projections.

Figure 20.2. Basic Assumption

	Pre Publication	Year One	Year Two	Year Three	Year Four	Year Five
Number of issuses		5	10	12	12	12
Average Circulation (000)						
Subscriptions		192	326	413	436	439
Newsstand		70	109	157	180	200
Total		262	435	570	616	639
Subscription price		$15.97	$15.97	$15.97	$15.97	$15.97
Newsstand price		2.50	2.50	2.50	2.50	2.50
Subscription Mailings						
Pieces (millions)	.1	6.0	6.0	6.0	6.0	6.0
Response rate	7%	7%	6%	5%	4.5%	4%
Bad debt	40%	40%	40%	40%	40%	40%
First renewal	40%	40%	40%	40%	40%	40%
Subsequent renewals	60%	60%	60%	60%	60%	60%
Average Total Pages/Issue		79/84	89/94	99/108	118/128	138/148
Average Advertising Pages/Issue		29/34	39/44	49/54	59/64	69/74
Advertisint Rate						
Black & White page		$3,000	$8,000/ $9,200	$11,000/ $11,600	$12,000	$12,6000
Four-Color page		$4,500	$12,000/ $13,800	$16,500/ $17,400	$18,000	$18,900
Cost/Copy Printing & Paper		$.34/.36	$.38/.40	$.42/.46	$.50/.54	$.59/.63
Number of Employees						
Mechanical & Distribution	1	1	1	2	2	2
Editorial	6	10	10	10	10	10
Advertising	4	7	7	7	7	7
Circulation	5	5	5	5	5	5
General & Administrative	4	5	5	5	5	5

period plus at least five years of operations. These are on the cash basis because that is all that is important in a new venture. They should be brief (two pages are plenty) and in the normal financial style used in the magazine business. Sample figures are shown in Figures 20.1 and 20.2 on the preceding page.

Sample Financial Plan

Plans call for a test mailing of 200,000 pieces in December of Prepublication, First Year. This mailing will be designed to test in six or seven areas:

- Two or three copy approaches
- Two prices
- Hard and soft offers

Based on the results of this test, the decision of whether to continue the project will be made.

If the test is positive, the staff will be hired in September, Prepublication Second Year with regular publication March Year One. Mailings are planned for October (500,000 pieces) and December 1 million), Prepublication Year Two. The test mailing, however, may indicate that either larger or smaller mailings can be made at those times.

Cash flow results for five years and the major assumptions on which they are based are on the following two pages.

Development of these figures can require a good deal of time and work because this is when you really come to grips with what your publishing plans will be.

In arriving at these figures, it is wise to use one of the computer model programs that have been developed for magazines. Planning for a magazine is very complex because it is a business where there are three or more revenue streams in one product—single copy, subscription, advertising, and possibly others. These revenue streams are all interconnected. See chapter 57, "Use of Computer Models," for a discussion of models and their use.

The various revenue streams are dependent on decisions that are made in each area. Everything, of course, depends on the quality of the editorial content. The advertising rate depends on the amount of circulation. The amount of circulation can depend on the circulation prices—and can vary depending on the cost of obtaining it. Everything is interconnected.

WARNING

Don't present projections that are too optimistic. It is usually obvious and then no one will believe anything. On the other hand, don't present figures that are too pessimistic either. Some people, in producing their figures, reduce their revenue figures arbitrarily and put "cushions" into all the expenses just to be safe. The only problem is that they end up with a magazine that doesn't work—the risk/reward ratio is not attractive to any investor.

You should present figures that are as realistic as you can make them. Anyone who looks at projections knows that nothing will ever come out exactly as you have forecast, but if the figures are reasonably based, they can accept them.

After you have done the figures as realistically as you can, you should also have available "downside" projections—suppose everything is, say, 20% or so worse than you say. Is it still a good project?

Every potential investor will ask for these sooner or later—and you look a lot smarter if you have them available before they ask, although you don't include them in the Business Plan.

CHAPTER 21

Test, Test, Test—Find Every Possible Way to Take the Risk out of the Project

I STARTED OUT this book by pointing out that people buy magazines because they have interests and companies advertise in magazines because they want to reach people with those interests.

It's very easy for an entrepreneur to feel that potential readers "need" the magazine he is starting—and that advertisers will flock to reach those people. But our dumps are filled with the remains of magazines no one wanted to read. In financial circles, starting a magazine is regarded as being about as risky a business as starting a dot.com company.

There is a lot of truth to this. To repeat what we said earlier—it is just too easy to start a magazine. The failure rate is probably about 90%. It is also true, however, that the success rate for magazines that are carefully planned and tested is about 70% —which is way above the average for most businesses started in any field. This rate, of course, can be achieved only through careful testing, primarily of what the public wants to read, but also of whom advertisers want to reach. This testing can take several forms, which have been used successfully:

- Conducting focus group and in-depth research with potential readers to determine the degree of their interest in a proposed magazine.
- In the case of paid circulation magazines, conducting real-time testing of whether people will buy the magazine. This can be done through testing the sale of subscriptions and/or the sale of single copies.
- Testing whether advertising can be sold.

These tests will not ensure success, but they greatly reduce the failure rate for any specific project.

Determining the Public's Interest in Reading a Specific, As-Yet-Unpublished, Magazine

We are all familiar with the extent to which research people have invaded our lives. We are bombarded with written questionnaires in the mail. On the telephone we are asked for our opinions constantly about various subjects. We are accosted in shopping malls and other places by people with pads and pencils asking us questions. The TV people live and die by the Nielsen ratings, and people on the Internet seem to know everything about us.

We also know that not all of this research results in meaningful answers. Every poll is accompanied by a statement that there is a plus or minus of some percentage of accuracy. But this probable statistical error is just part of the total error, as we learn at every election when the actual results are tabulated. Witness some of the surprises such as the *Literary Digest* poll of the 1936 election, or the morning we awoke to find that Harry Truman had defeated Thomas Dewey for the presidency, to say nothing of the Bush-Gore debacle.

What we want to know is: Will people buy and read a magazine that has not yet been published? We will know the real answer to that question only when we have asked readers to buy either a copy or a subscription. We will never know whether the actual magazine will satisfy the desire they may have had when they first bought it until they renew a subscription or continue to buy single copies.

We can't simply send out questionnaires, telephone people, or intercept them at a mall and ask them if they would buy a magazine about, say, "single living" and get a meaningful answer.

For this reason the research community has developed some very sophisticated techniques for trying to evaluate the public's reaction to new products of various kinds. The two methods which are particularly adaptable for use in the magazine field are focus group and in-depth research.

Focus Group and In-Depth Research

Both these techniques aim to determine the participants' real thoughts and reactions about the subject being discussed. In-depth interviews are normally done one-on-one, while focus groups depend on magnifying the results of such in-depth thinking by utilizing the benefits of group dynamics. Where it is feasible, the latter method is preferable since you can get the feelings of a number of different people at one sitting.

Since everything in a magazine depends on the editorial product, your research starts by trying to find if there is a serious flaw in the basic concept of the proposed magazine.

A focus group consists of 10 to 15 carefully selected people who would be likely readers. They are asked to comment on your editorial plans while you examine their comments for possible flaws in your strategy. You can't expect them to tell you what should be in the magazine, although you will probably ask them that in the course of the meeting. As a basis for conversation, show them three or four issue plans. For the second round of focus groups, show them the pilot issue.

The focus groups should be moderated by trained researchers or marketing professionals who are familiar with the focus group technique and are skilled in getting the most out of group dynamics. No one connected with the magazine should conduct them—they are too biased about the project—and are not trained in the proper methods of conducting them.

It is usually not difficult to gather the people together, everyone loves to give advice, and you pay the members of your group a nominal amount. You can sit behind a one-way mirror and watch the proceedings, which are usually taped for later listening.

Depending on the nature of your magazine, you will probably have at least five or six groups so that a pattern of peoples' thinking will come through. If it is important to get reactions from different parts of the country, you will need more groups than that.

You will probably want to make sure that the leader asks the participants whether they would subscribe to your magazine—and how much they would be willing to pay. Most people can't resist putting in that question—just understand that the answer, while heartening to hear, is probably meaningless.

> *Lew Miller had for many years been the publisher of the very successful magazine for doctors,* Patient Care. *His experience will give you an idea of how useful focus groups can be. His proposed new magazine was called* Life Options. *It was to be devoted to helping people get through the major decisions they have to make during their lives—such things as Should I Get Divorced, Should I Retire and Move to Florida, Should I Disown My Third Child, and the like.*
>
> *We ran a series of focus groups. Half the groups thought the idea for the magazine was fine. But the others hated it. They only wanted to face those decisions when they had to—not worry about them all the time. This was a very strong signal that this was not a good idea for a magazine.*

You run one early series of focus groups based on the issue plans you developed. Continuing the process of taking the risk out of the project, you run a similar series of focus groups, with other participants, after you have a completed pilot issue.

This qualitative research is, of course, designed to tell us whether there is anything basically wrong with the concept of the magazine that would make people not want to read it. We are still left with the question of whether they will buy it and read it—or whether advertisers will buy advertising. There is only one way that I know of to test whether people will buy a magazine, or companies will buy advertising—that is by asking for the order.

There are three ways you can meaningfully test the potential sale of paid circulation magazines—by seeing if people will buy:

- Subscriptions through direct mail
- Subscriptions through subscription agents
- Copies on the newsstand

A further discussion of each of these methods is given in chapters 22, 23, and 24. Chapter 25 discusses testing the sale of advertising.

CHAPTER 22

Testing a New Magazine through Direct Mail

IF THE MAGAZINE is to have paid circulation, a direct mail test of the sale of subscriptions is almost always done, even when the eventual sale of copies may be primarily through single-copy sales. Why?

1. Statistically direct mail can give a very sound indication of the eventual reception of the magazine by the public, something that is very difficult to accomplish on the newsstand with all its uncertainties (see chapter 24, "Testing—Through the Sale of Single Copies").

2. While a direct mail test can be costly, it can be carried out without actually creating and printing the entire magazine, which would require you to actually go into business as well as to spend a great deal of money.

> **WARNING**
>
> A direct mail test will give you a very reliable indication of the response you will get from your first mailing campaign, but it will not tell you:
>
> - How well repeated mailings will do
> - How many of those who agree to subscribe will actually pay up when the time comes
> - The sale of subscriptions from any other source
> - Anything about the quality of the product itself
> - What the eventual renewal rate will be. This will depend on how readers react to the actual magazine when it is published.

The direct mail test will, however, give you a very good indication of the reaction of the public to the basic concept of the magazine and the way you plan to carry it out. Short of actual publication, there really isn't any other good way to test this.

This type of mailing is known in the business as a "dry" test because the product being tested is not actually being published. In fact, the first issue may be a year or two off. The recipients, of course, don't know this; to them it is simply an offer to subscribe to another magazine.

If the test is successful, the first major mailings (roll-outs) will take place just prior to the launching of the publication. For the test to be projectable, it must be performed at the same time of year as the roll-out, and both the test and the roll-out must avoid such disturbances as elections.

Since this is the first time direct mail has been discussed in this book—and since direct mail is so important to many magazines, we will go into detail about the test to give you some idea about how this very interesting—and useful—type of selling is done in the magazine business.

About Direct Mail

What works, works. What doesn't, doesn't. Don't try to figure out why. For instance, if the red envelope works better than the green envelope, use the red envelope.

The best time to mail is right after Christmas. That's why you get so many mailings for magazines (and other things) in January. No one knows why it is the best time. The second best times to mail are in June and September. Don't ask why.

If there are misspellings in your letter and it pulls well, don't dare to correct them for the roll-out.

The basic purpose of the direct mail test, which should never be forgotten, is to determine whether *anyone* wants to subscribe to the magazine. But, as long as you are testing, you try to learn as many other things as you can, such as:

- What copy approach works best
- What price works best
- What offer works best
- What lists work best

Copy Approach

It is important to test at least two different copy approaches (more if you can afford it). This means that two completely different direct mail packages (including the envelope, letter, order card or return envelope, and other enclosures) are written from scratch, often by two different skilled copywriters.

The copywriters, of course, are armed with all the material you have worked on which describe the magazine including a year's worth of issue plans which show the editorial approach. The pilot issue defines the physical size, number of pages, the logo, type of paper, and the artistic presentation of the pages. The business plan tells them who the readers are expected to be.

The two packages should be quite different. One might be a detailed explanation of what the magazine will be like, while another might emphasize the benefits the reader will receive, or emphasize the price, the premium (if any), or the offer.

The Price

The easiest way to establish the price is by looking at competing magazines, or those very similar to yours. Prices are usually determined by relating the subscription price to the cover price. For instance, if the cover price is $3 (or $36 for 12 issues a year), your regular subscription price would probably be $24, and you would use something like $15.97 in your direct mail piece. That way, if you want, you can point out the large discount from the cover price.

Don't forget the "magic 97s" as Eliot Schein, one of the best direct mail experts I have known, used to call them. Prices pull better at $11.97, etc., than at round numbers, as in any retail business.

Be careful about establishing too low a subscription price. Later, when you do your projections, you will discover that the subscription price is very significant in determining overall financial results. Once you have set too low a price, it is very difficult to increase it.

Number of Issues Offered

The calendar is not very important to subscribers. They do not take frequency into account in determining what price they will pay for a subscription. In fact, in most cases they don't really know what the frequency is, except for newsmagazines and a few others. Don't use a lower price because you start out by publishing only six issues a year.

The Offer

The offer is different from the price. Offers are usually described as "soft" or "hard" with variations known as soft-hard or hard-soft.

The softest offer might be, "Try three issues of the magazine free. When we send you a bill, if you don't want to subscribe, simply write 'cancel' on it and return it to us."

The hardest offer asks for cash or a credit card payment.

Any good test will have two or three different prices and both hard and soft offers. The soft offer normally does best, but if you can make a hard offer work, so much the better. Cancellations of soft offers often run 60% or more, while the cancellation rate for hard offers is considerably less, although lots of people feel no compunction about either canceling them or simply not paying.

Mailing Lists

The best lists for magazines are those of people who have subscribed to other magazines by mail. Second are those who have bought other items in the field served by mail. Compiled lists, such as all doctors, lawyers, etc., very rarely work.

The best list has to be the subscription list of a magazine that is most like yours. Chances are, however, that a competitor is not going to rent his list to a new magazine trying to get into his field. Try to think logically about the lists your competitors probably use—and others that should work well. You also want to be sure, if you can, that you test some very large lists that may produce large numbers of subscribers.

Projectability should be considered as well. To test 2,500 names of a list that totals only 7,500 is a waste of money and time. But a test of 5,000 names of *Washingtonian,* for example, can be projected for its "twins"—other city magazines. And, if *Time* works, so will *Newsweek.*

WARNING

Don't try to test too many factors in any one mailing. You will only end up confused as to what the results mean.

I recall the famous hundred-way test that was made by *The Saturday Review* many years ago. The magazine had been changed to four different magazines, each issued once a month, covering Arts, Education, Science, and World Affairs. The recipient was given the option of subscribing to any one, two, three, or all four of these.

When the results came in they were posted on a big wall for interpretation. In the end no one had any idea of what, if anything, they proved. Later, as you can imagine, the experiment—and the magazine—failed.

Timing of the Test

The best time to mail for subscriptions is the last business day of the year. Second best times are the Friday before the Fourth of July and the Friday before Labor Day. No one knows why, but that's the way it is.

While these particular dates are the best, mailings a few days different will not hurt the results much—and the chances are that there will be so much action by the major mailers that you will not be able to be precise about the date. A month's difference can be important—and some periods are complete disasters, such as the period between Thanksgiving and Christmas. You might aim for December 20 to January 20, June 1 to July 15, and August 20 to October 1.

It is foolish for a new magazine to test at any periods but the best. If the test fails, you will never know whether it was because no one wanted the magazine or because of the date you dropped the mail.

You can see that the good mailing periods force you into a timing cycle in your planning, whether you like it or not. Unfortunately, the three good mailing times are not spaced evenly. While mailing right after Christmas is best, you then wouldn't dare roll out before July. If you test in July, there isn't time to read the results and retest or roll out before December. You might be able to retest at Labor Day, and get the results in time to mail again after Christmas, but that may not fit your schedule for other reasons.

It takes time to organize for a test. A typical schedule might be (working backward):

Projectable results	February 10
Mailing date	December 26
Materials to lettershop for mailing	December 1
Mechanicals to printer	November 1
Final copy	October 1
Order lists	September 1
Hire copywriters	August 1

Direct mail printers and lettershops get very busy at the favorite mailing periods and good mailing lists are in great demand. If other customers are using the ones you want, you may not be able to get them. Be sure to make arrangements as early as you can.

When to Expect Results

We look for projectable results some 40 days after the mailing. But you will probably be eagerly counting them on a daily basis. Mailings do strange things. Sometimes the returns are very heavy for a week—and then they die. Other times they come in very steadily for a very long period without any peaks. It's better to wait a little longer to judge the results, particularly with a new magazine.

Test Mailing Costs

Suppose you make a test mailing of 100,000 pieces. The cost breakdown is something like this:

• Postage at current third-class rates (if you mail at first class, it would be much more)	$30,000
• Printing, depending on the size, number of different pieces, amount of four color, complexity	30,000

• Mailing house— labeling, inserting, etc.	5,000
• Mailing list (depends on nature of each list)	15,000
• Creative work (depends on the copywriters used)	10,000
• Mechanical preparation, typesetting, illustrations, etc.	10,000
TOTAL	$100,000

There are other costs when the returns come in. You will probably pay for the return postage (don't put anything in the way of getting the best response). If you get 5,000 returns, that will be about $2,500 at today's rates, but you won't mind paying for these.

You will get some, probably not much, cash from subscribers. You must either send it back or write each subscriber to ask if he wants it back. If you don't do that, put it in a separate bank account and don't touch it.

It's a good idea to send a card to everyone who subscribed telling them that you won't be coming out for a while. You also might send them a questionnaire asking what attracted them to the magazine, who they are, etc.—information that you might be able to use in selling advertising later.

SIZE OF THE TEST

The size of the test depends on the magazine, the eventual readership, the amount of money you have, and probably other factors. If you were going to launch a major magazine such as *People*, you would want to test as many lists as you could, a number of different prices, several copy approaches, and all sorts of other things. To do this properly you would use at least 500,000 pieces.

On the other hand, even in that case, you might want to start out with a much smaller test, say 100,000, just to see if *anyone* wants the magazine and then follow up with a much larger confirmation mailing with more extensive testing.

If your magazine is regional, or covering a relatively small interest group, you would tailor the size of the test for that. A new city magazine, for instance, might be successfully tested with just 25,000 pieces.

CREATING THE TEST GRID

It is important that the test give valid results. The test grid is the plot of what you test—and how you test one item against another. This must be carefully designed or the results will not be projectable.

Let's try one. Suppose you want to test in these ways:

- A—Control package. Created by Writer A. We chose it as the control because it is very descriptive of the magazine.
- B—Package created by Writer B.
- C—Package created by Writer C.
- Prices—$14.97 and $16.97
- Offers—Soft and Hard.
- 20 different lists—as many as we can afford.

Our plan is to take the six lists that we think will do best and test each of the variables against each other. That would mean that we would set up our grid with these headings:

- Letter A—$14.97—soft offer (Control)
- Letter A—$16.97—soft offer
- Letter A—$14.97—hard offer
- Letter B—$14.97—soft offer
- Letter C—$14.97—soft offer

Our statistician tells us that you need 10,000 names in each cell in order to have a confidence level of 95%. Anything else will not do. (Confidence levels are arrived at by very complex statistical calculations based on the size of tests and many other variables.)

If we have cells of 10,000 each, we will need a test of 300,000 pieces just to compare the different alternatives. Even if we cut them to 5,000, we still need 125,000, and we haven't done anything but test these six lists.

What to do? Compromise. Not as bad as it sounds because at this stage the thing we are really trying to learn is whether anyone wants the magazine. This is the grid we end up with—each cell having 3,000 names, even though our statistician tells us that the confidence level is only 85%.

Test mailing Grid

Writer	A	A	A	B	C
Price	$14.97	$16.97	$14.97	$14.97	$14.97
Offer	Soft	Soft	Hard	Soft	Soft
List					
#1	3,000	3,000	3,000		
#2	3,000	3,000		3,000	
#3	3,000	3,000			3,000
#4		3,000		3,000	3,000
#5	3,000		3,000		3,000
#6			3,000	3,000	3,000
#7–21	45,000 (3,000 each)				

Twenty-one different lists are being tested, all on the Control package. Each of lists 1 through 6 are tested on three of the different letters, prices and offers, all of which are tested against each other.

If you have made the kind of compromise above—and you probably have—you should do a confirmation mailing with more pieces to find out for sure what copy approach, price, offer, and lists work best before making a really major mailing

WHAT WILL THE RESPONSE RATE BE

In every seminar I have ever conducted someone asks "What response rate should we expect?"

There is no answer to that. Tell me what the magazine is all about, the universe of potential readers, the price, the frequency, and all the other factors, and I may be able to tell you what response rate you need to have a successful magazine—but what will it be on any particular magazine? That's why we are testing.

I can tell you one thing. It had better be pretty high or we don't have a chance of succeeding. In working out the projections for new magazines, we often call for response rates of 6% or 8%. When investors ask people in the business if these are realistic, they call them ludicrous, at which point the investors may then disappear.

The reason is obvious, though it may not seem so without an explanation. Most existing magazines are working with response rates in the neighborhood of 2% or 3% on mailings for new subscriptions. Of course they are. They already have their core circulation of 200,000 or 2 million and are reaching to get those last 2,000 new readers. This has to be very expensive.

We, on the other hand, are just beginning to build that core readership and, if there isn't enough interest for a high response, we had better give up now.

THE POSTAL SERVICE

I have been saying that the test mailing is the best way to get a reliable indication of the results of the first major mailing because it is so statistically accurate, but we are also at the mercy of the Postal Service. Third Class mail (now called Standard Mail) does not get all the care that First Class receives, particularly in terms of changes of address. The timing and percentage of pieces that are not delivered, as you would expect, are much lower with First Class.

And, from time to time we read about letter carriers who dump their mail in the sewer and other odd things happen. I remember the test for a new magazine where there was no response from a number of states. Didn't make any sense. Finally we figured out that, since this was a test, very few pieces were going to certain zip codes. This means that only a handful of letters were in the postal bags to those places—and the postal people thought the sacks were empty, so didn't bother to look.

INTERPRETING TEST RESULTS

We have done the test. We get results that look something like this:

Test Mailing Response

Writer	A	A	A	B	C
Price	$14.97	$16.97	$14.97	$14.97	$14.97
Offer	Soft	Soft	Hard	Soft	Soft
List					
1	6.1%	5.6%	5.4%		
2	7.2	6.0		7.5%	
3	4.3	4.3			3.8%
4	3.9	5.3		3.8	4.8
5	6.8		6.1		5.2
6	5.1		5.1	5.6	
7	4.8				
8	2.1				
9	8.5				
10	3.7				
11	2.8				
12	4.6				
13	7.3				
14	1.5				
15	3.9				
16	10.3				
17	2.9				
18	4.6				
19	6.2				
20	5.4				
21	9.2				

What do they mean? This is where the statistical half of the good circulation person comes in. As he will tell you, it's simple. You take the best letter, the best price, the best offer, and the best lists and you will then know that there are X lists that will produce Y% response when you roll out. If you are a particularly aggressive person, you apply a "lift" factor because of the time of year, the weather, who won the World Series, and other such factors.

The overall response rate was 5.3%, which doesn't sound bad on the surface, but that is just part of the story. After all, you have no idea of how many of those will pay—if it is just 40%, which is not unusual, the net is only 2.1%.

The response to the higher price at $16.97 was only 10% less than the $14.97. Those two dollars can be very important, you will find, when you do the projections.

The response to the hard offer was quite strong —just 9% less than the soft offer.

If the hard offer reduces the bad pay substantially, it can make a big difference.

Letter B seems to be clearly better than letter A, with a 10% increase in response.

Letter C seems to be a loser.

Better look at the response from different lists. To do this we put the lists in the order of their response level and include the total number of names in each.

Lists Ranked by Response

List #	*Response %*	*Total List Size*	*Total Estimated Response*	
16	10.3%	60,000	6,180	
21	9.2	80,000	7,360	
9	8.5	50,000	4,250	
13	7.3	120,000	8,760	
2	7.2	600,000	43,200	
5	6.8	400,000	27,200	
19	6.2	150,000	9,300	
1	6.1	250,000	15,250	
20	5.4	1,000,000	54,000	
6	5.1	375,000	19,125	
TOTAL		3,085,000	194,625	6.3%
7	4.8	475,000	22,800	
12	4.6	625,000	28,750	
18	4.6	300,000	13,800	
3	4.3	850,000	36,550	
TOTAL		5,335,000	296,525	5.6%

List #	*Response %*	
15	3.9	130,000
4	3.9	420,000
19	3.7	625,000
17	2.9	125,000
11	2.8	320,000
8	2.1	4,000,000
14	1.5	3,500,000

From this you can see that the very highest-ranking lists are relatively small, not unusual because these are the people most interested in the subject. At the bottom are some really big lists, probably a try at a compiled list and one of the newsmagazines.

But we seem to have a success. Lists with more than 3 million names pulled over 5%, with the average pulling 6.3%. Those with more than 5 million names pulled over 4%, with the average pulling 5.6%.

It appears that lots of people want our magazine, and since some of the lists have twins, the total is probably somewhat larger than shown here. Now we do some dreaming. Suppose we use Letter B and increase these response rates by 10%. Or suppose we use Letter B, increase the price by $2 and use a hard offer. We might increase the response by 33% and the net dollars by 50%.

It's time for realism. This was a pretty small test to be sure of all those conclusions. Let's reduce all the dreams by 20% and do a confirmation test of, say, 300,000 pieces.

WARNING

Be careful about test results. I recall the results for a test for *The Chicagoan*, a city magazine that got wonderful results from a mailing that featured an article by Mike Royko, an author well known in the area. The first mailing after the test mirrored the results of the test, but the results could never be repeated because they couldn't repeat the article. From then on, nothing very good happened and the magazine died.

HOW TO IMPROVE THE RESPONSE RATE

If we can send out fewer pieces and still get the same number of orders, our cost per order will be lower. There are a number of organizations that have, through extensive research, developed detailed information about the people who live in every zip code in the country. Among these are Claritis in New York and CACI in Arlington, Virginia.

If you take the results of your test and overlay it with the characteristics developed by one of these companies, you will probably find that zip codes with different types of people respond differently.

Suppose half the zip codes produce all your orders. The next time you mail, you eliminate the nonresponsive zip codes and you have to mail only half the number of pieces. (You may have to rent the entire list, but just use part of it.) Magazines that have been in existence for many years report that they do not get much benefit from this exercise in reducing the number of pieces mailed, but that it reduces the nonpay factor. You may be able improve this by taking advantage of some of the techniques described with lists that have been even further enhanced. See chapter 62, "Brand Extensions—Database Marketing."

A merge-purge is also often very useful. When you rent the lists that pull well, you will probably find that similar types of people are on the good lists. Since virtually all lists are on computers, you merge the lists, eliminate any duplicate names, and reduce the number of pieces you send out. Eventually you will probably want to merge-purge with your current subscriber list as well.

CHAPTER 23

Testing—Sale of Subscriptions through Agents

MANY CONSUMER magazines sell a great many subscriptions through independent agents that sell the magazines of many publishers. These are of several different types:

- Direct mail agents—These include those using stamp sheets such as PCH and AFP but a number of others have more recently entered the fray, including some publishers who are selling not only their own magazines but those of other publishers and those connected with some of the airline frequent flier award programs.
- Internet agents—Doing the same thing on the Net.
- School plan—Where schools are enlisted to have the kids sell subscriptions.
- Cash field—Selling door-to-door or by telephone.
- Paid during service—Also door-to-door or by telephone, but usually on an installment basis.
- Catalog agents—Selling to libraries, schools, doctors' offices, waiting rooms, and the like.

Details of the how these agents operate are discussed further in chapter 43, "Ways to Get and Keep Subscribers."

There is, unfortunately, no way to test a new magazine through these agents. You cannot really expect the agents to participate in selling a subscription for you and then have you later tell both the agent and the subscriber that the magazine was just testing and then refund the money, as you would if you had sent out your own direct mail.

About the first testing you can do with agents is to get them to try your magazine after it is launched—when they might provide a good source of new readers.

On the other hand, the various subscription agents will provide rough estimates of the volume they feel they can produce. Their instincts, based on their experience with so many other magazines, are very valuable. They will not, of course, guarantee any of their estimates of volume. They may be biased in their answers (for or against your magazine) because of existing relationships with other magazines—and they may not be familiar with the shifts in the interests of the readers your magazine is targeting.

CHAPTER 24

Testing—Through the Sale of Single Copies

BY FAR THE largest number of single copies of magazines are sold through the single-copy system, usually referred to as newsstand sales, consisting of national distributors, wholesalers, and retailers. This system and its current situation is described in chapter 47, "The Confusing Single Copy Sales Situation."

Single-copy sales are of great importance to many magazines because they are primarily sold on the newsstand—it is their lifeblood. For those magazines that sell well on newsstands, this is the most profitable circulation they have. For almost all consumer magazines, newsstand distribution of some kind acts to display the product to both readers and advertisers and often produces lots of subscriptions as a result of readers sampling copies. In addition, lively newsstand sales indicate editorial strength to advertisers.

On the surface it might seem that an easy way to test a new magazine would be by putting copies on the newsstands to see how well they sell. As you read the detailed description of the system, you will readily see why this is difficult for the average publisher.

The first problem is finding a national distributor who will take you on. With the enormous number of titles now being handled, distributors are wary about taking on another one unless they are convinced that it will be accepted by the wholesalers, the retailers, and, most of all, the public. While every so often a new magazine becomes a good seller on the newsstand, the vast majority do not sell well or are marginal at best.

The basic reason why a distributor will not take a new magazine on is because he does not think it will sell well. But other factors also come into play:

- The distributor may not want to take on a new magazine that may not continue to be published. Every added magazine involves going through the whole process of convincing wholesalers and retailers that they should handle it, setting up all the machinery and records that are needed, and taking valuable manpower from their operations.
- The distributor may be full-up with other new magazines or new clients and be unable to add to his line for the time being.
- The distributor may not want to handle the magazine because of its subject matter.
- The distributor may have a competing magazine.
- The magazine may be so unique that it will not fit into the normal distribution patterns that he has set up for most of his magazines.
- The distributor may be unsure of either the financial stability or the publishing ability of the publisher—and possibly both.
- The distributor may want promotional and other support that you are not able to give at this point.
- If a national distributor can be found, the new magazine still has to be accepted at the wholesale and retail levels. Chain store headquarters and/or regional approval must be obtained. This is where there is the most concern about the number of titles that can be displayed.

Because of these factors, it is awfully easy for a new magazine produced by an unknown publisher to get many returns with the bundles unopened from every level of the system.

Adding to the new publisher's problems is the fact that information about sales normally takes a very long time to obtain. More than one new magazine has been led to believe that sales were fine, only to find much later—and sometimes too late—that this was not true.

This is not to say that new magazines cannot be tested on the newsstand. There are at least two areas where this has been done successfully:

1. The major publishers who either own their own national distributors or who have very strong connections with the system, and lots of funds with which to finance not just a single test, but a series of issues, have often tested new concepts on the newsstand, sometimes with good results. They have also had their share of disasters, which you probably do not hear much about.

2. Many purely local magazines have been tested on the newsstand. In this case the publishers have been able to make arrangements for distribution, checkups, and promotion through personal calls and contacts.

If, of course, your magazine is going to be heavily dependent on newsstand sales, there is little that can be done without actually publishing and seeing how well it sells.

If you do test, you can do it in selected markets. This is very expensive because you must produce a test issue that will be as good as those that will follow. You will have to employ the same staff to produce it as will eventually be on board. Before you go to these lengths, better do financial models of testing both through the newsstand and through direct mail to see whether the risks justify the difference in cost. For a magazine that is programmed to eventually be a very major newsstand seller, this may be the less expensive—and surer—method, despite the cost.

WARNING

I am scared to death of trying to test a magazine that is not local through the system, unless you happen to own one of the national distributors. A valid test requires (at least) such things as:

- Test areas that are typical of the nationwide pattern.
- Distribution of copies and display that is typical of the nationwide pattern.
- Checkup of sales that is timely and is typical of the nationwide pattern.
- Promotion and publicity efforts that are typical of the nationwide pattern.
- Testing just one issue isn't good enough. Lots of people will try one of almost anything. You really will not have learned much unless you test a number of issues. This can be very expensive. It means that you have to go into business for sure.

The system does not lend itself to careful analysis and control which would enable you to make precise measurements of the kind needed for good testing. The whole complex is so large and with so many outlets of different kinds, that it is very difficult to fine-tune even one area for sophisticated testing. Even if this is done, extending the same procedures nationwide is almost impossible.

That does not mean, however, that no testing can be done. While you might not be able to be terribly refined in determining results, it is certainly possible to test on the newsstand in some areas to see if you have a big winner or not. You can also test to determine the result of different amounts of promotion so that you can gauge how heavily you must promote nationwide.

HORROR STORY

Book Digest, may its soul rest in peace, was launched in the normal way with a direct mail test that proved that it could be profitable. After the test, the magazine was started with a concentration on subscriptions.

About a year later, the publishers thought that it might be a good single-copy seller. So they decided to give it a try. They knew that they should not launch nationwide all at once. So they tried one issue in Columbus, Ohio, a city that seemed to be a good one for a reader's magazine since it was the home of Ohio State University. The wholesaler there was also the head of the wholesaler's association at the time and was quite enthusiastic. They put 40,000 in various outlets, using dumpbins in a number of supermarkets. At off-sale they got the report that the sale was 70% of the copies. They were golden!

They tested further by putting copies in three other cities nearby in the Middle West. Reports were not quite as good as the first issue in Columbus, but showed sales of over 50%. They were even more golden!

The next step was a roll-out nationwide with a million copies, but the reporting system, as we have said, was a little bit behind in giving information early—or at least good information.

A year—and $10 million later—it became apparent that *Book Digest* was not a good newsstand seller. They never did find out how many copies were sold in that first test in Columbus—just that it was less than 20%. Unfortunately they never were able to track down just how all those misleading signals developed. The system was just too confused and disorganized.

CHAPTER 25

Testing—Sale of Advertising

SOME MAGAZINES ARE almost completely dependent on advertising for their revenue. This is true for business magazines, most of which have controlled circulation, and even those with paid circulation derive most of their revenue from advertising. Some consumer magazines, too, are almost completely dependent on advertising for their revenue. For these magazines, even though the revenue comes primarily from advertising, it is still essential to test the editorial concept with potential readers through focus groups or in-depth interviews. No one wants to advertise in a magazine no one reads.

In addition to testing for readership, it is essential to test the potential for the sale of advertising. If you can develop focus groups with some of the potential advertisers, fine, but it may be difficult to get people to attend these sessions, although it might be possible at an industry convention or some other such event. An alternative is to have in-depth interviews with a number of the key potential advertisers to ask them whether they feel that the industry needs the kind of publication you are planning. People like to give advice, so it shouldn't be hard to set up these interviews, which will serve as a warm-up process for selling them advertising later.

You will never have a really valid test until you find whether the key companies will make firm commitments to advertise. One tried-and-true way to determine this is to go through all the motions of launching the magazine knowing that, if not enough key advertisers agree to buy pages, you won't start. Anything less than this will not give you a valid answer. This means that you print your pilot issue, develop your rate card, print a media kit, and announce the date of your first issue. You then approach the key advertisers as you normally would in selling advertising—through direct mail, telephone, personal meetings, and so forth. Set a goal for the number of pages you will need from these advertisers to determine whether you will actually publish when you said you would. If you reach it, you are in business. If not, you go home without spending an awful lot of money.

CHAPTER 26

What People Do You Need—And When?

FROM THE STANDPOINT of the people involved in the launch of a magazine, there are four stages you go through:

1. The Idea
2. Developing the Launch Scenario
3. Developing the Business Plan
4. Actual Publication

The Idea

You have an idea for a magazine because you feel that lots of people need communication about an interest you have. You probably do not work in the magazine business or any other communications media.

As the idea jells, you bounce it off a few others—and sometimes some of these people are drawn into the circle of those intrigued with the basic idea. Some of them may know something about the magazine world or even be connected with it.

It is rare, however, that any of you have had real hands-on, all-around experience in publishing a magazine, even if some are employed on a magazine. It's likely that no one has been involved in the start-up of a new magazine. Even if one has, every magazine is in a different business.

As you move on, however, it becomes important to determine what people you need, when you will need them, and where to find them. During the early stages, you are probably the only one completely immersed in the project.

Developing the Launch Scenario

By the time you have reached the stage of developing a Launch Scenario, you are probably the world's leading authority on the field to be covered and have just about all the facts, figures, and other data about the size of the market, the possible audience, the potential advertisers, and the key players, and have some firm thoughts about what the audience would be interested in reading.

What you are lacking, however, is knowledge about just how magazines are published, the techniques that are used in publishing, and the special skills needed. The last thing you should do in this field—as in any other—is to try to reinvent how it operates, so you had better get some experienced help.

The different types of functions performed on a magazine fall into five general categories:

1. Editorial, including art—The actual development of the content of the magazine.
2. Circulation—Obtaining and handling readers, whether paid or not.
3. Advertising—Selling advertising.
4. Production—Printing and distributing the magazine.
5. Administrative—Holding the whole thing together and handling the financial aspects.

Detailed descriptions of the functions performed in each of these areas are in later chapters.

Each of these areas requires the skills of real specialists. There are, fortunately, consultants and other outsiders who can supply most of these skills. Because there are, most of the functions needed in developing the Launch Scenario can be accomplished without hiring staff members and often other people can be found, particularly in the editorial area, who will help out for the sheer joy of creating something new—or because they believe in the project and would like to become connected with it at some time in the future.

Developing the Business Plan

The input of the entire future team is invaluable when it comes to developing the business plan. If money-raising is required, which is normal, the existence of a full team of skilled people has often made the difference between getting funded or not, so the more of these key people you can be identify early on, the better.

Key people are needed for most magazines in each of the areas sooner or later. Certainly a full-time editor, unless the publisher will be acting as editor, and usually an advertising director and circulation director will be needed. Even there the requirements differ, depending on the size and nature of the magazine. For instance:

- If your magazine is dependent on superior or unusual artwork or photojournalism, an art director may also be essential. If not, you may be able to use an outside art group to do this on a regular basis.
- You may be able to use an outside circulation service to handle both subscriptions and single-copy sales, but if the newsstand is key to your magazine, you will probably want your own single-copy manager. And, a magazine with large and complex subscription operations will need its own circulation manager. Subscription fulfillment these days is almost always performed by outside firms.
- You certainly will need your own people handling production and relations with suppliers, but they don't have to be heavyweights unless you have very unusual production requirements.
- You will want to have good and accurate financial controls and planning. Most investors consider the controller one of the most important, if not the most important, member of the team, but it may not call for someone who is overqualified.

Actual Publication

The number and types of people needed when actual publishing starts will vary depending on the nature of the magazine. For instance:

- A staff-written magazine will have different types of editors (but not necessarily more) than one that depends primarily on manuscripts from outsiders.
- A magazine such as *Scientific American,* which must rewrite technical articles so that they can be understood by lay people, requires editors with the special talent to do this.
- A magazine such as *ESPN,* with heavy dependence on photographs, will have picture editors.
- A magazine such as *Playboy,* which relies on newsstand sales, may have its own field force to check on the number of copies sent to different outlets and to police displays.
- Major consumer magazines have large advertising sales staffs with people who specialize in specific types of advertising, such as cosmetics, liquor, retail, and the like. And those that carry lots of car advertising usually have offices in Detroit. Other magazines may depend almost completely on the use of outside representative firms for the sale of advertising.
- Those with smaller potential revenue must tailor the size of the staff to what they can afford, so you will find some magazines with a total staff of just three or four people. As with everything else in this business, there are endless variations.

How Do You Find the Key People

This is one of those items that ranks high on the list of the most difficult things to do in starting a new magazine. It is difficult because most people who want to start magazines have never been in the business—or, if they have, their experience is with only one magazine. Even in working with that one magazine, they usually only really know well the people working in their specific area.

The magazine field is relatively small and, while magazines can be—and are—published anywhere, there are only few places that are even small centers for magazine publishing—and therefore for finding magazine people.

There is only one center for consumer magazines—New York. For business magazines, it is a little better—New York; Chicago; Boston; Cleveland; San Francisco; Washington, D.C., and a few other places are in contention.

If you plan on publishing anywhere other than in these places, you face the difficulty of finding experienced publishing people for the key slots. You really cannot expect to spend six months or so in New York looking for candidates, particularly before you have raised your capital. Even if you have found the people you want, they may not be willing to move away from the publishing centers. On the other hand, a couple of factors are going for you:

- Publishing is a very open field. People are very receptive to talking with just about anyone who calls—once at least. There are few secrets, most doors are always open. Gaining an audience with almost anyone is not difficult and people are very free in expressing their thoughts and giving advice.
- People in publishing are idea people. They are all intrigued with the idea of any new project, whether or not they believe it can succeed. You will find that many of them will try to be helpful.

The best way to find the potential key people for your team is through the networking technique, even though it is neither easy nor quick. Here are some places where you might be able to get started:

- Seminars held by *Folio,* the associations, and others.
- Publishing associations.
- Manufacturers, distributors, retailers, and others in the field you plan to cover.
- Potential advertisers and their agencies.
- Consultants in the field.
- Suppliers you may use, such as printers and fulfillment houses.
- Executive recruiters. While they normally only dig up names when they are on an assignment, they see a lot of people and may have names of some who could be helpful.
- Meetings or cocktail parties you attend.
- Other magazines in fields somewhat like yours.
- People at *Folio, Ad Age,* and other publications in the field.
- Advertising columnists in newspapers—*New York Times, Chicago Tribune,* etc.
- Book publisher.s
- Bankers or others in the financial field.
- Just about anywhere else you may go.

You will find that almost anyone is interested in hearing about a new magazine concept—at least for a little while. They like being in the know, and you never can tell where they will lead you.

Another way, if you can manage it, is to have your idea written up by *Folio,* a newspaper, or some of the other media. Remember that the media loves the media. You may find that people will be looking you up rather than the other way around.

Paranoia

Everyone who has an idea for a new magazine is certain that everyone he ever meets will want to steal it and beat him to the first issue.

> One would-be publisher met my wife, Hope, at a *Folio* seminar and told her that he wanted to ask me to help him get his magazine started, but was unwilling to tell me what the concept was. She, logically, pointed out that I would have trouble helping him if I didn't know what the magazine was all about. We never saw him again.

Later on you will, of course, ask anyone who is privy to your business plan and other inside information to sign a confidentiality agreement, but at this point, your problem is getting the magazine off the ground at all. There are a lot of people you will have to tell about it—or it will never happen.

I cannot guarantee that no one will steal your idea. I can simply point out that I have never heard of this happening—and that the process of starting a new magazine is so difficult, takes so long, and involves such enormous dedication that it is very unlikely that it ever will.

A Piece of the Action

Assume that you have found the stars you have been looking for. They are able, experienced, excited about the concept and ready to go. But they are employed elsewhere—and probably at salary levels far above anything you can—or should—pay at this point of your existence. They may also have large fringe benefits, excessive expense accounts, and pension or profit sharing plan amounts designed to make it hard for them to leave for another company. You, however, have two things that they may never be able to get where they are now:

1. A chance to join in the fun, excitement, and exhilaration of working on a new magazine with a team of others who are just as interested as they are—something few of us ever have the chance to do.

2. A chance to get a meaningful "piece of the action," which they probably will never have again. A piece of the action, of course, means a portion of the equity of the magazine at a time when it is probably worth very little, but that can be worth a lot after the magazine becomes successful.

There are a number of ways in which this can be accomplished, some more complex than others because they have been designed to take advantage of various income tax advantages. They generally fall into the four categories below. To determine which to use in your case requires the help of a skilled tax practitioner:

- Actual shares of stock—either given or sold to the key player at its low value when he joins. This is usually accompanied by an agreement to buy it back in the future at its then value.
- Options to buy stock at a low price at some point in the future when, presumably, it has a much greater value.
- Phantom stock—behaves the same way as actual shares by paying dividends and having a buyback in the future at its then value.
- Performance units based on the increase in value of the company at various times.

I have always felt that handing someone real stock certificates that denote actual ownership in the company (with voting rights) is the most effective way to lure the person you want. If you do it any other way, your potential employee might think "Hey, I don't want any old share of profits. I can get that where I am. I want to be an owner. I want to be a partner. We are starting this together."

You can't be niggardly about the amount you part with. The whole purpose of this exercise is to get the new magazine launched right—something about ten times harder than launching a moon rocket. To do this there are only two things you need—capital and the right team. Sure, you are doing it because you want to get rich—but more because you want to have the fun of starting something—and making it work. You will be rewarded in heaven, if nowhere else.

Don't be niggardly, but also don't be dumb. Make sure you have a buy-back provision if the key player doesn't prove to be key after all.

CHAPTER 27

The Magazine's Name

> **WARNING**
>
> When my publisher first read this chapter he told me it "lacked focus," which I'm sure he did not find about any other part of this book.
>
> After rereading and reworking it, I believe it hasn't improved at all from that standpoint. I have reached the conclusion that I just cannot define what makes for a memorable name, just as John Wanamaker didn't know which half of his advertising was useful, and which was wasted.
>
> So, enjoy this if you want, but don't expect to learn anything.

As a recent *Folio* article pointed out, naming a magazine is even more difficult than naming a baby. With a baby you don't have to worry about how it will look on a logo or whether it will have newsstand appeal. And it really won't matter if three other kids on the block have the same name.

This undoubtedly is the most subjective area in the magazine business. The name often seems to be most near and dear to the hearts of the founders of a magazine, probably because it serves as the symbol of the entire project.

There are lots of opinions about what is a "good" name, but there is no real way to measure the effect the name of the magazine has on its eventual success.

Since this is a very subjective subject, please excuse this very subjective analysis. It undoubtedly simply reveals my own probably irrational feelings.

A handful of magazine names will probably end up being considered "great," but I am not really sure whether it is because the name was great or whether the magazine using that name was so good that it would have made any name great.

On my very short list of great names are *Life* (but not *Look*), *Time* (but not *Newsweek*), *Saturday Evening Post, Playboy* (but not *Penthouse*), *Hot Rod, Rolling Stone, Fortune, Vogue, Gourmet, Prevention, Parents,* and *McCall's*—why, hard to say, but I think each reflects something more than just a magazine, perhaps a lifestyle, or a reflection of the times during which they were great magazines.

I guess my favorite, though, was *Casket & Sunnyside*, which was a magazine for funeral directors that I had the joy of consulting with for a time. It was, of course, the result of the merger of two magazines.

But I also realize that someone else may have a completely different list of great titles.

Most people starting a new magazine spend an awful lot of time worrying about its name—probably too much time. Suppose you ran into these well-known magazines for the first time, each of whose name was carefully selected by its founders:

Atlantic Monthly
McCall's
Star
Cosmopolitan
Essence
Time

From the titles, you wouldn't have any idea of what any of them is about.

Now, of course, each of these has become well established in its field. The original meaning of the name (if it had one) has disappeared. For its readers, *Time* no longer has any relation to hours and minutes, but simply is "that magazine," and has actually established itself as a brand of its own.

I doubt if the name picked for a magazine has ever been a major factor contributing to its success. But I am sure a poor name could contribute to the failure of some magazines—for instance, *Intellectual Digest, Kosher Home, Soldier of Fortune,* and *Human Behavior* must have been turnoffs. And even the well-known *Psychology Today* has suffered—after all, there were very few gift subscriptions sent to readers' mothers-in-law (or anyone else for that matter).

I feel a lot better about the names people have picked for magazines after reviewing those the dot.com people dreamed up for their companies. It is hard to fathom what a Teligent, an Aether, a Cendant, or an ILX is up to.

And I can see why the accountants at Arthur Andersen wanted to separate from the consulting group that calls itself Accenture, whatever that is. The name alone turns you off.

It is likely that a name that doesn't give you any idea of what a magazine is all about can make a launch more difficult than it might be otherwise. This may well have contributed to the demise of some recent magazines—*Savvy, Harrowsmith, Omni,* and *Lear's*—although it probably was not the only reason for it.

Sometimes the name that has been picked is an indication of a much deeper problem—that the founders don't really know what the magazine they are going to publish is all about. In other words, they haven't done their editorial homework (see chapter 18, "If You Can't Say It in Ten Words") and have not crystallized the basic concept of the magazine.

One like that, in my opinion, was *George,* which never decided what its editorial focus should be. It defined itself as being "for personalities who shape public issues," which gave it the right to discuss anyone anywhere. I understand that "George" was a symbol for George Washington, for reasons that are very obscure in my mind and probably in the minds of many others. (Washington's picture was hidden on the cover of each issue for reasons that escape me—a ploy they copied from *Playboy,* which has done the same thing with its Bunny on its cover since its inception in 1953.)

Features of a Good Name

Let's try to analyze the features of what would seem to make for a good name. There seem to be at least five points to strive for:

Descriptive of the Subject Matter

It seems logical that the name should give the reader a good idea of what the magazine will be all about. It just makes it easier for a potential reader to decide whether he would be interested in it.

A few that do this very well are:

Southern Living
Digital Photo
Firehouse
Muscle and Fitness
TV Guide
Teen
Arabian Horse World
dads
New York
Parents
Self

There are, of course, a host of others.

Some magazines have what their publishers feel are descriptive names, but may suffer because the average reader is not familiar with what the name is describing:

- *Organic Gardening* is completely descriptive, but until you know what organic gardening is, it is meaningless.
- *Mother Jones* says it all for its constituency, but not for the world in general.
- *Chronos* says something about time to Greek scholars, but not all of us will relate to that.
- *Chili Pepper* means it's about hot food but is a little obscure on the surface.
- *Content* may be understandable to those in the computer field who demean all of us in creative areas. They feel that everything that appears in any

kind of media is furnished by "content providers," obviously a second class occupation in their view. The publishers have caved in to this view through their choice of the title. (The name of the magazine is *Brill's Content* but Brill's was added only to avoid a conflict about being able to use the term "content.")
• *Buffalo Spree* is about the city of Buffalo, not a bunch of animals having a great time in Montana. I must admit, however, that it does give an impression of that city that most of us may not have.
• *Immersed* is about deep exploratory scuba diving, which you may never have heard of.
• *Live Steam* is known well only by hobbyists who love locomotive and other steam engines.

And, everything else said, you have to believe that, if a magazine needs a subhead to describe itself, there is a weakness—for instance, *Time,* the weekly newsmagazine; *Playboy,* entertainment for men; *Mature Outlook,* for vibrant people who enjoy life.

(About now you have probably realized that most of the magazines I described as having "great" names are not really descriptive of their subject matter, at least not without some explanation, so how can they be great? I guess this is just one more indication of how subjective this subject is.)

Distinctive and with Personality

It is also logical to seek a name that is distinctive so that there will be no confusion with other similar magazines. *Robb Report, Wink, Darwin, Smock,* and *Jet* are certainly distinctive, but hardly descriptive. Whether any of these has personality is questionable.

The most distinctive I have found so far, which might also be considered descriptive and, just possibly, with personality, is *Line 56.* I am sure you realize that this comes from Act III, Scene 1, Line 56 of *Hamlet*:"To be or not to be"—and that the magazine has to do with B2B e-commerce.

All except the most general magazines are addressed to special interest groups, and being distinctive is not easy. For instance—there are *Golf Digest, Golf for Women, Golf Illustrated, Golf Magazine, Golf Tips, Golf World, Golfweek, Golf News, Golf Traveler, The Golfer, Executive Golfer, Travel & Leisure Golfer, Junior Golfer, Senior Golfer, The Golfer,* and a whole raft of similar regional titles.

Even in that field some have tried to be different, although none of these seems to have yet made a real impression:

Fore
Tee Time
Tour
Schwing

This kind of sameness is relatively typical for most special interest fields, although few have this many entries.

Attractive

It certainly seems helpful if the magazine title can depict something attractive as well as being description and distinctive. It's hard to do this and still make it easy to understand what the magazine is all about. Only a few seem to have been able to accomplish this:

I Love Cats
Real Simple
Bon Appetit
Weddingbells
Win Magazine
Luxury
Vim & Vigor
Family Fun
Endless Vacation

Many have shown great creativity in turning a prosaic title into something attractive. Housekeeping doesn't sound like much fun, but *Good Housekeeping* is something entirely different. And the magazine *Cigar* isn't exciting, but *Cigar Aficionado* is something else. Here is the way some others have improved their titles simply by adding a word at the beginning or the end:

Beginning Words	Ending Words
All About Kids	*Adirondack Life*
American Baby	*Adventure Journal*
Best of Home Plans	*Air Force Times*
Better Homes and Gardens	*Allergy Hotline*
Celebrated Living	*American Survival Guide*
Chronicle of the Horse	*American Observer*
Elegant Bride	*Antique Trader Weekly*
Fine Gardening	*Architectural Digest*
First for Women	*Art in America*

Go Boating
Home Cooking
Inside Karate
Insight on the News
International Living
Joy of Collecting
Let's Play Hockey
Luxury Golf Homes
Modern Bride
National Geographic
Natural Living
Official Crosswords
Old House Journal
Our Animals
Popular Electronics
Practical Boat Owner
Quick 'n Easy Crafts
Smart Money
Taste for Life
That's My Baby
This Old House
Today's Homeowner
Total Health
Traditional Home
True Story
Voice of the Tennessee Walking Horse
Weekly Standard
What's Brewing
Your Health
Art News
Art Forum
Arts Alive
Atlanta on the Go
Beer Report
Bird Talk
Birding
Black Elegance
Bridal Fair
Cat Fancy
Coastal Living
Cycle Now
Disney Adventures
East Bay Express
Fishing Facts
Fishing Smart
House Beautiful
Motor Trend
Music Choice
Nashville Scene
Old Car Trader
Piano Today
Showboats International
Snow Goer
Soap Opera Update
Star Wars Insider
Valley Advocate
Wine Enthusiast

Capitalize on an Existing Reputation

It certainly helps to be able to connect with a brand that has already been established, such as:

Smithsonian
ESPN
Air & Space Smithsonian
O
Harvard Magazine
Asimov's Science Fiction
Sesame Street
Arthur Frommer's Budget Travel

In some cases that can even be another magazine, such as:

Cosmo Living
Sports Illustrated for Kids
Parents Baby
Better Homes and Gardens, Woman's Day, Family Circle, Sunset, and some others have special issue publications published at various times during the year
Petersen's Photographic
Rodale's Scuba Diving
Scholastic Parent & Child
Vogue Patterns
Teen People
Organic Style—playing off *Organic Gardening*

Capacity to Make a Good Logo

A name can sound very good, or seem good in concept, but look simply dreadful when it appears on the cover of a magazine. A good designer can develop a good logo for virtually any name. But it is certainly harder with a name that is either too long—or too short. And some combinations of letters create real difficulty.

Some that are too long include *Ladies' Home Journal,* which has been shortened to simply *Journal* on the cover; *Better Homes and Gardens* is just *Better Homes;* and *Blair & Ketchum's Country Journal* is now just *Country Journal*.

The short ones can be even more difficult. There isn't much you can do graphically with *W, M,* or *Us.*

And there are certain combinations of letters that are difficult to make attractive on the cover of a magazine.

I am sure you have figured out by this time that there are no real hard-and-fast rules about what makes for a good magazine name.

A few years ago I tried to rank a whole bunch of magazine names on a scale of 1 to 10 based on the desirable characteristics above. It turned out to be a fruitless exercise because some of those that rated lowest, such as *Money, Us, Working Woman,* and *National Enquirer,* seem to be doing quite well, thank you.

And other would-be magazines that ranked highest, such as *Who's Who, Rags, Plants Alive, Rona Barrett's Hollywood,* and *L'Officiel,* either died aborning or were put out of their misery later.

Hard work and brilliant ideas also don't necessarily yield a good name. I was on the board of a new religious magazine a few years ago. After reviewing some 500 different suggestions for a name, we unanimously fell in love with *A.D.* Only problem was that, after we went into actual publishing, few of our readers understood the connection with Anno Domini—and besides it was almost impossible to do anything graphically with it.

There also may be some magazine concepts that do not lend themselves to good names. Take the mature market, for instance—a difficult field in almost every way. Magazines that have failed have included those whose names hastened their demise:

Golden Years
Lear's
McCall's Silver
Longevity
Prime Time
Mature Outlook

There are now just three major magazines in the field:

- *Modern Maturity* (which seems like an oxymoron).
- *My Generation* (a spin-off from *Modern Maturity*).
- *New Choices, the Magazine for Your Health, Money & Travel*—which probably holds the record for changing its name. It started as *Harvest Years*, then became *50 Plus,* then *New Choices for the Best Years,* then just *New Choices,* then *New Choices for Living after Fifty,* and possibly a couple of other names, and now is in its present incarnation.

Everyone in this field seems to have trouble knowing what to call older people. Most of the regional magazines seem to have settled on using the term "senior," which is sort of innocuous—but a couple call themselves "Get Up and Go!" which I think is dreadful.

I actually favor "old folks," but have yet to make any headway with it.

Business Magazines

Almost all the business magazines are named to be descriptive of the function they perform in their industries, although a number of the newer entries in the technical fields, as you might expect, have gone afield to some extent, for instance:

- *Context*—Business strategies for the digital age
- *Profit*—Business to e-business
- *Red Herring, Upside,* and some others—Business of technology
- *The Big Picture*—Large-format digital printing
- *Twice*—Consumer electronics
- *Cheers*—Full-service food and drink establishments
- *Pro*—Lawn and landscape contractors
- *Direction*—Moving and storage

Hopefully the people in those industries are well acquainted with the titles that serve them, strange though some may seem.

Protecting Your Name

When you pick a name, you will, naturally, become very paranoid about protecting it. This will be true even though you now know that the name may not be that vital in the long run.

So far, at least, magazines have not had the problem that Internet companies have with their domain names, where anyone can pick one and own it without even putting it to use.

Legally, the person who has the right to use a name for a magazine is the one who first uses it and continues to use it. He can stop others from using it, or something like it, only if confusion would be created in the minds of whatever public is being served. This is all based, in the end, on old common law precepts and usually has to be determined by a court if there is a dispute.

After you think you have found the name that you want to use, you must try to determine whether anyone else is using it for a magazine. The first place to make a search is at the U.S. Patent and Trademark office in Washington. This is usually arranged by your attorney with someone down there who specializes in this kind of thing.

This, unfortunately, is not the end, because lots of magazines are started that never register their names. That does not stop them from owning the name. So, when you start publishing, you may find that someone you never heard of may claim he had it first.

You may also find that names that are registered are no longer being used. In this case, you probably will be able to use the one you want, but you had better consult an attorney first.

The current copyright law (passed in 1988) allows you to reserve a name with the U.S. Patent and Trademark office (PTO) even before its use as long as you actually intend to use it. Prior to this, the only way to protect a name was through use. It was common practice then to send out a periodic newsletter to people in many states so that the name could be shown to have been used in interstate commerce.

While it is still possible to do this, it is easier and less expensive to reserve the name.

If, after review, the PTO allows the name (because it has found no conflicting names and no one has opposed your use), you have six months to actually use it. This period may be extended to as much as twenty-four months on a showing of "good cause."

At the end of the period you must actually have used the name and must file an affidavit stating that you have done so. If you meet these requirements, the date of your registration will relate back to the date when you first reserved it.

To some extent the problem may be somewhat academic. You can be stopped from using a name only when it would create confusion in the public's mind or tarnish the name of a different kind of product with a well-established reputation. There may actually be other publications using the name you want that could not conceivably result in confusion or dilution.

Since the test of whether a name is like that used by someone else is whether there will be confusion, there are no hard-and-fast rules. The facts of each case determine the outcome.

Here are some of the more recent court findings on the subject with which I was involved:

- *PC Magazine* was started in 1984. Later that year, Ziff-Davis bought it from the founders. The entire staff mutinied and went to IDG (*Computerworld,* etc.) and started an almost identical magazine within two months, called *PC World.* Ziff tried to stop them from using that name, but lost the case.
- When Bob Guccione first started what was later called *Omni* magazine, he planned to call it Nova. WGBH, the Boston public television station that produces the science series called Nova for television, complained, and the court prohibited Bob from using the name for the magazine. (You have to wonder whether the judge would have ruled the same way if someone other than the publisher of *Penthouse* had been in the picture.)
- *Inc.* magazine tried to stop *Manhattan, inc.* from using "inc." in its name. It failed. The decision hinged on such things as the fact that the latter was a local, not a national magazine; the *I* in "inc." was lower case; and other seemingly insignificant details.

Sometimes the use of a typeface in the logo similar to that of another magazine can make the difference.

As you look at the various publishing fields, you will run into all sorts of names that seem to be very similar and you may wonder how there is not confusion. The examples of magazines serving golf mentioned above are an excellent case in point.

Other examples might be:

- *Parents* and *Parenting*
- *Woman, Woman's Day,* and *Woman's World*
- *Soap Opera Digest, Soap Opera Magazine, Soap Opera News, Soap Opera Stars, Soap Opera Update,* and *Soap Opera Weekly*

And there are lots of others of the same kind.

C H A P T E R 2 8

Raising Money

RAISING MONEY FOR a new magazine is undoubtedly the most difficult part of the launch process. Not only is it difficult, but it is also exhausting, depressing, time-consuming, and only joyful the very few times when someone says "yes"—and means it.

WARNING

You cannot imagine how difficult money-raising is. And it's really even harder than that. So, enjoy this if you want, but don't expect to learn anything.

Sources of Capital

At this writing we have just passed through a period when money for high-tech ventures was available as never before. The markets were high, feelings were good, IPOs were being launched left and right, and the amount of capital available seemed almost unlimited. Now we seem to have entered more normal times. The situation remains as it has been for a good many years for someone wanting to launch a new magazine. Capital for magazine properties has always been difficult to obtain and the boom in high-tech investing did not change that.

Here are the principal sources for raising money—and a review of the chances of attracting investments from each group.

Credit Cards

You may have read about people who have hocked themselves up to their eyeballs by using every credit card imaginable—and then launched a successful new project. There may be people who have done this, but I don't happen to know any of them, although I imagine that some entrepreneurs have used their credit cards to avoid starving at times.

Chances are that if you try this, you won't have enough to get started anyway. In any case, bankruptcy is always fitting.

Bank Loans

Forget it. Bankers need either hard assets or some other kind of collateral to make loans. One of the charms of the magazine business is that we don't need any machines or buildings or other hard assets to be able to publish, so there is no collateral unless you can get some investors to put it up, or to guarantee the loan.

Large Corporations

Forget it—at least for those large companies that are not already heavily into publishing. There was a time some years ago when a number of the major corporations had publishing properties among the businesses they owned, including ITT, Xerox, Litton, Norton Simon, and a few others. They have, however, all sold off their publishing activities because they were not enough like the parent companies' basic activities (which they understood better) to be worth keeping.

Government Bodies

The Small Business Administration (SBA) helps support banks and others who make loans and other investments. For a long time the SBA was prohibited from investing in anything that attempted to influence people—freedom of the press, you know, but this policy no longer obtains.

Virtually every state and many other governmental bodies have funds that they use to attract business. Their goal is usually to increase employment so when you approach them to help support a magazine, their first question is liable to be, "How many employees will you have?" Your answer "5 to 15 or so" pretty much closes the door.

But trying never hurts—you never know.

Foundations

There are lots of foundations, some of which have considerable amounts of money to dispense. Years ago the Ford Foundation supported a number of publishing projects, and Exxon and some others have helped out once in awhile. Chances are slim, but if your project fits a foundation's objectives, it might happen. You can find out about them and what their interests are at the Foundation Center whose headquarters is in New York.

Wall Street Firms

In a number of cases some of the investment banking companies have looked into new magazine concepts. Allen & Company and Oppenheimer have invested in several, but not in recent years. The capital for *Essence* was raised by E. F. Hutton. When these firms become involved, it is usually through personal investments by some of the partners. It's worth looking into if you have contacts.

One investment banking firm has set up a fund for investing in publishing—Veronis, Suhler and Associates. They have a policy so far, however, of not going into start-ups. Both John Veronis and John Suhler come from the magazine business—and both were formerly involved in launching new magazines. Perhaps there is a lesson to be learned there.

Some years ago one fund was founded to support new magazine ventures. So far as I know, no investments were ever made. I still think such a fund is a good idea, but I don't know of any that now exist.

Venture Capital Firms

Some of the most astute and helpful investors are in venture capital firms that have been set up specifically to help new ventures. Most of these firms, however, are now geared to high-tech ventures and do not look at publishing projects. Some others have been in magazine ventures and have a flat rule—no magazines—because they didn't work out.

There still are, however, some that can be approached. You must realize, however, that they review some 40 to 50 projects a week, and your chances are very limited. Among those that have venture firms are major banks, large corporations, insurance companies, and individuals who are able to attract capital from pension funds and the like because of their ability to develop profitable new ventures. Some of them have considerable amounts to invest.

Wealthy Individuals—and Sometimes Not So Wealthy.

Individuals sometimes invest in magazines, usually because they are very interested in the subject matter of the magazine. Most city magazines, for instance, were originally financed by groups of local wealthy individuals. If you can find people who are fascinated with the field you want to cover, give it a try. Better yet, see if you can gather a group of them together.

Publishers

This would seem to be the most logical place to find money because publishers understand the business and are not afraid of it. Until the past few years, however, it was virtually impossible to get publishing companies to even look at projects that were not invented within their walls.

In recent years, however, many publishers have reached the conclusion that they do not know any more about starting new magazines than anyone else, that all the good ideas will not be born within their companies, and that new magazines can probably be started better and with far less expense as independent entities than they can do it. (See chapter 12, "Start-ups: The Record for Existing Publishing Companies.")

Almost all the major publishers these days are willing to look at new magazine projects, but you must realize that they have internal agendas that may or may not fit, or that may even conflict with, your project. There is also the possibility that some of the executives will be jealous of giving you the opportunity to get rich while they are working for a relative pittance.

CUSTOMERS

For many magazines with paid circulation, the subscribers as a group become the largest investors in new magazines—but, of course, they don't know it. A number of would-be publishers have conceived of the idea of getting the largest advertisers in their field to become investors by paying for a year's advertising in advance. Advertisers have only very rarely been lured into such schemes. They only work out in very specific times and places where the advertisers' interests are clearly helped. In one instance Nike supported the launch of *Runner's World,* but this is not a usual event.

SUPPLIERS

New magazines have dealings with all sorts of suppliers who might help with financing by lending money or extending terms. These include printers, paper companies, and merchants; single-copy distribution companies; and others. In some rare instances, deals have been made with some of these suppliers and, sometimes, when the publisher owes enough, a supplier, normally a printer, will lend support to protect his investment.

When this is done, the publisher must be careful not to get locked into a situation that is later not to his advantage.

EMPLOYEES

Perhaps you will be fortunate enough to find key employees who are wealthy and are as interested in the project as you are, and who want to invest. Don't count on it. If this happens, you may later get into a partnership situation that does not work out well between you.

Why It Is So Difficult to Raise Money for Magazines

You and I know that magazine publishing is a high-profit, low-risk business, but many in the world, particularly those involved in financial affairs, do not agree with us. If you understand how they feel—and why they feel that way—perhaps it will help when it comes to raising money for a new magazine.

WHAT DOES THE MARKET SAY ABOUT MAGAZINES?

Financial people, in looking at any field, start by trying to find out how the public markets rate companies in the field.

The problem here is that there are only a handful of public companies that are primarily devoted to magazines.

In the consumer field are:

- Meredith—*Better Homes and Gardens, Country Gardens, Country Home, Family Money, Golf for Women, Ladies' Home Journal, Midwest Living, More, Renovation Style, Successful Farming, Traditional Home,* and *Wood,* plus books and other offshoots of these magazines.
- Playboy Enterprises—*Playboy* plus a cable channel and other offshoots.
- Primedia—Some 150 consumer magazines in specialized fields.
- Reader's Digest—*Reader's Digest* in this and other countries plus several special interest consumer magazines and extensive direct mail book, music, and other operations.
- Scholastic—Primarily the publisher of the *Scholastic* papers that are distributed through schools.

In the business field are:

- Three international companies with substantial holdings of business magazines in the United States—Elsevier N.V., Reed International, and United Business Media.
- Penton Media with more than 50 business publications and many trade shows.
- Three or four b2b newer entries.

As you can see, each of these operates in specialized areas, and while Wall Street likes to categorize companies, none really represents the situation of the magazine industry as a whole.

Other public companies whose publishing interests may be substantial, but which are overshadowed by their other operations, include:

- AOL Time Warner—Probably the largest consumer magazine publisher with *Time, Fortune, Sports Illustrated, People, Southern Living, Sunset,* and a number of other titles, plus associated book publishing operations—but with AOL, cable, and other activities that are much larger.
- Walt Disney—A few magazines among its operations.
- Martha Stewart—Two magazines.
- McGraw-Hill—Once the largest business magazine publisher, now dominated by its book, financial publishing, and other operations.
- Washington Post—Owner of *Newsweek.*

In the eyes of most financial people there is no magazine field—or at least there is no base to start from. And it is different from every other business they have to tackle since the companies they serve are dependent on the fields they cover rather than being focused on a single industry. To understand a large publishing company requires understanding all the various fields it serves—often a gargantuan task. Venturing into this unknown is something few financial people like to do.

A Very Public Business

By their very nature, magazines are in the public eye. Not only that, but since the media loves other media, magazines get far more than the share of publicity they deserve. This has led to a perception that magazines are a very risky business. You can probably recall seeing pictures on the front pages of newspapers and on TV of editors crying as a magazine is closed up. People remember the foldings of *Life, Look, The Saturday Evening Post, Spy, Coronet, The Saturday Review, Ms, Colliers*—and more recently, *Ge*orge, The Industry Standard, Sport, and many others. No matter that many of those magazines should never have been started in the first place, or that they had reached the end of their life cycles, the public's perception is that magazine publishing is a very difficult business.

Investors Must Relate to the Product

A golfer probably won't invest in a tennis magazine. If you don't relate to New Age thinking, or women's lib, chances are that you are not a good investment prospect for a magazine about either one. Yet many of these same people will invest in some high-tech scheme with a product whose use they don't even understand, as has been amply demonstrated in recent years.

You rarely have any idea of what potential investors are interested in, so you have to canvas an awful lot of them before finding even one who wants to discuss the subject you are covering.

The Unusual Economics of Magazine Publishing

Most financial people spend their lives working with businesses that involve tangibles—things you can touch and feel. In publishing, we don't need buildings, or machinery, or inventories. We don't even have many people. We do our accounting statements differently, without any cost of goods sold, gross profit figures, or depreciation, a concept with which financial people are not familiar. The unknown scares them. They don't know how to measure success in this unfamiliar business.

Most financial people are not aware of the high profit margins that can be earned in the magazine business and will stare at you in disbelief when you tell them that you can earn 30% to 35% profit on sales year after year.

Not Aware of the Sales Prices of Magazines

This negative may not be as strong as it once was after the last few years when the large sales prices of Petersen, Primedia, Ziff-Davis, Cahners, and other magazine companies have become known. It has also become relatively apparent to almost anyone that there are many buyers for almost any magazine.

Publishers and Financial People Often Do Not Relate Well to Each Other

Most publishers are not trained in financial affairs. Their knowledge of operating statements and balance sheets is not extensive. They rarely are skilled in discussing tax matters, depreciation policies, various ratios—or in the methods and joys of making deals, which is how financial people live.

Conversations between publishing and financial people often take place with each party working from a different agenda.

Some Investors Have Been Burned

A number of perfectly good investors have put money into magazines over the years, despite their original fears. Lots of them have either lost their investments or barely come out whole. The cry in many venture firms is: No magazines.

This, of course, really reflects on the investors themselves because they invested in the wrong magazines—or the wrong people. But when you start out being uncomfortable about the industry, it is much easier simply to avoid even investigating a new magazine than to blame yourself. When in doubt, as in baseball, fire the manager.

The Positives for Investing in Magazines

Interestingly, many of the positives are the same as the negatives, but viewed differently. For those who will listen, there are many compelling reasons for considering investing in magazines, but for those financial types who start out with a negative, or at best, an unknowledgeable mindset, it is difficult to see the other side.

A Public Business

The public character of magazines makes it very easy for investors to monitor them—certainly much easier than some high-tech venture that they don't understand. Consider that you can read the editorial content, you can count the advertising pages, and the circulation is audited. There are no real surprises.

This is very different from the all-too-familiar savings and loans or high-tech industries, where no one really seems to know what is happening, but in which they invest anyway. And when did you last hear that a company such as Boise Cascade suddenly discovered that the land it had purchased for $400 million was underwater and had to be written off? Somehow this doesn't make the front pages of the *Times* the way the fifteenth death of *The Saturday Review* did.

Profits Can Be Very Large

We know that the average profit for all consumer magazines is some 15% of revenue, and that this average includes the new ones, the dying ones, and those in a mature state. About the same is true for business magazines. Not many industries can come even close to that profit percentage.

The fact is that a great many magazines make enormous profits for many years of their lives, and the investment required to launch most of them is minor compared with almost any other business.

It's a Fun Business

Magazine people, their writers, and their advertisers are interesting, well-educated, idea-type people. They are fun to be around. More fun, even, than ball-bearing manufacturers.

It's an Influential Business

If I own part of *Washingtonian* or an architectural magazine, I can put it on my coffee table—and many of my friends will realize that I have an influence on what goes on in the city in which I live—or in the industry in which I work. If I own part of *U.S. News & World Report,* I can call the White House and talk to whomever I want without even donating a few hundred thousand dollars.

It's a Cash Business

There are not many of those. Consider these points:

- Subscribers pay in advance.
- Single-copy sales are remitted as the sales are made, and often with advance payments.
- Most advertising is paid very quickly, usually within 30 days of publication.
- You don't need to build a building, buy equipment, or invest in any inventory.

You May Find Investors Who Love Your Concept

Then you are really in clover. These are the people who might invest for the wrong reasons. I remember one sailing magazine that raised about

$2 million over a two-week period by going down to the local yacht club and talking with the people with the biggest boats. Incidentally, they didn't raise enough and the magazine failed—don't forget undercapitalization.

It's a Tax Shelter

Well, it used to be in a big way for certain magazines. There are still ways that some taxpayers can take advantage of the tax aspects, although these shelters are not as good as they once were.

Seed Money versus Major Financing

Seed money includes those amounts you need to get started, such as for developing the editorial concept, doing a pilot issue, and testing, which we discussed in chapter 17, "The Launch Scenario." The seed money is at the greatest risk because all you have at that stage is an idea, a concept, and, perhaps, a plan.

Major financing is the amount you need to take the magazine to a profitable state. It can range from a few thousand dollars to many millions, depending on the project and how it is carried out.

It would be wonderful if you could raise the seed money and the major financing from just one source at the beginning of the project; then you would have to go through only one fund-raising period rather than two or more. This rarely, if ever, happens. Instead, you will probably have to get the seed money first. Where do you get that? From the people you least want to approach—your family and friends. This includes people like your doctor, dentist, brother-in-law, aunts, uncles, stingy grandparents and the like.

Normally it is only after you have proven that the public wants your magazine that you can seriously start going after all those other major sources we discussed before.

Structuring the Deal

There are an infinite number of ways in which the financing deal can be structured. These methods depend on who the parties are and the creativity of the financial people involved. Here are some ideas that are general in nature, but that will give you an idea of some that have often been used. There are, generally, four different groups involved in the financing, each with somewhat different interests:

- YOU, and others of the founding group, whose primary interest is in getting the project off the ground—and, hopefully, becoming wealthy when it finally succeeds.
- SEED MONEY INVESTORS. Most likely they invested partly, if not entirely, for nonfinancial reasons and without a careful study of the financial aspects of the project. Chances are that they don't ever expect to get their money back, let alone make big profits, but they are the people who put up the money that is most at risk—and they should be rewarded handsomely for this when the magazine is successful.
- MAJOR INVESTORS. Probably professionals in the financial area, to a greater or lesser extent, who believe that money is more important than any other ingredient. They are there to make substantial profits over the long run.
- KEY EMPLOYEES. These are the people who will make the project successful, some of whom you have lured away from other jobs because of the chance to get a piece of the action, discussed in chapter 27, "What People Do You Need."

The portion each group gets is the result of a series of negotiations. These take place early, with the seed money investors, and they are relatively easy to deal with. The major investors come along later, when their participation is indispensable, and because of this, they have great bargaining power.

It may sound as if the entrepreneurs and employees will have a hard time of it—and get squeezed by the big money people. Fortunately, almost all major investors are realistic about the fact that the founder and the operators need a sizable incentive—or else the project doesn't have a chance. They know, too, that they cannot run it themselves.

The one given, which you must accept early on, is that you will not be able to keep a majority ownership of the project. The amount that you do keep is dependent on the skills and experience you bring to the party.

The nature of the transaction will vary depending primarily on who the major investors are.

If the Major Investors Are Individuals

The general relationship that eventually results is something like this:

Entrepreneur—and others who may have contributed time, talent, and effort in the early stages	25–40%
Seed money investors	10–15%
Major investors	45–60%
Employees	5–10%

The deal will probably get much more complex than this simple example. For instance, the entrepreneur may start out with just 15%, but get up to 30% if certain predetermined objectives are met.

Seed money investors usually get three to five times the percentage of ownership per dollar they invest compared with the major investors. The employees' share depends on their skill and experience.

The legal form of the venture can vary considerably. One factor in the calculation is that almost all the start-up expenses can be taken as tax deductions. Usually these losses are offered to the major investors as a "sweetener" because their out-of-pocket investment will be reduced by the tax benefits they can receive.

When individuals are involved, the organization is generally a limited partnership, a limited liability corporation, or something the Tax Code calls an S corporation. These forms of organization do not pay taxes themselves. They file tax returns that allocate income or losses to the partners or stockholders who then include them on their individual tax returns. Since there are almost always early losses, this is advantageous for them.

From a potential liability standpoint, the investors in either a limited liability corporation or an S Corporation are protected from liabilities as they would be in any other corporation. In a limited partnership they are protected from any liability in excess of the amount of their investment. If, however, they become active in the business, they cease to be limited partners and become general partners subject to all the liabilities of the partnership.

Limited partnerships or limited liability corporations are generally preferred because they are very flexible. The partners can agree to just about anything they want. This is more difficult to accomplish in the S corporation. For instance, the partners may agree to divide profits and losses in different ratios:

	Profits	Losses
Limited partners (major investors)	60%	99%
Entrepreneur and others	40%	1%

In this way the major investors get virtually all the losses in the early years for tax purposes.

If the Investors Are Venture Capital Firms

Venture firms do not often want to play the tax games discussed above. They are also sometimes organized as a Small Business Investment Company (SBIC) or a Minority Enterprise Small Business Investment Company (MESBIC). By doing this, the federal government through the SBA will add to the capital provided by the investors and thus increase the pool of funds available.

With these investors you may also end up with joint ventures, convertible debentures, preferred stock, short-term notes, mezzanine financing, warrants, guaranteed bank loans—and who knows what else.

If the Investors Are Publishing Companies

A publishing company may simply offer to invest the capital needed for a percentage of the magazine, plus an option to buy the rest at a later time for a price that is less than the fair market value is expected to be at that time. This is attractive to the publishers because they can continue to grow their operations at a much reduced cost compared with starting things themselves or buying other properties at their full value.

The publishers likely will insist that they have 80% of the magazine because with that percentage they are able to file consolidated tax returns—and then can apply the magazine's losses in the early periods against their other profits for tax purposes. The percentage ownership is not really important at this point as long as the buy-out provision is realistic.

Note that the publishing company can also be very helpful to the magazine—by buying printing, paper, and other items less expensively; using its clout with single-copy distributors; providing skilled input in developing and interpreting direct mail campaigns; and in lots of other ways.

ONE CREATIVE COMBINATION OF INVESTORS

Creativity has never been lacking in the financial community when it comes to making deals. Here is one scheme that has been used:

> *The publisher puts up no capital, but provides services to the magazine that are calculated to be worth over a million dollars, plus management oversight. The publisher has an option to buy the magazine at any time after five years for 70% of its then fair market value, which is determined through a formula.*
>
> *The new magazine gets many benefits from the relationship with the publisher, with no out-of-pocket cost, reducing its need for capital. The publisher is able to acquire an addition to its stable of magazines with no upfront cash and at a bargain price, knowing that there will be no competing bids.*
>
> *The venture firm, impressed with the stamp of approval of the publisher, the cost savings, and the other help the publisher will give, agrees to invest $2 million. The venture firm is also assured that there is a built-in buyer later when the magazine is successful. Investors almost always want to know what the "exit strategy" is for their investments.*

OBVIOUS WARNING

As you can see, these things can get very complex. Be sure you have competent financial and tax people on board for the negotiations.

How Do You Find Investors?

You probably know who your family and friends are—the ones who may invest for the wrong reasons—even though you will probably get some surprises, both pleasant and unpleasant, when you ask them for investments. Chances are, though, that you don't know any venture capitalists, wealthy individuals, publishers, or anyone else who can provide the major financing that will be required. How do you find them?

It's a lot of hard work. People these days call it "networking." Talk to bankers, lawyers, accountants, brokers, investment people, those who live in large houses, and anyone else who would seem to be able to lead you to these people. After you talk to the first round of these, ask them if they can lead you to others. This process will go on ad infinitum, if you do it right.

There are books that list the venture firms, their industry preferences, and the size of the investments they like to make. One of these is *Pratt's Guide to Venture Capital Sources* published by Securities Data Publishing. The venture people like to be listed because this is the way they hear of investment opportunities. In many cities there are regular meetings of venture firms where they hear proposals about possible projects. See if you can get invited to these—and hopefully get on the program.

There are many lists of wealthy people—the Forbes 400 is one. Major contributors to good causes is another.

If you want to try publishers, peruse SRDS and other such sources to find which companies might relate best to your project.

Things to keep in mind when looking for investors:

- Expect to be turned down very often. Also expect that lots of people will not answer quickly or will not have the good manners to tell you when they have decided against your project. This is nothing personal—some people just hate to say no.
- You will find that different groups of investors are interested in different size deals. The big venture firms may talk to you only if you are asking for $10 million or more. And there are other people who will do something only for less than $200,000. You have to find the groups that fit your the investment needs.
- In any venture deal, you will have to find what they call a "lead" investor. He is the one who will monitor the investment for the others. Once you can find one, he may be able to round up the followers.
- Investors like buddies. They will rarely invest unless one or two others are in, too. So don't expect one person or group to take the whole thing. Having several investors is healthy for you, too—less dictation or interference with operations.
- You may run into people called "finders." They will tell you that they can find money for you. It's all right to pay them a percentage of what they raise (so long as the investors know this), but if they ask for money up front, be very, very careful. I must also tell you that I have yet to find a finder who successfully raised money for a magazine, even

though they may have been able to do it for other ventures.

• When trying to raise money, go in all directions at once. Don't wait for any specific group to make up its mind or you may spend the rest of your life waiting. It can't hurt to have more than one on the string, even after the one you hope for does actually say yes.

• If you are dealing with a publishing company, you must also be aware that only rarely can one person make a quick decision. There are always internal politics, most of which you will not understand unless you are on the inside. So some very favorable—or unfavorable—initial reactions can change seemingly with the weather and the wind.

Steps Involved in Raising Money

The basic tenet in raising money is: Be overprepared. You will recall that the business plan was carefully written so that it would act as a door opener for investors, among other things. Unless you personally know someone, or have an introduction that can't be turned down, you will not get in the door without first sending something first—your very carefully prepared business plan. Here are some other points to keep in mind:

• Investing in your magazine is not priority number one for anyone you send your business plan to. Routine follow-ups on what they feel about your project are needed for most people. Be courteous in asking where things stand—and don't be a pest. Also, expect that you will never get an acknowledgment or a reply from some of them.

• Have all your supplementary material (list later in this chapter) ready to go, with copies available for anyone who wants them. Very different from the business plan itself—having more ready is better than less.

• Rehearse your pitch, not once, but several times.

• When you get an audience, take as many of your key players with you as you can. Don't forget that the investor is intensely interested in the people involved.

• Before you go see a real potential investor, do some dry runs with people you think would not conceivably be interested. Try some bankers and lawyers—and carefully record all their questions, objections, and other observations so that you will be prepared with the answers when the real investors ask the same questions.

While the chances are that you will have to raise money in two phases—seed money and major financing—you don't really want to wait to start on the major financing until the results of whatever testing you are doing come in. As soon as you have a good business plan and a pilot issue prepared, you should start talking to potential investors. When the test results come in, you may have them warmed up enough that you can talk seriously.

What Investors Are Looking For

Remember that most investors are financially oriented. They usually have firm ideas about what they expect from an investment in any start-up operation. There are lots of different ways of expressing what investors want. Some people like to express it as a percentage return on investment (ROI)—they might say 25% per year, or something like that. I have found that there are so many different ways of making that calculation that you are never sure exactly what they mean when they give you a figure, but you can be sure it's substantial.

A simpler way of expressing it might be "I want to get ten times (or some other number) my investment back if I sell out after five years." Here is the way you might want to develop a calculation of this kind for them. (Note that we are discussing cash flow—that's all important):

Anticipated cash flow from operations

Year 1	$ (600,000)	
2	(400,000)	
3	100,000	
4	800,000	
5	1,500,000	
High negative cash flow-during February of Year 2		$(1,200,000)
Investment required (includes a cushion)		$ 1,400,000
Per unit (assume ten investors)		$ 140,000
Sharing of losses (for the investors' tax purposes)		
Investors	99%	
Entrepreneur	1%	
Sharing of profits		
Investors	65%	
Entrepreneur	35%	
Value of magazine at end of five years		
$1,500,ooo x 10–15	$15,000,000 to $22,500,000	
(assuming a multiple of ten times cash flow—magazines sell for 10 to 15 times)		
Excess cash in company$ 2,000,000		
Total value of the company after five years		$17,000,000 to $24,500,000

Situation of holder of one unit
Investment $140,000
Less tax saving by usinglosses
($140,000 @ 39% tax rate)—
depends on current tax rates $ 55,000
Net investment $ 85,000
Value he received at sale
$17,000,000 to $24,500,000 x 6.5% = $1,105,000 to 1,592,500
Less capital gains tax @ 20% = $221,000 to 318,500
Net return $ 884,000 to 1,274,000
Return 10.4 to 15.0 times investment

As you can see, the projected figures in this case work out to ten or more times. The investor might feel that this is good enough. Because of differences in the tax consequences for different investors and as well as changes in the tax laws, the calculations can become much more complex.

What to Say When You See a Potential Investor

I wouldn't dream of trying to tell you how to sell (or charm) people. Each of us has his own personality. Of course, you must adapt yourself to the people you are talking to.

Here, however, are some thoughts:

- As you would with anyone you don't know, try to find out everything you can about the person—or people—you are going to see. Ask around, read anything you can find, try the Internet—and look everywhere else you can think of.
- You obviously are very enthusiastic about the concept of the magazine—and you have to be sure that this comes through. On the other hand, you must be observant enough to see when your audience is getting bored. Nothing can turn them off quicker than your going on and on in your enthusiasm. If you have a confederate with you, make sure that you guard each other against this—and interrupt when boredom seems to be setting in.
- Until you get there, you will never know whether he has read one page, two pages, no pages, or the whole Business Plan you used as a door opener, or, if it was a referral from someone else, how thoroughly the concept has been presented. Even if he says he knows all about it, you will not know whether he really understands it until the discussion gets under way. You don't want to bore him by repeating everything he already is familiar with, but you also want to be sure that he understands what it is all about—and you must correct any misunderstandings he has.
- Don't be put off by what appear to be very dumb or simplistic questions. Magazine publishing is not understood by many people—and the field your magazine covers probably is relatively obscure to the people you are talking to. Patient—and understanding—explanations may be wearying for you, but exciting for your audience.
- On the other hand, do not try to explain the entire publishing business as if you are an expert in it. You aren't—and this will become clear sooner or later. Explain what you have to—and get some expert to cover the parts you don't know thoroughly.
- By the same token, your job is to discuss the magazine, the field it covers, and how you will make it work. The people you are talking with are probably knowledgeable about financial, tax affairs and the like. If they want to discuss such things as the financing methods, that is a wonderful sign. It indicates that they are interested. But don't queer the deal by getting too deep into these areas where they probably know more than you do. Refer them to your accountants or lawyers or other helpers.
- Most of the people you will be talking to have met many other entrepreneurs. They know that you have probably spent many hours of work, lost lots of sleep, spent most or all of your assets, possibly gotten divorced, and who knows what else, to get to the point you have in the project. They don't really want to be told about this. They assume it, so don't discuss it.

It also doesn't help to tell them how long it took you to reach this point. If it's such a good idea, why did it take you so long to raise your capital?

In brief, your job is to stay out of details—and SELL, SELL, SELL the concept.

Material to Have Ready

While the Business Plan is the door opener and should not be more than 20 pages long, when you get to see potential investors, you must be as well prepared as you can. That means that you must be able to anticipate every question and every concern that the investor may have.

You should have with you a briefcase full of specifics, plans, write-ups, clippings, and anything else that might be helpful. Brevity is not as important as full explanations and complete details. Be fully prepared with copies of anything that will be helpful. At this point, don't be bashful about showing work that is in process. People like to be in the know—and they also like to be asked their opinions about things, even if they are not expert about them.

Here is what you should have available. It may seem to be a long list, but you should have considered almost every one of these items, so be sure that you have them all in writing.

Basic Concept for the Magazine

- Complete research into the field covered, number of people who should be interested, depth of their interest, demographics and psychographics of these people, etc.
- Focus group results for those that have been finished. If they have not been completed, include the detailed plans for doing them and the cost.
- Research into competing magazines, their circulation, advertising, and pricing. Have available copies of the magazines, their media kits, mailing pieces, and anything else you can get your hands on. Explain how you will differ from them.
- Research about other media—newspapers, newsletters, TV, Internet, etc.—covering the field.
- Launch Scenario—Perhaps with comments on how each step was completed, and results versus what you had expected.
- What you have spent so far. Also the time and expenses of those who have been involved. Other opportunities these people may have foregone, such as quitting their jobs.
- Situation about the copyright and/or trademark registration of the name of the magazine—or of sections, if that would be done.
- The Pilot Issue. If it has not yet been completed, the plans for it plus whatever parts are available, the design of magazine logo and inside pages, graphics that might be used, confirmation of writers, pasted up pages, or anything else.

Editorial

- All those detailed issue plans you prepared
- A graphic grid showing the pattern of the editorial matter, or whatever else your designer has prepared
- Whatever information you have about writers, artists, and others who have been contacted to provide material
- Names of people and their credentials on the editorial advisory committee if you plan to have one
- Methods of composing and laying out the editorial copy, including the extent of desk top publishing or other computerized methods to be used

Circulation

- Detailed research into the size and nature of the market for readers
- Prices for single copies, various length subscriptions, various types of subscriptions such as introduction, conversion, renewal, gift, or agent sold
- Marketing plans for single copies
- Marketing plans for subscription sales incuding sources and methods to be used, copies of any direct mail and other efforts completed or in process
- If controlled circulation, characteristics of those to whom the magazine will be sent and the methods of finding and qualifying them
- Plans for having the circulation audited by one of the well-known audit organizations
- Any data you can obtain about the circulation efforts of competing magazines

Advertising

- Details of the market such as types of advertising to be sought, target accounts, trends, and advertising in competitive magazines and other media, etc.
- Definition of the magazine's brand name and positioning
- Media kit as far as it has been developed
- Anticipated advertising rates for various types of advertisers and comparison with competitors
- Situation in the field regarding rate cutting, value added efforts, and the like
- Charter advertising rates you plan to offer
- Types of promotion efforts you will pursue
- Methods of determining research into the audience and into the readership of your magazine in the future
- Whether you will publish regional, demographic, special, and other such editions
- Whether you will give some advertisers exclusives in some categories—at least for a time

Ancillary Activities

- Description of list rental, reprints, classified advertising, T-shirts, and other sources off income arising from normal magazine operations
- Description and potential revenue and anticipated costs of other ancillaries, such as book publishing, catalogs, trade shows, and other longer term offshoots that can be developed based on the brand developed by the magazine

PRODUCTION

- Trim size
- Paper type and weight to be used
- Distribution methods, suppliers to be used, and cost for distributing single copies, subscriptions, controlled circulation, foreign circulation, airline copies, and any other circulation
- Printing method to be used; information about conversations with printers, paper suppliers, etc.
- Binding method to be used—side stitch or saddle stitch

GENERAL AND ADMINISTRATIVE

- Office—probable location, type and amount of space, cost
- Equipment to be purchased or leased and estimated cost
- Public relations and publicity activities

PEOPLE INVOLVED

- Method of organization
- Job descriptions of key people
- Detailed biographies and other information about the key people
- Pay scales, contracts, advertising commissions and other arrangements
- Fringe benefits to be offered
- Travel, entertainment, other policies

FINANCIAL

- Detailed printouts of the projections in the business plan
- Written description of the projections and assumptions on which they are based
- Downside projections
- Results of sensitivity analyses and other projections that have been made
- Accounting system to be used and types and frequency of reports to be developed
- Plans for developing budgets and other future projections

SUPPLIERS

Actual names and qualifications. Contracts where available. Before that, the methods for selecting them and estimated costs.

- Printer
- Provider of color separations, typesetting, and other such material, if any
- Paper supplier
- Single-copy distributor
- Freight company
- Advertising agency
- Research company for focus groups, other research
- Subscription fulfillment
- Circulation auditing organization
- Telephone system
- List broker

CONSULTANTS AND OTHERS TO BE USED

Names, qualifications, and estimated costs. Actual arrangements wherever they have been consummated.

- Magazine designer
- Editorial consultants
- Production consultants
- Postal consultants
- Single copy consultants
- Subscription consultants
- General magazine consultants
- Public relations firm
- Legal firm
- Accounting firm
- Financing consultants
- Insurance broker

FINANCING

- Methods being used to obtain financing.
- Suggested financing plan. It is good to have more than one plan to show that you are flexible.
- Types of people and organizations who are being offered the investment opportunity.
- Specifics of people who are being approached.
- Specifics of those who have already signed up.

WRITTEN OR VERBAL OPINIONS

- Readers
- Advertisers
- Employees
- Suppliers
- Consultants
- Bankers
- Investors
- And anyone else
- Lists of people the potential investor can talk with to discuss the project

CHAPTER 29

Now That You've Raised Money for a New Magazine . . . Here Are 186 Things You Must Be Sure to Do

CONGRATULATIONS! You have raised $30,000—or $300,000, or $3 million, or $30 million—to launch your magazine. What happens now?

You are embarking on the second hardest job there is—starting a new business. The hardest, of course, is raising money. You've already done that. The next phase is very different. First, let's agree on a few basic assumptions:

- Not many people have successfully started a new business of any kind.
- You have never started a new business.
- The business of magazine publishing involves attracting a part of the public to your product. And who can predict what the public will like?
- You are familiar with some aspects of publishing, but other aspects are foreign to you.
- You are not really sure how good each member of your team is.
- You have rounded up some money—and some investors—but you do not know them very well.
- You will get only one shot at the project.
- You are exhausted—and to some extent frustrated —from the money-raising activities.

So now what? Now comes organizing, planning, hiring, directing, buying, selling, negotiating, dealing, and doing all sorts of other things you probably have never done before. Will you be good at them? Who knows?

Below is a list of 186 things to do after you've raised money for the new magazine. Of course, not every item will pertain to every venture, but, taken as a whole, this list will certainly provide a useful checklist—for the publisher of a well-established magazine as well.

No matter how exhausted and discouraged you get:

1. Continue to resell the investors. You may need more money later.

2. Continue to resell your staff. They may not always remember that it is better to work longer and harder for you and receive less pay than they think they can get elsewhere.

3. Continue to sell the suppliers. They must continue to understand the importance of being connected with such a successful and prestigious magazine, and you may need them for extended credit at some point.

4. Continue to sell advertisers and agencies on the idea that they should place their ads in your magazine, even though they normally do not do this for new magazines.

5. Continue to sell your banker. When you need money later he may be able to furnish it.

6. Continue to sell everyone else you can find about the concept. Who knows when they might be helpful?

7. Work an 18-hour day every day, including Sundays and holidays. You will probably be able to do this for only two to three years.

8. Don't surprise the investors. Tell them everything, even if they think you are the greatest bore in the world.

9. Never, never, never find the need for midnight calls to investors for money you need tomorrow.

10. Get to know your competitors.

11. Overcommunicate with employees, suppliers, investors, advertisers, readers, and everyone else—or at least try.

12. Expect surprises in the quality of your employees. Some may even be pleasant surprises.

13. Listen to advice from your investors. Don't necessarily act on it. Some of them may have had experience in starting things.

14. Keep your investors from forcing you to hire their ne'er-do-well relatives.

15. Listen to publishing people and their advice. But remember that very, very few of them have ever been connected with a start-up, and even if they have, no two magazines are the same.

16. Get your spouse interested and useful in the project. It's cheaper and less time-consuming than a divorce.

17. Delegate authority and responsibility as much as you can, but don't abdicate anything.

18. Review every plan and every decision everyone makes.

19. Develop an organization chart and short job descriptions. Review and update them regularly.

20. Don't fritter your time away with minor projects.

21. Stay flexible.

22. Get wired into your company's grapevine. Be sure you can plant rumors, too.

23. Remember that *everything* is important when you start a new business—what kind of wastebaskets to buy, where the coffee machine is located.

24. Make sure you have good accounting and statistical records and that each month's results are known quickly.

25. Sell advertising even if you don't think you're a good salesperson. No one else has the same enthusiasm and dedication.

26. Budget on both the cash and accrual basis. As you learn more, change the budget as often as monthly if it is helpful. Use a computer model to make it easier. Keep investors informed of any change.

27. Project operations for several years ahead. Make changes as you get more information. Keep investors informed.

28. Join MPA, ABM, DMA, and/or other useful associations. Get to know others in the business. You can learn things, make friends, and find prospective employees.

29. Subscribe to *Folio, MIN, Ad Age,* and other periodicals.

30. Send yourself and your employees to programs run by the associations and other groups as they fit your situation. Maybe your investors would be interested, too.

31. Have a board of directors. Be sure it includes knowledgeable people who will speak up to you.

Investigate, negotiate, and make arrangements with

32. A law firm.

33. An accounting firm. Be sure you are audited every year.

34. An executive recruiting firm and employment agencies.

35. An advertising agency.

36. A subscription consulting firm.

37. A single-copy consulting firm.

38. A marketing consulting firm.

39. A public relations firm.

40. A publishing consulting firm.

41. A national single-copy distributor.

Investigate, negotiate, and make arrangements for:

42. Composition equipment.

43. Prepress equipment.

44. Printing.

45. Paper.

46. Subscription fulfillment.

47. Catalog, mail, telephone, and other subscription agents.

48. Office equipment and supplies.

49. Computer modeling.

50. Other outside systems like payroll, general ledger, and advertising.

51. Organize an editorial board if it will be helpful.

Seek out and hire:

52. The editor and editorial staff.

53. The advertising director and salespeople.

54. Advertising promotion people.

55. Advertising research people.

56. Independent publishers' representatives.

57. The circulation manager and other circulation people.

58. Subscription fulfillment people.

59. Single-copy salespeople.

60. The production manager and production people.

61. The controller and other accounting people.

62. An office manager.

63. Writers.

64. An art director and artists.

65. Secretarial and clerical people.

66. In seeking out and hiring, remember the equal opportunity laws.

67. Get to know reporters for the *New York Times,* the *Chicago Tribune, Ad Age,* and other publications covering the field.

68. Organize and carry out a carefully thought-out public relations program.

69. Determine the city of your headquarters.

70. Determine where the actual office will be—and what kind of effect you want. Remember that no one visits a publisher and that investors like the frugal approach.

71. Investigate, negotiate, and contract for space and facilities for your main office.

72. Investigate, negotiate, and contract for office layout and decoration.

73. Determine if and where you need branch offices.

74. Investigate, negotiate, and contract for branch office space and facilities.

75. Determine the phone system you will need.

76. Develop pay scales for employees.

77. Develop incentive plans for as many employees as possible.

78. Set up a routine for changing salaries.

79. Determine holidays, working hours, vacations, fringe benefits.

80. Investigate, negotiate, and contract with insurance people for fringe-benefit packages. Don't forget the plans set up specifically for publishing groups.

81. Develop stock purchase, option, or other plans for key employees.

82. Decide whether you will have pension or profit-sharing plans.

83. Determine expense account policies and procedures.

84. Get your employer's Social Security number and do other steps to comply with federal and state requirements.

85. Investigate, negotiate, and contract for business insurance of various kinds.

86. Establish your fiscal year.

87. Obtain the necessary copyrights and trademarks.

88. Consider company life insurance for you and other key people.

89. Name the magazine.

90. Have a logo designed.

91. Have a design for the inside of the magazine developed. Be sure it has the reader in mind.

92. Determine pay scales for outside manuscripts, artwork, and photographs.

93. Develop a contract for outside authors.

94. Set up schedules for things to be done by you and by everyone else.

95. Develop a system for checking on meeting these schedules.

96. Establish a reading file where copies of every letter and memo are placed. Read it regularly.

97. Decide on the best Postal entry points for the magazine.

98. Make the necessary arrangements with the Postal Service.

99. Determine when the first issue will be published.

100. Determine the publishing schedule thereafter.

101. Determine advertising closing date, editorial schedules, printing schedules, mailing dates, single-copy on-sale and off-sale dates, and other related schedules.

102. Decide on paper weight and quality.

103. Open bank accounts. Decide who can sign checks.

104. Have investors and staff get to know each other better.

105. Set up a regular reporting schedule for investors.

106. Develop schedule for number of pages in each issue depending on the number of advertising pages.

107. Decide whether to offer charter rates—or something else—to get early advertising.

108. Develop advertising rates.

Decide:

109. On whether to guarantee an advertising rate base and what it will be.

110. On subscription and single-copy prices.

111. On reduced introductory prices.

112. Whether to be perfect or side stitch bound.

113. On the size of the magazine.

114. On titles for the staff—and the layout of the masthead.

115. On the design of the stationery.

116. On how to train your employees.

117. On the in-house composition system.

118. Whether to do in-house or outside data processing.

119. Organize to develop classified advertising.

120. Make arrangements for renting your list.

121. Be sure to take advantage of all the tax opportunities offered to magazine publishers.

122. File all required tax returns.

123. Instill in all employees the attitude that the reader is a customer and should be treated as such.

124. Work to get the most out of the suppliers and professionals you use.

125. Set up committees and task forces to study and execute difficult projects.

126. Don't let any piece of advertising promotion or public relations get out of the shop without your OK.

127. Frequently get an updating of the status of advertising sold.

128. Be sure you have a good call report system for ad salespeople. Monitor it frequently.

129. Establish contacts with the key accounts and agencies, not only to help sell, but also to be able to monitor both the sales force and the attitude of the ad community toward your magazine.

130. Set up a credit-checking system for advertisers and agencies.

131. Set up a billing and collection system for advertising.

132. Be sure you have a complete file of ad prospects. See that they are intelligently assigned to salespeople.

133. Review all subscription sales plans.

134. Study the results of sub efforts and tests regularly.

135. Push the fulfillment house for fast and accurate data. Be sure you understand it.

136. Move into single-copy sales gingerly. Confine to specific areas to start.

137. Get to know the single-copy wholesalers —plus their marketers, route people, and distribution clerks.

138. Set up direct sales outlets with logical retailers not served by wholesalers.

139. Read every word of every issue before it goes out, if you can. Don't hesitate to insist on changes.

140. Review each issue after it has been published. Mark it up to show how things could have been improved. Give each issue a grade—75%, 45%, etc.

141. Do reader research on each issue to find out what was read.

142. From time to time hold focus group sessions with readers to try to improve editorially.

143. Make sure excess cash is invested wisely and safely. Ask the investors to help.

144. Have your circulation audited if you carry ads.

145. Develop audience research for advertisers.

146. Keep on testing for subs. You may find a breakthrough—or at least small improvements.

147. Set up regular meetings with the staff.

148. Know what to say when certain newsletter writers call.

149. Decide whether to have a company outing in the summer and/or a Christmas party. If so, decide what they should be like, whether spouses should be invited, and where they should be held.

150. Review each issue for printing quality.

151. Have regular directors' meetings at logical decision points.

152. Negotiate with foreign publishers for international editions.

153. Start planning for by-products.

154. Go over the layout for each issue for the least expensive printing imposition.

155. Review all printing and paper bills.

156. Decide when to change ad rates and/or the rate base.

157. Decide when to change circulation prices.

158. Insist on edit plans at least six months ahead.

159. Hold a retreat with key staff annually to rethink the entire project.

160. Review competitors' magazines, personnel, and operating methods.

161. Remind the editor that he is a marketer, too.

162. Remind the circ director that he is really a marketer.

163. Explore other ways to get subs.

164. Realize that you and your partners may not get along. When that happens, face up to it.

165. If one or more of your partners has to go, so be it.

166. If you have to go to save the project, so be it.

167. When you find that the edit product is not turning out as you had anticipated, do something. Fire the editor, get a new art director, hire a consultant.

168. Or go off and rethink the whole edit approach.

169. When you find that subscriptions are not coming in at the rate you anticipated, do something. Get a new sub director, hire a new consultant, have a new letter written.

170. Or go off and rethink the entire circ approach.

171. If single copy sales are not coming in as anticipated—or if you cannot find out how many are sold—do something. Get a new single copy director, get a new national distributor, hire your own field force, try new promotion devices.

172. Or go off and rethink whether you really have a newsstand magazine.

173. If ad sales are disappointing, do something. Hire a new ad director, change the promotion, try a new research approach.

174. Or go off to rethink whether your ad sales approach is right.

175. The office is in chaos. You wonder how the issues get out. Get a new office manager—or hire a new publisher to replace you.

176. Get rid of anyone who is not doing his job—whether he is an employee, a consultant, or a supplier.

177. If you are the misfit, take yourself out of the picture—fast.

178. You have already developed go/no-go points. Don't be so excited that you carry on even though the stop signal is there.

179. Something big is sure to go wrong. When it does, don't hide it. Tell investors, suppliers, and anyone else who might be helpful.

180. Have a party when an issue gets into the black. Make sure it isn't such a good party that you go back into the red.

181. Make sure you see your children on Christmas, Thanksgiving, and their birthdays.

182. Make sure the investors know early that you have a need for more money because things have not quite worked out right.

183. Let your investors know early on that you will need more money because of your tremendous success.

184. If it looks as if you will run out of money, don't dribble away what you have. Stop publishing and cut all drains until you can raise more.

185. If things look as if they will not work out, be the first to know it—and the first to admit it.

186. Forget about ever starting another business. Once is enough.

Part III:
The Various Operations in Publishing a Magazine

CHAPTER 30

Organization of a Magazine

THERE ARE THREE major interrelated functions that must be performed in publishing a magazine:

1. Editorial—Developing and presenting material the magazine's audience will want to read.
2. Circulation—Obtaining readers who are interested in the magazine's content.
3. Advertising—Selling advertising to companies that want to reach those readers.

A magazine has frequently been described as being a three-legged stool with editorial creating the product, circulation obtaining readers, and advertising paying for the whole affair. This is a little simplified and may not be completely true for all magazines, but it does emphasize the interdependence of these three equally important activities.

Necessary to complete the operation, but in a supporting role, are:

1. Production—Getting the magazine printed and delivered to readers.
2. Accounting—Keeping track of what goes on through the financial records.
3. Office and other services—Making sure that operations can be carried on efficiently.

There must also be someone to coordinate activities—usually called the publisher.

While each of the three key areas is absolutely necessary for a successful magazine, they are extremely different in nature—and each role calls for a very different type of person. Here are some generalized descriptions of who runs each (which, I am sure, will result in cries of protest from all three).

The editor is:

- Skilled in developing and presenting material that is of the most interest and/or value to his readers
- Imbued with serving, as well as influencing, readers by giving them as much useful information, advice, and entertainment as possible in as inviting a way as he can
- One who believes he understands the pulse of his readers (without, necessarily, the need of independent research)
- Curious, self-confident, and fearless
- In touch with sources of writing and graphic talents
- Very knowledgeable about the field served, and often considered to be one of its real experts
- Guardian of the independence of the editorial content
- Not always attuned to all the ways of marketing the editorial product
- Sometimes deploring of the tactics used by circulation and advertising as being too crassly commercial
- Sometimes somewhat introverted

The circulation director is:

- An unusual pairing of talents—the ability to creatively seek out sources of readers and methods for attracting them, and also an orientation toward the use of numbers and statistics in doing this
- Wired into the clubby circulation world where knowledge, but not secrets, is shared
- Knowledgeable about selling subscriptions

through many sources, as well as billing and renewal techniques
• Familiar with available lists, copywriters, subscription agents, and consultants in the field as well as subscription fulfillment operations
• Skilled in the interpretation of seemingly small statistical variations and in projecting circulation levels
• Generally reluctant to try new circulation sources
• Not often very knowledgeable about single-copy sales, although responsible for them

The advertising director is:

• Skilled in the sale of an intangible product in a one-on-one situation
• Creative in helping advertisers solve their problems
• Able to hire salespeople and/or independent reps and to train, motivate, and support them, as well as to develop incentive programs for them
• Generally more outgoing than those in editorial and circulation
• Often the spokesman for the magazine
• Convinced that more ads can cure any ills the magazine may have
• Creative in developing promotion campaigns, group meetings of advertisers, and other such events
• Personally well organized and scheduled, and willing to travel to meet with prospects at their convenience
• Good at using research to demonstrate the efficiency of his magazine

Normally none of the three, because of their orientation, inclination, and experience, is very knowledgeable about the overall operation of a magazine or about the other departments' operations. The publisher almost always comes from one of the three disciplines, most often from advertising, and may not be very familiar with the other two areas.

Decision Making

You can easily see that decision-making concerning the three interlocking parts of a magazine, each headed by a person with a very different personality and orientation, can be difficult. Yet agreement must be reached about such basic and vital points as:

• The editorial thrust of the magazine
• Selling points in acquiring circulation
• Attributes of the magazine used in selling advertising
• Number of issues
• Number of editorial pages—and the number in color
• Amount of circulation and the sources to be used
• Circulation prices
• Advertising rates
• Editorial independence versus advertiser pressure
• Whether to have demographic or geographic editions
• Whether to supplement paid circulation with some controlled (unpaid) readers
• Publication of special issues, their subject matter and function
• Other basic decisions affecting operations

It is not only these major issues that must be solved, but also seemingly minor—or issue-to-issue—decisions such as:

• Circulation wants to stick a renewal notice on top of the cover to boost renewals at a lower cost than more renewal mailings. The editor feels that the cover is the most important page in the magazine and must be seen by readers and prospective readers.
• Editorial wants to have a "well" of 16 edit pages to increase readership. Advertising wants to put ads next to all edit pages.
• Advertising wants to accept "checkerboard" ads, but this makes reading the editorial content difficult.
• Circulation wants to bind in subscription cards near the best editorial features, but this interrupts the flow of the editorial content—and advertising says "not covering those IBM ads."
• Editorial wants two contents pages (after the cover these are the second most important pages) at the very front of the issue, but advertisers want to be as far forward as possible.
• Advertising has a 32 page advertorial insert it would like to run as far forward as possible, but this destroys the normal layout of the editorial pages.

You can add to this list such things as where to place house ads, what subjects should be on the cover, the nature of the direct mail circulation efforts, and just about every other decision, small or large.

The production manager and controller can serve to leaven the decision making to some extent because they deal with all three of the major areas. A good budgeting process together with the use of computer models can also be very helpful (See chapter 52, "Keeping Track," and chapter 55, "Planning.")

In the best magazines there is a very collegial atmosphere. In others there is "creative tension" among the three areas.

More often than not, the approach of the advertising department wins out, with circulation considered last because the ads bring in the money (and because of the forcefulness of the advertising people). This undoubtedly has contributed to the frequent decisions by many magazines to push their circulations above their natural levels in order to increase ad rates, as well as many other less obvious mistakes.

Starting Up—When Publishing Is the Most Fun

That collegial atmosphere talked about above usually exists when you are planning and starting up a new magazine. All of you are excited, open-minded, full of ideas, having the fun of developing something from nothing, and wanting to know about all the aspects of publishing because you all want to be part of everything.

It isn't until later, when everyone is busy handling his own duties—and probably running into daily frustrations—that positions harden and the fun seems to drain from the process. (But read on about "Think Small"—it may help alleviate some of the headaches.)

Think Small

The best organization is the one-person shop.

Why?

Because every time you add an employee, you add a management task. And every time you add a further employee, you have multiplied that task not by two, but by four. The more people, the more you are in the management business, rather than the magazine business.

A basic flaw in most peoples' thinking—everything that can be done by your own people is automatically good. I suppose that's because man's basic philosophy is to build. If he builds bigger, then he thinks he must be building better, but, to build bigger obviously means having more people.

As organizations grow, the tendency is to add people to do things that might just as easily be bought outside. You know, "We do it cheaper that way because Joe is already on the payroll and, if he does it, we don't have to add the overhead and profit we would have to pay an outsider to do it."

Phooey!

A core of people, of course, is necessary to get the magazine out. But, the more skills that can be purchased outside, the better.

We are fortunate that a whole raft of talented people are available to do a great many things needed in publishing. Why should you consider them? Because you cannot be expert in everything. When you have your own people do things that can be done better by outsiders, you are not necessarily getting the best. I would rather have a $100,000-a-year person who spends all his time designing mailing pieces for two weeks of his life, for instance, than have a $30,000 employee who will never be a whiz do it every once in a while. You pay the outsiders only as you use them.

Besides, once a person is on the payroll, flexibility is lost. It is hard to fire a person who is not doing his job quite as well as you wish, so you just put up with it. If, on the other hand, you find you have the wrong outsider, simply change.

Where Consultants Can Be Most Useful

Here are a few of the many areas where you can use consultants to good advantage:

- In the production area, a consultant could:
  - Find suppliers and negotiate for paper and printing
  - Determine the best method and pricing for delivering subscription copies through the Postal Service
  - Find suppliers and negotiate for delivery of single copies
  - Audit calculations for price increases based on contract escalation agreements
- In the editorial department, a consultant could:
  - Design—or redesign—the magazine
  - Design each issue of the magazine
  - Critique the editorial content and design
- In the advertising department, a consultant could:
  - Develop the promotion campaigns
  - Design the sales compensation plan

- Sell advertising in certain regions—or take over the entire sales operation
- Evaluate the sales effort with advertisers and agencies
- A consultant in the circulation department could:
  - Develop the overall plan for obtaining and renewing circulation
  - Take over the entire circulation operation, or parts of it
  - Find suppliers and negotiate for subscription fulfillment
- A consultant might also do your long-range planning.

Organization Charts

For most organizations there are two organization charts. One is published, the other is the way things actually operate. We will be discussing the way a publishing company actually operates.

From the discussion so far, I imagine you might have reached the conclusion that the best organization would be a round one with editorial, advertising, and circulation all on an equal footing. Delightful as that may be in theory, experience has shown that somebody has to be the boss if anything is to be accomplished. The actual chart normally would resemble the one in Figure 30.1, below, with editorial, advertising, and circulation all reporting on an equal footing to the publisher, with production and administrative on a line below to indicate their lesser importance.

For many magazines the publisher also serves in another capacity—more often than not as advertising director or as editor (on many new magazines) or, rarely, as circulation director.

There are, of course, untold variations in real life, primarily because people do not fit neatly into the little boxes we would like them to, or because there are personality conflicts and they cannot work with each other. Some I have seen are:

- The art director independent of the editor—I marvel that this can work well at all.
- Production under the advertising director, since, with a magazine carrying lots of advertising pages, the layout of the magazine is most dependent on the ad pages carried.
- Just one promotion director who does promotion for both circulation and advertising. This seems strange since the nature of promotion for circulation is very different from that for advertising.

Figure 30.2 shows how it used to work at the *New Yorker,* and at some other magazines where there is complete separation of Church and State, with editorial completely independent of all the business operations. I always wondered how this actually worked in practice—for instance, who decides how many pages are in each issue?

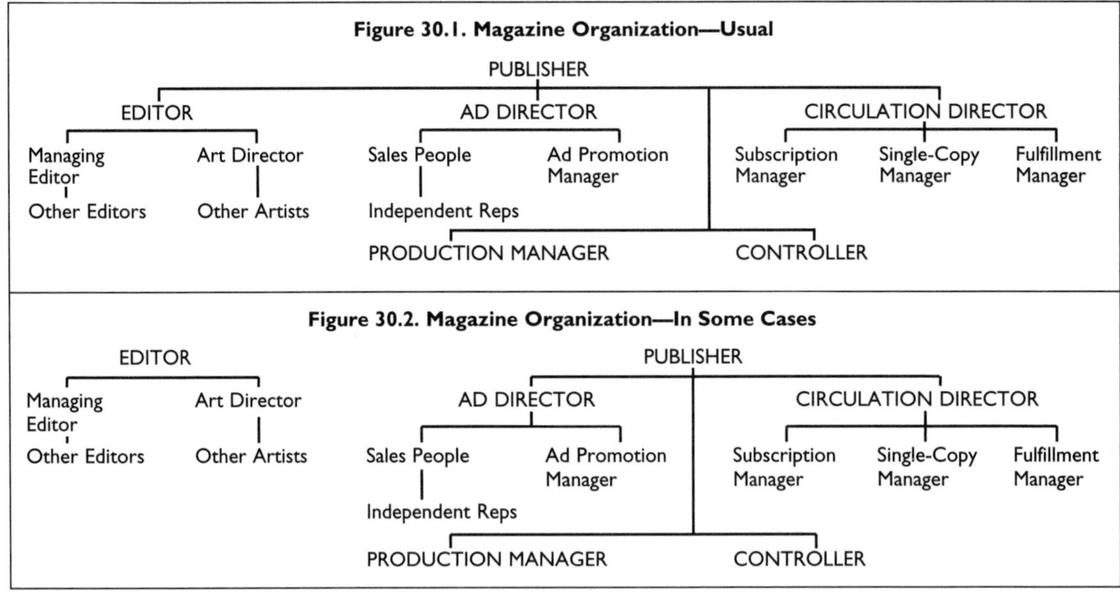

In the business magazine area, where copies are normally distributed on a controlled basis, the importance of advertising becomes more obvious. Of course, for those magazines with no—or very little—advertising, it has very little importance.

Printing, Delivery, Subscription Fulfillment

It is obvious that delivery of the magazines to readers is something that publishers rarely do for themselves—although even today some local publications take this on because it may be the only feasible way to get good delivery. (And who knows what is going to happen to the Postal Service as the Internet chips away at its basic business.)

It may be hard to believe, but not too many years ago virtually every magazine publisher thought he had to do everything for himself except make the paper and deliver his magazine to the reader.

The first 12 floors of that big green McGraw-Hill Building on 42nd Street in New York, which was built in 1934, have very high ceilings because of that publisher's need to have its own engraving plant for pictures and color work and its own presses for printing its magazines. If you go through Stamford, Connecticut, on the train, you will still see a large McCall's sign. The sign is all that is left of Conde Nast's engraving and printing operations.

It took some time—and lots of convincing—before almost all publishers gave up their printing plants (Meredith sold its plant in Des Moines only in the 1990s). Even today, Chilton and Penton, and probably some others, still own printing plants, but at least these are operated as separate entities disconnected from their publishing operations. Today virtually all publishers have contracted for printing with outside organizations that can do it better and at less cost.

These operations do not belong in a publishing company. They are foreign to all the other things that are needed to publish magazines, and they force you to make decisions that are completely at odds with the needs of the magazines—decisions such as keeping a magazine going because it fills up the printing plant. Besides, it is virtually impossible for a publisher to afford to keep the equipment up-to-date, as independent printers are forced by competition to do.

The same battle has been pretty well settled in another area that does not really fit with the rest of the publishing operations—subscription fulfillment. Virtually all larger publishers—and most smaller ones—now have their fulfillment handled by outside houses.

The decision involving fulfillment, aside from the fact that it doesn't fit, involves how you can best handle your readers. It took many a disaster, big and small, before many publishers realized that this type of operation simply does not fit with their other operations—and farmed it to firms that do it both better and cheaper.

But, as you will read in chapter 44, "Fulfillment: My Good Customer," this decision about fulfillment has hardly solved all the problems publishers have in serving their subscribers well.

Departmentalization

Most companies that have launched one magazine reach the point where they acquire others—or develop spin-offs of the original property. They start thinking in terms of centralizing some of the activities that are common to all the magazines they publish. Normally this would include production, management information systems, reader service, and subscription fulfillment, but often, perhaps unwisely, it includes art, photography, circulation marketing, single copy sales, circulation planning, and advertising promotion. The benefits seem so logical because you can:

- Attract and employ experts in their fields
- Consolidate vendor contracts and contacts
- Take better advantage of size in dealing with vendors
- Eliminate duplication of efforts

While there can, in some organizations, be benefits to this type of departmentalization, there is one very basic problem: For those who are running or working in the department, the department becomes their central focus rather than the magazines. In their minds at least, the department is more important than any one of the magazines it was created to serve. Control of the department's operations, activities, and their costs becomes very difficult, and it tends not to treat its in-house magazines as the real customers they are.

One day some twenty-five years ago, the publishing world was startled to hear about a magazine publisher with eight business magazines, some directories, and a few newsletters. This company deliberately moved its four profit centers into separate buildings in different parts of the New York City area.

Not only that, but the art department was disbanded, production activities were transferred to each individual magazine, and accounting functions were handled within each profit center.

The company had started some years before with just one magazine—and since then had purchased several others. As is normal, it brought all the properties under one roof, developed art, production, circulation, accounting, personnel, and office service functions to bring "efficiency" to these common functions.

Then the empires started to build, the departmental walls grew up, and the task of management became more important than editorial, advertising, and circulation.

The point was reached when there were more people in the various service functions than actively worked on the publishing properties.

How did the company get back to concentrating on publishing rather than on services? It made each magazine an independent entity, and to make the point stick and avoid future empire building, it physically separated the parts by locating them in different places.

Remaining in corporate headquarters were just three people who were available to consult, control, and plan for the future. They visited with each of the magazines every two weeks, went over progress, activities, and plans, but did not get into the minutiae of day-to-day activities. Not surprisingly, they did a better job of management than when everyone was located together.

If departmentalization seems to be best for some activities, there are a few ways to ensure that the people involved are serving the publications rather than perpetuating their departments.

- Each publication should have its own close-knit group of key people devoted only to its operations: an editor, advertising director, circulation director, controller, and production director. They deal with the corporate departments when necessary.
- The costs of service-oriented departments, such as production and advertising promotion, should be allocated among the publications on some logical basis so that they do not get out of control.
- The costs of supplier departments, such as art or photography, should be charged on a price schedule, just as if they were outside suppliers.

Market-Based Sales Operations

Many companies create groups of properties and assign teams to sell advertising for a number of the magazines, as well as trade shows, database marketing products, Web sites, custom publishing, and special events. Rather than knowing all the nuances of every product sold, they try to understand the objectives for the key accounts involved—a change from a sales focus to a marketing focus.

As you can imagine, this has its problems.

1. The sales forces devoted to selling the individual properties can be upset by such a plan because it cuts through the relationships they have built with advertisers—and can also hurt their incentive plans.
2. Each product has its own attributes and the group salespeople may not be able to fully appreciate each of them.
3. Some products can be shortchanged.
4. Selling can become quite complex.
5. Not many salespeople can sell more than one product successfully.
6. Compensation plans can get even more complex.

CHAPTER 31

Getting the Most from Outside Professionals

ONE OF THE least-known business arts—and it is an art—is using outsiders to help you understand and run your business.

I have been in the public accounting and consulting fields all my business life. I have seen clients who got the most out of me and my firm—and others who got a workmanlike job, but probably not as much as they could have from us.

I have been on the other side, too. I have had outside professionals work for me and my firm. I found that when I got the most out of them, it was usually because of what *I* did.

When I talk of outside professionals, I am naturally discussing those in the recognized professions, such as lawyers and accountants, but I also am including others such as:

- Overall management consultants
- Publishing consultants
- Production consultants
- Marketing consultants
- Editorial advisors
- Design experts
- Investment bankers and brokers
- Single-copy sales consultants
- Subscription consultants
- Direct marketing experts
- Executive recruiters
- Public relations people
- Research firms

The magazine industry is one of the few fields where there is a vast array of the best and most experienced brains and talents working as freelancers, consultants, or moonlighters. To get the most out of these professional outsiders, you must understand their functions, when you should use them, how they work, what kind of people they are, where to find them, how to choose the best ones, how to work with them, and how to pay them.

Why Use an Outside Professional?

There are any number of reasons why you might use outside professionals. These include:

- By specializing in particular areas, they can become more familiar with all their aspects than an insider can.
- They have seen how others do things—and which methods are best. By applying this knowledge and experience, specialists can save a great deal of time an organization might otherwise spend reinventing the wheel.
- They bring viewpoints that you cannot get from inside. They are not bound into the organizational structure or inhibited by the restrictions and politics that go with it.
- They are independent in forming opinions and making plans in a way no insider can be.
- By paying for only a part of a person's time, you can get much better talent than you can afford to hire on a permanent basis.

• You can avoid building a larger organization than necessary. Aside from the "think small" aspect, you eliminate the fringe benefits and hidden costs that accompany the hiring, housing, and administration of each added employee.
• They can counter the "not invented here" syndrome that seems to go with every organization.
• They can study a situation without the distractions that anyone within an organization has.

How to Know When You Need Outside Help

Sometimes it is obvious when you need outside help. Whenever anything legal comes up, you must have an attorney. Taxes can only be handled intelligently by professionals. Accounting and auditing matters require independent accountants.

Beyond these areas, we are talking about running the business—planning, buying, selling, handling employees and all the other things needed to operate.

I feel that any business, no matter how small, should have regular input from outsiders concerning its overall strategy, tactics, and planning. One approach is to have outsiders on a board of directors or board of advisors

Whether or not you have outsiders on the board, any business can benefit from a periodic review by an outsider—every year, every other year, and certainly not less than every three years. This type of review should be open-ended—"come look at my company and tell me how you think it can be improved." Not many people are capable of doing this. Most are specialists and should be used only in specific areas.

You probably need an outsider if:

• You have a feeling that profits are not as good as they should be.
• Your competitors are improving their positions versus you.
• Your people do not meet their deadlines, causing excess costs.
• Some of your people are antagonistic toward each other.
• The information you receive about operations is not very helpful—or is always late.
• You have trouble holding good people.
• You want to develop an acquisition program.
• You want to start a new magazine.
• Your costs are above industry averages.
• You want to start a pension, profit-sharing, or Employee Stock Ownership Plan.
• Your salespeople are making too much money.
• Your actual figures are nowhere near your budget.
• You have no budget.
• You have no long-range plan.
• You want to sell your company.
• Your single copy sales are declining.
• You need to hire a key employee.
• Your printing contract is coming up for renewal.
• You wonder if anyone is reading the magazine.
• The appearance of the magazine is old-fashioned.
• You want to launch by-products.
• Different departments are getting in each other's way.
• You don't like to pay taxes.
• You want to set up your estate in the best way.

What Manner of People Are These Professionals?

They are different from you. Their joy is in solving problems. They often are not even around when the results of their work comes in. Most of them probably would not be very good at the day-to-day job of following through. They get their jollies from working on a number of assignments at once, whereas most people become confused and lose their priorities if faced with this kind of life.

Most work alone, or in small partnerships. There are only a handful of large firms and these are mostly in areas where large numbers of people are needed on a repetitive basis, public accounting being an example.

The professional's role is to jump when a client calls, to work late hours and weekends, and to consider your situation to be just as important as you do.

The consulting business is one with an inelastic inventory-time. This means that it is a feast-or-famine business. Because of this, such working hours, attitudes, and tactics are vital.

Most professionals belong to associations that have written ethical standards that are somewhat different from those of most people. Confidences are sacred. Quality of work must meet certain standards. Educational levels are prescribed.

Not all professionals are the same. Most can handle only one area. There are only a few who are truly generalists and seem to know what helps get things done, no matter the subject.

Some like lots of new challenges. Others like to

work with a few clients on a long-term basis. Chances are that the greatest expertise will come from someone who does lots of different jobs for lots of different people. Maybe you need that—or perhaps you would prefer someone you can see often to bounce all sorts of ideas against, but who confines activities to a relative handful of clients.

To the new buyer of such services, the prices charged may seem to be enormous. But if you choose and use them correctly, it may be the best bargain you can buy. A good professional can make the difference between success and failure—or between great and small successes.

The prices paid to professionals are a function of supply and demand. With a fixed number of hours, the best command the highest fees. In fact, one of the things to watch out for are professionals whose fees are too low.

Why Some Professionals Have Earned a Bad Name

There are lots of hacks and hangers-on who give advice. If you are not experienced, you may have difficulty differentiating the good from the bad. Here are some things to watch out for:

- The long report that doesn't seem to say anything
- A seeming misunderstanding of the assignment
- Missing promised deadlines because of a need for further data and analysis
- Continuous additions of new projects
- A fee reduction because of a supposed misunderstanding
- A fee increase for the same reason

There are other warnings of this kind. The best professional wants to solve your problems and go on to something else. If nothing else is on the horizon, one who is not so good may try to drag your work on.

Finding and Choosing the Best

Leads to finding consulting help come from pretty obvious places:

- Associations
- Publications
- Publishers and their people
- Other professionals
- Suppliers
- The Net

Investigation is the most important step. Outside professionals should be chosen as carefully as employees. But how do you do that? You may never have hired an attorney or a consultant before. And, believe me, just because a person is called "Esquire" or has the initials CPA after his name, does not qualify him to help you.

Here is the textbook list of things to check out:

- Reputation
- History of performance
- Clients served
- Experience of clients
- Cooperativeness
- Inventiveness
- Repeat business
- Pertinent experience
- Fee arrangements
- Independence

I can't quarrel with any of those points, but they really don't give you a concrete idea of how to tell the best professionals from the others. To help simplify the process, let's first think of what a professional is expected to do. When you break it down this way, it becomes easier to know the kind of person to look for. A professional is expected to:

1. Define the problem or opportunity—probably the most difficult and valuable part of the job.
2. Investigate the available facts and opinions.
3. Assess the capabilities available within your organization, money, people, facilities.
4. Be able to work with you and your people.
5. Assess alternative solutions, their costs, benefits, risks, and likelihood of accomplishment.
6. Develop alternate plans and outline the optimum one and the steps needed in its implementation.
7. Sell you and your people on accomplishing the plan.

Here are the three steps in your investigation:

1. Check credentials and general reputation.

- What was the original source of the individual's name?
- Who has recommended for—and against—him? How well do you know them?
- What stature and reputation does he have?
- What professional organizations does he belong to?

- How active has he been in those organizations?
- What was his history before becoming an independent professional?
- What is his educational background?
- Has he been active in civic and charitable activities?
- Have any clients given public recognition to the help given them?
- Do clients use him for repeat assignments?
- Is there any question about keeping information confidential?
- Has he been able to work for competitive companies?
- Does he appear often on association and other programs?
- Does he contribute articles to magazines?
- What is his area of expertise?
- Is he known as someone who "tells it like it is"?
- Is he known as a winner?

2. Check with people who have hired him.

- How did you come to hire him in the first place?
- What assignments has he tackled?
- Have you hired him more than once?
- If not, would you?
- Overall, has his work been successful?
- Have you implemented his recommendations?
- What is his greatest strength?
- What is his outstanding weakness?
- Was all the information kept confidential?
- Was the work done on time?
- Our problem is_________. Would you think he would be good for this?
- Have you recommended him to others?
- Is he easy to work with?
- Did he do the work in conjunction with you and your people—or alone?
- Did he antagonize any of your people—how?
- Does he pussy-foot about difficult solutions?
- Has he done work for any of your competitors?
- Did you have a hassle about the fee?
- Was the fee worth it?

3. Interview him yourself.

- Does he understand your problem?
- Can you understand what he is saying—or does he talk in jargon?
- Do ideas pop out as you discuss the project?
- Will it be done alone or in conjunction with you and your people?
- Does he feel equipped to do the specific assignment? Why?
- Is he excited about the assignment?
- Does he communicate well with you?
- Do you think he can relate to your people?
- Can you stop the assignment if things are not working well?
- How deep in the organization will he go?
- Does the fee arrangement seem fair?

The good consultants know the other good ones and often have developed working relationships, formal or informal. If you can find a true professional in one area, he probably will lead you to others in different fields. If you can find one with really recognized stature, you may have it made in all areas.

Don't hire a firm. Hire either an individual or specific people within a firm. Large firms have good people, but you cannot expect everyone to be top-notch in working with you and your specific situation.

Don't necessarily expect to find everything you need in one place. While some firms establish a standard of excellence, they rarely can cover everything equally well.

Don't trust anyone who cannot be exposed to your most important information. If there cannot be complete confidentiality—or you are not willing to disclose everything—don't start.

The best usually get around a good deal because they are in demand—and because it is good for their business. They will know lots of people, will get to meetings, will probably often be asked to appear on programs and to write articles. This gives you a chance to get to know them before making a commitment.

The best professionals don't withhold ideas. Even at an initial meeting you will find them sparking with thoughts about your situation.

Rarely do you want an outsider to attack your situation by going into an ivory tower or a trance—and voila—producing a solution. You want someone to work *with* you and your people. The more the outsider does this, the better the job will be and the more your people will get out of it.

The best do not want to waste time and will refuse an assignment if you won't seriously take steps to implement change. Good professionals are liable to ask point-blank whether you will take their recommendations seriously.

Of particular importance is the ability to do the specific task you have in mind. Your outside professional must understand the assignment, have the qualifications to do it, and want to do it. He must also relate to you—and vice versa. If not, you may have a disaster.

Be sure the professionals you hire have the courage of their convictions. A mealy-mouthed professional is worse than worthless. He must be willing to speak frankly, hopefully in a nice way.

In certain types of assignments knowledge of the specific industry is of great help. In others, it may actually be a detriment: It is possible to be too bound up in the system—whatever it is—to bring any new insights.

In assignments such as organization studies, marketing approaches, and other broad areas, a good professional is useful no matter what the industry involved. Even if it is an industry alien to him, don't underestimate the ease with which he will become oriented to it. The principles are common, only the terminology is different.

When in doubt about whom to use, choose the best you can find even if it will cost more. The cost-benefit ratio in almost every case will weigh very heavily in your favor.

The best recommendation has to be from one or more clients who have used him on a somewhat similar assignment—and subsequently rehired him for further work. The strongest endorsement (which is sometimes difficult to find out about) is where a professional represented one party in the sale of a business to another company. When the latter company had need for the same kind of representation, it hired the individual who had previously been on the other side.

In checking what other clients think of him, see if you can go two or three deep in the organization. The best outsiders leave a job with the respect of lots of people—not just the one who hired him.

Working with Outsiders

When you have about decided to work with a particular person, bring him in to discuss the project and how to approach it. It is important that you both understand what is supposed to be done and how he will go about it. In many cases this can be agreed upon verbally, as can the fee and billing arrangement.

In more complex assignments or more structured companies, it is a good idea to get an engagement letter outlining the job, the steps to be followed, the method and time of reporting, and the billing arrangements.

If you don't know him well, you may want to start with a small assignment before beginning anything major.

Telling Your People

Some people in every organization worry whenever *any* outsider is brought in. The initial introduction and an explanation of the assignment is imperative. Cold memos just will not do. The list of those to be informed and the order in which they are informed can be very important.

You should very carefully plan exactly how you will explain things to your people: the assignment, the professional's introduction, his background and stature, the method of operating, those who will be involved, the data that will have to be accumulated, the results you hope for, and the eventual reporting methods. Emphasize that everyone involved will get the final results.

Emphasize, too, that all employees should be completely frank, open, and honest in their remarks, no matter whose toes are stepped on—including yours. Assurances must be given that nothing anyone says will be passed on as a particular individual's comment.

If it is an extended assignment, make arrangements for office space, secretarial help as needed, and other amenities. Be sure to give him a copy of your internal phone book.

The Basic Approach

The basic reason for using outsiders is to bring a skill, knowledge, and time resource into your organization to complement those you already have. Since it is a person, and not a machine, all the techniques for getting the most out of people should be employed.

You and the outsider (and whomever else you want) become a task force, whether you call it that or not. To get the most out of the task force, you must have its members excited and interested—and you must develop as much liking, respect, and coordination as you can.

If it works the first time, you will have developed a permanent resource that becomes more valuable as time goes on because of the outsider's knowledge of you and the company.

You Are the Quarterback—Things to Do

Make yourself available. Find time not only to discuss the project, but also to break down those roadblocks that some employees will inevitably set up.

One of the best working relationships I have had involved the president of a medium-sized publishing company. Every morning before office hours we would sit for half an hour to discuss progress from my viewpoint and his. He also acted as my appointments secretary. Aside from making it easier to get to see people, it showed everyone on a day-to-day basis that he was solidly behind the project. It also gave him a chance to get feedback from his people.

Don't hesitate to put forth your ideas—and have others in the organization do the same. The good professional doesn't care where the answer comes from. Even if your solution is not perfect, it might lead to a better one.

Challenge him. He is a problem solver and will react positively. I recall that, when discussing a difficult tax situation, my old boss, J. K. Lasser, used to say, "Don't tell me it can't be done. Tell me how to do it." With that attitude, we were able to accomplish things taxwise that no one else could.

Make every meeting a businesslike one (as you should all meetings). Send out an agenda and whatever background material would be useful in advance. Tell each participant what you expect to accomplish. Assign responsibilities and set deadlines. You will get better results faster and cheaper and you will impress the professional who wants to solve problems, not socialize at meetings.

Make sure he has all the information needed. Withhold nothing. If you do, you are not going to get the best from him. What is so secret in the magazine business? With an ABC report and a few copies of the magazinea anyone can approximate your P&L. In addition to the business facts, tell him of your personal situation and that of the other key people, as far as you know. Reveal your dreams, your hopes, your worries.

No matter how long he is around, he can never know everything about your company. Don't expect him to. Tell him more than you think he needs to know.

If he asks for more information, have it prepared quickly. It may be stuff you should have at your fingertips. Make sure to study it yourself. He may be trying to tell you something in a subtle way.

Do everything to position him as one more member of the team.

He should be exposed to as many people as possible to learn things they might never tell you.

Have him go to company functions so that he can see people interact. If there are committee meetings, have him sit in.

Expect that some of your people will resent the use of any outsider. They may feel it is a reflection on them, whether it is or not. On top of this, every organization is afflicted with the "not invented here" syndrome.

Make sure that everyone who was involved significantly sees or hears the final report and has a chance to comment on it. Usually he will give you the report first so that you can censor it. I cannot, however, recall that any changes were ever made after a first meeting of this kind.

In some situations, the best solution cannot be found through empiric thinking, but require a participative, maybe even a brainstorming, approach. In that case, have him run a meeting, chair a task force, or take your people off on a retreat.

If you are using several outsiders, have them compare notes on how to work with you, how the organization operates, trouble spots, and the like.

Things Not to Do

- Don't ask him for help in irrelevant areas. I have seen an outside art director asked for his opinion about whether a particular magazine would be attractive to lots of advertisers or not. He gave his opinion, which he probably should not have. Worse than nothing.
- Don't try to get it for free. The good professional will tell you lots of things for nothing, but no one likes a chiseler, subtle or otherwise. You may get something—but not the best.
- Don't try to tell him how to do the job. If he doesn't know, you shouldn't have hired him in the first place. He may surprise you by interviewing some people at their desks, others in a conference room, and still others at lunch or over cocktails. This is not just chance, he knows that different people are at ease in different places.

- Don't expect him to run the business for you. He is a problem solver. You still must make the decisions.

Incidentally, it's nice to tell him the results of his help later. He might be off on the next assignment and never be able to ask.

> **WARNING**
> After the consultant leaves, do something! Even if it is only to tell your staff that you have decided to do nothing—let them know, and why. Otherwise you lose credibility.

Diagnosing the Trouble—The Consultant's Skill

Most people in a company think they know what the problem is before the consultant is called in. Very often they are looking at the symptoms rather than the basic causes, and the consultant spots something different from what everyone expected.

I recall one situation where there was a very long lead time between the closing dates for editorial and advertising copy and the publication date. Everyone assumed that the schedule had been put together wrong and just needed tightening up.

It turned out to be an organizational problem instead. The production department handled every bit of copy that went to the printer. The advertising service department handled the receipt of ads, billing, and record keeping. This department was not allowed to follow up with the agencies. This had to be done by the salespeople who really didn't know precisely what was needed.

The result was too much handling—and confusion—which resulted in excess cost as well as a very long lead time.

The solution, which seemed simple but turned out not to be because some departments had to be broken up, was to move the entire function to each individual magazine where there was more knowledge and more interest in the magazine and its advertisers. Result—savings in cost and valuable lead time and better handling of the customers.

Don't be surprised if the outsider's solution is something you have heard before. Almost always someone somewhere in the organization has already thought of the answer.

In another case, single-copy sales were slipping badly. Those in circulation realized that the editorial product needed improvement—cover lines, blurbs, livelier pages—but could not get that point across to the editors. The outsider saw this and successfully got the changes made—something the circulation people could never have accomplished.

Methods of Reporting

The outsider's report can take the form of simple verbal reports; a letter; presentations with slides, flip charts, or even film; or long written reports.

Some assignments require written reporting—development of job descriptions, systems studies, valuation of a company, or the creation of a chart of accounts.

Some clients demand written reports. In many cases this results in a seemingly endless number of pages that read like (and may well be) boilerplate.

Where it can be done I favor a visual-verbal presentation rather than a written one. This is usually in the form of a live presentation using slides, flip charts, or other visual devices.

- A written report is usually very time-consuming and can increase the cost of the assignment considerably.
- A written report necessarily contains a great deal of detailed information. It is probable that somewhere there will be a mistake, small though it may be. This can make some people feel that the entire report and its results must be incorrect—and therefore worthless.
- The object is to get action. A live presentation can focus on the truly important and ignore many details. This is difficult in writing. In case you feel that the verbal-visual approach is not dignified or formal enough, let me assure you that I have made many reports of this kind with flip charts in my own handwriting to some of the largest corporations. After the presentation we have the flipcharts reproduced in reduced form for all those involved.

How Professionals Are Paid

There are a number of ways that professionals are paid, depending on the nature of the work and the desires of the parties. In the end it all comes down to paying for the time spent.

Individual consultants normally charge so much per hour, with the rate based on what they feel they are worth. For those in demand, that figure can continue to increase depending on their popularity.

Large professional firms normally have formulas based on the cost of the consultant's salary and fringes for an eight-hour day. This is generally 1.0% to 1.3% of the salary per eight-hour billable day. It may appear that the large firm charges more than an individual or small group—and many times they have been accused of this. But the firm provides a good deal of support, research, and know-how behind the scenes, and usually several people work on an assignment, each billed at his own rate. Senior people do not waste time doing junior work. In the end, you come out at about the same place for similar work.

Billing should be done frequently enough that both parties can recall what work has been done. I favor twice a month. Normally rough estimates are made of each phase of the work so that both parties know about what is involved.

Firm Quotations

A firm quotation is usually provided by the professional as a range of figures. A difficulty is that assignments normally expand in unexpected ways that are not included in the original estimate and that are not worth discussing with the client. For this reason, quotations normally have a good margin for error. On the other hand, where the actual time comes in lower than expected, the best professionals bill only for the time involved.

It is usually best to divide a large job into phases, then a firm quote can be made for the early phases with quotes on the later ones made only after more is known. The client, can, of course, stop the assignment after each phase.

Contingent Fees

In certain types of work, contingent fees are common:

- Executive search—About 33% of the annual compensation of the person hired. Some firms charge only if they are successful. If the employee does not work out, the search is repeated without charge.
- Brokerage for buying or selling a business—Normally at a percentage of the price, although often a flat amount is agreed to either before or after the transaction. Some like to work on this basis and bill for their time plus a balloon payment if the transaction is consummated. In many deals the actual price is obscured by tax gimmicks, contingent deals, and other items, so the percentage is rarely strictly adhered to but serves as a basis for discussion.
- Finders fees—Normally also on a percentage. Some finders also ask for something up front whether successful or not. Deal carefully with these people.
- Cost reduction activities—In certain areas, such as short-interval scheduling, a percentage of the perceived saving per year is the fee.

Retainers

Some professionals and clients like the security of retainers—so much per month for, say, 10% of the consultant's time—or for three days a month, or the like. This kind of arrangement is a function of the people involved. It can easily lead to dissatisfaction and the need for renegotiation if either party feels he is not getting his money's worth.

On the Come

More than most businesspeople, professionals may be convinced to work without pay on some occasions, to be compensated later. This often takes place when a new venture is started, when money is being raised, and the like. Professionals like to help people at these times. They also may see the opportunity for a long-term large gain. In some cases they will take a portion of the equity of the project rather than be compensated at normal rates. This, of course, is quite frequently done in the present dot.com world.

Some Hours Are Worth More than Others

Once in a while the outsider will accomplish something in a very short space of time that is worth far more than the normal billing rate. It is common, then, for the parties to negotiate a substantially greater amount.

Expenses

It is normal for out-of-pocket expenses to be added to the other charges that outsiders bill. This would include travel and the like, but not bills for phone charges, copying, secretarial, and the like. If they are such small-timers as to bill for these little charges, you shouldn't be using them in the first place.

CHAPTER 32

Basics of a Magazine's Editorial

Editorial Is the Key to Every Magazine's Success

WE HAVE SAID it before, but it bears constant repeating. A magazine exists only because its readers have interests that they want communication about. If the editorial content does not do this, the magazine cannot succeed.

Every magazine is in a different business. There are an infinite variety of magazines:

- Consumer or business
- General and special interest
- National, international, or appealing to only a small regional area
- Addressed to news, how-to, display of new products, entertainment, or think pieces
- Content consisting only of directory material or price quotes
- Published at any frequency from quarterly to weekly, or even daily
- Circulated free, through paid subscriptions, or on the newsstand
- With circulation in the millions, or just thousands, or just hundreds
- Supported by lots of advertisers, or just a few, or without any advertising
- Published by profit-making enterprises—or by governmental, religious, or other not-for-profit organizations
- Aimed at people of different ages, different sexes, different income levels, different ethnic backgrounds, different educational levels, in different businesses, and with just about every other difference humans can have

There is no editorial formula that fits every magazine—or only rarely, any two magazines. Each must present material in the way that will be of most interest—or value—to its particular readers. The ways in which this is done are infinite—and must be specially designed for the subject matter and audience being addressed.

Because of this, my comments on the editorial area will necessarily be confined to those things that are common, such as crystallizing the editorial content—sometimes discussed as defining the editorial mission. This was discussed earlier in chapter 18, "If You Can't Say It in Ten Words or Less." Whatever you call it, it is essential that everyone connected with the magazine know what its editorial mission is—and that this mission is consistently pursued.

Editorial Functions

The basic function of the editorial department is to develop and present material that the magazine's audience will want to read in a manner that is most inviting to that audience. Depending on the basic thrust of each magazine, this may be in the form of news, picture stories, entertainment, how-to information, or just about anything else.

This can be a difficult assignment. It requires that the editor understand the audience the magazine is trying to reach. While the editor may not be personally involved in the subject matter, he will necessarily have to become one of the greatest experts in that subject—and in how to make it attractive for the readers.

The editor also has the task of creating a completely new product every time an issue is produced. This does not mean, however, that he must reinvent the magazine for each issue. As we discussed earlier, crystallizing the editorial concept is vital to the success of every magazine, but once the editorial concept has been crystallized, each issue is an exemplification of the formula for carrying out that concept. Creativity is an element in carrying out that formula—but you don't have to reinvent the concept for each issue. In fact, you must be careful *not to deviate from that concept*—or you will destroy the very essence of the magazine.

The Editor

- Is devoted to carrying out the editorial mission as it has been defined. Through research the ideal editor continuously reexamines the need for changes in that mission, and is willing to reposition the magazine when necessary.
- Understands that it is only through the pages of the magazine that casual readers become permanent readers.
- Is imbued with the idea of communicating with readers and potential readers by making the magazine as useful and as readable as possible, as well as by developing interactive communication devices in the editorial and other areas of the magazine.
- Is an expert, perhaps the most expert, about the field served.
- Serves as spokesperson for the magazine and the field to the public at large, through various media and meetings, potential advertisers, and those in the circulation chain.
- Knows about sources of information, outside authors, artists, and others.
- Understands the need for appealing graphics and the ways in which they can be used to help communicate the editorial content.
- Can find, hire, and supervise a superior staff.
- Can plan editorial content for many months ahead as well as to meet frequent deadlines.
- Knows about the economics of magazines, the place of editorial in the mix, and ways of controlling costs.
- Believes in the need for editorial independence—and knows how to achieve this in a practical world.

Where Many Editors Fail to Reach the Ideal

The average editor is probably more introspective and less outgoing than his counterparts in the advertising area. Because of this, it is not surprising that, when publishers (using that word in the sense of the boss of the magazine) are chosen, the vast majority come from the advertising area rather than from either editorial or circulation.

Too many editors do not want to be interfered with and also want to retain a mystique about the creative process with which they are involved. Many also have a deep-seated worry about being too crassly commercial.

Few have any great desire to become public spokespeople for their industries, although there have been some very notable exceptions—for instance, John Fairchild, who was the dean of the women's fashion world when he commanded *Women's Wear Daily;* John Mack Carter, who spoke frequently to women's groups when he was editor of *Good Housekeeping;* and Hugh Hefner, whose life in *Playboy*'s bunny world is well known.

Relationship with Advertising and Circulation

To be successful, a magazine must be able to perform the three basic activities with great coordination and the methods for carrying them out. This is not always easy to achieve when specifics come up about such things as:

- The editor may want a certain number of editorial pages in each issue—and wants those pages placed so as to be as attractive to the reader as possible, while the advertising director may want many advertising pages at the front of the book with editorial matter adjacent to every advertisement.
- The advertising director may want the largest possible amount of circulation so that the advertising rate can be increased, while the circulation director does not want to spend too much for new subscriptions or to obtain readers who will not renew.
- The circulation director may want to use a sweepstakes approach in obtaining subscriptions,

while the editor wants to attract only new readers who are most interested in the content.

- Many other such major disagreements—as well as many more lesser ones—all brought about by a necessary difference in perspective.

These three people, as they should, have different viewpoints about the key to success:

- The editor knows that the success of the magazine stems from the editorial product he is producing.
- The circulation director knows that the increased circulation is the result of the techniques he uses to obtain readers.
- The advertising director knows that the profits come from the increases in advertising that he develops through superior promotion and selling activities.

To some extent, each of them is correct. In the best of all possible worlds, the editor will convince the others that the established editorial rationale and the editorial content are very sound and very saleable to both readers and advertisers.

More than that, the editor must be sure that both circulation and advertising are selling the magazine the editorial department has created—and not some other product that they feel is more salable. If the latter happens, then schizophrenia has set in—and the magazine is doomed to failure.

To be most successful, the editor will help both the circulation and the advertising people in developing their promotion for the magazine to be sure that they are selling the product he is editing. He will also assist the advertising people—not in actually selling advertising, but in explaining the editorial rationale and how it is carried out. In addition to one-on-one meetings, this includes addressing various luncheons and breakfasts that are arranged with advertisers and agencies.

The editor will discuss the editorial thrust with the copywriters for circulation copy—and even meet with various groups of national distributors, wholesalers, and retailers involved in the single-copy sales chain when that can be helpful.

In the business magazine area the editor will be instrumental in working with those organizing trade shows, in addressing them, appearing on panels, and helping organize programs and attract speakers.

The Editorial Staff

There is no ideal size or type of editorial staff. I have seen successful magazines that are edited essentially by one person with just about everything else done by part-timers or outside organizations of one kind or another.

I am also familiar with magazines, most of whose editorial material is purchased from outsiders, running some 100 edit pages a month, which have over 70 full-time staff members. I wondered just what all those people do.

Newsmagazines, of course, must have larger staffs because of their frequency and the nature of the beast. On the other hand, most business magazines need only some 10 to 20 full-time editorial people.

The number of bodies will also vary considerably depending on how much of the composition and prepress work is done in-house versus by outside organizations.

Editorial Job Descriptions

- EDITOR OR EDITOR-IN-CHIEF. Overall responsibility for the editorial staff, direction, and content, including both art and text. Responsible for special publications, books, and other products.
- MANAGING EDITOR. Coordinates editorial, art, and production to ensure that the magazine is turning out each issue of the magazine in acceptable form and on time. Supervises copyediting and proofreading staff to ensure that the magazine is factually and grammatically correct. In charge of making sure that broad plans are in place for editorial content a year in advance—with specific plans for at least four months.
- ASSOCIATE EDITOR OR SENIOR EDITOR. Responsible for planning and writing features in a specialty area and for all editorial work in that area. Supervises assistant editors, freelance writers, designers, and photographers.
- COPY EDITOR. Copyedits, proofreads, and prepares copy for the printer. Responsible for the accuracy and flow of copy through the editorial department to the printer.
- ASSISTANT EDITOR, EDITORIAL ASSISTANT, EDITORIAL RESEARCHER. Assistants at various levels in the department. Some may perform the duties normally associated with a secretary, but that title is rarely used in the editorial area.
- WRITER/REPORTER. Researches, writes, and edits material in assigned subject areas. Attends functions

and shows. Keeps current on magazines, newspapers, and other publications in areas assigned.

• EDITORIAL RESEARCH DIRECTOR. Responsible for the direction and management of all research and fact-checking functions to ensure editorial accuracy.

• ART DIRECTOR. In charge of planning and executing the graphics for the magazine. Oversees photography, illustrations, and art production.

• EDITORIAL SYSTEMS MANAGER. Responsible for the operation and maintenance of editorial electronic facilities including training and support of all editorial users. Coordinates editorial systems with the other internal systems as well as with external sources and suppliers.

There are lots of other titles used by various magazines, such as senior writer, staff writer, photo editor, fiction editor, fashion editor, cartoon editor, news editor, research editor, and so on. It often appears that editorial titles are really morale boosters for those in the editorial department.

Editorial Organization Chart

Because of the variety of types of editorial material in various magazines, there is great variation in the way different editorial departments are organized. Below is a chart that might indicate some of the major things to be considered.

The managing editor, of course, occupies a central position because he normally is in charge of scheduling and actually seeing that all the pieces are in place and that the magazine gets out on time.

In some magazines, the art director seems to have almost equal status with the editor and operates semi-independently, although the organization chart may not indicate that. I believe it is important that the art director be an integral part of the editorial team so that the graphics and layout of the magazine are directed toward making the communication to the reader as good as it can be. The editor, of course, should set parameters to be followed in terms of readability versus so-called artistic creativity. Some thoughts about current trends in this area are discussed in chapter 33, "The Editor as a Marketer."

USE OF OUTSIDERS

There are few areas of business where you are able to use creative and talented part-timers as much as in the editorial side of a magazine. Available to the editor are some of the world's greatest

- Authors
- Writers
- Photographers
- Artists
- Designers
- Reporters

Figure 32.1—Editorial Department Organization

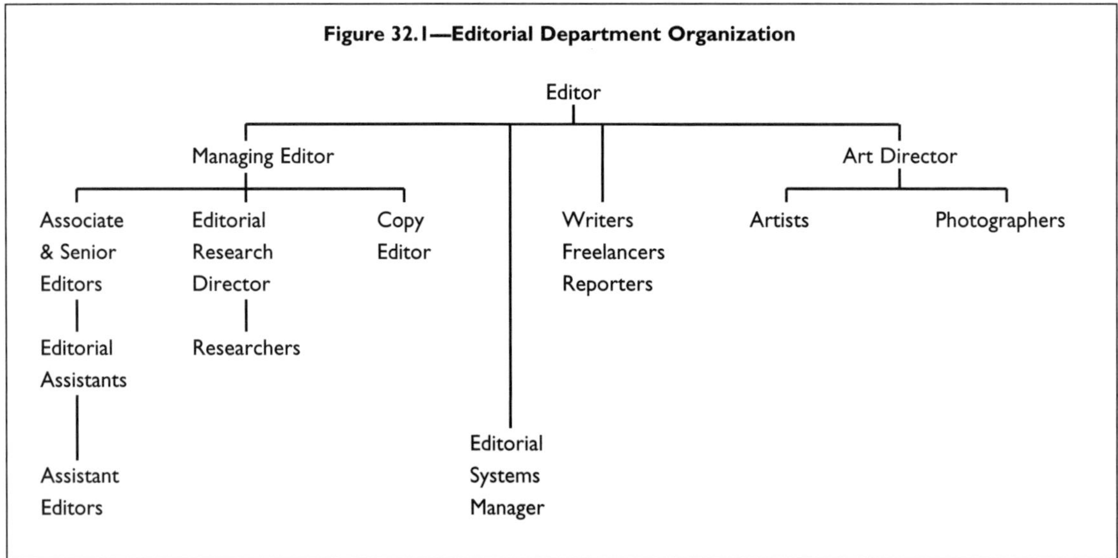

There are also stock photo houses from which you can find pictures of almost anything without having to commission special assignments. You can even find people who will help edit the magazine, do proofreading, and do anything else you may want. That is why a single editor may literally be all some magazines need.

Payment for these outside services is normally on a negotiated basis, although new magazine publishers can often obtain good terms based on the promise of future regular work.

Advisory Board

It is common practice for new magazines—and for many older ones, too—to have an editorial advisory board. These are particularly useful for business magazines and consumer magazines in specialized fields.

The listing of the names of prominent people in the field on the masthead of the magazine as members of the advisory board adds to the stature of the magazine, particularly when the people actually doing the publishing are not well known.

Surprisingly, it is usually not difficult for publishers to attract well-known figures to agree to be on such a board. I guess we all like a little recognition, no matter how prominent we may be.

In most cases the board actually has very little, if anything, to do. They usually have little desire to go to meetings, although that sort of thing might be arranged if there are industry conventions where it is convenient. It is useful to bounce ideas off the members, let them in on future plans, and, in general, make them feel part of the operation without having to spend much time involved in it. Often they are willing to write articles for the magazine with no more than token compensation.

Compensation for the advisory board is normally not needed unless they must attend meetings and the like. Token awards, of course, are always welcome.

Editorial Independence

Editorial independence—often talked and written about but rarely defined. The various associations in the field have rules defining what should and should not be done to remain independent. A great many of the pages in Steve Brill's new magazine, *Content,* are devoted to the subject. Recently there was a brouhaha about the Internet bookstore Amazon.com and the book reviews it ran. As the Internet continues to grow in its unregulated state, there are bound to be many more breaches of independence, as well as many more ethical and legal breaches.

In a previous incarnation I was a CPA. There is no field where independence is more required than in public accounting. It is the lifeblood of the business. In the end, I believe, independence is a state of mind that cannot be defined or legislated. It is essential, but either you have it, or you don't.

I have the feeling that many editors hide behind the shield of editorial independence when they want to avoid doing things they don't like to do, such as visiting advertisers. Of course editors should not go out to visit advertisers with the rate card in hand—and of course they should not let advertisers read editorial copy before it is printed—and they should not let an ad for Chevrolet be placed on the page opposite an editorial piece about what a great car a Chevy is.

But editors *should* visit advertisers to explain what they are trying to do editorially, and they *should* let them know what types of subjects will be carried in future issues so that the advertisers can run ads having to do with the same subjects. Those ads will actually enrich the overall coverage in the magazine.

More difficult independence situations arise, I believe, with respect to custom publishing, where a magazine is developed for a single company—or with advertorials, where so-called editorial pages are mixed with advertisements for a group of advertisers covering a single subject. These, it seems to me, should be off-limits for the editors of a magazine, and, if they are published at all, the editors of the magazine should not be the ones to develop them.

Number of Editorial Pages

The number of editorial pages, of course, gives no indication of the usefulness of a magazine. The newsmagazines determined long ago that there should be a certain number of pages in each issue because that is the number needed to cover the news—and it is all you can expect a reader to handle once a week.

The same kind of thinking cannot be applied to other types of magazines—or to those that publish less frequently. There must, however, be some kind of relationship of editorial and advertising—or the magazine will not seem to be giving full value to the reader.

Most magazines develop a figure for the minimum number of pages for each issue needed to cover the subject—and a maximum number that the staff can intelligently develop. Then, in order to avoid an every-issue discussion, magazines develop a scale to be followed as shown in chapter 55, "Planning."

EDITORIAL COSTS

It sometimes comes as a shock to editors to find that for most magazines the amount spent on developing the most important part of the magazine, the editorial content, is the smallest item in the budget, but that's the way it normally is.

Editorial costs are also the easiest item to control since they consist only of the staff plus outside purchased manuscripts and artwork. Costs are normally monitored through a single figure for the editorial cost per page.

The primary way editorial can throw a magazine's cost structure out of whack is in the number of editorial pages, and the number printed in four-color. This requires strict control.

BY-PRODUCTS AND BRAND EXTENSIONS

A number of profitable by-products can be created by the editors right out of the pages of a magazine. These not only provide additional income, but also get readers more involved with the magazine and reinforce its position as the authority in its field. Included are:

- Reprints of articles. *The Harvard Business Review,* for instance, does a flourishing business in these.
- Collections of material in book form such as the *New Yorker*'s series of cartoon books.
- Special issues devoted to specific subjects. *Better Homes* and other shelter books have whole series of special interest publications (SIPs) devoted to gardening, house plans, decorating, and the like.

In the business magazine field there may be even more opportunities:

- The entire trade show business, that now threatens to overshadow the magazines in some fields, started out as a by-product of various magazines.
- Special daily editions are published at trade shows.
- How-to books, tapes, and films are developed based on material from the magazines.

Beyond these, of course, are the more diverse activities that have been developed based on the aura the magazine creates, which are covered in depth in chapters 59–65, covering brand extensions.

EDITOR VERSUS CONTENT PROVIDER

It has only been in recent years, with the growth of the computer industry, the Internet, and all their adjuncts, that the term "content provider" has come into vogue.

It happened, of course, because those who are technically oriented are more interested in the methodology of getting messages from one place to another than in the message itself. They think the delivery method is more important than what is being delivered. That same kind of thinking probably took place with the advent of the printing press.

Adding to this lack of appreciation of the editor's role is the fact that, up until now at least, the vast majority of material used on the Internet does not appear to either require or to have used the services of skilled editors.

This type of thinking is one of the major reasons why so few of the many attempts to publish magazines, newsletters, books, or any other creative material using computer technology as the delivery method have succeeded. It is also undoubtedly the reason why the graphics and design of material sent by computer are still so dreadful.

This is not to say that the Internet will not eventually become a major carrier of well-designed, interesting material. This may happen when those in charge of these delivery methods learn that the key to profitable business lies in the quality of the editorial material presented, and not just the "content provided."

CHAPTER 33

The Editor As a Marketer

WARNING

My publisher feels that I am "talking down" to editors here. (He is, of course, an editor himself, so is particularly sensitive about this.) After rereading it, and contemplating the overwhelming importance of the editorial product as well as the horrors some magazines pass off as being compelling for the readers, I decided to leave it as originally written.

But, dear editors, please note that I have also said a few unkind words about advertising, circulation, production, and management people as well from time to time in this book.

I AM WELL aware that many editors consider each issue of a magazine as a kind of sacred literary event, packed with deathless prose and beautiful graphics. To these people the concept of being a marketer is crassly commercial.

But even deathless prose is useless if no one reads it. Shakespeare's plays would have been of no value if no one came to see them, and Michelangelo's paintings would have been wasted had they not been displayed in the Sistine Chapel where there was sure to be a good audience.

One of the editor's prime jobs involves being the reader's best friend—making it easy for him to understand and read your magazine and letting him know how to find the old familiar parts as well as introducing the new and exciting. Repeating some of the very obvious basic truths about magazines:

- Each issue of a magazine is a consumer product with a very short shelf life.
- People will read only what they are interested in.
- Most people do not really enjoy reading for its own sake. It is hard work for a great many—and there are many other conflicting influences.
- People cannot read something if they don't know it exists—or cannot find it.
- The easier you make it, the more people will read.
- The more interesting you make it, the more people will read.
- The more involved a reader gets, the more his interest is stimulated.

Add to these:

- Artwork is useful only if it helps reading and understanding. Otherwise, it is not only useless, it is actually inhibiting for the reader.
- The best place to market a magazine to a reader—and to an advertiser—is in the pages of the magazine itself.
- You must invite, lure, entice, or even trick readers into reading.
- You will never really know what readers read unless you ask them.
- The editorial content has more to do with developing continuous readers—and renewals of subscriptions—than anything else.

Editorial Marketing Techniques

I cannot tell you what subjects will interest the

readers of your magazine—or how you should approach these subjects. There are, however, time-honored and proven techniques that are useful in increasing the readership of any magazine.

Some of these techniques may involve hard work. Others will result in interesting clashes with the art director, the advertising director, the circulation director, and others in the organization. Even the editor may differ with the necessity for some, and I am sure he will be able to find other, better methods for accomplishing the increases in readership, which is what we are all after. But, since these methods all have to do with the heartbeat of the magazine that is basic to its success or failure, they are worth discussing.

THE LOGO

You are launching a new magazine. You already have agonized over the name of the magazine (see chapter 27, "The Magazine's Name") and spent many hours, and possibly dollars, having a distinctive logo designed. The logo is your brand. At this stage of the magazine it is not known at all—certainly not the way the *Time* magazine logo is known or *The Wall Street Journal* look is recognized.

You will, of course, use your distinctive logo on your letterhead and in all your circulation and advertising promotion. That distinctive logo, in its distinctive typeface, should also be used on every page of the magazine—and wherever the name of the magazine is used in the text. *Time* and *The Wall Street Journal* do not bother to do this, but they no longer feel the need for recognition, although it wouldn't be a bad idea for them either.

THE COVER

The cover is the most important page in any magazine. If it is used correctly, it is the first and probably the best opportunity you have to lure a reader inside.

There are several characteristics of a good cover. Beauty, while nice, is not necessarily one of them.

1. It must identify the magazine. This ties in with the need for a good logo that is distinctive, large enough to be seen, and in a position to be seen.

2. It must identify the issue of the magazine—so that there is no confusion about whether a reader has already seen that issue.

3. It must attract your attention, or it hasn't accomplished anything.

4. It must lure the reader into opening the magazine.

5. It must exemplify what the magazine is all about.

A good cover is obviously the lifeblood of any magazine that wants to sell well on the newsstand, but it is also important for subscription copies—you want to make sure people look inside.

Newsstand magazines forever labor to develop covers that will help them sell more copies. It's worth your while to become a newsstand junkie—visit the stands and see just what techniques they use. You will find catchy cover lines, alluring—or interesting—pictures, big question marks, all sorts of different colors, and goodness knows what else to convince you to buy the magazines.

The Seven Sisters and other women's magazines have worked very hard on this and are good examples to copy—except for one thing. They compete so hard that they look alike. If their logos were covered up, you would have difficulty knowing which magazine is which—and often you might find it hard to discern one issue from the next.

All sorts of testing devices have been set up to help these newsstand magazines know what covers will sell best. To my knowledge, however, no real answers have been developed that will work consistently. I have sometimes suggested that they take the covers out of the hands of the editors and hire package designers to create them instead. This has not been received too kindly.

So many magazines compete for space on the newsstand that it is a tribute to the ingenuity and persistence of the American public that they are able to find the magazines they want at all.

In many cases only a portion of the cover can be seen on the newsstand. It is vital, then, that the logo be prominently displayed—and in the right place. For a number of years Petersen Publishing (*Hot Rod, Motor Trend,* etc.) ran their logos vertically along the spine of the cover so that they could be seen.

While the importance of the cover is obvious for newsstand magazines, it is just as important for copies delivered by subscription. You still have to get the recipient to look inside.

Don't Cover the Cover

For reasons that I do not understand, there seem to be trends these days for magazines to use wrappers or false covers when they send magazines to subscribers. Or to hide the cover under renewal subscription offers, invitations to buy the publisher's books or other products, or advertisers' outserts. Sometimes other items are bound or polybagged together with the magazine when it is sent out—resulting in the cover being completely covered up, to say nothing of the difficulty in getting the magazine out of the polybag.

This is one of those areas where, as editor, I would do battle with the circulation and/or advertising people. Polybag—or do anything else you want when you send out the magazine—but don't ever hide my cover. I want readers—and so should the circulation and ad people.

Who Is the Magazine For?

I don't really know why, but it is rare for a magazine to tell its potential readers and advertisers who it is edited for. This may not be necessary for old, established magazines, or at least they may not feel it is, but it certainly could be helpful when you are first launching a magazine.

In many cases, of course, the title itself describes the magazine—or the publishers think it does. But why make life any more difficult that it has to be?

Here is the way some relatively new magazines have described themselves, none of which seem very meaningful:

- *More*—Smart Talk for Smart Women (It's really for women over 40).
- *Brill's Content*—The Independent Voice of the Information Age (It's really to see how impartially the media covers stories).
- *Mountain Freak*—For freaks like us.
- *New York Lawyer*—For lawyers on the verge.

Many other new magazines don't give you a clue, such as *Talk, Jane, Details,* and *Icon.*

Some thath seem helpful:

- *Sisters in Style*—For today's young black woman.
- *Folio*—The Magazine for Magazine Management.
- *Kirkus Reviews*—The Journal for America's Most Important Readers (It is circulated primarily to librarians).
- *Guns & Gear*—The newsmagazine and equipment guide for huntersand shooters.
- *Columbia Journalism Review* has a statement on its masthead: "To assess the performance of journalism . . . to help stimulate continuing improvement in the profession, and to speak out for what is right, fair and decent."

It would seem logical for a new magazine to make a real point of who it is edited for—and to try to make that audience feel important while it is doing that, as *Kirkus* does.

Contents Page

Many readers ignore the contents page, but for those who use it, here is another place to lure the reader into looking further into the magazine.

The contents page can be particularly important because one of the basic concepts of a magazine is that no one is expected to read everything in an issue; the contents page gives readers an opportunity to choose what interests them.

In recent years many magazines have improved their contents pages by adding short descriptions of what a reader will find in each piece, and they often use two pages rather than just one to do this. Some give a brief précis of each piece, which is very helpful.

Many have also added small pictures or other graphics from the pages inside to the contents pages. This is a great idea if the pictures are easily related to the articles, but too often they are just strung out on the page and serve to confuse, rather than help, because you cannot tell what pieces the pictures relate to.

Whatever else you do with the contents page, don't forget to:

- Make sure the type is large enough to be easily read.
- Have the descriptions of articles understandable—and not so cutesy that you have no idea of what the piece will be about. The venerable *Fortune* and *Forbes* are both guilty of this.

• Put it in a fixed location in the magazine, hopefully very far forward, like page 3 or 5 (another item for argument with the advertising director who wants that page, too). If *Time* can do it, so can you—and note that *Business 2.0,* devoted to the dot.com world, has it on the inside cover and the first inside page!
• Follow a pattern in its presentation so that readers become familiar with it and can easily find the columns they always read.
• While you follow a pattern, make sure you have a surprise for the reader every so often.

THE LAST PAGE

Lots of people start at the back of a magazine when they pick it up. While most magazines these days use the last page for a sort of endpaper of editorial material, it might be worth advertising some of the exciting features on that page with a mini—or perhaps whole—contents.

What better place to advertise the next issue than in the present one? *Playboy* uses the last page to do this with, of course, pictures.

COMING ATTRACTIONS

One of the editor's jobs, in addition to getting each issue read, is to make casual readers into permanent readers. It is often said that the circulation people obtain readers, but renewals are the result of the editors' work. Be sure to tell readers what to expect in the future.

SERIALS

What ever became of the idea of carrying discussions from one issue to another to ensure that those reading will have to buy the next issue, like the serials we used to go to the movies to see when I was a boy, or the soap operas on TV today? I recall that *Redbook* did this when it was primarily a fiction magazine, with whole books serialized over a number of issues. And weren't Dickens's books published on a serial basis?

SINGLE SUBJECT ISSUES

Many magazines seem to feel that, every so often, a subject is of such interest and importance that an entire issue should be devoted to it. I have always felt that there must be very, very few times when this should be done—and that it goes against the entire concept of a magazine being something that no one reads cover to cover.

It also serves to drive away those readers—and there are always some—who have no real interest in that one subject.

Why Do They Make Life So Difficult for the Reader?

HOW CAN I FIND THAT ARTICLE?

I'll bet you can pick up any magazine you want and will not be able to find the same words used as the title for an article in these four places:

- Cover lines
- Contents page
- The article itself
- The run-over page of the article

In fact, I'll bet that you will have a lot of trouble even identifying the same article in all those four places.

Someone worked very hard to develop the headlines and decks for each piece—why change them when you are developing the cover and the contents page? If we are doing everything we can to get the reader to read our magazine, why make it difficult? Perhaps this is part of getting the reader involvement in the magazine we also work so hard to get—or is it just laziness?

HOW CAN I FIND THAT PAGE?

• Contents pages tell us what pages different pieces are on.
• Runovers tell us the pages on which we can find the continuation.
• Advertiser indexes tell us what pages the advertisements are on.
• Crossword puzzles tell us what page the solution is on.

But I can't find what page I am on!

In many magazines these days most pages don't have numbers anymore—and when they do, they confuse rather than help.

Take a recent issue of *Wired.* The first page

number I could find was 35. From there, through page 121, exactly twenty-five had numbers on them, and these numbers were not correct because there was an unnumbered insert in the middle.

I thought this must be something that only publishers of new magazines devoted to computers and the Internet did, until I happened on a recent issue of *Business Week.* This was really wild:

- Per numbering system—the magazine had 152 pages plus cover for a total of 156.
- Actual count—228 pages plus gatefold cover for a total of 234.
- Of the 228 inside pages, only 104 had any kind of page number.
- There were three sections of 12 pages each labeled something like 76E8, which meant that they came after page 76, if you could find that.
- It had one 36-page section labeled something like F.15, with no hint of where you might find it.
- It had one 4 page section not labeled at all.

(Incidentally, in that issue there were lots of items that suffered from the same title deficiencies in the contents mentioned above—plus a bunch of editorial pieces that never made the contents at all.)

Do the editor and the publisher really want the reader to be lost? And do the advertisers want that, too?

This should not be difficult to correct, given our current computerized world. I don't think advertisers would mind having a page number inserted tastefully on the bottom of their ads, even if they are bleeds: then the advertiser indexes might be even more useful.

Readability

I am a nut about the fact that a magazine, which normally consists primarily of text matter, should be easy to read. Unfortunately, too many of today's magazines make it difficult for a reader.

I am not an artist or a designer, so I cannot tell you all the technicalities of how to accomplish the most readability, but here are some very obvious things that seem to be ignored by too many of today's magazine designers:

- The type size must be large enough to be easily read.
- Some classic typefaces are easier to read than some of the newer, more "creative" ones.
- Solid blocks of gray type are inhibiting and must be broken up in various ways.
- Reverse type is almost impossible to read.
- Tint-blocks behind the type make it more difficult, and sometimes impossible, to read.
- For blocks of type, sans serif type is much harder to read than that with serifs. This is not necessarily true of headlines.
- Mixing many type styles and sizes is inhibiting to the reader.
- Ragged right is easier to read in some instances than justified type.
- In other instances the reverse is true.
- Illustrations that are relevant to the text are helpful, those that are not relevant are inhibiting.
- Captions should be placed where they logically belong, under the illustration, or else they confuse things.

There obviously are many other rules of this kind. It is probably also worthwhile exploring the FOG and other indexes that are designed to help make the text easier to read through the use of short paragraphs, short sentences, and short words.

One of my favorite examples about readability involved the editor of a new magazine who had two pages in which to fit a piece she had commissioned. The text was so compelling that she couldn't bear to cut a word, so she ran the article on the two pages in 6-point type with, of course, a tint-block behind it. Completely unreadable.

Some Ways to Help the Reader Out

Luring Readers into Reading within the Article Itself

We have already talked about the use of cover lines, the contents page, and coming attractions. There are also many devices that can be used in the article itself to hook a reader, such as:

- A catchy—or inviting—headline, sometimes in question form
- Decks below the headline
- Blurbs and call-outs
- Speedbars
- Boxes with interesting material

- Pictures and their captions
- Charts and graphs
- Perhaps a short précis for those who don't want to read the whole piece (the *Harvard Business Review* and the *Journal of Accountancy* do this)
- The news section presented in newsletter style and form
- Information about the author, his qualifications, and perhaps some interesting tidbits—in the article rather than on the publisher's page

If you do enough of these gimmicks, the reader will probably understand the key points without wading through the entire piece if he doesn't want to.

> NOTE: Developing these kinds of lures is not easy. It takes a great deal of imagination and much more time than simply editing the piece itself. But, if it helps get readers to read, it is worth it.

READER INVOLVEMENT

It goes without saying that an involved reader is a better reader. The kinds of things that can be done to involve readers are limited only by the editor's imagination. They include standbys such as:

- Puzzles—crossword and other
- Contests
- Games
- Questionnaires
- Opinion surveys, where you also give readers a warm, fuzzy feeling about the magazine by asking their advice
- Bingo cards for more information or reprints

SOME FUN PIECES

It sounds frivolous, but consider some oldies that always seem to get readership, such as:

- Brief looks back at historical events in the field covered
- Horoscopes
- Lists of strange statistics a la *Harpers*
- Reprints or digests of material from other sources
- Cartoons
- Answers to FAQs

Editorial Research

The basic job of the editor is to know what his readers want and to give it to them. Unfortunately, editors are fallible, and readers do not know what they want until they see it.

Most editors I have known like to rest their cases on the opinions of the readers as expressed in the letters they receive. This is almost invariably a tiny number compared with the total readership—and I am always suspicious that the ones the editor favors were written either by him or by his friends.

The best editors, of course, are also very curious about just what the readers are interested in, and like to do professional research into that. Periodic focus groups are helpful.

I do not believe that editors should depend on their readers to tell them what they would like to see in the magazine. Nor do I believe that surveys of what readers like about the magazine are very useful in determining what the content should be (although such information may, at times, be useful for advertising purposes).

What is most informative, of course, is finding out just what the readers have read in the magazine, page by page. It doesn't matter whether they agree with it or not.

I favor continuous research into this. It can be done fairly simply and inexpensively through asking a small fraction of the readers through mail surveys what they read. It's best to do this with every issue—and then you will see patterns emerge.

Design, Artwork, Layouts

Too many new magazines, in my opinion, have been taken over by their art directors, most of whom are imbued with the concept of doing things differently. The idea that the graphics are there to support, supplement, and be a partner in the communications process seems to have gotten lost. The current trend results in camouflaging the message, rather than helping to reveal it. And, apparently, the editors involved on many magazines seem to have lost their power to direct the art people.

Perhaps I simply grew up in the era when good graphics were dictated by what looked good on the printed page, while today we have been brainwashed by TV and the Internet. Good graphics don't seem to have transferred often from print to this more visual world, which is always in motion. They haven't even learned yet (readily apparent when you view things on the screen) that the most readability comes when you put black type on white space. Or that reverse type is terribly hard to read.

Adding to this problem is that just about anyone now can design and lay out pages with the currently available computer programs. Unfortunately, just about anyone seems to be doing it. Just because it is easy to do doesn't mean that you can do it well.

The result, of course, has been that the graphics very often inhibit rather than assist the communication of the magazine's message. Such things as beautiful effects in black and white—and wonderful pages made up just of type without illustrations—seem to have been forgotten.

The Editor's Control of Pages

In many magazines the editor has no control of the editorial pages. From a readership standpoint, the most attractive pages are in two-page spreads, but these have become a rarity in many new magazines in favor of advertisements facing editorial pages.

In many magazines the "editorial well," where readers could browse at their leisure seeing only editorial material, no longer exists, to the obvious detriment of readership.

Wasted Editorial Pages

Editorial pages are precious—and expensive. It is foolish to waste any of them on material that no one will read. Some areas that could be reduced:

- Mastheads. The fashion today is to list the name of every single person who has anything to do with a magazine on a masthead. These now cover somewhere between a third of a page to two pages. Of what value are all those names, most of which are of advertising, circulation, and business people, to the average reader?
- Editorials. There are undoubtedly times when issues are so important that your opinion would be helpful to the readers, but it is hard to believe that this is true every time you publish an issue. I suggest that you do some research on the readership of the editorials—and after that, cut most of them out.
- Publisher's Page. As a reader, I don't often really care how or why you decided to discuss the things carried in this particular issue. I also have no interest in how you decided to pick Joe Blow to write for you. If you think the writer is really of interest, tell me about it on the piece that he has contributed, where it will be more meaningful. And if you want to give credit to specific editors, give them by-lines as the newspapers and newsmagazines do.
- Overly Long Pieces. Length does not very often make for thoroughness. It is usually a turnoff for most readers.

Reposition and/or Redesign

There will, of course, be times when it is wise to reposition the editorial content of the magazine as well as to redesign the graphics. When that time comes, just do it, but don't make a big brouhaha about it with the readers—remember, they liked it the way it was before. I recall when Clay Felker, one of his generation's truly great editors, took over *Esquire* and decided, wisely, to gear it for a younger audience. He made a big announcement about it in the magazine. This was fine, except that some 90% of the existing readers were not part of that younger audience—and would have torn him limb from limb if they could have caught him.

C H A P T E R 3 4

Basics of a Magazine's Advertising

The Income from Advertising Is Vital for Most Magazines

WHILE A FEW magazines do not take advertising at all, and a number of others have very little, most magazines depend on advertising to produce revenue to pay for the costs of developing editorial material, of obtaining and servicing circulation (the cost of which is often in excess of the income received), of printing and distributing the magazine itself, of paying for administrative costs—and then producing substantial profits for the owners.

From this standpoint, of course, advertising plays a key role as the third leg of the three-legged publishing stool.

Most advertising is known as display advertising and is sold as full or fractional pages, with many advertisers taking two or more pages in succession—and some creating more exotic forms such as checkerboards on two-page spreads or gatefolds on the cover. Most magazines also sell classified space in smaller units—and they often sell directory listings. Inserts of two or a great many more pages are becoming more popular. Insert cards are frequently bound in by direct marketers, and in some cases advertisements are sent along with the magazines in some sort of shrink wrapping. The ingenuity of publishers and advertisers in finding unusual ways of presenting ads is impressive.

For most special interest consumer magazines advertising is of two kinds:

- Generic—Closely connected with the field served, such as food and cosmetic ads in women's magazines
- Nongeneric—Of interest to consumers in general, such as ads for automobiles in those same women's magazines

For business magazines, of course, almost all the advertising comes from suppliers to the field covered, although even here, nongeneric ads are sometimes carried.

Advertising Rates

Unlike many other forms of media advertising, rates for magazines are published on a rate card with different rates for different sizes of ads and discounts for frequency. Ads in color and those on the covers and certain other positions are charged more because of the greater readership they receive, not because of the larger cost of doing this. There are often discounts for increases in advertising over the previous year, for advertising in more than one of a publisher's magazines, and sometimes special rates are created for specific advertisers.

Advertising rates are generally related to the amount of circulation a magazine has, the strength of the interest of the readers in the magazine, and just who the readers are. For instance, on a per thousand circulation basis:

- *Good Housekeeping,* a general-interest women's

magazine with about 4.5 million circulation, charges about $40 per thousand.

- *Vogue,* a women's fashion magazine with about 1.1 million circulation, charges about $50.
- *Modern Bride,* a magazine for brides with about 400,000 circulation, charges about $96.

Business magazines, with their smaller circulations made up of readers intensely interested in the fields covered, run well over $100 per thousand.

For many magazines, lower rates are often charged for mail order, books, or other categories. Sometimes special rates are charged for such ads as those for hotels and resorts in travel magazines. They are felt to be of greater interest to readers and in many ways supplement the editorial content of the magazine.

Advertising Price Negotiation

For a very long time the advertising rate cards for magazine were sacrosanct, with anyone cutting rates considered to be a kind of outcast. All this changed a number of years ago and now most magazines, both consumer and business, have allowed themselves to be treated as commodities. Rate cutting is rampant. This was probably the result of a transfer of advertisers' experience in the broadcast field, where the buying of time has always resembled an Oriental bazaar.

While this situation is not as pleasant as it was in the old days, publishers have learned to live with it, and it reflects the way things are done in most areas of business.

WARNING

One of the by-products of this situation is that statistics about advertising-dollar income in magazines are somewhat misleading, particularly when you are measuring against figures of many years ago. These figures have been developed for many decades for the major consumer magazines by PIB. Traditionally they have been measured by taking the ad pages in a magazine and multiplying them by the card rate—making no allowance for the off-the-card discounts publishers may be granting advertisers. The dollar figures are now overstated more than they were 20 years or so ago, but current year-to-year comparisons are quite valid. The figures for number of pages are, of course, not affected.

Value Added

Rather than giving in completely to advertisers' requests for discounts from the rate card, most publishers provide "value added" services for advertisers.

This is not really a new concept, but rather a new term. Decades ago, publishers provided what was then called "merchandising" help. This took the form of hangers in grocery stores saying "as advertised in *Life*" and the like. Today the list of things done, many of which cost the publishers very little, include:

- Reprints of advertisements
- Editorial reprints
- Hangers and countercards for retail stores
- Use of subscriber lists for sampling purposes
- Product research
- Premiums for the advertisers' or retailers' sales forces
- Events tailor-made for a specific advertiser
- Special positions in the magazine
- Writing and design assistance for direct mail
- Writing and design assistance for advertorial projects
- Inclusion of special questions in publishers' research projects

You can view this as unnecessary expense for the publisher—or, more positively, as a complement to the aura a magazine has created, as well as to its pulling power.

Barter Advertising

For many years the only barter advertising carried by most magazines involved travel for sales meetings. The corporate barter industry, however, has become much more sophisticated and successful in marketing its services in recent years. Travel barter is now used for the normal travel of editorial and salespeople—and barter opportunities have been developed for many other costs a publisher might incur.

Inserts

Advertisers frequently print their own advertisements, which are inserted in a number of magazines. They often are on heavier weight paper than usually run in the magazines and stand out because of that. Often insert cards are used by mail order advertisers, as well as by the publishers themselves. Special rates are charged for inserts, which usually have little relation to the costs of handling the inserts, but are geared to generating the same percentage of profit as normal advertising.

ADVERTORIALS

One or more advertisers sometimes inserts pages (perhaps 8 or as many as 64) that contain not only advertisements but editorial matter that may resemble that in the magazine. These are called "advertorials" (though ABM and MPA like them to be called by kinder words such as "special advertising sections"). These pages are usually tagged on top as "Advertisement" and never use the same typeface and graphic look of the magazine itself. The editorial matter is generally not prepared by the magazine's editors so that they can maintain their objectivity. Many magazines will not allow their editors to prepare advertorials. Some of these publishers, however, have custom publishing divisions that will do the work (see chapter 66, "Custom Publishing").

WARNING

Advertorials, and inserts to a lesser extent, are an intrusion on a well-constructed magazine and can easily confuse or irritate readers. They are usually placed where they will impede the flow of the issue, where the pages are not numbered, and not all readers realize that the inserts are not part of the magazine itself. On the other hand, TV has infomercials and interrupts virtually every program with endless commercials, which is even more annoying.

Advertorials represent substantial income for the magazine—and also serve to make an issue fatter than it might otherwise be, which in some, but not all, cases is a plus.

PER INQUIRY AND PER SALE

Some mail order advertising is paid for on the basis of so much per inquiry (p.i.) or on a percentage of sales resulting from the ad (PS). This is generally considered as a method of rate cutting—or of desperation—on the part of a magazine, but more than one new magazine and many older ones have resorted to it.

Advertising Agencies

Almost all the display advertising in magazines is prepared by advertising agencies and delivered to the publisher ready for the printer. In the current computer age, some publishers have arranged to have the material sent electronically direct to printer (DTP) in which case the publisher does not handle it at all. This, of course, saves everyone involved both time and expense, although not the chore of making sure that the correct ad arrives in time and is placed in the right spot in the magazine.

Advertising charges are normally paid by the agency, which withholds a 15 percent commission. This agency commission is a holdover from the days when the agencies were considered the agent of the publisher in obtaining the ad.

These days, of course, almost all agencies work on a negotiated basis for their fees with their clients, with many fees based on the results that the advertising actually accomplished. The 15 percent paid for space placed in magazines has become simply part of the overall settlement between the advertiser and its agency.

Some smaller magazines, those that are local or in specialized fields, design and produce the ads for the advertisers and, of course, do not pay a commission on these.

Advertising Department Functions

The advertising department is in charge of obtaining the advertising for the magazine. This involves the direct selling of the advertising as well as the preparation of sales presentations for prospective advertisers and developing and coordinating the use of promotional material for the magazine.

The sale of advertising almost always involves one-on-one selling opportunities with various people at ad agencies as well as at the client companies. Magazines also often make major presentations to groups of advertisers and agencies.

Advertisers and agencies are scattered throughout the country and sometimes abroad. The larger publishers have salespeople in branch offices in various cities. Others use independent representatives to sell for them or, in some cases, make special trips to visit their larger customers.

The Advertising Staff

Advertising Director

The advertising director is in charge of selling advertising in the magazine both through direct selling and promotional activities and is responsible for the management of the advertising sales department, sets department policy and procedures, is accountable for attaining advertising goals or quotas, is responsible for recruiting and training sales personnel, supervises the salespeople and independent representatives, and is responsible for the record keeping, billing, traffic, and other such functions covering advertising.

He may be the only salesperson or may oversee a staff, depending on the size of the magazine. The staff includes all the salespeople, branch office salespeople, independent representatives, and the backup staff that generate the promotion and research, as well as those who arrange scheduling and keep the records.

He evaluates the need for research; meets with the advertising staff to discuss problem areas, how to break into a new product classification, and coverage of industry conventions; and coordinates the work of full-time salespeople and out-of-town representatives.

He must work in close coordination with both the editors and the circulation people and, as discussed in the editorial and other sections, come to grips with some sticky situations that may arise among them.

Other Staff

- Sales Promotion Director. Plans and develops promotional programs in support of advertising space sales including promotional copy and artwork for sales efforts, and special promotional presentations and events. On some magazines, the promotion director is responsible for promotion and marketing for both advertising and circulation purposes. It has always seemed to me that the functions and strategies for selling advertising and circulation are so different that they should be handled by different people.
- Marketing Services Director. Develops market data, materials, and special advertising rates to support the sales staff.
- Research Director. Plans, develops, and executes all research projects to analyze existing and potential markets, improve the magazine's image, promote the magazine, and support advertising space sales.
- Marketing/Promotion Art Director. Responsible for visual character and quality of advertising/promotion material.
- Promotion Copywriter. Responsible for creation of ideas for promotional material, using selected features from the magazine as well as research data, and the writing and presentation of such promotional material.
- Branch/Regional Manager. Responsible for the sale of advertising pages to accounts located in an assigned geographic area.
- Advertising Sales Representative. Calls on and makes presentations to clients and advertising agencies to sell advertising pages. Services and maintains current accounts. Develops new business.

> **WARNING**
>
> Not many people can sell advertising. It involves all the difficulties any salesperson has in selling anything, but, added to this, these salespeople are selling an intangible product—one where the benefit to the advertiser normally can never be measured.

Most magazines assign their salespeople to handle accounts based on geographic territories, for obvious reasons. In the consumer field, however, it is common practice for the major magazines to have specialists for various types of advertisers, such as fashion, cosmetics, or travel. These salespeople, of course, are very well known in the areas they cover.

While face-to-face selling would seem to be the ideal in selling advertising, a great deal of space, particularly in special interest, regional, and business magazines, is sold on the telephone with little or no personal contact, except, perhaps, at industry meetings.

An uncounted number of books and articles have been written, and courses conducted, for salespeople. MPA and ABP conduct courses regularly to help with their training. Although it would be redundant to repeat this information here, one point bears repeating: Salespeople should constantly remind themselves that they are doing consultative selling, the goal of which is to assist the buyer in buying advertising that will help him sell more of his products. They are not "just peddling space."

The method of compensating advertising salespeople is peculiar to the magazine business and is discussed in chapter 38, "Compensating Salespeople."

Independent Advertising Representatives

It may not be economic for a publisher to establish offices in every geographic area—or to have its salespeople cover certain types of advertisers. There are independent advertising representatives located in many cities and in foreign countries selling advertising for more than one publisher. In some cases, these reps will take over the entire ad-selling operation for a publisher. Both very large and very small magazines—as well as those in between—use reps.

The reasons for using independent reps include:

- Representing the magazine in areas where, because of the small number of potential advertisers, it may not be economic to set up your own office.
- They may do a better job than your own people because:
  - They are motivated to sell since their compensation comes entirely from commissions.
  - They normally are experienced salespeople who do not need training.
  - They know the territory and the advertisers in it and can gain quick acceptance for your magazine.
- The compensation is usually fixed at a percentage of sales.
- They can be used to get started in an area where you may later introduce your own salesperson.
- If you hire the wrong rep, making a change will probably not be as difficult as it would be to change an employee.

Reasons for not using an independent rep include:

- They may not have as complete an understanding and the same fervor for, your magazine as your own people have, and you may lose direct contact with the advertisers.
- They may just skim the cream in the territory rather than going after all the advertisers that should use your magazine.
- You may choose the wrong rep firm—or be handled by the wrong person within the firm—and lose a great deal of business and time getting established in an area. If this happens, there may also be a residual negative reaction about your magazine.
- You may lack the sense of control that you have with your own employees.
- There may be difficulties in handling accounts when the advertiser is in one area and the ad agency in another.
- You may not prepare the rep to work for your magazine as thoroughly as you do your own people.
- It may be more costly.

The success you have with rep firms can depend a great deal on how you treat them—you will have much more success if you make them just as much a part of the team as your own people: visit with them, ask their advice, have them at your sales meetings, etc.

The use of rep firms is most common on the West Coast, in the South, and in the Southwest. A number of companies also use them in Detroit where it is very difficult for an outsider to break into the automotive community. Few publishers use them in Chicago, and over the years I have found only one New York rep who did a really good job, because almost every magazine feels a need to have its own people in that center of the advertising world.

While a great many publishers use reps successfully, I have also encountered a few who felt that it was better to spend the money to fly their best salespeople to various areas to be sure their magazines were adequately represented—and also to impress the advertisers with the attention they were getting.

Compensation for reps is normally the result of a negotiation and usually ends up at somewhere around 15% to 20% of the net income sold, depending on who pays the travel and entertainment expenses. A new magazine will normally have to guarantee the rep a certain amount per month during a start-up period.

Use of Outsiders

As in other areas of the publishing industry, there are a number of outside organizations that can be helpful to the advertising department, including:

- Market research companies
- Promotional companies that will design and produce media kits and other promotion
- Ad tracking companies that provide competitive market statistics such as share of advertising dollars and pages

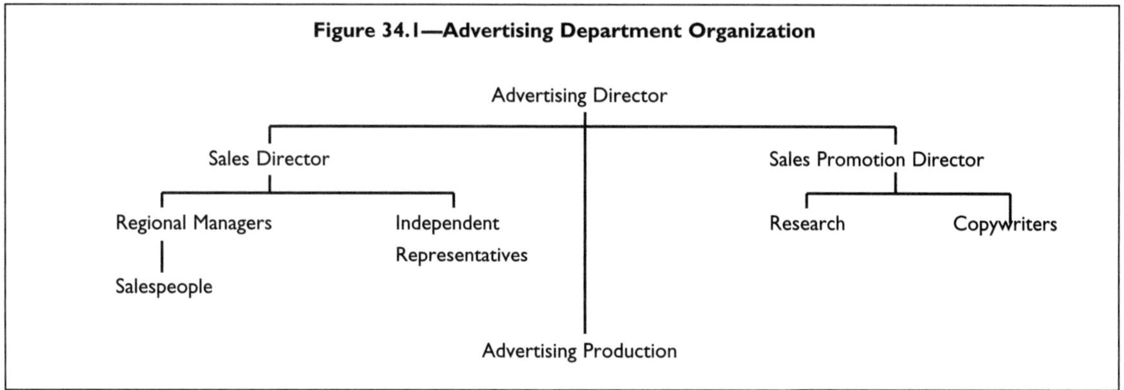

- Sales consultants who will do everything from critiquing the selling, promotion and research operations to helping select and train salespeople
- Organizations that have record-keeping systems specifically designed for advertising

Advertising Costs

Monitoring the costs of the advertising department is relatively simple through the use of two statistics:

1. The percent costs of net advertising income.
2. Advertising costs per advertising page.

While these costs will probably be out of line at the start-up of a magazine, they should be kept within the bounds of industry averages as reported in the cost studies conducted by MPA and ABM after the initial push.

CHAPTER 35

Advertising—Positioning

Positioning of a product or service in the marketing world is defined as the creation of a distinct identity, image, or concept via advertising, public relations, or other techniques. A product is usually positioned to appeal to buyers with specific needs or desires. To say it another way, it means finding something unique or different about your product—something that makes it stand out in the minds of your customers.

Or even more baldly, positioning is giving all the reasons why someone should buy advertising in your magazine rather than spending it somewhere else (without demeaning the competition because that would not be seemly).

Positioning for any magazine consists of two things:

1. Positioning magazines as a class
2. Positioning of the specific magazine to appeal to buyers of advertising in the field it serves

In selling advertising, it is important not only to explain the positioning of the specific magazine, but also to take care not to pass lightly over the positioning of magazines in general. These days, particularly, people need reminding of the basic attributes of magazines versus seemingly more exotic new media.

Positioning of Magazines As a Class

Magazines operate in a world that includes many other media—newspapers, network and cable TV, radio, outdoor media, newsletters, direct mail, telemarketing, pennysavers, trade shows, and, most recently and notably, the Internet.

The unique attributes of magazines are explained below. MPA has done a great deal of research on some of these points and has brochures and other material that can be useful. This material is primarily devoted to comparisons of magazines with TV since these are the two media that vie most for national consumer advertising.

ABM has developed similar material supporting the positioning of magazines, including a wonderful list of 50 reasons why a company should launch an ad campaign.

Attributes of Magazines That Attract Advertisers

• Magazines Are Universally Read. Nine in ten adults read at least one magazine a month, and virtually every market segment can be reached by magazines.
• Each Magazine Is Devoted to a Specific Interest. Each singles out a precise industry, profession, market, or group of people with specific demographics and/or lifestyles; each is read for specific information pertaining to that interest; and advertising that is related to the specific interest becomes an addition to, rather than an intrusion on, the magazine's editorial content.

Nature of Magazine Readers and Reading

• Readers are Self-Selected. People buy, pick up, or request a magazine specifically because they want to read about the subject covered.
• What They Read Is Also Self-Selected. You read

what you are interested in and get on with your life, unlike broadcast media where you must absorb things serially, or the Net where you must know how to narrow your search in a sea of information, and never really know how many things you may have missed.

• Readers Love Their Magazines. The relationship between a magazine and its readers is personal and intimate, one-on-one. Because of the interest in the subject matter, magazines are read thoroughly and have high credibility with their readers.

• Reading Is Habit-Forming. For the foreseeable future, at least, people are going to insist on seeing things printed on paper.

• Reading Is a Participatory Activity. Reading requires effort. The reader does not sit back and wait to be entertained. He reaches out for specific information and devours it.

• Reading Is User-Friendly. You determine the rate at which you read. You can read whenever you want, as much or as little as you want, and as often as you want. You can read many times faster than you can listen—but you can also skim, stop, review, or reread material.

• Magazines Have an Educated and Affluent Audience. Magazine readers are better able to comprehend written material and act on it. Magazine readers also generally have higher incomes than the general population.

Physical Format

• Conducive to Reading. Magazines are easily portable. Readers can read wherever they are. Magazines can be picked up and reread many times. They can be kept permanently.

• High Graphic Impact. Reproduction values in magazines can result not only in beautiful pages, but also in very true-to-life illustrations.

• Extensive Information. There is more room on magazine pages for very detailed explanations and information than in other media.

Marketing Assists

• Interactive Opportunities. Readers have ample opportunities for feedback: Phone numbers, addresses, and Web addresses can be included. Bingo cards, coupons, order forms, mailing lists, and other interactive devices are available.

• Detailed Information about Readers. Demographics, psychographics, buying habits, and lifestyles of individuals are available.

• Secondary Readership. Pass-a-long readership is considerable.

• Can Reach Market Segments. Readership can be segmented geographically, demographically, and in other ways.

Benefits for the Advertiser

From an advertiser's standpoint, all this means that advertising in magazines in general is credible, and that in a specific magazine is even more credible because it is targeted to a particular interest.

Because of the targeted nature of magazines and the fact that the reader—and what he reads—is self-selected, the advertiser is reaching those most interested and most likely to buy when they are in the mood for learning more about the subject.

Because of the physical nature of a magazine, interactive response devices can be used; it can be read at any time and in any place; it can be read and reread; and it can be kept and referred to later.

Since the advertising is related to the subject matter of the magazine, it is an adjunct to the editorial content. This interest is heightened because of the personal and intimate relationship of readers with their magazines and the fact that reading is a participatory activity that requires effort and interest on the reader's part.

Because the audience is more educated than most, it is better able to comprehend advertising messages and to act on them

All this gives the advertiser the impact of a high-powered rifle on the best prospects, resulting in far better cost efficiency than any other media. Added to this are the pass-a-long readers who are not included in the basic circulation.

Through geographic or other editions, smaller advertisers can limit their appeal to those in specific geographic areas or with specific demographics. Larger advertisers can test different approaches to these different groups—or even to every nth name of the entire audience.

Adding to the advantages are the advertiser's ability to present true-to-life graphics and extensive details about his products and services. He also has detailed data about the readers and their interests that are not available for most other media.

For general advertisers, the audience has higher income than the public in general.

WARNING

All the material above is designed to showcase the advantages of magazines versus other promotion media, but don't be too antagonistic to the other media.

In the end, they are trying to help the advertisers just as you are. There are some ways in which each of the other media can accomplish results that magazines cannot. In fact, you will probably use direct mail, TV, radio, the Net, and all the other media yourself from time to time.

Often a combination of different media will be best for an advertiser. When that is the case, the smart magazine publisher will try to help develop the package that will be most useful through joint ventures and joint presentations with representatives of the other media.

At times business magazines and consumer magazines may find themselves vying for advertising. This is particularly true, for instance, when *Business Week, Fortune, Forbes,* etc. go after the same advertisers as magazines in specialized fields. Witness the current trend for advertisers of prescription drugs to appeal to consumers directly, as well as to the medical fraternity.

Positioning a New Magazine in a New Field

If you are launching a magazine in a field that never existed before (or one that no one previously recognized), your task is to explain what the field is, who the readers might be, how many there are, and how you will reach them. You also must define who the logical advertisers are, how you will reach them, and how you will explain to them why they should advertise.

For this kind of magazine, competitive positioning is not needed, but it is good to compare the magazine with other magazines in somewhat different fields that have been successful. A good example of this is *Stratos,* as discussed in chapter 20, "The Business Plan."

Positioning a New Magazine in an Existing Field

Some creativity is needed in positioning a new magazine that is competing with already established magazines in an existing field.

If it really has a unique editorial focus or editorial format, then it is offering something that no other magazine offers. This would be true of a splinter magazine in an existing field. A good example of this is *Elan* as discussed in chapter 20, "The Business Plan."

If it doesn't, and very few magazines do, then you have to look for ways to describe it that sets it apart from the competition. Positioning does not depend only on your magazine's strengths. Seasonality, technological advances, government regulations, or your creativity may propel you to the forefront of your category.

The types of things you might point to as being unique are:

- Editorial Leadership
    - The first to fill a market need—more impact, greater readership, and longer visibility
    - Industry exclusives of various kinds—a different point of view, a survey, a directory, new facts
    - Exclusive articles by well-known people
    - Awards that have been won
    - Editor who is a leader in the field
- Advertising
    - More pages and/or more revenues than the others
    - Larger gains in pages; if not that, larger share of the market, or a larger gain in that share
    - Lower cost-per-thousand circulation
    - Lower absolute cost per page
    - More new advertisers—or more leading advertisers
    - Testimonials by one or more leading industry spokespeople
- Circulation
    - Better quality circulation—for instance, greater affluence
    - Reaching more decision makers
    - Exclusive in reaching a specific market or a specific segment of the market
    - Getting to the readers first because of the publishing schedule
    - Controlled circulation reaching all the decision makers while your competitors are paid, but not reaching them all
    - Or just the opposite—readers who are willing to pay for their magazine
    - Reaching many readers that the others bypass
    - The only one with audited circulation

- Readership
    - Research studies showing that your magzine is the choice of people in the field, is most useful, has most pass-along readers, is most involved, etc.
    - Testimonials from influential readers
    - Responsiveness as shown by reader inquiries, phone calls, coupons clipped
- Pricing
    - While your basic rates may not be lower, your cost may be less because of various discounts. Magazines are always discussing the "efficiency" of their pages
    - Various merchandising services offered without additional cost
- Format
    - Different size, different frequency, better reproduction quality, better paper, better binding

If you want to get a feeling for how consumer magazines handle this positioning process, you might get the media kits of the magazines trying to serve girls from ages about 12 through 24. There are three incumbents—*Seventeen, Teen,* and *YM*—as well a very new magazine—*Teen People*—vying for advertising to this age group.

In the business magazine area, you might review those magazines serving the advertising field, which is changing very rapidly because of the computer, cable TV, the Internet, etc. Take a look at the media kits of *Ad Age,* the *Ad Week-Brand Week-Media Week* group, as well as *Brand Marketing, Target Marketing, Direct, Direct Marketing*, and *DM News.* They are probably among those periodicals you should be reading in any case.

CHAPTER 36

Advertising—Sales Tools

Media Kit

THE BASIC ADVERTISING selling tool is the media kit. It should tell the whole positioning story that you have carefully developed. It is the item buyers will keep and have handy when considering your magazine. It would normally contain:

- Copies of the magazine
- Rate card or cards
- Explanation of the field covered
- Positioning of the magazine within the field and against its competitors
- Circulation audit statements
- Editorial calendar, highlighting special issues
- Results of syndicated and other research studies
- Recent articles from the magazine
- Testimonial letters from satisfied advertisers
- Articles about the magazine
- Material testifying to the stature of the editorial product and the editors, such as biographies of the editors, editorial awards, and the like
- Comparisons of readership, cost per thousand circulation, research results with competing magazines
- "Value added" benefits that are available, such as research studies
- Anything else that seems helpful to an advertiser

Most media kits consist of attractive folders with pockets on each side where different pieces of information can be inserted. By putting different items in it, you can tailor-make a kit for each advertising prospect, as well as keep the information up-to-date.

The kits should have tabs and be of a size that can fit in a file drawer so that they can easily be filed and found when wanted. While having an advertiser or agency get the complete media kit in hard copy form is preferable, many magazines also have much of the data available on the Net.

> **WARNING**
>
> Some kits, unfortunately, seem to end up being a mishmash of pieces of paper of various sizes, different typefaces and colors, and some good—and some bad—copy.
>
> I favor having a booklet, as well designed and edited as the magazine itself, that tells the whole story in a structured and coherent way. This will, of course, have to be supplemented by circulation audit reports and other current information, but the less loose stuff, the better.
>
> While having an advertiser get the complete media kit in hard copy form is certainly preferable, many magazines also have much of the data from their media kits available on the Internet.

Rate Card

The rate card is a listing of a publication's advertising rates together with information needed for advertisers who are planning to use the magazine. The internal design of the rates and their relationship with each other (the percent markup for four-color versus black and white, the percent discount for a half page, etc.) can do a great deal to steer advertisers to buying more space—or space that is more profitable for the publisher.

The rate card should contain at least:

- Basic advertising rates for black-and-white, two-color, and four-color ads of various sizes and frequencies

- Rates for covers and other special positions
- Rates for regional, demographic, or other editions
- Rates for special types of advertising, such as mail order, books, etc.
- Discounts of various kinds such as dollar volume, renewal, consecutive pages
- Additional charge for bleed, if any
- Printing requirements—page sizes, method of sending copy, etc.
- Deadline dates for insertions and sending copy
- On-sale dates
- Information about the advertising sales forces, locations of offices, and where to send material
- Advertising contract terms

Many publishers also include selling material along with the rates so that the card may be being several pages long and a mini-media kit.

Most of the information should also be made available in SRD and on the Internet.

Circulation Data

Advertisers are, of course, most interested in readership: how much there is, who the readers are, how loyal they might be. The basic data—and sometimes the only data—is found in the circulation statements of the magazines and, in abbreviated form, in SRDS. The data come in various forms:

- Sworn to by the publisher
- Audited by the ABC
- Audited by BPA International
- Audited by other independent audit organizations or accounting firms

The vast majority of paid circulation magazines are audited by ABC, although BPA does some. Most controlled circulation magazines are audited by BPA, although ABC does a number of these. See chapter 42, "Circulation Audit Organizations."

Many publishers do not have their circulations audited. While the sworn circulation statements of many publishers may be perfectly accurate, there is always a question in readers' minds as to just how much the numbers have been inflated. History has shown that circulation is often considerably overstated.

You must be careful to differentiate between actual circulation and claims of the "Number Distributed to Various Places," "Guaranteed Paid and Controlled." Advertising people may feel that these do not give real information about the number of buyers or readers.

A knowledgeable reader of the audited statements of paid circulation can learn a great deal about the relative strength of competing magazines by comparing such tables as:

- Circulation versus the Rate Base (for the magazine that has one)
- Circulation per issue—subscription and single copy
- Subscriptions sold at basic versus lower-than-basic prices
- Duration of subscriptions sold
- Channels of subscription sales
- Use of premiums
- Bulk subscriptions versus individual
- Circulation by county size
- Post expiration copies included
- Geographic analysis of circulation
- Renewal percentages (now authorized for publication by ABC by those magazines wanting to show it)

At this writing ABC and BPA had just decided to reduce the requirement for paid circulation from 50% of the published price. New types of information may now be reported that will increase the usefulness of their statements.

Controlled circulation audit statements can also be helpful through an analysis of the number of subscriptions specifically requested by the recipient versus those sent from lists and other sources, as well as the recency of the request or the makeup of the lists.

In the business publication area, competing magazines in a field agree on the categories into which the readers are classified. A magazine that doesn't feel that these titles are a good representation may simply decide to be audited by ABC rather than BPA (or vice versa) and avoid having to be directly compared with its competitors in the way they have agreed.

Both ABC and BPA have issued booklets that describe the various items listed on their audits and how to interpret them.

Consumer Magazines— Syndicated Research

This type of research is used only by the very largest consumer magazines. It is very expensive and very detailed research about magazines' readers. Like the Nielsen ratings for TV, it is subject to many arguments about the accuracy of the methods used and of the results obtained. For some magazines the results may vary considerably from one period to another.

The organizations that do this research collect information from a cross section of the population on a statistical and geographical basis. They measure heavy-to-light usage of a great number of specific products. They also collect personal data such as education, income, age, property ownership, how long a magazine is kept, and psychographic information about the readers. Prominent in doing this type of research are Simmons Research, A. C. Nielsen Corp, Arbitron, J.D. Power and Associates, Roper Starch Worldwide, Harris Interactive, Yankelovich Partners, and The PreTesting Company.

Included is not only the primary buyer of the magazine, but the pass-a-long readership, which for some magazines can be considerable.

HISTORY

Syndicated research got started back in the 1950s when the major magazines tried to prove that their audiences were larger than those of the new guy on the block—television. This effort, of course, failed for what are now very obvious reasons, but had a great deal to do with the death of *Colliers, Life, Look,* and the *Saturday Evening Post* (as it was then), and the near death of a number of other major magazines as they tried to outdo TV with numbers.

Consumer Magazines— Other Research

Most larger magazines in competitive fields have research performed by well-known firms so that they can tell advertisers more about their readers. A relatively standard list of information is developed including such things as:

- Gender
- Age
- Number of people in household
- Education level
- Household Income—average and median
- Ownership and value of home
- Ownership of passport
- Value of securities owned
- Vocation
- Ownership of second home
- Ownership of cars
- Pass-a-long readership
- How long copy of magazine is kept
- Readership of articles on specific subjects
- Readership of competitive magazines

In addition, depending on the field covered, data are collected to determine the demographic and/or psychographic characteristics of the readers by finding out about such things as:

- Ownership of specific types of goods
- Plans for buying such items in the future
- Amount spent per year on items in the field
- Time spent, and how it is spent on things related to the field

Added to this there are often questions relating to their opinions about important subjects in the field covered. The answers can be used both as editorial material and to develop knowledge about trends in the field that will impress advertisers.

Research for Business Magazines

Business magazines generally want to prove three things to advertisers:

1. They cover all the companies in the field. For the majority of magazines that are distributed through controlled circulation rather than paid, this is done when they select the companies to which they send the copies.
2. The people to whom they send the magazines have a major buying influence within the companies. They do this through the job titles selected—and later through questionnaires to those to whom they send the copies.
3. The recipients read their magazine versus the competitors in the field. This is done through research into such things as:

- Which magazines do you receive?

• Which ones do you read regularly (how many issues)?
• Which single one is most important to you?
• If you could receive only one of them, which would it be?
• Questions about specific articles in the magazines.
• What do you do with the copies—keep them or pass them to someone else?

Once again, it is also useful to try to develop material that can be used editorially—as well as to impress advertisers with your knowledge of the field.

Research Must Be Credible

I pointed out above that the multimillion-dollar syndicated research is at times subject to severe criticism. Whenever there are competing magazines, or other competing media, your research is going to be carefully examined—and any flaws pointed out.

Surveys made by publishers themselves are always suspect. The wording of the questions asked and methods used in asking them can lead to misleading answers, as we all know. Mail surveys where fewer than 50% respond, despite more than one request, are very suspect.

To have your research believed, it is always best to have it performed by an independent research organization. Even that may not be enough—it's better if it is one of those companies that is well recognized by the advertising community.

CHAPTER 37

Advertising—Promotion

SAL MARINO, who for many years was the CEO of Penton Publishing, used to say that promotion managers should never report to sales managers because of the great differences in their functions.

Sales concerns itself with personal, across-the-table contacts. Promotion is largely concerned with long-range group-to-group contacts and communicates with words and pictures. While promotion cannot have the effect that individual selling has, it can reach a great many more prospects all at once with its selling messages—and can also sometimes develop sales by itself.

Promotion is not simply an adjunct to the selling operation. It is much more. The dictionary defines it: the activity of increasing popularity or sales by advertising, displays, events, public relations, and other techniques.

Magazine people should understand promotion better than anyone else because that is what they are trying to get prospective advertisers to buy.

Usually there are at least three main areas where promotion can be used by a magazine:

1. To sell advertising in the magazine itself by explaining the specific way such advertising can benefit—or has benefited—companies with products or services serving the field.
2. To demonstrate the magazine's knowledge of what is going on in the field covered.
3. To bring wider recognition for what the magazine is doing in the field being covered.

From time to time we have seen promotion campaigns that, for a time at least, catapult magazines into orbit. Consider the promotion by Oprah of her new magazine, *O,* or by the ESPN network of *ESPN,* or of *George* when it was first launched.

Promotion of a magazine can and does take all sorts of forms both prosaic and exotic. Creativity is always rampant, if not necessarily beneficial, in this area. Some useful promotion:

- Advertise in the trade press. After all, if you don't do this, you are indicating that you don't believe in advertising yourself. If you do use such advertising, it should be carefully and creatively crafted to show your own prospects just how advertising can be used to help sell. It should not be just the showboat ads that so many magazines use.
- Develope a useful newsletter to send prospective advertisers, telling not only about your magazine, but also about what is going on in the field that might be of interest to them. The idea, of course, is to demonstrate your closeness to the field.
- Participate in industry conferences and seminars.
- Sponsor a major event whenever there is a really critical issue being faced in your field.
- Tell about market research and editorial research you have carried out.
- Make sure that prospects know about special issues, members of your advisory board, any editorial or other changes such as frequency, circulation, personnel, or other items.
- Sponsor events that will put your magazine on

the map, just as large corporations do with golf tournaments and the like.

• Provide testimonials from advertisers and readers.

• Put on breakfasts, lunches, dinners, and other affairs for advertisers and agencies where your magazine's knowledge of and place in the field is dramatically demonstrated.

• Promote the editorial content and the editors who have created it, including such things as the awards they have won.

• Get publicity through broadcast appearances and write-ups in newspapers and in the other media. Since the media love the media, this is never too difficult.

The list is almost endless—and is limited only by the creativity of those in charge.

CHAPTER 38

Advertising—Compensating Salespeople

ONE OF THE essential, but more difficult, tasks in publishing management is the development of a compensation plan for advertising salespeople. Ask any publisher at just about any time about the system he is currently using and he will almost invariably tell you that it isn't working as well as he expected—and a change is under study. About the only consistent feature in most companies is that the system is changed every three to five years.

This is not as surprising as it may seem. Different people may be involved as time goes on. Economic conditions change. Company profits can have ups and downs. Salespeople mature—and may become more or less productive. Customers change. The place of a magazine in its life cycle can make a big difference.

There seems to be a need for a periodic review of any basic system. The chances that one magazine's system can be applied to any other are very slim.

Because of the great variety of magazines and plans, we will not discuss any specifics in the way of dollar amounts or commission percentages.

Objective of Your Compensation Plan

The objective is to develop the *most profitable* sales (not necessarily the most sales) at the least cost. This means that the first step is to determine which are the most profitable sales in both the short and long run. Besides this the plan must:

- Result in a living wage
- Be equitable to all salespeople
- Give a fair value for services rendered
- Result in competitive pay
- Steer salespeople to the most desirable types of sales
- Not result in overcompensation
- Be simple to understand and to administer

It's not easy to get all this into one plan.

I do not believe that all salespeople can be led in any direction by putting a compensation carrot in front of them. Certainly there are a few who are like that, but there are just as many who will work just as hard and effectively for a straight salary as for a commission, and there are all kinds of people in between. But as long as there is just one who will respond part of the time to an incentive, you had better build one in, difficult or not.

Cash Compensation Methods

There are a number of ways of determining the cash payments to be made to salespeople. These vary from a straight salary to straight commissions and include everything in between.

STRAIGHT SALARY

This sounds like the simplest, and it is in many respects, but there must be a periodic renegotiation. When that time comes, there must be a reason for changes. That reason normally has to do with results, so there is not as much difference between a straight salary and a commission as may appear.

A straight salary is used:

- Almost always for a person who cannot quickly achieve a sales level high enough to earn a living wage on a commission basis
- For someone whose work is more of a service nature, such as handling a group of large customers
- When selling is a team effort, or the result of heavy research and promotion, and the sale cannot be attributed to any one individual
- When territories or assignments are changed and it's necessary to put a salesperson on a straight salary basis for a time
- For some people who simply work better this way than with a direct incentive

Straight Commission

This is based on the sales in a territory or for specific accounts. It might seem to be the most equitable and the easiest to administer, but it isn't that simple. The potential of different territories varies. In a time of a recession, the salesperson may not earn an adequate wage, no matter how hard he works. More than once a straight commission plan has had to be amended when a recession struck. On the other hand, in some instances the salesperson may reap the benefits of a windfall that he may not really deserve.

From a control standpoint, too, there may be difficulties. When a salesperson is doing well, he can become quite independent. This can make it difficult to change territories or assignments, even though this may be best for the magazine.

Many attempts have been made to ameliorate the difficulties inherent in both the straight salary and straight commission plans. These can work for a time but must always be subject to adjustment for changes in conditions, the magazine, and the salespeople.

In the end, like all compensation, any plan eventually comes down to individual negotiation. The plain fact is that it is very difficult to quantify the contribution any single person makes to an operation.

Combination Plans

Some of the combinations of salary and commissions that are commonly used include:

- Salary plus year-end bonus. This combination gives recognition to the results of a year, but without a specific formula.
- Draw against a commission. This is an attempt to give greater certainty as well as to level out earnings throughout the year. It does not, however, eliminate the basic problems of the straight commission. In many cases publishers have had to allow people to keep their draws, even though they were not completely earned, because of an unforeseen recession or problems with specific advertisers.
- Salary plus commission. This guarantees the salesperson a base, no matter what, while retaining the incentive of a commission. This is usually paid for sales over a certain amount, called a "bogey" or "quota." Most publishers try to arrange that the salary will be around 70% or 80% of the total compensation, although this varies. Bogeys are determined in a variety of ways. Most common is a percentage of sales in the territory for the prior year, although this is adjusted for the potential in the territory, the stage of the salesperson's development, ad rate changes, and other factors.

Commission plans differ as much as the ingenuity of the people who create them. They can be a level percent of the sales produced or can rise in steps as sales increase, under the theory that this gives more incentive to sell additional business.

Sometimes they decline in steps, a practice that at first may be difficult to understand. The reasoning is that a salesperson can handle only so much business well. If you keep increasing the commission, he will earn a great deal, but many potential customers will not be covered.

The obvious thing to do at this point is split the territory, but, if the salesperson is earning too much, there will be resistance. Since he is obviously one of the best, the choice is: (1) split the territory, give lower overall pay, and risk losing the salesperson; (2) split the territory but guarantee the individual's pay until it can be built up again; or (3) retain the original plan and not gain additional sales.

None of these is acceptable, so you try to avoid the situation by reducing the commission rates as sales increase.

Sometimes the percentage is geared to net sales less salary and expenses. This is an attempt to relate to the relative profitability of each person.

You would expect that a commission based on

dollar sales would be most logical, since a dollar earned for a color charge is just as good as one for the basic page. But the number of pages sold may be a better measure (1) if the profits from color or other charges are not in the same proportion as those from the basic page sale, (2) if the salesperson has no influence over the advertiser's use of color, (3) if the need to fill the magazines with pages is paramount, or (4) if the publisher wants to avoid increasing the commissions when advertising rates are increased.

In a few cases, commissions are determined on a group basis. This might apply to all the people in an office or to a group that handles one category of advertising.

OTHER COMPENSATION ALTERNATIVES

Creativity is often also used: to avoid income taxes, to enlist husbands or wives to spur their spouses on, to convert ordinary income taxes into capital gains, or for psychological reasons. For instance:

- Payment of expenses. Beyond those for normal travel and entertainment, but still so closely related to the business that an individual may be able to deduct them for tax purposes. These might include club initiation fees, dues, and expenses for the purchase or rental of an automobile.
- Fringe benefits. These are part of the compensation package, as they are for all employees. Medical, pension, and profit-sharing plans are certainly all pluses to employees, but the effect on sales would be very difficult to trace. In some cases key employees, salespeople as well as others, may be granted special benefits such as dental payments, college education for their children, and other such items.
- Stock, stock options, phantom stock. Sometimes these are given (or sold) to very key employees in all departments to make them feel that they have an ownership interest and to give them a chance to gain major benefits at capital gains rates. This type of incentive is particularly helpful in luring people to join a new magazine.
- Opportunity bonus. This is granted for developing certain types of business, for each new account sold, for upgrading the amount an advertiser uses, for a page in a directory in addition to the magazine, or for any other item the publisher is pushing.
- Prize. These reward extraordinary performance. The prize might be a trip for the leading salespeople and their spouses, or attendance at the "winners" sales meeting at some exotic place.

THE SALESPERSON AS AN INDEPENDENT CONTRACTOR

Some people deal with their salespeople as independent contractors who are running their own businesses, even though they work for only one organization. The theory is that if the salespeople feel that they are in business for themselves, they will work harder and spend less. The company avoids payroll taxes and other fringe benefits. The employee can deduct part of his expenses as business costs for tax purposes more easily than if he were on the payroll, and he can also set up his own retirement plan.

The key disadvantages are that there may be the loss of control, and that the IRS will come down heavily on both the company and the salesperson. Better investigate this carefully before agreeing to it.

SETTING UP A PLAN

Simple though most plans seem in concept, in practice there are many decisions, compromises, and negotiations that must be contended with.

Unless you are a new magazine, the problems start because you already have salespeople who are being compensated in some manner—and you cannot change their pay levels or methods without some good reason. You may have to resort to some elaborate and ingenious calculations to develop a formula that results in a good incentive, does not change the present pay levels much, and can be applied fairly to all. In some cases, exceptions have to be made for certain salespeople to develop a plan that will stand the tests of both fairness and time.

ADMINISTRATIVE DIFFICULTIES

On a day-to-day basis, all sorts of relatively minor points come up. Some individuals are very picky and legalistic about their rights. At times you may wish you had never started the plan, but you are dealing with the most important item the salespeople have—their income—and you must do it fairly. Some of the frequent areas of difficulty are these:

• Split commission. Often an advertiser will be in one city and its agency somewhere else. They must be called on by different members of the sales staff. The commission is split between them, normally equally, but in some cases, in some other ratio.
• Increase in advertising rate. If the commission is on a page basis, there is, of course, no effect (which may not be ideal). If it is on a dollar basis, the salesperson may be getting pay increases for no real increase in productivity. The situation can be handled in a number of ways, ranging from no benefit to full benefit, with most publishers settling on about half the amount of the rate increase in figuring the individual's commission.
• Increase in cost of living. Salespeople suffer from inflation along with everyone else. Keeping their compensation at an adequate level can be handled in a number of ways—they can be allowed commission on part or all the advertising rate increases, or they can be included in any overall company wage increases, for instance. There is always the danger, however, that the cost of selling will then get out of line.
• Credit and collection. Most publishers try to keep the sales staff out of the credit and collection process. From the credit standpoint, it is felt that the sales staff would be too free in granting extensions, and collections do not involve a salesperson's real skill and could ruin relationships that he has built up. On the other hand, commissions normally are paid only on amounts collected, so the salesperson has a stake in the payment. This division of duties often results in clashes between sales and accounting people.
• House accounts. Everyone has some accounts on which no commissions are paid. These are serviced by the publisher or someone else who is not primarily a salesperson. Periodic review of these is needed to be sure that they might not be handled better in the normal course of advertising sales.
• Windfalls. At times an advertiser will embark on a blockbuster campaign for which the sales staff can take no real credit, but on which there would normally be a large commission. This is usually handled on a case-by-case basis.
• Split territories. At times a territory becomes too big for one individual to handle and the publisher wants it split with another person. This often happens when the first salesperson has done an excellent job, but just has too much to handle. Normally some kind of phased formula is arranged to give that individual several years to get sales back up to the previous level in a smaller territory.
• Differences in territories. Some territories do not have the potential of others because of a lack of prospects, but it is still important that they are covered well. How do you adequately compensate a person who may be doing a fine job, but who cannot earn the commission he deserves because of the nature of the territory? This is done through a special compensation arrangement giving him a few lucrative accounts in another area, or in other creative ways.
• New salespeople. They can rarely earn enough to fit into a commission plan. This is normally handled through a salary or nonreturnable draw adequate for his existence, plus an understanding of just when he will enter the compensation plan.
• Low-profit business. At times a publisher will accept business that does not yield the normal profits (a large insert, a remnant, and the like). In this case a special arrangement must be made.
• Noncommissionable work. Some salespeople are asked to do work on which they cannot earn a commission. This might include training a new staff member, developing promotion material, or many other things. If this type of work becomes meaningful, an adjustment is required.
• Sale of different products. Although it is pretty axiomatic that a salesperson is most effective when working on only one magazine, there are a few who can work on two or more effectively. At times it is the only way a territory can be covered adequately. Difficulties arise because you do not want any of the magazines to be neglected. The system must take into account that one product may be easier to sell than another, that the salesperson has a liking for one more than the other, and that one page rate is much higher than the other, so the commission is higher.
• An individual's pay gets too high. It is easy for a salesperson and his family, like the rest of us, to become accustomed to spending an additional amount. As in golf, the best we have ever done becomes "normal." This can happen when the compensation seems to be higher than an individual's efforts are worth, even though the formula in the plan works out that way. Although most managers profess that they do not care how much a person is paid as long as he produces the business, in practice this feeling may not carry through. There is, too, always the fear that if someone earns too much, he will become unmanageable. The answer is: change the plan, and hope you can hold on to the employee.

• Expense account limitations. Every company has some limits to the amount of expenses salespeople are allowed, whether the rules are written down or not. It is difficult to set hard-and-fast rules because situations vary. Some salespeople can use expense accounts very effectively. Others have little need for this. And, of course, filling out an expense report has become a high art form in some firms. Most companies today require coach airplane travel, limit meal and hotel costs (with different amounts for different cities), and designate the conventions each staff member attends. The overall approach, however, in the magazine business is not toward penny-pinching in the expense area. A few companies do not separately reimburse salespeople for their expenses, but increase their compensation and let them take care of expenses individually. Most publishers feel that they lose some control under this policy and that some people will become niggardly to the detriment of sales.

Changing the Compensation Plan

While everyone tries to set up a plan that will last for all time, there inevitably are times when a change is needed. This should not be done lightly or just because there are complaints.

No plan is perfect, as you have probably gathered by now. There are always exceptions and adjustments to be made and there will always be complaints. Changes require reorientation and new adjustments. In the end there is some kind of negotiation with the salespeople each year in any plan, no matter how carefully it has been designed.

CHAPTER 39

Getting Started in Advertising

YOU HAVE YOUR major financing—or at least you feel that it will be available in the foreseeable future. Now it is time to develop a strategic marketing plan for selling advertising.

You actually are probably farther along the path to doing this than you realize. In going through the start-up steps of crystallizing the editorial, developing issue plans, holding focus groups, printing a pilot issue, writing a business plan, testing for circulation, and seeking a staff, you have probably developed a great deal of the material that goes into a marketing plan. In addition you will need to consider:

- The specifics of the publication timing schedule

> **WARNING**
>
> We discussed the timing of the first issue in the launch scenario earlier. You have done a lot since then, and conditions may have changed in the marketplace. Chances are that the timing you had previously done may not be the most advantageous. It is worth revisiting the thinking you had previously made. Whatever you do, make sure you plan the first issue bearing in mind the fall advertising planning season for most advertisers. Give yourself enough time to do the selling job—at least six to nine months.

- The advertising plan, which must include detailed research about potential advertisers:
  - Who they are, where else they advertise, who are the bellwethers, names of key players at the advertisers and agencies
  - Location of advertisers and their agencies so that you know where to locate your salespeople and where to concentrate efforts so that there is the least cost in meeting with the most potential clients
  - Acquiring testimonials from key players
- Make arrangements with:
  - Independent reps if you plan to use them
  - An advisory board and consultants
  - ABC or BPA for a circulation audit at the earliest possible time
  - SRDS for a listing as soon as possible
  - A printer, single-copy distributor, the Postal Service and other suppliers

- The Media Kit (see chapter 36, "Advertising Sales Tools"). You already have the pilot issue, editorial plans for a year (which you may have to update), positioning of the magazine, biographies of the editors, and other key pieces. You also have the results of your focus groups and test mailing. You will need to complete the details of the rate cards, including the charter rates.

Rate Card Structure

The structure of the rate card—the relation of half pages, color pages, covers, inserts, and the rest to the black-and-white one-time rate—can be quite important in luring different types of advertisers. David Orlow has done a great deal of work in defining how to accomplish this.

The basic principle: The advertiser should pay

extra because of the additional impact that color or a cover position, for instance, has on readers—just as advertisers pay higher amounts for the most popular TV shows.

Rather than trying to recalculate the perfect rate card—or to reinvent one—a new magazine would be wise to copy the structure that competing magazines, or others most similar to it, are using. Saves lots of time calculating—as well as explaining.

Charter Advertising Rates

You are a new and unknown magazine and must make it easy for advertisers to use you. Chances are that your rates will be much lower than any competing magazines on a dollar basis (although not on a cost-per-thousand circulation basis) just because you will not have much circulation to start with. If you simply offer reduced rates, you may find that you have committed to rate-cutting for the rest of your existence, and no one will believe any rates you publish thereafter.

A better practice—and one that is often done—is to make a charter offer. This can be done most easily by offering two pages for the price of one —or three for the price of two. You must be careful in doing this. You don't want the first issue to be relatively fat with new advertisers, while those that follow appear to be pamphlets. This makes it appear that advertisers will not stick with you. You avoid this by offering the charter rates only if the advertiser agrees to run his three insertions in each of the first three issues—or some other such arrangement.

- Develop some "quick and dirty" research among the people who responded to the direct mail subscription tests about their demographics.
- Develop some value added benefits.
- Develop the promotion program (see chapter 37, "Advertising—Promotion").
- Let the world know you are in business—that means the press, the trade press, the people in your field—and if you are a consumer magazine, try for TV and radio coverage.

While you undoubtedly have a very long list of potential advertisers, do not try to call on all of them prior to the first issue. Confine your selling efforts to carefully constructed attacks on the leaders in the industry whose appearance in the magazine will do a great deal to help bring the stragglers in later. Of course, you cannot ignore the others—keep them informed.

WARNING

At the start-up of a magazine, calls on the advertisers are probably more effective than calls on agencies because the advertisers usually understand the field they are in better—and can make decisions without inhibitions about what the client will say.

You should not, however, ignore the agencies—they can shoot you down. One method of taking care of some of the agencies is to arrange group meetings with the large ones where you can tell your story to lots of their key people with the assistance of your editor to explain the editorial approach of the magazine

It is probable that, at the beginning at least, the entrepreneur will be the best salesperson because he is the most enthusiastic, knows the subject best, and is, after all, the founder. People will want to see you. When you appear, don't forget to stress the financial stability of the venture.

How Advertisers and Agencies View New Magazines

You had better face the fact early on that there will be no great rejoicing in the advertising world that you are starting a new magazine. The advertisers and agencies in your field may simply feel that they will have to see yet another set of salespeople—and add to the numbers in their computers when they have to decide where to place advertising.

The best you can hope for at the beginning is benign tolerance. They will probably put up with your visits—but, please, not too many of them—out of the goodness of their hearts.

Put yourself in the place of the ad director or the brand manager in a company—or the account executive or media director in an agency. They are well aware that the failure rate for new magazines is high—and that includes even those started by magazine companies with deep pockets and lots of know-how. They may even have had some experience in putting ads in one or more magazines that didn't make it.

Those within the advertiser company are supposed to know the fields they serve intimately, and do not want to be tagged as the guy who put ads in a failing magazine. For those in the agency, there is an even greater fear of making this kind of mistake—it may mean the loss of a client.

What They Look For

The type of analysis they will make will seem superficial compared with what you have gone through with potential investors. It will start, as always, with an understanding of the editorial approach and your ability to show that people will want to read the magazine. After that, you will probably find that advertisers are more interested, not in the subjective excitement they see in the magazine, but in comparing it with other media they have available—something they normally like to quantify through the computer and its ability to massage numbers.

Here is a précis of an analysis SRDS made back in 1990 about what media buyers had to say about the subject:

- Financial strength of the company. Existing companies are more likely to have the staying power for a launch than an entrepreneurial enterprise. History has not proven this to be true, but the logic is hard to dispute.
- A good business plan.
    - Does the plan communicate the magazine's editorial positioning clearly—and differentiate it from other magazines?
    - Do the editorial and art staff have track records with other successful titles?
    - Have they created a pilot issue that delivers what they have promised?
    - Is it targeted to an audience that will grow?
- Can the magazine reach its readers at a reasonable cost?
    - If the price is higher than similar magazines, is there some added value to make readers want to buy it?
    - If the subscription offer is too rich, with many free issues, a sweepstakes, or attractive premiums, why are these incentives needed?
- Does the magazine intend to have its circulation audited by ABC or BPA quickly? If not, what other data are available to determine the circulation or what the newsstand percent of sale?
- What kind of partner is the magazine for the advertiser? Do the ad reps bring ideas, are they responsible, have they delivered what they promised?
- What's happening to the category the magazine is in?
- Are the ad rates in line with what similar magazines charge? If they are higher, is some other incentive being offered such as positioning opportunities that might not be available in existing magazines where present advertisers have the key spots? A charter rate helps, and new magazines usually have absolute dollar rates much lower than existing ones because their circulations are lower.

CHAPTER 40

Basics of a Magazine's Circulation

NOTE: A seemingly disproportionate number of pages will be devoted to circulation in this book because it is the one major area of the business—the care and handling of readers of a serially distributed product—that is unique to magazine publishing and therefore requires more explanation.

CIRCULATION IS THE most difficult part of publishing a magazine. The basic reasons for this are:

- You are dealing with the public and you can never be sure how they will react.
- Circulation is not one single thing, but the result of picking up readers of many different kinds, in different places, in different ways, at different times, at different prices, and at different costs.
- Unless you have a magazine that can make profits from circulation alone, it cannot be considered all by itself, but only in conjunction with the advertising income based on the amount and type of circulation.

Most publishers historically have not understood the circulation function and its workings very well. It is often considered to be a necessary evil. Something always seems to be going wrong—and, since there are so many things to go wrong, something usually is. Improvements are measured in minute percentages

Lots of managements still think of circulation as a dirty, grubby, nickel-and-dime service-type business. That picture persists from the old days when the circulation director sat in the middle of a bunch of noisy Speedomat or Eliot stencil-making machines, or, worse yet, with Pollard-Alling plates flying from floor to ceiling and around his head.

It is even hard to communicate with circulation people because they talk about such weird things as "nixies," "idiot marks," and "prematures."

Circulation, along with editorial and advertising, is one of the three equally important legs of a magazine's three-legged stool. Because of (1) the nature of circulation, (2) the types of people who are in charge of it, and (3) its history in many companies, it gets much shorter shrift in most magazine operations than either editorial or advertising. Very rarely has a circulation director become the publisher of a magazine, and many editors and publishers really do not understand the circulation activity or its importance.

Circulation consists of acquiring, communicating with, and renewing readers for a magazine. These readers do not appear suddenly en masse, but must be attracted from many different sources in a great many different ways. Since there are, literally, thousands—or millions—of readers for any one magazine, very detailed records are needed. Success, contrasted with the excitement that a major editorial article or the sale of a 12-time advertising schedule generates, often comes from an increase in the response to a mailing from 2.4% to 2.5%.

The good circulation director must possess three very different qualities:

1. Creativity in developing ways of reaching and attracting readers. Even if he cannot write copy or do design work himself, he must be creative enough to recognize what works best.

2. An understanding of statistics. This is a mass business where small differences in returns, cancellations, bad debts, and renewals can make the difference between success and failure.

3. The ability to deal with infinite detail. There are thousands of orders, many low-paid clerks, computers that don't always work—and lots of other details that just cannot (and do not) go right all the time.

Nature of Magazines versus Other Products

A magazine is *not* just a commodity. It is a unique product delivered serially to readers who are intensely interested in its subject matter. It is not, on the other hand, a sacred literary event. After the magazine has been printed and bound, it is a consumer product just like a bar of soap, and should be sold as such. Its advantage is that it is much more exciting than soap. Its disadvantage is that it has a very short shelf life, but so do eggs and many other products.

Types of Circulation

Paid Circulation

Someone has bought either a single copy or a subscription. The magazine has received income—and this proves to advertisers that someone thought enough of the magazine to pay for it—what better indication that he truly wanted it?

Almost all consumer magazines—and many business magazines—have paid circulation. For those with no, or very little, advertising, it's the only way they can make a profit. For those that depend on advertising, most advertisers expect paid circulation primarily as proof that the recipients really want the magazine.

Controlled Circulation

The term "controlled" is, of course, a euphemism for free. The word "controlled" was coined many years ago by publishers of business magazines to indicate that copies went only to those having certain job classifications that advertisers wanted—and to no one else. In most cases, these magazines also develop some other kind of evidence that the recipient wants to receive it, even though he did not pay for it.

Most business magazines today depend on controlled circulation, based on the concept that the magazine reaches all the people who have a major buying influence in a certain business field. Some other business magazines continue to depend on paid circulation. (Interestingly, the advertising and marketing area is one in which paid circulation is still strong—note *Advertising Age, Ad Week,* and some of the other leading magazines.)

HISTORY

Acceptance of the concept of controlled circulation for business magazines was reached only after some very bitter fights among the major publishers. There were actually two associations of business publishers, one for paid, the other controlled, that took potshots at each other for many years. It was only after McGraw-Hill, then the largest business publisher and a strong advocate for paid circulation, adopted controlled circulation for some of its magazines in the 1960s that peace came about and the associations merged into the present ABM.

Some consumer magazines depend only on controlled circulation, such as the airline inflight magazines. (The readership of these magazines is apparent to advertisers.) Others include those sent to mothers of new babies, the alternative weeklies in many cities, as well as many others.

A few consumer magazines supplement their paid circulation with a certain amount of controlled circulation. This includes: (1) Copies that are put in physicians' waiting rooms and other public places where multiple additional readership may take place, (2) copies in hotel rooms or on airplanes, and (3) copies purchased in bulk and sent by various organizations to lists of people they are interested in.

Amount of Circulation

Rate Base

Since ad rates are usually based on the amount of circulation a magazine has (expressed as CPM or cost per thousand), a number of the consumer magazines in highly competitive fields guarantee (or state) a rate base of at least so much circulation for advertisers. Usually if this rate base is not achieved, a pro rata reduction is made in the ad rate—or some other accommodation is made, such as running another ad free. In many cases it is important that the rate base be reached for each issue, although usually it is stated as an average for the period.

In the case of the store-sold magazines, such as *Family Circle* and *Woman's Day,* where the amount of circulation varies considerably by the time of year, different rates are charged and different rate bases are offered seasonally.

In recent periods, with the changes that have taken place in the singl-copy sales area and the problems the direct mail circulation agencies have been having with their sweepstakes offerings, the number of publishers willing to offer rate bases has declined somewhat.

NATURAL CIRCULATION LEVEL

Every magazine, consumer or business, has a level of circulation that we call "natural"—meaning those readers who are most interested in the subject-matter and who can be reached without undue strain or expense. This level will, of course, change as peoples' interest in the subject matter changes. The precise point of what is natural is difficult to define, except as shown by the cost of obtaining—and renewing—circulation.

Theoretically, at least, a magazine at, or somewhat below, its natural circulation level will be able to command the largest number of ad pages at the highest rate, although many publishers still try mightily to offer circulation far above the natural level.

HISTORY

The validity of this concept was amply proven back in the 1960s when *Life, Look,* and the *Saturday Evening Post,* among others, tried to outdo TV in the number of readers they could produce. They spent so much money acquiring circulation that, in the end, their losses put them out of business (or, in the case of the *Post,* into a completely different role).

The temptation still exists for publishers to push circulation to the highest level possible in order to get a higher ad rate—as well as to show more circulation than its direct competitors. This leads—and I am sure will continue to lead—to tension between the advertising people and those in editorial and circulation. Advertising tries to get the editors to change the product so that it interests more readers and to get circulators to dig up more happy readers using who knows what methods. It often also leads to the schizophrenia of ad people trying to sell a magazine and an audience as they would like it to be—but one that really does not exist.

As mentioned often in this book, getting above the natural circulation level—or not recognizing that that level may have declined—is one of the surest ways to kill a magazine.

Single-Copy Sales

THE SYSTEM

When most people think of magazines, I imagine that they instinctively have in mind newsstands (or, more properly, supermarkets and other outlets that actually handle the bulk of these sales). The system for distributing and selling most single copies is a huge and complex business that is discussed in more detail in chapter 47, "The Confusing Single-Copy Sales Business."

It is a very wasteful distribution method since more than half the copies rather than being sold to readers are shredded and sold as waste paper. This same system also handles the sales of mass-market paperback books.

Several different types of magazines are found on newsstands:

- Major consumer magazines that derive most of their circulation through single-copy sales, such as *Family Circle, Woman's Day, Cosmopolitan,* and *Playboy.* There are now only some 13 magazines that sell 500,000 or more copies this way.
- Major consumer magazines for which newsstand sales are an important source for selling copies although they have even more sales through subscriptions, such as *Time, Sports Illustrated,* and *Better Homes and Gardens.* The newsstand also acts a good sampling device for getting subscriptions.

- Consumer magazines aimed almost entirely at newsstand buyers with very little or no subscription circulation or advertising such as *Family Circle's Home Crafts, Hustler, Baseball Digest,* and *Celebrity Magazine.*
- Annuals and one-shots (specials), of which there seem to be an endless supply.
- Comics and puzzle magazines.
- Many other consumer magazines that are placed in these outlets primarily for sampling by the public and to be seen by prospective advertisers.
- A handful of business magazines in a few fields such as advertising and entertainment in the cities where these activities are centered.

Single-Copy Sales—Direct

Some specialized consumer magazines have considerable sales through retailers that serve their readers—for instance, *Rolling Stone* in music stores, golf magazines in golf shops, pet magazines in veterinarian offices.

Magazines should enter into direct sales of this kind only after careful planning. The business of contacting retailers, arranging and policing displays, agreeing on pricing and the amount to be remitted to the publisher, and collecting can involve a great deal of time for the publisher's staff. Often the task can be simplified by selling the copies directly to the retailers without the option of the publisher accepting unsold copy returns, with the retailer keeping 50% or so of the cover price, rather than a much smaller amount if the publisher were to accept returns.

WARNING

More than one publisher has worked very hard to develop direct distribution, only to find that collecting from small retailers is difficult if not impossible. Better to use some system of up-front payment.

Subscriptions

For most consumer magazines—and for those business magazines that have paid circulation—the emphasis is on subscriptions. This simple statement opens a Pandora's box of further discussion.

There is no single way of getting and keeping subscribers. The good circulation director gathers subscribers bit by bit from many different sources, each with its own characteristics. It is a very imaginative activity that involves extreme creativity, the handling of many thousands of customers, weighing costs and pricing to develop the amount of circulation producing the optimum financial results, and the melding of all this to produce a relatively consistent number of readers for each issue. In doing this, the circulation director will do a great deal of testing of various copy approaches, prices, timing, and almost everything else.

The circulation director must:

- Obtain new subscriptions directly by the publisher in a number of different ways
- Obtain new subscriptions through various independent agents
- Get as many of these subscribers to renew at the most favorable rates. These are all discussed in chapter 43, "Ways to Get and Keep Subscribers."
- Fulfill these subscriptions. This involves receiving them, collecting for them, changing their addresses, renewing them, answering subscribers' complaints, and making sure the magazines are addressed correctly when they are sent out. See chapter 44, "Fulfillment: My Good Customer J002684RO6JIBD23C."

WARNING

The subscription acquisition game requires constant pressure to get new subscriptions. Consider an average consumer magazine (if there is such a thing). Suppose you buy 1,000 new subscriptions (the word "buy" is used advisedly, because that is really what you do). Renewal of these will be at about the percentages shown below.

Initial subscriptions 1,000			
Conversion (first renewal 40%)		400 remaining after a year	
Second renewal	60%	240	2 years
Third renewal	65%	156	3
Fourth renewal	70%	109	4

You are in a never-ending round of buying new subscriptions just to stay even. And, if your circulation is above its natural level, the renewal history gets even worse.

Controlled Circulation—Business Magazines

Business magazines—and some consumer magazines—carefully develop lists of people serving the target field being covered who would be of most interest to potential advertisers. These are specific people doing specific jobs in companies that buy the products used in the field. They "qualify" to receive the magazine.

In order to further qualify these people—and to quantify the influence they might have in the purchasing process within their companies—the publisher also tries to get them to "request" the magazine individually, just as paid circulation magazines try to get people to subscribe. The more who are qualified—and request the magazine—the greater the value to the advertisers. Of course, the more recent the qualification and the request, the better.

This circulation is usually supplemented with names from lists of people who seemingly have the qualified titles, but who may not have requested a subscription. The idea is to be able to claim complete coverage of a particular field.

All this is audited by ABC and BPA in much the same way paid circulation is audited.

List Rental

Most magazines rent their subscription lists to other direct mailers. These lists usually can command relatively high prices because they consist of people who not only have evidenced interest in a specific subject, but who also have either paid for their subscriptions or have indicated they want to receive a controlled circulation magazine.

The list rental business for a magazine can provide a pleasant but not enormous profit at very little cost and with very little trouble. Like everything else, the business is more complex than it might seem at first because buyers will first want to test portions before renting the entire list, or may want to rent only what are known as "hot names" (those that have subscribed during only the past three months, or some other such selection). Almost all publishers have list brokers handle the rental for them in return for a commission.

In recent years, some publishers have worked to turn their simple subscriber lists into databases containing a great deal more information. These can be used in many ways by the publishers—and are sources of considerable further income from advertisers and through rentals as discussed in chapter 62, "Database Marketing."

Circulation Department Functions

The circulation department is in charge of obtaining circulation of various kinds; handling the subscribers in many ways; collecting single-copy and subscription revenues; keeping records of all kinds, including those for subscribers; planning the methods of obtaining and renewing subscribers; and handling everything else having to do with this area.

Often in multipublication houses, the circulation function is performed by a central department serving all the magazines because of the similarity of the operations performed for the different magazines. This department can be staffed with specialists in direct mail, single copies, subscription agents, fulfillment houses, and the other areas of circulation.

There is one great disadvantage to this kind of setup: None of these people has as his prime function the circulation of any one specific magazine, and a magazine works best when a small group of people dedicated to it in the three essential areas of editorial, circulation, and advertising are working closely together, with the success of that single magazine foremost in their minds.

Where there is a centralized circulation department, it is wise for each magazine to have its own circulation director, independent of that department, with the ability to utilize the department's services as he would with any other outside supplier (although not all multiple publishers follow this practice).

The Circulation Staff

- CIRCULATION DIRECTOR. Directs and coordinates circulation marketing efforts and all record keeping concerning circulation, including the fulfillment of subscriptions, to ensure maximum prof-

Figure 40.1. Circulation Department Organization

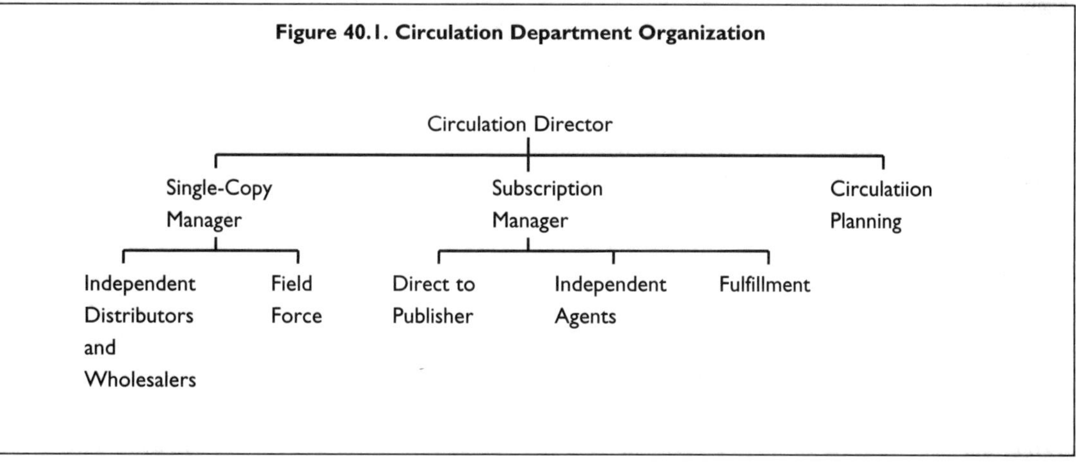

itability. He is directly responsible for budgeting and analysis of single-copy and subscription programs, list rentals, and database planning and maintenance.

- SINGLE-COPY MANAGER. In charge of all single-copy sales; relations with the national distributor, wholesalers, and retailers connected with the system; as well as any direct single-copy distribution by the publisher. If the magazine has its own single-copy field force (which a few major magazines use in order to supplement the field forces provided by the national distributors and wholesalers), it would report here.

- SUBSCRIPTION MANAGER. In charge of getting and renewing subscriptions using all desirable means including direct mail and other direct-to-the publisher methods, as well as the various subscription agents. If the magazine has specialists in direct mail, subscription agents, or telephone marketing, they would report here.

- PLANNING MANAGER. In charge of developing and analyzing results as well as projecting future operations, usually using a computerized magazine model.

- FULFILLMENT MANAGER. In charge of subscription fulfillment and relations with readers, whether performed within the company or by an outside organization.

Magazine Pricing—Single Copies

For those magazines that sell well on the newsstand, the cover price is arrived at as the result of careful testing of the effect price changes have on the sale. In some cases, special issues are priced higher than the regular issues.

For most other magazines, where the single-copy price may not affect the sale of copies as much, the price for single copies is arrived at empirically. Very often it is developed so that the subscription price is a bargain. *Dog Fancy* is typical in that it can advertise to subscribers that they are paying just 54% of the single-copy price. The single-copy price is $3.99, or $47.88 for 12 issues. Listed subscription price is $27.87—just 58 percent of the single-copy price. Most magazines offer further discounts for subscriptions and the difference becomes even larger.

CARDINAL RULE

Every magazine, even those that are circulated on a controlled basis, should have a price on the cover—the higher you can realistically make it, the better! Otherwise you are putting yourself in the same class as a catalog or any other throwaway.

Magazine Pricing—Subscriptions

The pricing of subscriptions is a sort of never-never land. Here are some of the many different prices that were charged by two magazines recently:

	Time		People	
	Issues/ Price	Per Issue	Issues Price	Per Issue
Single cCopy		$3.50		$2.99
Regular subscription	54/$69.92	1.30	52/$103.38	1.99
PCH Offer*	18/$7.92	.44	20/$35.80	1.79
PCH Offer*	26/$19.24	.74	24/$47.76	1.99
Professional	54/$39.97	.74	52/$51.74	1.00

*Includes postage and handling

There were also different prices charged on insert cards, renewals, and other sources. These two magazines are both published by Time-Warner, which has a very sophisticated circulation operation. The various prices were undoubtedly developed after careful testing.

It appears from these prices that *Time* magazine, which is in a very competitive field with *Newsweek* and *U.S. News & World Report,* is very close to, or perhaps above, its natural circulation level and seems to be reaching for those last few readers. *People,* on the other hand, is primarily a newsstand magazine and does not have the same kind of direct competition, so its subscription prices can remain relatively high.

Note that the direct mail agencies normally have as part of their agreements that they can offer the lowest price available.

It is normal practice to upgrade the price of subscriptions with each renewal, aiming eventually to reach the "regular" price. This sometimes is done in two or more steps. It is an interesting business where your best customers, those who renew most, are given the opportunity to pay more, the longer they stay with you.

Testing

Testing is a way of life in the circulation business for both consumer and business magazines. You are dealing with such large numbers and expenses in making subscription efforts or single-copy sales that you must test before going all out with what may be very expensive roll-outs nationally.

It is also a very statistical business, where differences of tenths of percents mean either success or failure.

Use of Sophisticated Computerized Magazine Models

Magazine publishing is an unusual business in that it has several revenue and expense streams all involved with a single product. In order to understand the economics of the business—and to balance the results of these various streams—computerized models of a magazine are used by virtually every magazine today in doing its planning. "What if" games have become a way of life in most publishing companies.

The most complex part of the model has to do with the circulation area because there are so many different sources, income streams, and expense items. In many companies, the circulation people do the modeling of their activities and then meld their models with the other operations of the magazine since they are mutually dependent.

Modeling is discussed in more detail in chapter 57, "Use of Computer Models."

Subscription Fulfillment

Fulfillment involves all the subscription record-keeping activities—receiving and recording orders, handling billing and collections, changing addresses, answering queries (usually and pleasantly called in the field, "complaints"), and developing statistics.

Today most magazines farm their fulfillment out to independent service bureaus, even though there are a number of very sophisticated computerized systems available that publishers could use. It is usually done outside primarily because it is an operation that is foreign to the basic functions of a magazine, just like printing. It can normally be done better and cheaper by outsiders.

The negative of this is, of course, that you lose some control over the handling of your most precious customers—your readers. Many publishers of higher-priced periodicals with relatively small circulations have found it better to do their fulfillment in-house, where customers can be handled individually. See chapter 44, "My Good Customer J002684RO6JIBD23C," and chapter 45, "Outsourcing Subscription Fulfillment."

Use of Outsiders in Circulation

There is an almost endless list of outside people and organizations that are used in the complex circulation area. In addition to firms that perform fulfillment, there are some that will take over the entire circulation acquisition operation. This can be particularly helpful for a new magazine that needs the skills of experienced people.

Among the other outsiders are:

- Single-copy consultants
- Single-copy field representatives in various parts of the country
- Subscription consultants
- Direct mail consultants and specialists of various kinds, such as copywriters
- List brokers
- Mail monitoring services
- Sellers of foreign copies and subscriptions

Control of Costs

The income and costs of circulation come in bits and pieces (some quite large) from many sources. Control and understanding of each of these is essential. The study of detailed computerized information and the magazine models mentioned above are invaluable in keeping up-to-date about these.

This is a complex subject—details can be found in the chapters on subscriptions (43 and 46) and on single-copy sales (47 and 48).

CHAPTER 41

Current Circulation Situation Confronting the Major Consumer Magazines

MANY OF THE major consumer magazines have pushed their circulations up about as far as they can go in an effort to develop the highest ad rates as well as to be the leaders in their fields. It is very questionable whether they can maintain the levels they have reached.

Three problems that have arisen in recent years have made the acquisition of circulation both difficult and expensive:

1. SINGLE-COPY SALES. The system has changed considerably in recent years, with the major retailers taking control (see chapter 47, "The Confusing Single-Copy Sales Business"). This has resulted in a contraction in the number of wholesalers from some 500 to about 60 (with just four handling 90% of the business). Retailers, rather than the publishers or wholesalers, now take the lead in deciding which magazines are carried and in the financial arrangements. In the long run this may be very beneficial because the old system was unwieldy and inefficient in many ways.

In the short run, however, for many magazines, particularly those with the most sales, this has brought about a large reduction in the number of copies sold. While the publishers, the remaining wholesalers, and the retailers have been working to develop better methods, it will take considerable time for these to be agreed upon and put into place in this huge and complex operation.

2. SUBSCRIPTIONS DERIVED FROM DIRECT MAIL AGENTS. Many of the largest magazines have depended on the direct mail agencies, operating primarily with a sweepstakes approach, for large numbers of subscriptions. The major agencies, PCH and AFP, have come under considerable well-publicized pressure from local, state, and federal authorities to make sure their efforts are honest and not confusing to the public.

While the agents and the publishers are quite willing to make changes to avoid misunderstandings, this whole brouhaha has resulted in very sharp declines in the number of subscriptions that can be delivered by these agents—as well as a major reduction in the amount of the subscription price that they are able to remit to the publisher. While this remittance was always a small percentage of the price, averaging about 15%, it is now closer to zero.

3. SUBSCRIPTION FIELD AGENTS. To try to make up for the losses in single-copy sales and direct mail agent subscriptions, publishers have been pushing harder to sell subscriptions through other sources. One method, which can develop many subscriptions in a relatively short time, involves field selling agents who sell subscriptions either door-to-door or on the telephone. They operate in two ways—as cash field or paid during service agents (see chapter 43, "Ways to Get and Keep Subscribers"). The remit to publishers from these subscriptions is generally quite small.

These agents, most of which are relatively small and scattered around the country, have always been difficult to control. They frequently present subscriptions that were not ordered by the subscribers, and sometimes they are harassed by local authorities and Better Business Bureaus—often with good reason. Many years ago the MPA had a committee to control them (the XYZ committee), but it has always been difficult.

Many publishers have used these agents for many years in a relatively small way to meet their advertising rate bases. With the present shortfalls in both single copies and in subscriptions from the direct mail agents, pressure has been exerted to obtain more subscriptions through these field agents.

Recently some well-publicized problems have arisen in this area too, which will make it difficult for them to continue to produce additional subscriptions.

The result of these three problems has been that many magazines are having a hard time holding their circulation levels. A number have reduced their advertising rate bases—and the chances are that more will do this.

Adding to the changes that have been taking place in the circulation world for consumer magazines, as of this writing, the ABC and the BPA have just abandoned the 50% rule (subscriptions must be sold at 50% of the published price in order to be counted as paid circulation). This was originally instituted because the Postal Service would give reduced prices for carrying subscription copies only if they had been sold for 50% of the published price, but this no longer obtains.

This is a major change in the circulation picture. No one at this point is sure what effect this change will have, if any, although opinions of all kinds are being bandied about.

The Internet to the Rescue?

Like the cavalry, the Internet may have come along just in the nick of time. Not only can it be the source of both new and renewal subscriptions, but the use of e-mail can also reduce costs considerably. The magazines covering the computer, Internet, and allied fields have had good success, for obvious reasons, selling and collecting for both new and renewal subscriptions on the Net.

Time-Warner has already announced that it has obtained millions of new subscriptions over the Web for its many magazines and expects to increase this as time goes on. Many other magazines have begun efforts using the Web. Results have been slow so far, but in the long run, this may become a major subscription source. It is discussed further in chapter 43, "Ways to Get and Keep Subscribers."

CHAPTER 42

Circulation Audit Organizations

HISTORY

The concept of having independent audits of circulation arose early in the twentieth century, primarily in connection with newspapers, when the ABC was established. The BPA was established after WW II to audit controlled circulation business magazines. (ABC at that time would only handle paid circulation.) Other recognized audit firms include VAC and CAC, while some publishers have their circulation audited by accounting firms.

THE TWO MAJOR accepted circulation audit organizations, ABC and BPA, are tripartite owned—by representatives of advertisers, advertising agencies, and publishers. Traditionally their services were based on auditing the circulations of print publications—newspapers, consumer magazines, and business magazines. For many years that was all they audited. Today both organizations audit controlled circulation and also have taken on the auditing of Internet hits, trade show attendance, and other kinds of audience research that is accepted by advertisers and agencies. The areas that they serve are expected to continue to expand as requirements change.

The agencies' audit procedures are similar to those used by financial auditing organizations and they are given free access to publishers' records in order to do this.

Circulation results are reported by the publishers in "pink sheets" that are widely circulated in the ad community twice a year. Actual audits are performed annually and differences from the previously published results are then circulated. Material changes from the pink sheets are, of course, an indication to advertisers of inadequate records, either intentional or inadvertent.

Over the years, strict definitions have been developed of exactly what is included in the various categories, often after lengthy arguments among competing publishers. Some of the definitions leave a reader with less than the complete information he needs to analyze the circulation strength of a magazine. It is only recently, for example, that ABC has allowed the reporting of renewal rates by those magazines that feel this is important information—but it still is not required for all magazines.

Imperfect though the data may be, it is far superior to anything else available and, for the major consumer and business magazines, is the foundation for advertisers' decision making (although other types of research are also depended on). It is also far superior to any research developed by any other media.

While many business magazines have paid circulation, the great majority use controlled (free) circulation. Business advertisers are most interested in knowing that the magazines reach all the people who can influence the purchase of their products in the fields they serve. While payment for a subscription would indicate that the recipient wants to receive a magazine, the relatively small cost of a subscription for most businesses is deemed to be no more indicative of interest than a request by the recipient that he is interested in receiving the magazine.

For this reason, audits of most business magazines consist of recent requests to receive the magazine. Audited results normally segregate this requested circulation from that which is based only on job titles, association lists, and other such material—and the recency of the requests is indicated.

Publishers with controlled circulation normally qualify readers in much the same way they would ask for paid subscriptions, through mail and other direct means.

CHAPTER 43

Ways to Get and Keep Subscribers

THE ACQUISITION AND renewal of subscriptions involves some of the most sophisticated selling methods in all of business. Books have been written about different parts of it.

This is simply an introduction to the subject to give you a background about the many different sources that can be used and a sampling of the thinking that goes into the process.

Subscriptions are basically obtained in two ways—direct to the publisher and through agents of various kinds.

Direct to the Publisher

DIRECT MAIL

Direct mail is by far the largest source of new subscriptions. This is not surprising because:

- Lists of just about everyone are available in many different forms. In recent years many of these lists have been enhanced to make them more useful—see chapter 62, "Database Marketing."
- Through direct mail you can pinpoint people who should be interested in the magazine who have not only the demographic but also the psychographic characteristics you may be looking for.
- Results are statistically predictable. Even relatively small tests give sound indications of what major mailings will bring.
- The public has accepted direct mail as a means of selling lots of goods. That same public has also been trained to expect magazine offers and is accustomed to buying magazines this way.
- The level of sophistication in the use of direct mail is very high. The three essentials of a direct mail piece—the offer, the list used, and the copy approach—have been finely honed.
- "Merge purge"—the practice of merging all the lists made in a major mailing—eliminates duplicate names, reducing the number of pieces sent. Overlaying the lists used with geographic and demographic research can also help pinpoint the most likely buyers.
- Mailing only to certain names after the use of regression analysis is often used.
- "Hot lines"—mailing to people entered on lists in the last three months or so rather than entire lists—are common. The newer the names, the better the response.
- Computer letters, sweepstakes, tokens, and all sorts of other devices are used to increase response.

But there are—and always will be—some inherent weaknesses in direct mail:

- It is expensive—and it becomes more so as costs, particularly of the Postal Service, inevitably rise.
- There are some good prospective subscribers who do not ever buy by mail.
- As with any selling method, when you have reached a certain level of saturation, the cost of acquiring more orders goes up very sharply.
- Only certain periods of the year work well for direct mail. This restricts the times when it can be used and results in peaks and valleys of cash requirements. See chapter 22, "Testing a New Magazine through Direct Mail."
- Some magazines lend themselves better to other selling methods.

- Outside events such as elections, hurricanes, and snowstorms can negate the best-laid plans of the smartest publisher.
- Postal delivery can be erratic both in timing and performance.

The Internet

One of the great benefits of the Web for magazines should be in the acquisition and renewal of subscriptions because:

- Every mailing by a publisher involves printing and postage, as does every response, while correspondence on the Net costs little for either party.
- Most payments on the Net are made through credit cards, eliminating costly collection efforts by publishers and mailing of checks by subscribers.
- Since correspondence is almost instantaneous, delays in the start of subscriptions should be substantially reduced. The familiar "please wait four to six weeks for delivery" should be a thing of the past.
- "Complaint mail" will be reduced, with a resultant cost saving.
- All of this should result in a much reduced cancellation percentage.

Most magazines are just in the testing phase of handling subscriptions that way. Those in the Web or computer businesses, of course, are wedded to e-mail and have had very long and good experience with it.

My informal experience, unfortunately, in looking at renewal notices, insert cards, and the like, for most consumer magazines indicates that only a few so far seem to be trying very hard to take advantage of what can be done on-line. Only a handful try to get people's e-mail addresses. Part of this may be because the publishers' Web sites are usually in the hands of the editorial people—and little shrift has been given to the needs of circulation.

The cost of sending direct mail for new subscriptions is somewhere in the $400–500 range per thousand, and it is rising. E-mail is only $50–80. If it can be made to work on only a portion of the new subscriptions, it is well worth the trouble. Good e-mail lists, of course, are not as available—and usually are quite expensive.

In using e-mail for subscriptions, in addition to the normal tips on designing direct mail, keep in mind the following:

- E-mail that looks like spam is unwanted.
- Don't forget to emphasize privacy.
- Give the prospective customer a compelling reason to give you an e-mail address.
- Ask permission to contact by e-mail and to share names with other marketers.
- Keep in constant touch because e-mail addresses change frequently.

Insert Cards in the Magazine

These come in many different forms, from simple bind-ins to blow-ins and gift orders. Most publishers do not confine their inserts to just a couple of cards per issue, but keep adding cards as long as the number of responses increases. The cards generally work in both subscription and newsstand copies.

You may wonder why they use those annoying blow-ins. Simple—when they fall out, the reader has to do something with them—and the response increases.

Insert cards are a good and inexpensive source for getting subscriptions. They are very easy for readers to use, the readers have already sampled the magazine, they take advantage of pass-along readership, and, since magazines have a long shelf life, may give results for a long period. The number of subscriptions obtained is limited, however, generally somewhere around 1% of the subscription copies, and about twice that for single copies.

Exchange Advertising

These are free exchanges of space with other magazines. The only cost is that of running the other magazine's ad in your magazine. Its use is limited because there is only so much available space—and only so many magazines that you might want to exchange with.

In some cases, direct competitors will exchange space. This is not as wild an idea as it may seem, because in every study I have seen of direct competitors' circulation, there is always a surprisingly small amount of duplication.

The usual exchange is for ads in an equal number of copies in each magazine. A new magazine, of course, will not have as much circulation as an older one, so the deal is made for promises of space in the future.

Advertising in Other Print Media, Radio, and TV

Freestanding inserts in newspapers have been successful for some city magazines. TV, while expensive, has been effective for some of the news and other magazines. Radio is inexpensive. Cable networks with their focused programming should provide an added source for some of the special interest magazines.

Advertising at regular rates in other magazines rarely pays, nor does the insertion of magazines in catalogs.

Gift Subscriptions

Some magazines have been able to get as many as 25% of their subscriptions from gifts. These magazines apparently have a very unique hold on their readers.

Most magazines make efforts to obtain gifts—but only at Christmas. Those that have developed large numbers do not limit their efforts to that period, but try throughout the year on as many occasions as possible for people to send gifts.

Partnership Marketing

This is a relatively new approach whereby the publisher creates programs for a third-party customer who buys subscriptions, usually in bulk, and sends them to its own customers or prospects. Banks, insurance companies, and real estate companies are typical prospects for these programs. To date, the subscription is sold for at least half the regular price (to satisfy the former ABC requirements) plus a small marketing fee for binding in the partner's message. It is unclear what effect the elimination of the 50% rule by the audit organizations will have.

The publisher gets subscriptions at considerably lower cost than many other methods and can target the readers the partner wants. This may also extend the magazine's reach to population segments in which it may be underrepresented. And it also may lead to incremental ad tie-in sales opportunities.

The partner gets a cost-effective vehicle for delivering a message that can be personalized by announcing the gift to the recipient.

Arranging these partnerships, of course, involves a new kind of selling for the circulation people.

Catalog Partners

A somewhat similar approach has been found effective in partnership with catalog companies that are already advertisers. The catalogers use a subscription offer at an introductory rate to close the sale with their customers, and the subscription is added to the order. From the magazine's standpoint, there is no promotion, cancellation, or collection expense.

Telephone

In some instances telemarketing has worked very well for selling new subscriptions. Years ago Norman Cousins made a very personal pitch (recorded of course) for *The Saturday Review* that was quite effective in selling three-year subscriptions for $25. Today we all get so many calls that they are like spam on the Web—a terrible nuisance—so telemarketing for magazines is pretty much confined to renewals, where the response is still quite good.

White Mail

White mail simply refers to mail where the source cannot be tracked—the term grew up because it referred to "Aunt Minnie writing a letter to the editor" to subscribe, in contrast to most subscription orders that come in on subscription forms of one kind or another. They are always nice to get—but there are rarely many.

Stuffers in Packages

These can be quite effective at very low cost, depending on the field the magazine serves. Stuffers are normally in department store billings, in flour bags, in shoe boxes, in frequent flyer mailings, and the like. The sources are limited only by the creativity of the circulation people. In some cases the company doing the stuffing gets a portion of the subscription price. Sometimes you simply pay them a fee. Most publishers try to find ways to get their advertisers to join in these subscription efforts through using their lists or including their products as premiums, etc.

So-called "take-ones" (subscription blanks) are often placed in airports, retail stores, boxes on street corners, and other such places. They are inexpensive and produce a limited number of subscriptions.

PRICING

The pricing of subscriptions is both an art and a science.

As with everything having to do with subscriptions, the prices charged for different types of efforts are the result of careful testing of both the response and the pay-up. Most prices are much lower than the cost of single copies—and usually are less than that for a "regular" subscription.

A new magazine, while it will undoubtedly follow most of the pricing structures of existing magazines, should take care to set its prices at the higher levels of magazines in its field. If it doesn't start out that way, it will quickly fall into the trap so many existing magazines are in—of selling only on price.

THE OFFER FOR A NEW SUBSCRIPTION

The offer in a new subscription solicitation is different from the price. It, too, is based on careful testing. As was discussed earlier (chapter 22, "Testing a Magazine through Direct Mail"), the offers vary from soft to hard—and everything in between.

PAY-UP

A subscription is not really a subscription until payment has been received. Soft offers invite readers to cancel if they are not completely satisfied after receiving one, two, or up to twelve copies. Generally a publisher will receive payment for soft offer subscriptions of less than 50%.

Payment for hard offers are higher than that, but still may be only about 70%. People have been educated to understand that, no matter what the offer was, you will not make a big affair of trying to collect $15 for a subscription if they want to cancel, so many treat a hard offer the same way as a soft offer.

The pay-up, of course, will vary with the nature of the original source—insert cards and gifts will be higher than cold mailings, for instance.

Subscription Agents

There are a seeming plethora of different types of agents that sell magazine subscriptions in many different ways. Remittance rates to the publisher vary with the circulation size of the magazine—and in some cases can go down to zero or below. The principal agents are given in the sections that follow.

DIRECT MAIL AGENTS

These have been, most notably, PCH and, until recently, AFP, and some smaller players. For a very long time direct mail agents have been a major source of subscriptions for many of the larger consumer magazines. A few years ago, the number of subscriptions that could be obtained started to decline—no one is quite sure why, but it seemed to coincide with the time when the agents increased the number of mailings and made major efforts to sell items other than magazines.

Recently, in addition, there have been a number of well-publicized legal cases about the so-called misleading advertising of the sweepstakes, as well as proposed congressional action defining exactly how the sweeps offers should be made. This has resulted in further declines in the number of subscriptions obtained. There has been great anguish in some publishing houses about how to replace the lower responses from this source, although they still attract a good number of new readers—and are well worth using.

These agents offer subscribers the lowest introductory prices used by the magazines. The remittance rate to the publishers has never been large and, because of the present troubles, has dropped from an average of about 14% to about 5%. Because of the reduced price approach, and the subscriber's loyalty to the agent rather than to the publishers, when renewal time comes, some are developed through the publisher's renewal series and others through the agent, again at a low remittance rate.

The advantages for the magazine in using these agents are:

- No upfront cost
- No collection cost
- Opportunity to mail in quantities a magazine could not afford
- Publisher can confine its own direct mail efforts to the best lists rather than going broadcast at enormous cost
- The readers select the magazines they want
- The subscribers are just as good for advertisers as those obtained directly by the publisher

School Plans

Operated by Reader's Digest and some others, these agents sell subscriptions for a long list of magazines through teachers (and their pupils). They are a good source for some magazines at a remittance rate somewhat higher than the direct mail agents (usually about 7%). The kids get prizes and the schools are given maps or other classroom equipment for their efforts.

College Agents

Several agents operate on campuses. Remit rates average about 19%.

Cash Field

These are primarily telephone operations (with some door-to-door) by crews or Mama/Poppa teams that travel to neighborhoods and sell groups of subscriptions to individual families. The average order has to be large and the subscription terms long (three years or more) because of the expense of the activity. Renewal rates, therefore, are terribly low.

Many advertisers do not feel that these are really good subscribers who want the magazines, but actually their demographics are just as good as those sold in any other way because the subscribers select the magazines they want from long lists.

This source can produce lots of subscriptions in a very short time when needed. The average remit to the publisher is about 12%.

As with other field operations, there is often harassment of the salespeople (sometimes deserved) by Better Business Bureaus and local authorities.

Paid during Service (PDS)

This is another field method, usually by telephone, that sells a long list of titles. In this case, the sale is made and then installments are paid over a year or so. The total contract must involve a large dollar amount for it to be worthwhile for the agent, so a number of different magazines are usually sold with quite long terms. Remit to the publisher averages about 8%.

Catalog Agents

There are a handful of agents that sell subscriptions as a service for libraries and other organizations that buy lots of different magazines. These are usually done through catalogs that list hundreds of magazines. The library normally pays full price for the subscriptions and the magazines pay a commission—20% or so—to the agent. A magazine may be able to increase this type of business by sending sample copies to libraries since they cannot be familiar with all the magazines that are available.

This is good business for publishers, but the number of subscriptions is limited. Renewals come through the agents without any effort by the publishers.

Waiting Room Agents

Some subscription agents have developed a service that sells groups of magazines to doctors, beauty parlors, and other places where multiple readership occurs. These subscriptions are useful for publishers because they add pass-a-long readership, increase the opportunity for insert card subscriptions, and offer a sampling device they could not get otherwise.

In-Flight Agents

Copies of popular consumer magazines are often put on airlines. Some of these are through a direct approach to the airlines, but more are handled by agents. The process involves having the airline buy the subscriptions so that it counts as paid for circulation audit purposes. The publisher buys a binder or pays the airline in some other way. The net result is a zero remit to the publisher. These subscriptions are obviously good for sampling, for insert card responses, and for developing multiple readership of copies.

The Internet

A number of organizations sell subscriptions on the Web to a great many magazines. The prices charged are in the same range as those of the direct mail agents, but the remit to the publisher is much higher, about 20%. Up to now, this source suffers from the fact that the buyer must look for the magazine, rather than the other way around.

There are also a number of unauthorized people selling subscriptions on the Web at prices they set without approval. This is an extension of the unauthorized type of sale that has been prevalent in the PDS and cash field areas for many years. Policing is difficult, but possible.

Cooperative Mailings and Card Decks

These joint mailings have included magazines to some extent, but so far at least, have been relatively minor players in the sale of subscriptions.

Prices, Offers, and Pay-ups for Agent-Sold Subscriptions

Price will, of course, vary for each source. Pay-ups will normally be substantially greater than for those sold directly. This helps in fattening up the number of subscribers, but the amount remitted to the publisher is so small that it is not significant.

On the other hand, a switch of subscriptions from direct mail agents to field agents results in a great increase in the average price by the subscriber because field agents normally sell them at full price—although the publisher does not get any more. This can be attractive for advertisers.

Other Ways to Get Subscriptions

Magazine publishers have been able to profit for a long time using the well-known and carefully honed methods of getting circulation that we have been discussing. Little real exploration has been made, however, in developing new sources of subscriptions because, until recently, it really didn't seem to be needed.

With the current major problems in three major areas of circulation—single-copy sales, direct mail subscription agencies, and field agencies, it is time that publishers start to seriously explore some other subscription acquisition methods.

Through the Major Sources of Retail Sales

Supermarkets, newsstands, and other retail outlets are logical places for selling subscriptions as well as single copies. By selling subscriptions, the retailers could be relieved, to some extent, of the handling problems of such a time-related product as magazines. Some other sales options include:

- Catalogs and catalog stores. Some attempts have been made to include one or two magazines in specialized catalogs, but I am not aware of any testing that has been made of including magazines in the major all-inclusive catalogs.
- Book stores. They are already catering to readers, and the larger stores devote considerable space to magazines.
- Greeting card stores. Magazines make great gifts and are priced well. It would be easy to put subscription cards in their slots.
- Book and record clubs. The direct mail agents are already selling records—how about vice-versa?
- Retail operations on the Internet. For instance, Amazon.com knows the interests its customers have—how about selling them subscriptions in those areas?
- Wouldn't it pay for the direct mail agents to expand their sweepstakes to the Net?
- Other specialized retailers. These could include special interest magazines in their offers.

Through the Major Delivery Organizations

- The Postal Service, which is already heavily involved in the magazine business
- Federal Express, UPS, and others
- Newspapers using their delivery organizations

Other Possible Sources

- Through Visa, Mastercard, other credit card organizations
- Through libraries to their members and users
- Use of off-sale copies from the single-copy system as sampling devices in various areas where people congregate, such as waiting rooms and hospitals

Renewals

It must be apparent from the data on the various sources of new subscriptions that the first subscription is rarely profitable after you take into account the cost of sending the magazine to the subscriber. In fact, in many cases, the publisher loses money even without considering that cost. Most publishers speak of a source as being profitable if the subscription income covers only its acquisition cost, even though the cost of sending the copies to subscribers—or at least part of it—logically should be considered as well.

Profits from subscriptions come only on their renewal. In the last analysis, the renewal rate indicates how well the editor has done in keeping readers happy, but the methods for obtaining renewals are also very important. Like the other parts of circulation, obtaining renewals has become a high art. All sorts of methods and lures are used in addition to simply sending out renewal notices in the mail.

Methods of Obtaining Renewals

It is normal to start sending renewal notices about five to seven months before the subscription expires. Publishers continue to send them as long as the amount they bring in is greater than the cost to obtain new subscriptions to replace them. The number of notices varies with the original source of the subscription. You will sometimes see as many as twelve, although the average is about eight or nine. For field-sold subscriptions, only one or two notices are sent—and some publishers don't send any because the renewal percentage is so low.

Most renewal notices are sent by direct mail, but some publishers attach renewal invitations to the magazines themselves, usually by hiding the cover under a huge renewal offer. And, for many, one of the final efforts is by telephone.

The percentage of cash received with renewals is much higher than for new subscriptions, but there are still many who will cancel or not pay up.

There are different ways of handling the pricing of renewals. Most publishers attempt to get the price up to the full price. This may be done in steps. For instance, if the original subscription was sold for $15.97, the first renewal may be at $17.97, the second at $19.97, and finally up to the full $24.

Conversions versus Renewals

The first renewal is called a conversion—and the record of these is kept in infinite detail by original source so that projections can be made of the conversion rates of future new subscriptions. Second and subsequent renewals are known simply as renewals, and these days careful records are also kept not only of the original source but also of every renewal by original source.

Advance Renewals

Publishers often try to get renewals many months before expiration with some sort of come-on, such as "Renew now before the price is increased." This effort gets cash in earlier than and many circulation people believe it also increases the total renewal response.

It also gives the publisher an opportunity to renew subscribers who were originally sold by agents—and who might otherwise renew through those agents at a much lower remit to the publisher.

Renewal at Birth (RAB)

You have just subscribed to a magazine. You have sent in your money, so you are our friend. Wouldn't you like to subscribe for two years instead of one? Sometimes this offer is made in the billing series even before you have paid. Cash is received earlier, the cost of renewing is avoided—and many believe the total renewal response is improved.

Continuous Service

Surprisingly, it has been only recently that publishers have begun seriously testing the concept of automatic renewals. Perhaps it has been because in the past they used to think of them as "till forbid"—and now have figured out the more customer-friendly approach of "continuous service."

Early reports indicate that they result in more than a 10% increase in response rates because you put the force of inertia on the side of the marketer. It also saves considerable expense in sending repeated renewal and collection notices.

The techniques for accomplishing this are still being tested using such approaches as credit cards for payment, avoiding RABs, not featuring it in promotion (but confining mentions to the order card), and not stepping up the price. It appears, so far, that it could go a long way to improving the renewal history at somewhat less cost than at present.

One of the Internet agents advertises that subscribers will be offered renewals, through its service, at the lowest price available. I have always wondered why the PCH and AFP have not offered a renewal service. It would seem so logical for them to act as the reader's agent to take care of all his magazine wants.

Renewal Rates

Every magazine is different, of course, but overall renewal rates for consumer magazines might come out something like this:

Conversions

Direct to publisher	
Direct mail	40%
Internet	Probably 30
Insert cards	45
Exchange ads	30
Other media	30
Gift	55
White mail	50
Stuffers	40
Agents	
Direct mail	20
Internet	20
School	25
Cash field	10
Paid during service	10
Catalog—Renew through agent	
Waiting room—Renew through agent	
In-flight—Renew through agent	

Note that these percentages represent the number who renew through the publisher's efforts, probably at a stepped-up price. The renewals of subscriptions sold by direct mail agents, which are renewed through the agents, is probably another 20%—but, of course, at a much lower remit.

Renewals

First renewal of a conversion	60%
Second renewal	65
Subsequent renewals	70

Who Is a Good Subscriber?

A puzzling question that just about every publisher would like to have the answer to—but I am not sure anyone does.

- Easy to obtain the first time?
- Renews at a high rate?
- Subscribes for three years rather than one year?
- Demographically attractive to advertisers?
- Gives lots of gift subscriptions?
- Pays up promptly?
- Buys lots of other products of the publisher?
- All of the above?
- Or what?

Even more valuable would be a formula for determining the lifetime value of your subscribers, bearing in mind all the ways in which you can earn profits from them.

CHAPTER 44

Fulfillment: My Good Customer J002684RO6JIBD23C

CONSIDER THE CONDITION of the potential subscriber way out there in some obscure ZIP code area in a Nielsen C or D county, or, if he's lucky, in an A or B.

He sends in some sort of card asking if you will accept him as a subscriber. Often he trustingly sends money, too.

Then he waits to see what will happen. He might even forget that he subscribed—it takes *that* long to get his first issue. Often his first contact is the return of his canceled check. Aha! You do love him after all.

But he had the misfortune to send in his order on the wrong day of your updating cycle—and the fulfillment operation is behind schedule anyway. And, if you don't need him to meet your circulation guarantee, you might start him next July when things are slow. He'll never know what happened. He may even think someone has sent him a gift when the magazine finally does arrive!

This sordid saga could go on in the same vein through virtually all the steps in most magazines' dealings with their subscribers.

The Abused Subscriber

Most publishers just don't think of subscribers as customers. But they are. And probably the most valuable ones they have. Consider the position of the subscriber:

- He doesn't know when his first copy will be sent.
- He doesn't know when his last copy will be sent.
- If something goes wrong, he doesn't know how to ask for a correction.
- His copies come with some weird hieroglyphics above and sometimes below his name and address.
- He is never sure he is paying the lowest possible price for his subscription. And, indeed, may not be.
- If he moves and tells the magazine, he has no way of knowing he was heard from unless, through some legerdemain, copies start arriving at the new place.
- If he asks for a correction, an enormous period elapses before he hears anything—and sometimes he never does. So he writes again and again.
- Sometimes he continues to receive issues after his subscription has expired. We are serving him in arrears, but he doesn't know that.
- He may have a subscription that won't expire for 20 years, but doesn't know that and continues to send in money. No one tells him.
- Sometimes you ask him to renew when he has just received his second issue.
- Often you ask him if he wants to renew before new higher rates are put into effect. But he is never sure what this means.
- Since he is a long-time loyal subscriber, he is allowed to pay more for his subscription than a new subscriber.
- If he pays promptly, he gets no benefit from that, but pays the same amount as those who wait three months.
- He wonders what other things you are doing with his name and address.
- If he lives in some undesirable (for advertisers) area, he may never be asked to subscribe.

My thesis is simple: subscribers are customers—and should be treated like customers. In fact, they are probably the most important customers you have.

Circulation As a Marketing Function

I have advocated for a long time that the circulation director be renamed marketing director. Fulfillment should not be a dirty word in either sex or magazines. And subscription fulfillment should be treated as a major part of the marketing function.

Let me first explain *why*—and then give some examples of *how*—this might be accomplished.

Subscribers are important for a number of reasons:

- They pay you money so that they can read your magazine—and they pay in advance. This helps your cash position.
- If they renew, they pay again and again—and the expense of obtaining that renewal is much less than that of obtaining a new subscription.
- They are a source of other subscriptions—gifts, bind-in cards used by readers other than the original subscriber, etc.
- They form the loyal readership that you work so hard to sell to advertisers.
- They are the source of sales of other items

Renewing Because of, Not in Spite Of

A magazine is a creative product that develops a dialog—a warmth, a real communication—between the editors and the readers. Why shouldn't this feeling be continued through all the communications with the readers? Sometimes it seems that people renew in spite of the material we send them.

The most costly parts of fulfillment are the entering of new subscriptions and answering "complaints." (Complaints in our lexicon, of course, include such innocent questions as "Why didn't I receive my copy?" and "Why didn't you change my address when I asked you to?") Increasing the renewal rate reduces the number of new subscriptions that must be entered. Helping the subscriber understand what is going on reduces complaints.

Each renewal notice and each collection effort costs money. Isn't it better to communicate constructively if you can increase both the percentage of replies and the speed of replies from the customer? You will probably send no more pieces than you do now—but they will be different ones at different times.

I have listed below a few "Why Don't We's" in handling our customers. These are designed to stimulate thinking of ways to develop a real relationship with subscribers.

Why Don't We

- Carry through the personality developed in the magazine in all correspondence with subscribers, rather than sounding like a group of accountants in our mailings.
- When someone first subscribes, tell him such things as:
  - We received your subscription.
  - We are delighted and welcome you to our magazine.
  - Here are some interesting things you will find in coming issues.
  - Your first issue will be sent out ____ and you will probably receive it____.
  - You may cancel at any time.
  - If you want to change your address, here is a form to make it easy.
  - If you have any questions, here is a form listing those that are most frequently asked.
  - If you want to order reprints, here is a form and a price list.
  - If you want to contact advertisers, here is a form you can use.
  - This is our list rental policy _________. We think you will be interested in the merchandise that those who rent our lists offer.
  - You are paid through_______, when your subscription will expire. We will be asking you if you want to renew about _____.
  - Here is the imprint of your mailing label with your name and address. Please be sure it is correct. The code lines are explained in the diagram.
- Offer to sell other magazines to subscribers as a service to them.
- Offer other very logical products as a service.
- Send the first issue of a subscription right away even if it must be done off the normal fulfillment line.
- Sell the product and not the price for both new and renewal subscriptions—or at least in addition to the price.
- Ask readers' opinions about the magazine every so often.

- Ask those who do not renew, why they didn't.
- Have a reduced price for prompt payment.
- Separate postage so that we can let the reader know how much of the price involves the Postal Service—and also be able to pass along the inevitable postal price increases.
- Stop selling at innumerable different prices.
- Try a continuous service method.

WARNING

This—almost word for word—was the major part of an article I wrote for *Folio* back in 1974. I am sorry to say that so little has changed that this same piece could be reprinted today.

Complaint mail—Yes, we still call any communication we receive from a subscriber by that label. If that doesn't exemplify the attitude publishers have about their customers, I don't know what does.

It is all part of the feeling publishers have that readers will put up with anything. The same attitude is sometimes shown on the editorial pages—see chapter 33, "The Editor as a Marketer."

Biggest Magazine Failure

Magazines show their obvious disregard of their readers best by that wonderful phrase "allow 3 to 4 weeks for your first issue." (The worst I have seen was from one of the Internet subscriber services: "Please allow 4–10 weeks from the time you place your order for your subscription to start or stop.")

Amazon.com would never tell me that. Everything is sent out at least by Priority Mail, if not by Federal Express, UPS, or Express Mail!

I can get a mattress delivered by truck within a day!

Dell will build a computer to my specs and get it to me in less than a week!

What on earth are you publishing people doing all that time?

Obviously not caring for me as a customer.

Of course you don't want to spend extra for sending a copy off-line. But perhaps it will be worth it in having a happier customer whose pay-up and renewal will be increased!

And I realize that you don't want to overprint an issue just to serve new subscribers (who you are not sure will appear), but you are quite willing to print three copies for every one you expect to sell on the newsstand—and you can predict the number of subscriptions much better than the newsstand sale. (How about sending some of those unsold newsstand copies to first- time subscribers rather than to the shredder?)

CHAPTER 45

Outsourcing Subscription Fulfillment

Consumer Magazines

ALMOST ALL consumer magazines have outsourced their subscription fulfillment to fulfillment houses—highly computerized large independent firms—which make a business of handling the millions of necessary transactions. Even the largest publishers have reached the conclusion that, while fulfillment is very important, it is an operation that is foreign to the rest of the publishing activities. Keeping up with the latest equipment and programming needs as well as hiring, training, and supervising the many employees required are more than they want to be involved with. They also have memories of the disasters in their own shops where umpteen thousand subscriptions were thrown away—or stuffed into a drawer—never to be seen again.

These days fulfillment operations are able to:

- Address magazines directly on the press, without using labels
- Develop a different magazine carrying different pages for each subscriber
- Comply with the Postal Service's requirements so that they pay the least possible postage for the best possible service
- Personalize just about anything that is sent to a subscriber
- Deliver statistical material derived from the entry of subscriptions and renewals directly to the computer models publishers use for their planning (without human intervention)

Unless there are very unusual circumstances, it would be foolish for a new consumer magazine to consider developing its own circulation fulfillment system, even though there are a number of fine programs available. It might make sense only if the circulation will be very small—and in a highly concentrated field where personalized hand-holding of each subscriber is vital.

CHOOSING A FULFILLMENT HOUSE

Choosing a fulfillment house that will cater to a magazine's size and nature, of course, is a delicate process. It is even more difficult than choosing a printer. After all, the fulfillment people are dealing with the most precious commodities you have—your faithful customers. If they are handled badly, they will blame you—just as you blame Tiffany's when they don't take care of your jewelry wants nicely.

You hire a fulfillment outfit basically because this kind of massive, but detailed, operation does not really fit in a publishing house. And you have heard many stories about other publishing companies where a few thousand subscriptions were thrown away, many readers were told just what was thought of them, or renewal notices were forgotten about. There are so many things that can go wrong in this kind of operation!

If you are new to the publishing business, you may not, however, have heard about some of the same kinds of disasters that have occurred in some of the largest fulfillment houses, more than one of which has gone out of business because of them (names withheld to protect the guilty).

Working with a fulfillment house, then, necessarily has to be an even closer partnership than that with your printer—see chapter 51, "Printing, Paper and Distribution."

The steps you go through in choosing one are mostly the same, but even more vital—the fulfillment people must understand the magazine business: how it works; its economics; the importance of subscriptions and keeping readers happy; and the needs of the publisher for sound and timely statistics about new subscriptions, renewals, prices, and everything else that has to go into the computer models used in planning.

Overseeing a Fulfillment House

No matter how closely your supplier is allied with you, when you have outsourced your subscription fulfillment, you may find that it is process oriented. It does not really understand the business you are in. Detailed instructions and close supervision are essential in order to have your customers treated as well as you would like them to be. It is also helpful to give them a glossary of the terms that are generally used in the field you are serving so that their telephone people can relate better to your customers when they have questions. In the end, you will really know how well they are handling your subscribers only by adopting such practices as:

- Seeding the subscriptions with tracking and decoy names and allowing some of these to expire
- Seeding all direct mail tests
- Making phone calls and writing to their customer service department, as if you are a reader
- Reviewing all subscriber correspondence

Most fulfillment houses these days do a workmanlike job, but it is hard for publishers to forget the many disasters that have occurred over the years. While most of these suppliers would also like to be involved in the development of databases—and other by-product businesses devoted to them—few publishers even now have enough confidence to turn this type of business over to them.

Use of the Internet

Publishers are just learning how the Internet can help make input into their computers easier, more accurately, and less costly by:

- Letting readers buy subscriptions—or get free trials—by inputting their own names and addresses
- Sending renewal notices, and receiving responses that can be entered into the records at virtually no cost, through e-mail
- Doing the same with reader inquiries (complaints)
- Allowing readers to view and change their own order information on-line
- Receiving payments through credit cards

Fulfillment for Business and Smaller Magazines

While a great many business and smaller magazines also outsource their fulfillment operations, it often makes more sense for them to do it in house than for consumer magazines because:

- Circulations are smaller.
- Considerably more information must be maintained about each reader, such as size of company, nature of company, and job title.
- Efforts may be made to sell trade shows and other products and services to the readers, and records of these are needed.
- There is an even greater need to be sure customers are well-handled because of the close relation of readers and advertisers.
- Database information about the different groups of readers can often be sold separately. (See chapter 62, "Database Marketing.")

CHAPTER 46

Subscription Source Evaluation

WARNING

This is a very complex subject. It is full of calculations, assumptions, results, numbers, etc. If you are not in a mood to concentrate, it is late in the day, or you have had too much to eat, try reading it some other time.

If you don't like this kind of stuff at any time, get a skilled editor to summarize it all for you.

As discussed in the last chapter, a magazine's circulation is made up of a lot of small numbers of readers derived from various sources. A paid circulation magazine can make it—or not make it—based on the skill with which it obtains that circulation. This calls for an understanding of just what the income and costs are for different subscriptions, depending on the price, method, and cost of sale; renewability; and lots of other things, as we will see.

Let's get a few things straight at the start:

1. Very few magazines make a profit from the sale of copies alone, whether they are single copies or subscriptions. Advertising, which is based on the existence of that circulation, is needed for most profitable operations. Having said that, the caveats are that many newsstand annuals and specials are profitable. Then there are those country-type magazines published by Roy Reiman in Milwaukee that do not carry advertising but are very profitable. A cheer for him and a few others.

2. The first subscription from a subscriber normally does not produce more income than the cost of obtaining that subscription, and very often the cost is substantially larger than the income received. A few sources produce more income than the acquisition cost—insert cards, gifts, and some others—but there are not enough of these to make for a profitable magazine.

3. If you add all the income received from a subscriber over the years (including, of course, all the renewals), usually, but not always, that will amount to more than the cost of first obtaining the subscription plus the cost of renewing it one or more times. Of course, only a minority renew once, let alone time after time.

Because of this, the sophisticated publisher makes very careful—and detailed—evaluations of the cost of obtaining and renewing subscriptions. This is absolutely necessary in order to avoid being badly misled about where he stands in total, as well as about which sources are most valuable.

To evaluate each source requires detailed calculations based on the various income and cost factors. To make it more difficult, a number of these items can vary considerably. The key things (but not the only things) you must keep track of include:

- For the initial subscriptions—and for each renewal
  - Orders received.
  - Number of those orders that are paid for. Many are cancelled—and in other cases payment is never made.
  - Number of issues to be served.
- Direct cost of acquisition for both new and renewal subscriptions including:
  - Selling materials—direct mail, advertising, postage, etc.

- Commissions to agents
- Response cards or envelopes
- Billing costs
- Issues of the magazine that are sent to those who ordered but later cancel or do not pay

The figures will, of course, be different for each magazine. The detailed description of the calculations needed are beyond the scope of this book—but the following examples of the income and costs resulting from these calculations for subscriptions obtained from different sources may give you an idea of the economics.

Direct to Publisher

Direct Mail

This is the largest source of subscriptions for most magazines. There are lists of everybody everywhere, so theoretically there is no limit to the number of subscriptions that can be obtained this way. Practically, however, as responses decline, activities must be curtailed.

The world of direct mail involves the use of a great many different lists; mailing at various times of the year; the use of different copy, price, and offer approaches; and a great deal of testing. Its practice has become a high art in many companies. Most publishers keep detailed records evaluating the results of each list and each mailing.

The figures shown below, of course, represent the results in a very simplified manner. So that you will not get mired in a raft of detailed calculations, I have included here just the basic assumptions and the financial results, but not the calculations used to reach these conclusions.

I have assumed a monthly magazine of standard size with issues of 100 pages each. I have also assumed subscriptions of a year with average costs for lists, mailing pieces, postage, and return postage. I have also added in as an acquisition cost the expenses of the copies delivered to those who do not pay, including postage and fulfillment—but none of the costs of the copies for a paid-up subscription. (This cost for nonpaid subscriptions can be sizable and is frequently omitted when people make calculations of profits from subscription efforts.)

First Subscription

There are five factors that can make a big difference in the overall profit or loss in obtaining the first subscription from a new subscriber.

Two of these—the quality of the mailing piece and the time of the mailing—are most important and must be kept in mind, but are impossible to include in these sample calculations.

The purpose here is to give you an idea of the effect of each of the other three important characteristics:

- Response rate
- Pay-up rate
- Price

Base Calculation

Let's start with these assumptions as a base for our calculations:

A monthly magazine of 100 pages per issue

Initial subscription sold by direct mail:

Price $15 for a year
Gross response rate 5%
Cancellations and nonpayment 40%
Net paid-up rate of 60%, or 3% of pieces mailed

Results:

Amount received for each paid subscription	$15.00
Total of all costs, except for copies sent to paid-up subscribers	$22.20
Net cash cost per subscription obtained	$(7.20) **A**
This means that to get 10,000 new paid subscribers would cost some	$72,000

(And that 5% response rate is by no means a low response.)

Renewal of subscriptions over four years:

At $18 per year.

Gross response rate	First year	40%
	Second year	60%
	Third year	65%
	Fourth year	70%

Cancellations and nonpayment of 10% for each renewal

Net response rate	First year	36%
	Second year	54%
	Third year	58.5%
	Fourth year	63%

Results from renewals:

Amount received from renewals per original subscription	$13.30
Total of all renewal costs, except for copies to paid-up subscribers	$4.10
Net income from renewals per original subscription	$9.20 **B**

Total new and renewal net per original subscription $2.00 over five years **A+B**. That means that you made $20,000 from those 10,000 new subs over the five-year period.

But, of the 10,000 subscriptions initially purchased, all you have left are:

After first renewal	3600
second	1940
third	1140
fourth	720

And those that didn't renew had to be replaced with new subscriptions.

Effects of Changes in Key Factors

Here we first show the effect of each change, and then total the result of all the positive changes, and then of all the negative changes, to give an idea of how great the profit-and-loss swings are from seemingly small differences.

Initial Subscription Purchased

Positive changes	*Better*	*Negative changes*	*Worse*
Price: Increase $3	$3.00	Decrease $3	$(3.00)
Response: Increase 1%	2.80	Decrease 1%	(4.20)
Pay-up: Increase 10%	3.40	Decrease 10%	(4.10)

As you can see, each factor has a large effect.

Increase all three	8.80 **C**	Decrease all three	(12.90) **D**
Total profit	$1.60 **A+C**	Total loss $(20.10)	**A+D**

Per subscription—it would cost $201,000 to obtain 10,000 subs, if all three items were negative.

Renewals—per original initial subscription purchased

Positive changes	*Better*	*Negative changes*	*Worse*
Price-Increase $3	$2.20	Decrease $3	$(2.20)
Response rate			
Increase 10% 1st renewal	2.60	Decrease 10%	(2.60)
Increase 5% later renewals	.70	Decrease 5%	(.60)
Increase all renewals 3%	.20	Decrease all	(2.80)
Increase pay-up rate 5%	1.30	Decrease 5%	(1.20)

Once again, each factor has a large effect.

Increase all three	8.10 **E**	Decrease all three	(5.00) **F**
Total profit	17.30 **B+E**	Profit	4.20 **B+F**

Total—new and renewal—

Best **A+B+C+E** $18.90 Profit: or $189,000 on 10,000 subs.

Worst **A+B+D+F** $(15.90) Loss: or $(159,000)

Subs remaining after five years	
Best:	1,390
Worst:	340

What you can learn from all these figures:

1. Seemingly small changes can have an extreme effect.
2. The subscription game is a constant one of getting new subscriptions to replace those that do not renew.
3. Price is an important factor, but no more so than response and pay-up rates.
4. More than anything else—you had better understand the economics of the subscription game, or you are dead.
5. It is very costly for any new magazine to build its circulation base because of the problem of replacing nonrenewals. But, after five years or so, you will have almost as many renewed subscriptions as new ones—and then you will be able to level out and reduce the annual expenses.
6. Because of this, when you start a new magazine, you should go out for subscriptions as fast as you can at the beginning so that you can reach that breakeven point sooner.
7. The situation for each magazine is very different. For a magazine that depends primarily on circulation for its income, it is essential to stick with those lists that will produce profits after just a few years of renewals, while a magazine that is heavy with advertising at good rates may be able to afford subscriptions that lose money for some time.
8. Computer modeling is essential in this business.

INSERT CARDS

These cards are, of course, put into both subscription and newsstand copies. Experience has shown that the more cards you use, the better chances of a response. It also has shown that blow-in cards are particularly effective.

Since the users of these cards have seen the magazine—and the cost of obtaining them is much smaller than through direct mail—this is a very desirable source. Problem is that there are only so many of them. You might anticipate that you will receive 1% of the circulation from cards in subscription copies, and 2% in single copies. This, of course, will vary depending on the magazine and all sorts of other factors.

Costs are very much less than direct mail, consisting only of the cost of the cards and their insertion in the magazines plus the return postage and the copies of the issues sent to those who do not pay. Prices and renewal characteristics are usually very much the same as direct mail.

Using the same basic pricing, cancellation, and renewal characteristics as with direct mail, an insert card subscription will produce a profit (before sending copies, of course) of $4.40 (versus a loss of $7.20 for direct mail), and after five years a profit of $12.60 (versus a profit of $2.00 for direct mail).

Gift Subscriptions

These are a sure winner for most magazines. Once again, however, the number that can be attracted is limited—and will depend on the subject matter of the magazine. They are normally sold at a price somewhat below the normal prices for direct mail, say $13 versus $15 in this case.

It is hard for a donor not to renew these subscriptions for the donee. And, if he doesn't, you still have a chance to get a renewal from the donee. So renewals and pay-ups are always higher than for direct mail.

The result in this example would be a profit of about $4.10 for the initial subscription (versus a loss of $7.20 for direct mail) and $13.70 after five years (versus $2.00). Because renewals would be better, there would remain 1,650 subscribers rather than just 720 for direct mail..

White Mail (Unsolicited Subscriptions)

Perhaps the best of all subscriptions, these come in without any known effort by the publisher. There are, unfortunately, only a handful—and I mean only a handful. Experience has shown that, in this business at least, word-of-mouth does not produce many unsolicited subscriptions, although it may help in other ways. They produce a profit of something like $11.40 for the first subscription and $20.60 after five years.

TV, Cable, and Radio

A few magazines have, at times, had good experiences with selling subscriptions over the air. These usually, but not always, have been connected with programs that are related to the subject matter of the magazines. The difficulty, of course, is in the high cost of producing the promotion packages and buying time on the outlets. There are no real generalities that can be used to estimate acquisition costs.

Web Sites

If the use of Web sites becomes a really major source of subscriptions and renewals, as Time-Life believes, they could well revolutionize the economics of the magazine business. Make these basic assumptions: (1) Sales can be made without any cost for mailing pieces, (2) most of the billing and collecting will be eliminated through the use of credit cards, and (3) with the payment through credit cards, the cancellation of subscriptions will be substantially reduced. You have essentially turned a loss operation into a profitable one.

I have made a calculation to compare with direct mail using these so-far unproven assumptions:

- Initial subscription
  - Bad debts and cancellations of the original subscription reduced to 20% from 40%
  - Acquisition cost at $5 per subscription versus the cost of mailings and billings
- Renewals
  - Bad debts and cancellations reduced to 5% rather than 10%
  - Renewal cost at $2 per subscription versus the present costs

Results show that the initial subscription will deliver a profit of $9.50 compared with a loss of $7.20 shown in the direct mail basic case—and a total profit over 5 years including renewals of $22.50 versus $2.00 for direct mail. The number of subscribers remaining is also substantially higher.

Other Direct Sales Sources

Magazines have creatively developed many other subscription sources—through telemarketing, freestanding newspaper inserts, exchange advertising with other magazines, inserts in manufacturers' packages, inserts in billings (particularly with department stores), use of card decks, by running special events for readers, and other ways limited only by the publishers' imaginations.

Any of these may be successful in selling a number of new subscriptions at lower costs than some of the direct mail efforts. They often, however, require considerable time to organize and test by the publisher's staff.

Agent-Sold Subscriptions

Direct Mail Agents

Many of the largest-circulation magazines, and others, have depended on direct mail agents for a good percentage of their subscriptions. To repeat, these plans call for the sale of subscriptions at the lowest price offered anywhere. The demographics and other characteristics of the readers are just as good as those from other sources. Renewals through the publishers' efforts are only about half as good as from other sources. But that is because many subscribers renew through the agents rather than through the publishers.

With the brouhaha and many lawsuits in recent years about the sweepstakes activities of these agents, results have declined considerably and the remit to publishers has been reduced from some 10% to 25% to much less. They still are, however, the source of many subscriptions. And the financial results for the publishers are far better than a good many of the direct mail efforts they would have to resort to if they tried to replace them.

Differences in the calculations from direct mail are principally:

- First subscription
  - Price—$12 versus $15.
  - Elimination of direct mail costs in favor of a remit from the agent of about 5% of the price.
  - Pay-up—95% versus 60% for direct mail.
- Renewal subscription
  - Price for first renewal—$15 versus $18. Subsequent renewals the same price as for direct mail.
  - Renewal rate for first renewal—20% versus 40%. Subsequent renewal rates the same as for direct mail.

Results:

- Initial subscription—No profit or loss versus a loss of $7.20 for direct mail.
- Renewal profit—$4.10 versus $9.20 for direct mail.
- Total profit for five years—$4.10 versus $2.00 for direct mail.
- Subscriptions at the end of five years for 10,000 original subs—360 versus 720 for direct mail.

Cash Field or PDS Subscriptions

These organizations, using primarily door-to-door and telephone sales methods, are often subject to problems with the local authorities. Subscriptions are usually sold for full price and for lengthy terms because of the agents' costs for this type of selling. I have assumed here no remit from the agent.

The resulting calculation may still be better than that for some mail-sold subscriptions. Differences from direct mail are:

	Agent	*Direct mail*
Initial subscription		
Term	3 years	1 year
Price	$36	$15
Remit to publisher	0	NA
Pay-up rate	100%	60%
Direct mail, billing costs	None	Lots
Renewals		
Renewal after	3 years	1 year
First renewal rate	5%	40%
Pay-up rate	90%	90%
Results		
Initial subscription	No P or L	Loss $7.20
Renewal profit	$ .70	$9.20
Subs at the end of five years	200	720

Internet Agents

Several agencies have been established on the Web. At this stage they have not yet become major suppliers of subscriptions for publishers and the terms of their operations have not settled down. They seem to be selling on the same terms as the direct mail agents, but offer "continuous service" for subscribers. Remit rates are about 20%. These would seem to be very attractive.

There are also a number of unauthorized agents selling subscriptions on the Web whom the publishers are taking steps to close down. Presumably they are passing the subscriptions they get to publishers through the PDS or cash field agents.

Catalog Agents

These are about the best subscriptions you can get. Problem is—there aren't very many. These agents sell subscriptions primarily to libraries. They usually sell them at full price and the publisher receives about 80% of that price. The agent renews the subscriptions automatically, so there are no costs for renewals.

These are obviously wonderful—too bad there aren't many.

Other Agents

There are other agents—through credit cards, using airline mailings, and even other publishers acting as agents at times. I have not heard of Priceline conducting an auction for subscriptions yet, but that is bound to come in time. Their income and costs should be evaluated in the same way.

Term of Subscriptions

In the complex subscription world, all sorts of other devices are used to get more subscriptions, lengthen those you have, increase renewal rates, increase the amount the reader pays, and almost everything else. Among the most common are:

- Continuous service—No real long-term experience yet, but logic indicates that there should be higher renewal rates at considerably lower costs.
- Short-term initial subscriptions—Theoretically a six-month trial will cost the publisher less than a full year because he does not have to send as many copies before the renewal. On the other hand, it also will result in an earlier need to replace the non-renewals.
- Three-year versus one-year—Usually given at a discount. You get the money up front, but less in total. But you save the costs of renewing and replacing the subscription each year.
- Early renewal—Often offered, particularly, but not always, when a price increase is in the works. Said to improve the overall renewal percentage.
- RAB—With your first bill you are offered the opportunity to lengthen your subscription. Sometimes results in earlier cash receipts and a later need to search for renewals. Usually works.

CHAPTER 47

The Confusing Single-Copy Sales Business

WHILE IT IS the most public part of the picture, the sale of single copies is the most confusing area of the business.

Revenue from single-copy sales of magazines declined in 2000, probably for the first time in recent history. They were $4.4 billion versus $4.6 billion the year before.

It is still a huge business, estimates are that some 2 billion copies of magazines are sold a year. Some 4,400 different titles are sold at about 175,000 different retail outlets. This means that 40 million copies are sold on a timely basis each week to the people who want them—a rather remarkable feat.

Retailers and Confusion

The sale of single copies is, of course, dependent on the retail industry. Magazines are among the highest-profit items retailers sell, with a gross profit margin of some 34% and an inventory turn much higher than just about anything else in the store. Major retailers have come to understand this—and also to appreciate the fact that a broad spectrum of different titles covering different reader interests is important.

The confusion comes about for several reasons:

1. Over 90% of the single copies are sold in stores where the principal activity has nothing to do with magazines—supermarkets, mass merchandisers, convenience stories, bookstores, and some others. Actual newsstands and stores principally devoted to the sale of magazines are just a minor part of the mix.

2. Magazines are very different from any other product in these stores. There are an awful lot of magazines, they come from many different publishers. They differ in nature because each appeals to people with different interests. And a magazine is not like any other product in that each has issues that are displayed at different intervals.

3. The methods of handling and selling magazines is different from anything else in most stores:

- They do not go through the store's warehouse, but are brought directly into the stores by wholesalers. Therefore, they do not go through the store's inventory and are not accounted for in the same way as other products.
- Displays are often arranged by the wholesaler's rather than the store's personnel.
- The magazines that are displayed—and the number of copies of each—are often determined by the wholesaler rather than by the store.
- Special racks are built (and periodically changed) to hold magazines at the checkout counters. The cost of these is normally shared by the magazines that use them. Negotiations for these are unlike the store's normal operations.
- Each issue of each magazine has an on-sale and an off-sale date to which the retailer must adhere.
- At the time of off-sale, the remaining copies must be returned to the wholesaler. This requires another handling and another accounting operation.

- The store does not purchase the magazines, as it does almost all other products, but accepts them on consignment. The store keeps only a portion of the selling price. This differs from the accounting treatment normally followed.

4. There are problems with magazines' UPC code (the bar code used in most outlets for checking out) that is the basis of the accounting for sales of just about all kinds:

- Not every magazine is careful about the location or the clarity of the code on the cover since it sometimes interferes with the cover presentation.
- There is not yet any provision for including the issue of each magazine in the UPC system, so that accounting by issue cannot be accurate.
- There is considerable "shrinkage" of the magazines delivered to the stores that cannot be accounted for. Some of this must have been going on forever, but it has surfaced only recently with more strenuous investigations into the way the single copy business is carried on. Included are such things as theft (not of dollars, but of copies of the most popular magazines, usually taking place in the back room—testimony, of a kind, to the desirability of the magazine); misscanning; delivery shortages; and miscounting on delivery, on returns, or anywhere else in the process.

5. Not included on this list is the time-honored system of "prematures"—the practice some retailers follow of returning unopened bundles of magazines—usually those with high cover prices—when they are short of cash to pay for shipments.

6. While publishers want to sell single copies, they are competing with these sales by selling subscriptions to the same magazines using extensive advertising, including insert cards in the copies themselves, which offer the magazines delivered by subscription at very much lower prices. Retailers are not happy with the competition.

7. The nature of publishers. Single-copy sales are the prime focus of only a few publishers. Not only are most publishers also interested in getting circulation through subscriptions—but they often think of circulation only so that they can sell advertising.

Many publishers think of single-copy sales as a dirty, grubby, nickel-and-dime business that they do not really understand or enjoy. (Not that there aren't some people in each company who know the field well.) Not only that, but the magazines do not even deal with the retailers directly, but do it through the national distributor and wholesaler.

Even today, after all the publishing mergers that have taken place in recent years, no one publisher dominates the single-copy scene in a way that would enable it to force changes. The top 25 single copy magazines, which account for more than half the sales, are owned by 13 different publishers.

8. The growth in the number of titles. The number of magazines, specials, and one-shots has been increasing—and will continue to do so. This has put great pressure on the sale of any one magazine through single copies just because there are so many titles trying to be seen on the stands. Consider how the number of titles vying for space (including one-shots) has increased:

Today, there are 4,400 titles, while in 1990 there were 2,800 titles, and in 1980, only 2,400. Total single copies of magazines sold have declined slightly, while the sales of the major titles have declined by about 40%.

9. Major changes have taken place in the retailing area. Major chains now dominate most retail businesses, with an increasing trend toward national rather than regional chains. This consolidation has brought about a greater interest on the retailers' part in controlling the way magazines are handled and sold—as well as in the amount of payment they exact for doing this.

Consumer shopping patterns have also changed, affecting the places where magazines are sold. Mass merchandisers, drugstores, and bookstores are replacing convenience stores in importance in the sale of magazines:

	Today	*1993*
Supermarkets	44%	43%
Mass merchandisers	15	9
Convenience stores	7	16
Drugstores	9	8
Bookstores	10	6
Other	15	18

Future Anticipated Improvements

The greater interest displayed by the retail chains beginning in 1995 has brought to light many of the shortcomings of the system that has been in existence for many years. In the long run, the changes that are being forced on the system should bring about a number of improvements in the distribution and selling of single copies.

Pressure from the retail chains has forced an overnight contraction in the number of wholesalers and in the recognition that some very basic changes were needed. The various parties involved, under the leadership of the MPA, have formed the Magazine Retail Council, consisting of retailers, wholesalers, national distributors, and publishers. This group has held several retail conferences to study the situation.

The first tangible result has been the Mercer Report, a study of the single-copy magazine channel by Mercer Management Consulting. Recommended was a two-stage program that should result in both improving the sales of magazines and reducing handling costs in the overall system.

1. The first stage involves the development and implementation of Cooperative Standards for Magazine Retailing (COSMAR). The problems with the system as it has been operating are very basic—and should have been addressed long ago. But this was difficult given the multiple entities operating in the field and the differences of magazines from the normal activities in the retail business. They have primarily to do with duplicate handling of the magazines and returns, lack of adequate record keeping, the shrinkage mentioned above, and other such mundane, but vital, matters.

2. The second stage is the development of scan-based trading. The ultimate goal is to eliminate virtually all the handling of the copies and to computerize record keeping through Paid on Scan (POS), which will eliminate all of the hand work. A system of this kind has already been successfully implemented by Barnes & Noble, the book-selling chain.

All of this will take several years to accomplish—particularly since this is seldom the uppermost project on most retail chains' agendas. Along with the changes should come much-improved sales data. From this, a basic change in the marketing approach should emerge; from being based on the "push" system, where you put out the number of copies you would like to sell, to a "pull" system, where the readers determine the number of different copies to be displayed. It should also help that the chains will apply their marketing know-how to magazine problems.

In the end, this should result in the sale of many more copies of more different magazines, the reduction of returns, and more profits for everyone in the chain. But at this point, the end is not even on the horizon.

A Brief History of the Single-Copy Sales System

After World War II, single-copy sales were dominated by the American News Company, which had a virtual monopoly in the business. In the 1950s an antitrust action broke this monopoly. Replacing it was the system involving national distributors and wholesalers. This was awkward and inefficient but somehow accomplished the job of distributing millions of copies each week.

Here is the how the system operated:

The Publisher

The publisher's only job was to publish the magazine. Some of the largest publishers also had field forces to oversee the distribution and display of their magazines, covering for the inadequacies of the national distributors and wholesalers, who were concerned with hundreds of titles.

The National Distributor

The distributor, the agent of the publishers, acted as:

- Banker—Billing and collecting for the magazines it handled and remitting its share to the publisher. For most established magazines, the distributor paid the publisher for a major portion of the anticipated sales before the on-sale date of the magazine, with the remainder paid some months later.

• Administrator—Taking care of all the paperwork and record keeping and arranging for the shipping of copies.

• Marketer—Opening new outlets for magazines; developing advertising, promotion, and public relations materials; and performing other marketing functions. This included having field forces of permanent or part-time employees to help in the distribution of the magazines locally, to oversee display, and the like.

• Buffer—Between the publisher and wholesaler, acting as the direct contact with the various wholesalers.

Wholesalers

Some years ago there were about 1,100 wholesalers, each of which had a virtual monopoly in its section of the country. With various consolidations, this number was reduced to about 200 by 1970, still operating in local geographic areas.

They did the physical handling and distribution of the magazines. They received the copies, allocated them to the dealers, physically distributed them and placed them on the stand, handled returns, collected from the dealers, and did whatever marketing was needed locally.

Dealers

Their only function was to take care of the actual sale to the customers.

How the System Worked

The standard amount paid for copies sold was 20% of the cover price to retailers, 20% to wholesalers, and 5% to 12% to the national distributors, with the remainder to the publishers. Some retailers, for instance, those in the New York City area with its traffic problems, were able to exact a somewhat higher tribute.

For many years, records of the draw (the number of copies placed on the stands) and the sale were kept for only about 200 of the best-selling magazines, under a system called Order Regulation. With the advent of computers, better records became available for many more magazines, but really good counts had seldom been achieved, and final sales results were not available for a number of months after the off-sale dates. Most publishers rarely had timely and accurate data about sales.

Retail Display Allowance (RDA)

In order to obtain entry into many large retailers, publishers paid an additional amount, generally 10%. To comply with Federal Trade Commission requirements, this was paid in the form of an RDA —presumably to get the retailers to prominently display the magazines (in actual fact, magazines such as *Playboy* and *Penthouse* paid it for copies that were not displayed at all in some places, but were kept under the counter). This allowance theoretically had to be offered to all the retailers in a geographic area, but in actual practice, publishers paid it to only those retailers who realized they could demand it. The allowance was not paid immediately, but some weeks later, either by the wholesaler or the publisher, based on voluminous and wasteful record keeping—a very awkward system.

At times over the years some of the major retail chains tried to bypass the system by working directly with publishers, but, while this threat hung over the industry, nothing ever really came of it.

In 1995, as the chains became more powerful, a number of the major retailers put their magazine businesses out for competitive bidding to the wholesalers. This, of course, changed the entire system.

Over the past few years, major wholesalers have bought out almost all the regional wholesalers, until today four wholesalers are handling over 90% of the magazine business. Because of the pressure on prices exerted by the retailers, as well as the difficulty of serving major geographic areas, profit making in the wholesaler business has become very difficult. Pricing pressure has also been brought to bear on the publishers. Part of this pressure has been taken care of through the RDA, but the amounts publishers receive of the cover price has been reduced in most cases.

There are now only six large national distributors, three of which are owned by large publishing companies. Since the change, however, a number of smaller distributors have emerged, covering local geographic areas, specialty markets, non-traditional chains, and independent stores, and handling direct distribution by publishers. Some of the national distributors have also joined in some of these activities.

This whole change essentially put the retailers in charge of the business, which, in the long run, should be good. But up until now, the inadequacies, while identified, have not been addressed in any significant way.

CHAPTER 48

Getting Started in Single-Copy Sales

JUST ABOUT ANY new consumer magazine—and a number of business magazines—would like to sell single copies, or at least be displayed on some, if not all, the available locations. If nothing else, it is a source of new readers. If the sales are good, they demonstrate the vitality of the magazine and its attractiveness to readers. It is also a showcase for advertisers and good public relations, no matter what field the magazine may be covering.

The approach a new magazine publisher takes toward single-copy sales, like everything else in this business, depends on the nature of the magazine and the field it serves. Let's try to break the approaches into some that different types of publishers might try.

Large National or Regional General and Specialized Magazines

If single-copy sales will be necessary, or even meaningful, for your magazine, your best bet would be to get a national distributor to handle it through the chain of wholesalers and retailers.

What is meaningful? This would include magazines that might be striving for over 100,000 copies sold each issue through the single-copy route. There are now fewer than 100 of these that are audited by ABC or BPA plus, of course, even more that do not depend on advertising to any great extent, as well as one shots, specials, annuals, comics, puzzle books, and who knows what else.

The first step involves getting one of the national distributors to take you on. As a single title, this may not be easy unless it is obvious that you have a chance to be a good addition to their stable of titles. They will be interested in such things as:

- How big a factor you might eventually become
- Whether you can achieve a good percentage of sales of the draw
- The cover price
- Whether you are directly competitive with one or more titles they are now handling
- Whether there are logical placements on the display racks (women's magazines with other women's magazines, car magazines with other car magazines)
- The likelihood that the chains will adopt you for inclusion in their lists of preferred titles
- The amount of handling that will be necessary to help you launch
- Their judgment about the your possibility of success
- The strength of your staff
- Your financial capabilities

If one of them does take you on, you will be faced with the job of getting into the major chains. While the national distributor will help you with your marketing, the time they can allot to any one new title is very limited, so you will have to assume much of this effort.

This involves getting national or regional headquarters of the chains to authorize the magazine to be placed in the chain's stores. You might be turned down because of the nature of the content, because the chain does not believe it will sell well, or because there is a limit on the number of magazines they are willing to display (they all have limits).

In most chains the individual store manager has ultimate discretion about which magazines will be displayed. A further approach, then, must be made to each store manager. This is normally done by the wholesaler, the national distributor, or the publisher.

Smaller National or Regional General Interest or Specialized Magazines

There are a handful of distributors that specialize in magazines that are seeking selective audiences and that want to be on certain newsstands, but that will not generally sell well. They work with newsstands such as those in Harvard Square, Grand Central in New York, bookstores, and other places where magazines hope to sell small numbers of copies to their particular audiences.

They normally send copies to these newsstands through the mail, with the postage charged to the publishers. The remit to the publisher usually amounts to about 40% of the cover price.

City and Other Local Magazines

City and other local magazines, with their obvious attraction for local wholesalers, newsstands, and other outlets—as well as the ability to do their distribution themselves or to use local trucking operators—may be able to bypass the normal distribution channels that magazines must go through.

Business Magazines

A few business magazines arrange to place single copies at selected stands in cities where their readers are liable to congregate; for instance, *Advertising Age* and *Variety* in New York and Los Angeles.

CHAPTER 49

Basics of a Magazine's Production

PRODUCTION IS CONCERNED with the development of the physical product and its distribution to its readers. From a reader's standpoint, very little has changed in the production of a magazine in the past hundred years. He still receives copies printed on paper in black and various colors, with pages stapled together. There is both editorial and advertising material. And he can either pick it up at a newsstand or other store, or have it delivered through the mail.

He might notice that the reproduction of pictures is much sharper; that some of the artwork is wild and funky; that the paper is not as heavy as it used to be; that page numbers are sometimes either not there at all or rather strange because of regional or demographic editions; that there are funny cards inserted throughout, some of which may even address him by name; and that there are strange codes and marks around his name and address on the cover—but physically magazines have not changed much in an awfully long time.

Actually, however, the methods of developing and reproducing the material that is presented on the pages of magazines have been revolutionized since World War II.

Technological Changes

In almost every area of the production process great strides have been made toward automating things and improving the quality, speed, and cost involved. Taking the areas one at a time:

HISTORY

I grew up in the era when hot metal was used to set type using a Linotype machine, with adjuncts such as a Ludlow machine and hand setting of type for headlines, statistics, and the like.

The publisher delivered copy either to the printer or to an independent type shop, and through a back-and-forth sending of materials and proofs several times, there finally emerged fully made-up pages that were made into metallic plates, which were then put on the press for printing.

Most large publishers had their own flat-bed letterpress machines. Some also had their own engraving plants for doing both black-and-white and color illustrations.

Because each editorial item required the time of the type shop to produce, when the billing for composition came along, costs were itemized—a headline cost so much, as did putting a group of items in a box, or starting a story with a large capital letter (had to have a "runaround" of type). When the bill came in, it usually consisted of a "laundry list" of what had been done, with some 50 or 60 items listed. A publisher could often reduce his costs by carefully controlling the extras he asked for.

The most expensive were "author's alterations" —changes that were made after the material had been set. It cost so much if the material was in galley form, a higher charge if it was in page form—and it was horrendous if made when the material was on the press.

PRESSWORK

Just about all longer run printing is now done by the photo offset process with the longest run magazines produced by rotogravure. Flat-bed sheet-fed presses are hard to find, with even relatively short runs produced by the web process from rolls of paper. Speed on these presses often exceeds fifty miles per hour. (In the old days they had to cut the rolls up to fit the flat-bed presses.)

All aspects of the presswork are controlled by computers that regulate the speed, color quality, ink, registration, and just about everything else. They can even change from one roll of paper to another on the fly without stopping the presses.

BINDING

Many binding operations have now been attached at the end of the presses so that separate binding lines are not required. We used to take the sheets from the presses and truck them over to the binding machines.

Computerization of lists, plus the use of ink-jet printing, has enabled publishers to do selective binding. This way individual magazines can be designed for each subscriber—and regional, demographic, and other editions can be produced automatically and addressed on line. At this point not many publishers have taken full advantage of all these capabilities, but they soon will.

PAPER

Paper manufacturing, too, has benefited from computerization of the process. Lighter weight grades have become possible, as has recycled paper, with excellent color reproduction qualities. Efforts are currently being made to introduce Supply Chain Management to the paper-making process and to apply "just in time" inventory concepts using Electronic Data Interchange (EDI). This should be very productive for major publishers and for large printers who often supply paper for many magazines.

COMPOSITION AND PREPRESS

Perhaps the most evident changes from a publisher's standpoint—composition, artwork, platemaking, and other prepress operations—can all now either be performed or directed by the publishers, rather than being farmed out to third parties.

Desktop publishing, to which many publishers converted at great cost in recent years, is no longer enough. The trend is rapidly moving toward automating even more of these processes. Publishers now have to be conversant with a new vocabulary including digital prepress, Computer to Plate (CTP), Extensible Markup Language (XML), SWOP color standards, Stochastic Screening, and Portable Document Format (PDF) to take full advantage of these new techniques. Quark and Adobe are competing for the best method of doing layout and editorial production. Digital cameras, remote proofing, and telecommunications networks are also needed. All this not only speeds the process, but reduces handling and costs.

These improvements will eliminate the need for one intermediate supplier—the prepress house (which is now often part of the printer's responsibility). All composition, printing, and binding operations will be handled directly from the publisher to the printer. Printers these days are offering help in developing DTP operations and are willing to install equipment for transmission, to train your staff, and to assist with the conversion. And one of these days it will be possible to handle magazines without the use of even one piece of film. Following that will come digital presses.

WARNING

You can easily get bogged down trying to understand all the technical operations and jargon while you really should be concentrating on publishing your magazine. It is enough to recognize that all this is going on—and to get help with the technical parts rather than getting too immersed in them.

WARNING

I worry a good deal about desktop publishing. It seems to put a premium on the ability to understand and use computers rather than on artistic presentation. This has resulted in some of the most God-awful presentations that have ever been seen. Hopefully these newer techniques added to desktop programs will not result in further deterioration of the look of some of our magazines. Certainly something for publishers to be concerned about.

Single-Copy Distribution

Publishers have benefited from improvements made by the trucking industry plus printers' efforts to provide joint shipping for a number of magazines, as well as those resulting from the consolidation of wholesalers in the industry and the greater interest taken by retailers in magazine operations (see chapter 47, "The Confusing Single-Copy Sales Situation").

The One Weak Area—Distribution of Subscription Copies

Magazines are still dependent on the Postal Service for the distribution of subscription copies. While it has made some strides in recent years toward bar coding, computerization, improved containers, and handling, there have been no real breakthroughs.

It has been difficult to make real changes in this large and unwieldy organization. Periodic price increases have been necessary for it to continue to be profitable. When combating these increases, publishers have always brought up the threat of "alternative delivery," but to date have not been able to point to—or to develop—any better, or even equal, method at a reasonable cost.

The Consolidation of Suppliers

The trend toward consolidation that has overtaken just about all businesses these days has also been evident in the printing and paper fields that are so important to publishers.

With the sale of World Color Press to Quebecor in 2000, the four largest printers handle about 40% of the magazine printing business in the United States—and just about all the really long-run business. A similar consolidation trend has been taking place with the smaller printing establishments that handle shorter run magazines.

WARNING

More worrisome for publishers in the long run is the future viability of the Postal Service. The foundation of the operation is First Class mail, which is carried at higher rates. This has already been seriously eroded by the movement to the Internet of many personal letters, as well as the sending and paying of bills. Hopefully publishers will join this parade by increasing the use of e-mail in the subscription process.

The Postal Service received substantial price increases beginning in 2001. It has already announced one small rate increase and has initiated steps for even larger ones. For a time it threatened to cease Saturday deliveries, but backed off. Other moves will undoubtedly follow.

Incidentally, few readers may recall that back in about 1980, the Postal Service, long before the Internet, made an effort to launch its own e-mail. The effort was half-hearted and was closed up soon after it started. Too bad.

The same has been true of the paper business with Finnish companies purchasing two of the largest American companies. UPM-Kymmene has taken over Champion and Stora Enso Oyi has taken over Consolidated. These two companies now produce some 40% of the world's coated paper. This has been followed by the merger of two major American companies—Mead and West Virginia.

This consolidation can be both good and bad for publishers. The large companies can be more fully equipped and have the capital to keep up with the latest improvements—but the choice of suppliers has been considerably curtailed, limiting the bargaining ability of the publisher. There have already been clashes between paper companies and newspapers concerning the availability and pricing of newsprint.

CHAPTER 50

Production and the New Magazine

Production—The Largest Cost

THE LARGEST COST for any publisher is that of the paper, printing, binding, and distribution of the actual copies. Control of these costs is not easy even if you have a good production manager; he cannot control all the factors that impact expenses. In addition to the outside influences, every department in a magazine has a hand in making decisions that affect production costs. Because of this interdependence, control of this largest area of expense is never as tight as one would like.

Wasteful habits in editorial can lead to late copy and excessive corrections. Positions that have been promised to certain advertisers can lead to expensive printing because of the difficulty of fitting these pages into economical forms. Poor estimates by circulation can lead to printing too many (or too few) copies. Management decisions can lead to excessive numbers of both pages and copies.

By the same token, production department decisions can have an impact on the operations of other departments. The type of equipment can limit the number and placement of color pages. If too long a lead time is needed for the printer's receipt of copy, late news may be missed—or some ads may have to be left out.

Contributing to the lack of tight control is the technical nature of the production process. Most publishing people are not as familiar with paper, printing, and distribution as they should be because it is not their priority. Even a good production department cannot know all the latest ins and outs of the field because its primary duty is a daily one of producing a good magazine on time.

There are two levels of decisions that can affect production: Basic decisions and issue-to-issue decisions.

Basic Decisions

TRIM SIZE

What should your trim size be? These days almost all magazines are so-called standard size—eight and a half inches by eleven inches or somewhat smaller. There are several reasons for this:

- Just about any magazine printer is equipped to produce this size, while there are only a few that can produce other sizes economically.
- If you are on the newsstand, most racks are made for this size.
- Almost all ads are designed for this size.
- The reading public is used to this size.

It is worth exploring sizes slightly smaller than standard. Both paper and postage costs are based on the pounds of paper used. The newsweeklies, *Sports Illustrated, People,* and some others are at eight inches by ten and a half inches (89.3% of eight and a half inches by eleven inches) and sizable cost savings. Most monthly magazines are only fractionally larger than this in one or both dimensions. Presumably this has to do with the press equipment they use.

A few magazines choose to be larger to create an impression. *Globe, National Enquirer,* and others of their ilk are nine and a half inches by eleven and three eights inches because of their desire for exposure at supermarkets. Newspaper-delivered magazines and the alternative weeklies are still larger in size and are printed on newsprint. There are also a few news-type magazines such as *Advertising Age* that go up to ten and seven eights inches by fourteen and a half inches, although not all news magazines find this necessary.

A handful of magazines are in the nine inches by eleven inches or nine inches by twelve inch area, including some (but only a small minority) of the art, women's fashion, music, and travel books. Others include *Business 2.0, Smart Money, Town & Country,* and *Cigar Aficionado.* Many other magazines that had been large some years back have reduced to more standard sizes.

There are, of course, also a few digest-sized magazines, and some of the kids' magazines are smaller than standard. While this means less paper and postage costs, it also entails a smaller ad rate—and some advertisers may not want to convert their ads to these sizes.

My conclusion is that any new magazine had better be standard-size unless it has an overwhelmingly good reason for being different.

Type of Paper

Coated stock may be necessary for good reproduction if you carry lots of advertising or for certain kinds of pictorial editorial, but some publishers have found that super-calendared or other less-expensive uncoated stock is good enough.

If you are not going to carry much advertising, you can confine the coated stock to the cover and just a few inside pages, all of which you may be able to run through the press at the same time with considerable savings.

Some publishers have reduced costs by printing part of their magazines on bulking stock. This is less expensive, lends a change of pace to the editorial content, and may bulk up a thin magazine.

What paper weight? Reproductive qualities on paper as light as 24 pounds are very good, although there might be some show through—and the lighter the paper, the lower the cost. Perhaps you could use this light-weight paper and then bulk up a thin magazine with a heavy cover and some insert pages.

Recycled paper? Only if you can get it at a reasonable cost—and its use is important to you or your readers.

There was the publisher of one new magazine whom I accused of using cardboard (coated of course) on the cover with heavy cover stock on the inside to make the magazine look classier. You can lose your shirt doing this type of thing—and readers are not really impressed.

Issue-to-Issue Decisions

There are, of course, myriad decisions to be made for each issue. A few can have a very big impact on costs.

Number of Editorial Pages

Readers seem to be willing to put up with a huge number of both editorial and advertising pages in their magazines. Consider the telephone-book-sized magazines in recent years in the bridal, computer, business, women's fashion, and some other fields.

For the new magazine, however, the question of controlling the number of editorial pages is important for its very survival. Unnecessary edit pages can be terribly costly—and I never met an editor who was satisfied with the number he had to work with.

The simplest way to handle this situation is to determine the minimum size of the magazine that will satisfy readers—and the maximum number of pages your editorial team can successfully prepare. Then, to avoid arguments each issue, develop a scale depending on the number of advertising pages. For instance:

	Editorial Pages	*Total Pages*
Minimum	50	
Maximum	80	
If 60 advertising pages	54	114
70	58	128
80	62	142
90	66	156
100	70	170
110	74	184
120	78	198

There has to be, of course, some leeway so that an editor can borrow from one issue and pay back in another when the content requires it.

PUBLISHER ORGANIZATION

Excess costs—as well as headaches and hard feelings—can very easily occur in the handling of the many pieces of copy, illustrations, and ads needed in putting out an issue of a magazine, as well as in instructions about the details of the production needs, such as the number of copies to be delivered to various places, the placement of pages in color forms, and the like.

It is worth the time and effort to carefully organize the scheduling of an issue and the relationship with the various people at the printer's to avoid misunderstandings and other problems such as missing deadlines. It makes for a smoother lifestyle as well as a vastly less expensive production operation.

If you find it necessary for your people to visit the printer when putting each issue to bed, something is wrong. It is a sign of disorganization and lack of planning—or the wrong printer.

Major Areas to Be Careful About

- Have larger printing forms been used wherever possible? It is usually less expensive to print in 32-page forms than in 16's—and then cut them to be bound in different places in the magazine. The same, of course, goes for even larger forms if they are available.
- Are four-color forms being used in the most economical manner? It is easy to get a feel for this. Count the number of color pages in the color forms. If it is not over 50% of the fou color pages available, investigate.
- Is the use of editorial color carefully planned? When color forms are being used solely for editorial matter, see whether they could have been put into forms containing advertising color at considerable savings. It is also amazing to see the visual effects a good art director, when pressed, can achieve with only black and white or two color to work with.
- Is the advertising department promising special positions without taking into account the extra expense? Often special positions are requested by habit rather than need and advertisers can be persuaded to take something else.
- Are covers and special sections being run in the most economical way? Sometimes covers and inserts can be run together and then cut apart with considerable savings. It may also be possible to gang-run covers for several issues and save money.
- Some very costly and unnecessary items are overtime charges, rush work, alterations on page proofs (if you still have them), and stopping the presses.

CHAPTER 51

Printing, Paper, and Distribution

Choosing a Printer

WHILE PRICE is always a consideration in choosing a printer, the most important factors are how his equipment and know-how fit the printing of your magazine. This includes:

- Composition and Prepress. How much up-to-date digital equipment that you want to take advantage of does he have and know how to use?
- Presses. How do they relate to your magazine as to speed, size of printing forms, quality you require, paper you will use, page size of your magazine, and other factors? Most printers these days have very similar presses, but their configurations may be different. There are printers who specialize in long runs, and others in shorter runs.
- Binding and mailing equipment. If yours is a large-circulation magazine, you will probably eventually have different editions—regional, demographic—as well as personalization that requires special binding and ink-jetting equipment required by sophisticated subscription fulfillment.
- Distribution skills and relationships can be important. Knowledge of Postal Service requirements is imperative, as is the ability to drop ship at times and to jointly ship and comail your magazine with other magazines. A postal substation at the plant can be helpful.
- Location. For magazines with substantial amounts of advertising, one of the most vital points is a location that will result in lower postal rates for subscriptions. That's why most of the major magazine printers are in the middle of the country.
- Flexibility. Chances are that you will have trouble meeting deadlines at the start-up of your magazine. A printer who is too busy may not be able to accommodate your needs.
- Willingness to be your partner. You probably have never dealt with all the problems of launching a publication, even if you have previously worked in the business. The best supplier relationship will be a partnership where the printer shares his know-how with you (to say nothing of the possibility that you will be late in some payments), rather than a stiff arm's-length relationship. This may actually be the most important factor of all.

WARNING

Be sure your printer is thoroughly familiar with magazines. Magazine printing imposes certain routines and disciplines that are not available in the normal commercial shop. Techniques are needed that not only help the printer in doing the job, but will also save the publisher many headaches and extra work.

WARNING

The temptation is great to demand greater quality than the magazine and its readers require. This can elevate the prices you pay for paper, printing, and probably everything else. Before you set your quality standards, take a look at what similar successful magazines do to see what quality is satisfactory for them.

THE PROCESS OF CHOOSING A PRINTER

It can take a long time to choose a printer. It is not just a question of asking for bids. You cannot intelligently go about choosing one in a casual or haphazard manner. Prepare carefully. If you feel ill at ease—or if a lot of money is involved—be sure to get an experienced consultant to help.

There are still lots of printers around, despite the consolidation that has reduced the number from prior years. Presses and binding equipment seem to be relatively standard, yet there are vast differences in the way the various pieces are configured, as well as in the adjuncts that are added to them.

1. Develop a list of what your magazine will be like:

- Number of pages. Black and white, four color, inserts, card inserts, etc. Include an estimate of the different sizes of issues during the year.
- Cover printing. Special ink or varnish required.
- Frequency.
- Trim size. Variation that would be acceptable to fit the equipment used.
- Paper type and weight. Alternatives that would be acceptable.
- Average pressrun. Variations in issues and pressrun for special issues.
- Regional and/or demographic editions and their pressruns.
- Publication date and anticipated closing date.
- Copies to be mailed by the Postal Service—and the number by different classes.
- Copies to be bulk shipped.
- Mailing and other distribution methods to be used.
- Anticipated composition and prepress methods to be used.
- Binding method—saddle or perfect bound—or unbound.
- Other specifications.
- Be sure to ask bidders for suggestions for changes in the specs that would make for lesser cost or improved timing.

2. Develop a list of printers who potentially may be able to handle your magazine.

3. Call this list to determine their interest. Get a list of their equipment and capabilities. Get a list of their present and former customers to get a feel for whether your magazine will fit their operations.

4. Send those who are interested and who could conceivably handle your requirements your list of information above. Ask them to make preliminary bids in two ways: (a) price lists of items to be performed and (b) a sample bill for an issue with detailed specifications.

5. Check with present and former customers of those that seem to be likely prospects.

6. Visit the plants of the likely candidates to discuss such things as:

- Ability to handle your work
- Understanding of your requirements
- Your ability to work well with your account executive
- Meeting with key employees to get a feel for their capabilities, flexibility, and other requirements
- The capabilities, efficiency, and cleanliness of the plant
- Relationships with the Postal Service and whether there is a branch at the plant
- Relationships with other shipping services
- Flexibility in meeting schedules, payment of bills, and the like
- Ability to purchase good quality paper
- Pricing of paper, including their handling charges and insurance
- Ability to fit with your composition and prepress methods and standards—or your ability to fit with theirs
- Ideas they have for improving your operations
- Willingness to partner with you—and to give you help as well as advice on improving your operations

7. Decide on the three to five most likely candidates.

8. Tell them to sharpen their pencils and present final quotes using the specifications as they understand them from your meetings. In getting the data this time, you will probably adjust your specifications considerably as a result of your conversations so that you can fit the requirements of your magazine to each bidder's equipment—and get figures from each that are comparable so that you can make an intelligent decision.

9. Reach a decision and work out a contract with the lucky winner, which should not be very difficult

at this point. Naturally, you will need your attorney at this stage.

Hints

- The location of the plant near you should not be important. In fact, it normally works out better if the printer is not near enough to be visited very often.
- Many publishers want their magazines delivered at the beginning of the month. By scheduling yours during the printer's slack time, you may be able to get reduced prices. Few readers are tuned to the date you publish, unless you are a weekly.
- Paper waste is inevitable in the printing and binding process. It can amount to a substantial amount of money. A good practice is to agree on an allowable percentage—and then split any savings achieved with the printer.
- You should agree on a percentage overrun above the print order. This varies depending on the length of the run. No underrun should be allowed.
- Just about any printing contract calls for price escalation in the event of labor, ink, and other cost increases. You should first agree on the method of calculating these escalations—and then insist on the right to audit the calculation. This is highly technical and requires skilled costing techniques, so you will probably need help. But the difference in cost can become tremendous.
- A long-term contract is preferable for both parties. It should contain reasonable cancellation provisions for lack of performance on either side, major changes in specifications, sale of either company, and other normal provisions.

> **WARNING**
>
> Some printers have what they call a "Kennel Club." To qualify, a magazine must be a "dog." You attain membership by bargaining so hard that the work is underpriced, the publisher uses processes that are not conducive to efficient printing, or you have forced inadequate prices when negotiating at renewal time.

PURCHASING PAPER

Paper is manufactured by a relatively small number of companies in the United States or in several foreign countries. Recent consolidations have reduced the number. Because of the large investment needed for paper-making operations, these are all large concerns. It is normally manufactured in a limited number of grades and qualities.

The availability and pricing of paper is cyclical, depending on changes in demand—and when the manufacturers build new plants. When it is in short supply, you may have difficulty getting paper at all, and then not at a good price. (The major magazine publishers all have investments in paper mills to ensure that they will be able to get paper when they need it.)

Like all industries, paper has its own standards, customs, terminology, and ways of doing things that sometimes are difficult to understand. Competition, however, is fierce because they are essentially dealing in a standard commodity.

Basically you have three possible choices for buying paper for your magazine:

- Directly from the manufacturer
- Through a paper merchant
- Through your printer

You also may seem to have the opportunity to buy paper at auction on the Internet, but this hardly seems an effort in which you should participate when you are launching a new magazine.

Since you are not a major publisher, you will not be welcomed by the manufacturers. Chances are that your printer will be able to secure all the paper you will need easier than you can get it through any other source. It will probably be less expensive than if you buy it and have it delivered to him since the savings you obtain in price may disappear when you add in the charges for storage, handling, financing, and insurance.

Delivery

SINGLE COPIES

If you expect to have substantial single-copy sales, the expedited delivery of these can be important. On-sale dates must be met or nothing will work. This obviously will require considerable investigation of various shipping methods to various parts of the country, timing of the printing and binding of the copies, as well as their segregation if you have regional editions. This, of course, is a whole world with which you are probably not familiar.

If your printer handles a number of other newsstand magazines, he can probably be very helpful. In fact, this may be an important factor in choosing the location of your printing. Shipping costs and times can be very important factors. Coshipping with other newsstand magazines can save a great deal of money but requires careful coordination of schedules—not only with those of the other magazines, but also with those of the printer and your editorial and advertising people.

Chances are that a consultant would be helpful in developing the best plan—and in reviewing it from time to time.

SUBSCRIPTIONS

Dealing with subscription delivery is a world unlike any other, although the Postal Service people try to be as helpful as they can. Some things to consider are:

- Different rates for different types of postal service—first class, standard class, periodical class, etc.
- Some of these rates are simple. It costs one price to send a first class letter anywhere.
- The rates having to do with magazine delivery are particularly complex. They are partially per piece, partially by distance, partially by weight, partially by the amount of presorting of addresses, and on and on.
- There are complex rules about what kind of materials, other than the basic magazine, will be accepted at the magazine rate.

Not only that, but there have been periodic rate increases, and there will be more and more of them because of the inefficiencies of the Postal Service and the effects e-mail and the other parcel delivery services are having on its basic income.

Over the years, publishers have become very adept at designing their operations so as to minimize their postal costs through such methods as using lightweight paper, organizing their mailing labels to best fit postal requirements, comailing with other magazines, shipping copies to different postal zones and entering them there, choosing the location of their printers, and, for the largest circulation magazines, printing in several locations.

Publishers have also been in the forefront of negotiations with the Postal Service during the periodic rate hearings, and sometimes have threatened to develop alternate delivery methods (but have not, to date at least, come up with any better or less expensive alternative).

A new magazine should not treat this area lightly. The costs involved are great, and delivery schedules are important. Most magazine printers can be helpful, but chances are that it will be worth exploring your particular situation with the Postal Service people directly—and probably with one of the consultants in the field.

CHAPTER 52

Keeping Track of What's Going On

THIS CHAPTER IS really about accounting, which is the way we keep track, but I didn't want to scare some of you away.

Basic Concepts

ACCOUNTING—WHY DOES IT EXIST?

The only reason: Accounting exists to help you run your business better. If you don't care about that, you shouldn't bother with accounting. Just get a desk with a large drawer. When the money comes in, stuff it in the drawer. When you have to pay a bill, take some of it out. No sense of keeping all those ledgers, journals, and other records.

You might, of course, find that you get a good deal of e-mail from the Internal Revenue Service and other public servants, but think of all the time and aggravation you will save.

As long as you're going to have to keep records, you might as well keep those that will be most useful and perhaps even take advantage of the information you get.

We will approach the subject in a number of ways:

- Explain some of the principles of good accounting and then show how these should be applied to the very different business of magazine publishing.
- Give examples of periodic reports that are most useful in analyzing what is going on—and how to use them.
- Present the statistical information that is most helpful in supplementing the basic reports.

We will not go into how you accumulate this data, develop a chart of accounts, and get the figures into the reports. Those are details that your financial people will know how to do.

Along the way we'll discuss the fascinating situation involving subscription income and expense and some other aspects of the business. Examples will be used as they seem helpful. I will also throw in some ideas, a few of which might seem somewhat unorthodox, but which I have found to be helpful.

SOME BASIC ACCOUNTING PRINCIPLES

Accounting principles can be as complex as tax laws, but the ones used in developing the most helpful information for a magazine are very few, very easy to understand, and based on common sense.

- ACCRUAL VERSUS CASH BASIS. There are two basic methods of keeping records. The cash basis is just what is sounds like: You record income as you receive the cash, and record expenses as you pay them. While knowledge of the cash flow of a business is important, clearly this method is not very helpful in running a business. Receipts may be received right away—or long after they are due.

> You may pay bills immediately—or after 120 days. So, if you record things only as the cash comes in and goes out, you can't match it with things as they happen, and you won't really be able to know whether you are doing things well or badly.

Under the accrual method, transactions are recorded in real time—as events occur. Advertising income for the January issue is recorded on the publication date of the magazine, even though the cash may not be received for some time. By the same token, the expense of printing the magazine is recorded on the same date, even though you may not pay the printer until later. This is obviously the best way to keep track of things—as they happen.

- MATCH INCOME AND EXPENSE. If you record the income from the January issue on its publication date, then you should also record all the costs that apply to that issue at the same time, so the printing, paper, distribution and most other expenses will be recorded on the same date. This gives you an accurate picture of the relationship between income and costs.

- ACCOUNTING. This follows the way the business is operated. If the figures are to be useful, they must relate to the way things actually take place, not to some arcane formula, and not for the convenience of the people keeping the records. Costs are grouped in the way the magazine is operated. We'll show these groupings later.

- ALLOCATION OF EXPENSES. In most companies, there are people or departments that have activities in more than one area. A promotion director, for instance, may develop advertising promotion for two magazines. To get the most accurate profit figures for each, his salary should be partly charged to each.

- IT SHOULD BE PRACTICAL. You can develop income and expense items in exquisite detail, but we are trying to run a business, not launch a spaceship. For instance, we could have that promotion director keep detailed time records to be sure that the allocation of his salary is precise, but it isn't worth the trouble, so we estimate the breakdown. The same goes for many other allocations.

- ACCOUNTING FOR SUBSCRIPTION INCOME. The one part of magazine accounting that needs explanation is concerned with subscription income. We said earlier that income and expenses should be recorded at the time the event takes place, but, when we sell a subscription, nothing really takes place until we send a copy of the magazine to the subscriber.

  To make the figures we use most meaningful, we record income for each issue at the time it is sent to the subscriber. If we sell a subscription for $12 we should take one dollar into income for each issue. Otherwise our monthly profit will be misstated. What do we do with the $12 when we receive it? We have to record it somewhere, so we set up on our accounting records something called Deferred Subscription Income. This account contains the amount we owe the subscriber for future issues.

  This is a simple enough concept. The only problem is that this amount we owe subscribers then shows up as a liability on our balance sheet, which makes it appear that we have large debts when those subscribers actually are the biggest asset a paid circulation magazine has. It is often difficult to explain that this seeming distortion is good, not bad, for the publication.

  When you are starting a new magazine with paid circulation, this anomaly is bound to pop up. Be forewarned that you will probably have to explain this accountant's fiction to potential investors.

- ONE PRODUCT WITH MANY REVENUE STREAMS. A magazine receives income from subscriptions, single-copy sales, advertising, and possibly other sources. These are all interrelated and it is important to understand the relationship of these revenue streams to each other in order to make intelligent decisions. This is very different from almost all manufacturing, trading, or retailing businesses. The traditional accounting practice of measuring cost of goods sold and gross profit against sales used in other businesses is meaningless here, even though some publishers mistakenly try to use it.

APPLYING THESE PRINCIPLES TO MAGAZINES

The principal income items are, logically enough:

- Advertising
- Subscriptions
- Single copies
- Other items tangential to the magazine, such as list rental and sale of reprints

The expense items are divided into the normal operating areas of:

- Mechanical—paper, printing, distribution
- Editorial—development of the content
- Advertising—sale of advertising
- Subscriptions—acquisition and fulfillment
- Single-copy sales costs
- General and administrative

Since this is the way magazines operate, this is the way the accounts should be set up.

Accounting by Issue

Ideally you would like to know the profit or loss for each issue, but in practice some compromises are made. Magazines issued more frequently than monthly normally use a monthly rather than an issue basis, although some weeklies use 13 periods a year to even out fluctuations. Magazines issued only six times a year may account every two months.

Accounting by Magazine

In a multipublication house you account for each magazine separately. How else can you know which are profitable? Expenses incurred for more than one publication are allocated among the publications. Expenses incurred for more than one department within a publication are allocated among the departments involved. Revenue and expenses not connected with magazine publishing are segregated so that the results of the magazine operations alone can be determined.

Accounts to Be Kept

A list of the accounts that are common to just about all magazines are shown by department (see chapter 54, "Records You Might Need"). Naturally, each magazine may not have all these categories and may have some not listed. The important thing is to keep it simple enough so that it is easily understandable. Too many details just lead to confusion and nit-picking. You can always dig in to find further details if you want to.

Useful Periodic Reports

Viewing Operations in Several Different Dimensions

You can learn a lot by looking at the numbers in various ways. In the sample operating statement (Figure 52.1) are figures:

1. For the single month versus the year to date. This helps spot trends.
2. Compared with the same periods for the prior year. Shows if you are better or worse.
3. That show percentages each expense item is to income to make the data more meaningful.
4. Compared with the budget to help understand what is happening versus what had been planned.

Statistical data provide even more useful information by displaying relationships.

The sample form (Figure 52.2) includes:

- Pages. Advertising, editorial, other, and total—and the percent advertising is of the total. This indicates the trend of advertising pages; tells whether the number of editorial pages is in line, both in absolute terms and as a percentage of the total; and tracks the number of other pages (make-goods, house ads, charitable, and the like). Some publishers also break advertising and editorial pages into black and white and four color.
- Average copies printed. Subscription, single-copy draw, others, and total pressrun. Indicates the trends of paid circulation. Also shows the number of free and wasted copies.
- Cost per copy. For printing, paper, and postage per subscription copy, and shipping per single copy. These vary, of course, with the number of pages in an issue. The cost per copy is also useful for comparison with subscription and single-copy revenue per copy.
- Cost per thousand pages printed (sometimes called CPM or cost per thousand copy pages). Obtained by multiplying the average pressrun by the total pages. This helps in tracking cost increases and in spotting wasteful production practices. It is also useful in planning and in comparing costs with other magazines.
- Advertising rate. Per page. Usually the one-time black-and-white rate is used.
- Advertising revenue. Per advertising page.

Figure 52.1. Operating Statement

Current Month							Year to Date					
Last Year		Budget		This Year			This Year		Budget		Last Year	
Amount	Percent	Amount	Percent	Amount	Percent	INCOME	Amount	Percent	Amount	Percent	Amount	Percent
$	%	$	%	$	%	Advertising, net of agency, cash discounts	$	%	$	%	$	%
						Subscription—accrual						
						Single copy, net of estimated returns						
						Other, net of direct cost						
						Total Income						
						EXPENSES						
						Mechanical						
						Printing, Prepress						
						Paper						
						Distribution						
						Salaries, fringe benefits						
						Other						
						Total Mechanical						
						Advertising						
						Salaries, fringe benefits						
						Commissions						
						Travel and entertainment						
						Promotion, advertising						
						Other						
						Total Advertising						
						Editorial						
						Salaries, fringe benefits						
						Travel and entertainment						
						Manuscripts, artwork						
						Other						
						Total Editorial						
						Circulation						
						Salaries, fringe benefits						
						Travel and entertainment						
						Promotion						
						Fulfillment						
						Other						
						Total Circulation						
						General and Administration						
						Salaries, fringe benefits						
						Travel and entertainment						
						Occupancy						
						Office Costs						
						Professional feels						
						Insurance						
						Other						
						Total General and Administrative						
						Total Expenses						
$	%	$	%	$	%	Operating Profit or (Loss)	$	%	$	%	$	%

Shows the trend of revenue. Comparison with the advertising rate above indicates whether the mix of color and black and white is changing and if off-the-card discounts are being given.

• ADVERTISING COSTS AS A PERCENT OF ADVERTISING REVENUE AND ADVERTISING COST PER ADVERTISING PAGE. Costs include just those having to do with selling the pages, not the cost of copies or of printing. This shows whether the cost of selling advertising is getting out of line.

• FUTURE ADVERTISING PAGES ON ORDER. Indicates future success. Includes the number of pages in house (not just promised) compared with the number in the prior year—a very simple, but significant, figure.

• EDITORIAL COSTS PER EDITORIAL PAGE. Reveals excessive costs that might not come to light when measured only as a percent of revenue.

• SINGLE-COPY DATA. Draw, percent of sale, revenue per copy. Essential for measuring success here. Unfortunately, since the information often is several months old, it is not always the good gauge we would like.

• SUBSCRIPTION DATA. New subscriptions, subscriptions sold, average length, revenue per copy, promotion cost per copy, accrual revenue per subscription copy, and subscription cash per copy. Shows the vitality of this complex area. The number of subscriptions sold and the average length give an idea of the readers' feelings about the magazine. The revenue and cost per subscription sold indicate profitability. It is helpful to compare the income per copy on the accrual basis with that on the cash basis. This, plus information on subscription cash received, gives indications of what future profits from subscriptions will be. This area has to be supplemented with details developed by the circulation department. See chapter 46, "Subscription Source Evaluation."

• SUBSCRIPTION DATA. Renewal—similar information.

• FULFILLMENT COST PER SUBSCRIPTION COPY. Helps spot trends in this cost.

• NUMBER OF EMPLOYEES. A simple measure that can very quickly indicate if the payroll is getting out of line.

Accounting in Multipublication Houses

If you publish a number of magazines, some employees will probably spend time on more than one magazine. If the situation is this simple, allocation of their salaries and associated costs (payroll taxes, fringes, etc.) based on an estimate of the amount of time spent is normally adequate.

Large companies tend to set up service departments to handle functions that are common to all the magazines. These usually are:

- Production
- Advertising promotion
- Circulation

Other departments are sometimes set up that are, in essence, supplier departments to the magazines, including:

- Composition
- Photography
- Art
- Direct mail
- Subscription fulfillment

Every multipublication house also has general and administrative costs that apply to the overall operation rather than to any one magazine, including:

- Executive
- Accounting
- Personnel
- Maintenance
- Office services
- Corporate

In addition, some large companies tend to have staff functions that do not directly serve any one magazine, such titles as:

- Group president
- Director of manufacturing
- Editorial director
- Advertising director

It may also be useful, in addition, for the organization to have some centralized services, but the fewer, the better.

My feeling is that the more functions specifically working for a single title, the better. I believe in an organization where each magazine operates as an

Figure 52.2. Statistical Data

Current Month				Year to Date		
Last Year	Budget	This Year		This Year	Budget	Last Year
			PAGES			
			Advertising			
			Editoral			
			Other			
			Total			
			% Advertising of total			
			AVERAGE COPIES PRINTED			
			Subscription			
			Single-copy draw			
			Other			
			Total			
			COST PER COPY			
			Printing, Prepress			
			Paper			
			Distribution—Subscription			
			Distribution—Single Copy			
			Total			
			THOUSAND PAGES PRINTED			
			COST PER THOUSAND PAGES			
			Printing, Prepress			
			Paper			
			Distribution—Subscription			
			Distribution—Single Copy			
			Total			
			ADVERTISING			
			One-time black and white rate			
			Income per Ad Page			
			Cost per Ad Page			
			% Ad Cost of Ad Income			
			Future Ad Pages on Order			
			EDITORIAL			
			Cost per Edit Page			
			SINGLE COPY			
			% of draw sold			
			Net Income per Copy			
			SUBSCRIPTIONS—NEW			
			New Subs Sold			
			Average Length			
			Income per Copy (Cash basis)			
			Promotion Cost per Copy Sold			
			Income per copy (Accrual basis)			
			SUBSCRIPTIONS—RENEWAL			
			Renewals Sold			
			Average Length			
			Income per Copy (Cash basis)			
			Promotion Cost per Copy Sold			
			Income per copy (Accrual basis)			
			FULFILLMENT			
			Cost per Subscription Copy			
			EMPLOYEES			
			Number			

independent unit with all its people working for that magazine and nothing else. Each then has its own:

- Publisher
- Editor
- Advertising director
- Circulation director
- Controller

I recognize that I am in a minority position and that most often larger publishers have all the different types of departments and titles above (plus probably several others).

If you have these departments, the problem is how to keep track of them—and, more important, how to measure what value they are contributing, versus their cost (not always easy to do).

These non-direct-line groups are usually of three different kinds and their costs should be allocated in different ways:

- SERVICE DEPARTMENTS. They provide a service to the individual magazines. You should accumulate their costs, and allocate them on some logical basis. For instance: The production department might be allocated based on the number of issues, number of pages, total production costs, or a combination of these; the advertising promotion department on the amount of promotion spending; and the circulation department on the amount of circulation.
- SUPPLIER DEPARTMENTS. They do things that could be purchased outside. The best way is to develop a price list and charge each publication just as if you were dealing with outside companies. In this way, equitable charges are made, there are comparisons with outside firms, and the departmental costs may not grow at an uncontrollable rate.

  Some companies with departments of this kind give the individual magazines the option of buying from the in-house departments or from outside firms. This helps control both costs and quality.
- GENERAL AND ADMINISTRATIVE (that means Overhead). These costs really cannot be allocated in any precise way. But they should still be applied to the individual magazines to get an idea of the real profitability of each after all costs are included. Common formulas used are:
  - Total sales
  - Total sales plus total expenses
  - Number of people

Data Developed Less Frequently

The basic reports are useful on a monthly basis, but once or twice a year it is good to review such additional information as:

- Payroll by department and in total
- Fringe benefits as a percentage of salaries
- Advertising dollars and pages per issue versus the prior year and versus competition
- Advertising rates and discounts versus competitors'
- Sales produced by each advertising salesperson versus the total of his salary, commissions, and expenses
- Details of subscription efforts by source—and of conversion and renewal rates by source
- Details of single-copy sales by issue
- Comparison of circulation results (and circulation audit reports) with those of competitors
- Circulation prices versus competitors'—not just the published rates, but those actually charged for various types and sources of subscriptions
- Complimentary copy list
- Costs of extras in printing and paper

If you are a member of MPA or ABM, be sure to make a careful analysis of your costs versus those developed periodically in their cost, salary, and other surveys.

Natural Classifications

It is useful every so often—maybe once a year—to take a look at the expenses for a magazine and/or a company according to their natural classifications (all the travel, or messenger, or rental, or salaries, etc.). When you do this, you may find that you say to yourself, that's just too much to spend on a particular expense.

Did You Get Your Money's Worth

In the same vein, while it is good to compare costs with last year and in other ways, every so often you ought to take an empirical look at such items as your cost per editorial page. Have you really gotten $2,500 worth of value from the average page? If the average was $2,500, some must have cost $4,000. Which ones? Were they worth it?

FIVE-YEAR REVIEWS

Don't forget once a year or so to line up the accounting and statistical figures for the past five years to see what has happened. You'll be amazed at what you can learn.

It won't hurt to add to this comparison what has happened to your competitors in terms of pages, prices, etc. Compare your data, too, against the trends in the industry as a whole, which you will find from studies made by MPA, ABM, other industry associations, and, sometimes, other magazines.

Some Misguided Approaches

NO ADMINISTRATIVE COSTS CHARGED TO START-UPS

Some publishers do this. The theory is that you would not be able to reduce the administrative costs if you didn't have the new operations. This is simply a ploy to make the losses of someone's new pet project look smaller. In actual fact, chances are that a start-up operation will consume more of the G & A costs than the older properties (and probably more of various other peoples' time as well). This is time and effort that otherwise could be spent constructively elsewhere. These costs should be applied to every operation—startup, loss, or whatever.

CONTRIBUTION TO ADMINISTRATIVE COSTS AND PROFIT RATHER THAN A P & L FOR EACH PROPERTY

Some publishers, rather than showing a profit or loss for each property, develop something called "contribution to administrative costs and profit." The theory is that the publisher of an individual magazine has no control over these costs. This is true, but it distorts thinking. The contribution figure is arrived at by charging all direct expenses against each magazine, but not making any provision for administrative costs. You then have a composite statement that might look something like this:

	Sales	*Expenses*	*Contribution*	*Contribution % of Sales*
Magazine A	$2,000	$1,600	$400	20.0%
B	5,000	4,500	500	10.0
C	7,000	6,000	1,000	16.7
	$14,000	$12,100	$1,900	13.6
Administrative costs			1,400	10.0
Net profit			$500	3.6%

As you can see, the company as a whole earned only 3.6%, yet the publisher of each magazine had the feeling that he was running a magazine earning 10% to 20% of sales. But, with administrative costs allocated on any reasonable basis, one or more of the magazines is actually not profitable, and even the best is not earning much. For instance, suppose we allocate based only on sales:

	Profit	*% of Sales*
A	$200	10.0%
B	—	—
C	300	4.3

Hardly an exciting performance.

In addition to showing misleading numbers, this approach fosters thinking on the part of the managers that automatically depresses overall profits because they may believe they are doing a bang-up job when they are really barely breaking even.

PROFIT FROM ADVERTISING VERSUS PROFIT FROM CIRCULATION

Some publishers try to determine where the profits came from: advertising, subscriptions, newsstand, or perhaps other areas.

I recall one magazine that carefully applied against advertising sales only the costs of printing, paper and postage of the advertising pages, plus the cost of selling those pages—and ended up with a big profit from advertising. Then it applied against circulation income the costs of selling and fulfilling that circulation plus the editorial expenses and had a big profit from circulation. When it deducted from these two profits the costs of paper, printing, and postage of the editorial pages and administrative costs, it had a loss. The two profits it computed were meaningless.

The point is that a magazine is one product with two—or more—revenue streams that cannot be separated. You cannot think of just one part at a time, each is part of an integrated whole that must be considered in total.

Grossing Up the Figures

So far we have been talking about revenue figures on some kind of net basis: advertising net of agency commissions and cash discounts; single copy sales net of national distributor, wholesaler, and retailer payments; agent-sold subscriptions net of the agents commissions; by-product sales net of direct costs.

We do this because that is the money we actually have to play with, and against which our expenses must be measured, which seems the most meaningful way.

Once in a while it is interesting to look at the same figures based on the full amount the magazine's customers paid, rather than what we received. This is called "grossing up" the figures. Some of the results are startling:

	Net	*Grossed up*
Advertising, net of agency commissions and 2% cash discount	$ 5,000,000	$6,000,000
Single copy, net of national distributor, wholesaler, and retailer payments	2,000,000	5,000,000
Agent-sold subscriptions, net of agents commissions	1,000,000	6,500,000
Direct-to-publisher subscriptions	4,000,000	4,000,000
List rental, etc., net of direct costs	300,000	450,000
	$12,300,000	$21,950,000

As you can see, we have just converted a $12 million business into a $22 million one.

I have seen this method used when presenting a business for sale; it is meaningless, but it makes it look bigger. In some of the statistical studies of MPA and ABM this approach is used to make other points.

The Floating Break-Even Point

This was not, as you might suspect, invented by Amazon.com or one of the other dot.com companies, but is a concept discovered a long time ago by one of the larger publishing companies that had lots of experience launching new magazines and wanted to justify them.

Here's how it works:

1. You carefully project the results for the new magazine for five years. This shows that it will break even in the third year when there is 250,000 circulation and 400 advertising pages.
2. After publishing for a year, you project that it will break even when there is 350,000 circulation and 600 advertising pages with much higher future profits (the principle of expanding expectations).
3. After two years' experience, you *know* it will break even in the fifth year with 450,000 circulation and 800 advertising pages with even bigger profits.
4. After three years, you are certain it will break even some day.

Some Wilder, but Terrific, Ideas

Make up Next Month's Operating Statement Today

I have always been bothered by two things people say:

1. Accounting results are just history and arrive too late for you to take corrective action.
2. The figures, when they finally arrive, always seem to contain some surprises.

There is no reason for either of these feelings in the magazine business because you can make up next month's operating statements right now. The day you accept the last ad for an issue, a financial statement accurate within 1% can be produced. (Note that I said "accept the last ad." This is not necessarily the official closing date—or the date you receive the actual copy for the ad, which is probably even later.)

When you accept that last ad, you know how many pages will be in the issue—and how the forms will be laid out. If you are on a monthly schedule and have very large circulation that requires some time to print, you can develop the operating statement for the September issue in June, which is when the last ad pages are accepted. That certainly is not history!

Even if you don't get the figures that early, what an improvement for most publishers—to have the August figures in July, instead of waiting for all the bookkeeping steps and detail to be finished, some time between September 15 and 30, which is normal.

Here is how you do it. All income and expense items for a magazine are either issue-related or time-related.

Issue-Related Income Items

Advertising income can be determined when the last ad is accepted. Today's computer programs can tell you within minutes the exact income from that ad, including the extra charges and various discounts.

Single-copy sales income is at best an estimate until several months after the off-sale dates because of the complexities of developing good data through the system. These estimates are just as good when made a few months ahead as they will be a month after publication.

Subscription income. Almost all publishers defer subscription income and know far in advance what it will be for an issue for the vast majority of the subscriptions. The only place where a problem may exist involves expires, renewals, and new subscriptions. But a sophisticated circulation department must estimate these very closely to determine the print order, so they can do it for this purpose as well.

Issue-Related Expense Items

Paper, printing, and distribution can be determined very closely once the pressrun, number of pages, and layout have been fixed. There will be a few unknowns such as the exact number of copies printed because of overruns, the precise amount of paper waste, and any extra printing costs, but these can be estimated based on previous experience.

Sales commissions are a by-product of the advertising income calculations.

Subscription fulfillment costs are a by-product of the subscription income calculation.

Editorial costs, including purchased manuscripts, artwork, and photos are known at the time of making up the issue.

Time-Related Items

All income and expense items not related to the issue are booked as they are incurred with no attempt to pin them to specific issues.

List rental, reprint, and other income are not assigned to an issue, but are included at the time of billing. These are normally small in the overall picture. Where they are substantial, they are prescheduled and can easily be estimated.

Salaries, other than salespeoples' commissions, are quite constant. Hirings and leavings are usually known early, as are changes in pay. Fringe benefits contain no surprises. Promotion, both for advertising and circulation, is scheduled far in advance, as is research. Travel is predictable and other administrative expenses are rarely unexpected.

Fixing Profit (I may get thrown out of the accountants' union for this one)

Our operating statements are upside down!

They carry profit as the last item on the page. It seems only to be the result of what is left over from sales after we have paid everyone, and we always talk about looking at the "bottom line." Why don't we make the bottom line the "top line"?

In the same way, the owners' equity on our balance sheets, which should be the most important item, is way down on the lower right-hand corner. In logical sequence at least, it is the last item to be read. Our British friends know better—their balance sheets are backward and upside down to us, but owners' equity is at the top left where it is the first thing you see.

This backward thinking fits with some other things publishers do. For instance, we put the most important story in the right-hand column. It should be on the left because we read from left to right.

I know how the operating statement got that way. It's us accountants. We're better at subtracting expenses from sales than the other way around, but in this computer age, we should be capable of doing it either way. When you put profit at the bottom of the column, your thinking is warped. It doesn't give the proper importance to the reason we are in business.

Even worse are those people—and there are lots of them—who set up their statements this way:

- Expenses
- Income
- Profit or loss

The minute I see figures set up in this sequence, I know I have a loser on my hands. He doesn't have a profit motive.

Profit, not expense, should be a fixed item—and the first fixed item. If we cannot make the rest of the figures fit, then something else should be changed—or the method of doing business should be radically altered.

This is a whole new way of thinking for most of us—but it puts the emphasis where it belongs—on what we are trying to achieve. This simple change in concept can have a radical influence on how we conduct ourselves.

There is more to it than simply developing the concept that profit is fixed. A change in the manner of making operating statements is needed because a whole new mind-set is involved. Here is one approach:

A CITY MAGAZINE

Operating Statement
(In thousands)

Profits		
	Fixed	$ 500
	Additional	200
		700
Sales—Net		
	Advertising	2,400
	Subscription	2,500
	Newsstand	500
	Other	100
		5,500
Costs		
	Mechanical	2,200
	Advertising	500
	Editorial	400
	Circulation	1,300
	Administrative	400
		4,800

We have accomplished a rather remarkable thing. The first item is the most important one!

Strange—the way we now do it is completely contrary to the way we do just about everything else. I don't know of any football team that consciously says, "We'll give the other guys 24 points, and if we can score more, we'll win." But that's the approach our normal financial statements take.

About now, you should be asking: "What, specifically, have we accomplished?"

1. The focus is on profits, not sales or costs.
2. If the fixed profits cannot be achieved, something else must change, but not that. If this means a change in the way of operating, so be it.
3. If there is no way of achieving the fixed profit, let's get out of the business. This may make us stop so many of those efforts that go on year after year—with good results to be achieved next year—every year.
4. If it's a new business, and if the fixed profits can never be achieved—or will take too long—let's not get started.
5. Management time—the most precious commodity we have—is not wasted on fruitless pursuits.

The same approach can be applied to some other tools used in business, for instance, the "break-even approach." I don't want to know what the break-even formula is. I want to make money. Let's change this to the not-very-catchy "minimum acceptable profit approach."

CHAPTER 53

Using the Figures—A Case Study

WE HAVE BEEN discussing the concept of looking at the accounting figures, not just in a single dimension, but in three, four, or more ways. Here is a quick and very brief example of how they can be used as a diagnostic tool.

Let's try it for A Magazine, using abbreviated figures. I will go through it step-by-step just as New Buyer did it before he bought A Magazine on September 1, Year 2. This way you can see how the information builds up and becomes more meaningful. I will use just the figures for Year 1 and Year 2, but, of course, New Buyer would have looked at data for a number of years back.

He first obtained the figures for the first six months of Year 2, shown below in Table 53.1:

Table 53.1

Six Months	This Year Actual	
Income		
Advertising—Net of agency commission & cash discounts	$3,600,000	54%
Subscriptions—Accrual	2,580,000	39%
Single copy—Net of returns	280,000	4%
Other—Net of direct costs	240,000	3%
Total	6,700,000	100%
Expenses		
Mechanical	2,400,000	36
Advertising	800,000	12
Editorial	500,000	7
Circulation	2,800,000	42
Administrative	1,100,000	16
	7,600,000	113
Operating (Loss)	$ (900,000)	(13)%

New Buyer quickly realized that Old Owner was not numbers oriented since all he had on the sheet were the bare figures for the period (New Buyer added the percentages). Pretty hard to learn much from this except that for six months the magazine was doing close to $7 million of business and managed to lose almost $1 million.

He also realized that this was a business that was dependent on advertising for profits and that the costs of obtaining circulation were almost as much as its income.

Undaunted by the large loss shown, New Buyer decided to look into the trends, so obtained the figures for the prior year (Table 53.2).

WOW! Every income item is way up—a total of $1.4 million. Happy that he had looked further, New Buyer wondered why profits were down by $400,000 with this great showing. Better look at the statistics for Year 2 to see what we can learn. It took a little persuasion as well as digging to get figures (Table 53.3).

Doesn't seem to be anything obviously out of line in mechanical, editorial, or fulfillment costs. Ad pages at 45% of total is not bad.

But another WOW! There are a full six months' ad pages on order, probably meaning another increase in sales. And the subscription cash received is almost a full million dollars more than the accrual figures. So, on a cash basis this is better than a break-even!

Table 53.2

Six Months	This Year Actual		Last Year	
Income				
Advertising—Net of agency commission and cash discounts	$3,600,000	54%	$2,880,000	55%
Subscriptions—Accrual	2,580,000	39%	2,100,000	40%
Single copy—Net of returns	280,000	4%	140,000	2%
Other—Net of direct costs	240,000	3%	160,000	3%
Total	6,700,000	100%	5,280,000	100%
Expenses				
Mechanical	2,400,000	36	1,700,000	32
Advertising	800,000	12	580,000	11
Editorial	500,000	7	340,000	6
Circulation	2,800,000	42	2,160,000	41
Administrative	1,100,000	16	900,000	17
	7,600,000	113	5,680,000	107
Operating (Loss)	$ (900,000)	(13)%	$ (500,000)	(7)%

Table 53.3

Six Months	This Year Actual	Last Year Actual	This Year Estimate
Pages			
Advertising	500	400	500
Editorial	560	440	500
Other	40	40	40
	1,100	880	1,040
% advertising to total	45.5%	45.5%	48.1%
Average copies			
Subscription	400,000	375,000	380,000
Single-copy draw	70,000	50,000	70,000
Other	5,000	5,000	5,000
Pressrun	475,000	430,000	455,000
Mechanical cost per copy	$ .84	$ .68	$ .74
Mechanical cost per thousand pages	4.59	4.49	4.27
Advertising revenue per ad page	$7,200	$7,200	$7,000
Advertising cost per ad page	1,600	1,450	1,120
% cost of revenue	22.0%	20.1%	16.0%
Future ad pages on order	480	260	400
Editorial cost per edit page	$893	$772	$640
Single copies sold 30,000	20,000	40,000	
% of draw	42.9%	40.0%	57.1%
Net revenue per copy	$1.56	$1.17	$1.50
Subscriptions sold	200,000	220,000	170,000
Subscription years sold	240,000	260,000	210,000
Revenue per copy sold (cash)	$1.20	$1.28	$1.20
Promotion cost per copy sold	$ .80	$ .64	$ .96
Revenue per copy served (accrual)	$1.08	$ .79	$ .90
Subscription cash received	$3,460,000	$2,460,000	$3,020,000
Fulfillment cost per copy	$.10	$.10	$.10
Number of employees	36	30	28

Better look further—may have a real sleeper here. Better compare statistics with the prior year.

WOW a third time. Not only are ad pages up, but the revenue per page is higher too (higher rate). Single copies sold are up, the percentage of sale is higher, and the price seems to have been increased as well. Subscriptions continue to sell well even with a price increase.

This is a hot property!

Still a few things to wonder about before making an offer for the business.

Old Owner did not have a budget system, of course, but New Buyer wormed out of him an estimate he had made in the fall covering the first six months of Year 2.

This showed that Old Owner had been aware of the growth that would take place in advertising and subscriptions, but had overestimated the single-copy sales.

It also showed that he had expected considerably lower costs in several areas:

Editorial pages—actual 60 more than he had estimated.

Mechanical costs per thousand copy pages—actually higher than he had estimated, and above those of the prior year.

These two items increased the total mechanical costs by some $300,000 above what they should have been.

The actual cost of selling ad pages—some $500 per page above his estimate and considerably above the prior year.

Editorial actual costs per page up—by some 15%.

Administrative costs—up about the same percentage.

The number of employees, which had been expected to decline by two, had actually increased by six.

All this indicated that the operation was out of control and, even allowing for some optimism on the part of Old Owner, that substantial profits should have been earned.

And to think that we learned all that from a handful of figures on just two pages!

CHAPTER 54

Records You Might Need

TO DEVELOP THE data needed for the operating statements, you will need to keep track through various accounts in the accounting records. You will undoubtedly have more accounts than the monthly statement uses so that it is easier to analyze for specifics when desired. Classifications that might be set up to produce the operating statements are generally as shown below—but feel free to expand or contract this list as needed.

Advertising Revenue

- Display advertising income (gross)
- Agency commissions
- Cash discounts
- Short rates (added charges for failing to earn frequency, volume, or other discounts originally contracted for)
- Frequency rebates (added rebates not originally contracted for)
- Guarantee refunds (because of failure to reach circulation guarantees or rate bases)
- Allowances (credits for poor reproduction, disputed items, other complaints)
- Classified advertising
- Advertorials, special sections, insert cards, and other special items

Detailed records in the advertising department also tally the premiums paid for color, bleed, covers, special positions, and other such items, as well as discounts for mail order, retail, and other categories.

For some magazines it is useful to show the gross advertising income less the various discounts on the operating statement.

Subscription Revenue

- New subscriptions by source:
  - Direct mail
  - Insert cards
  - Gift
  - White mail
  - Web
  - Direct mail agent
  - Field agent
  - School agent
  - Catalog agent
  - Other
- Renewal subscriptions

Subscription revenue is the gross amount received by the publisher before deducting the costs of promotion and selling commissions to agents, but after deducting refunds, cancellations, and other losses on charge orders not collected. Some publishers record agent-sold subscriptions on a net after commission basis.

Detailed records are kept of all this and much more information by the circulation department.

Single-Copy Revenue

- Newsstand
  - Sales
  - Returns
  - Charges for returned copies
- Direct
  - Sales
  - Returns
  - Charges for returned copies

Estimated returns are set up when each issue is published. This is adjusted to actual as later figures are developed.

Other Revenue—Net of Direct Costs

- List rental
- Reprint
- Postcard pack
- Other

Major by-product activities such as book publishing and Web sites would have their own operating statements.

Mechanical Expenses

- Salaries, including payroll taxes and fringe benefits
  - Executive
  - Other
- Travel and entertainment
- Prepress
- Printing, binding, distribution
- Paper
- Subscription postage
- Subscription shipping
- Wrappers or envelopes
- Single-copy shipping
- Other

Prepress may include composition, color separations, and other items depending on the degree of computerization and digitization of the operations. These may be assigned to the editorial department depending on where the purchasing responsibility lies.

More detailed records are kept by the production department about individual cost items.

Advertising Expenses

- Salaries, including payroll taxes and fringe benefits
  - Executive
  - Salespeople
  - Clerical
- Commissions to salespeople
- Commissions to independent representatives
- Travel and entertainment
- Promotion (including free copies to advertisers, presentations, sales aids)
- Advertising
- Research
- Circulation audit
- Merchandising
- Branch office costs
- Other

At some point be sure to measure the costs of each salesperson (salaries, expenses, etc.) against the income he produces.

Editorial Expenses

- Salaries, including payroll taxes and fringe benefits
  - Executive
  - Editors
  - Artists
  - Clerical
- Travel and entertainment
- Manuscripts
- Artwork, photos, cartoons
- Research
- Branch office costs
- Other

As mentioned above, prepress activities may be charged here depending how the magazine is operated.

If there are substantial manuscript and art purchases, which are purchased in advance of publication, they may be inventoried and charged to expenses as used or written off.

Subscription Expenses

- Salaries, including payroll taxes and fringe benefits
  - Executive

  - Promotion
  - Fulfillment
  - Clerical
- Travel and entertainment
- Promotion
- New subscriptions by source
  - Direct mail
  - Insert cards
  - Gift
  - White mail
  - Web
- Direct mail agent
  - Field agent
  - School agent
  - Catalog agent
  - Other
- Promotion—Renewal subscriptions
- Billing and collecting costs
- Fulfillment (outside and/or inside costs)
- Other

As with subscription income, details of subscription acquisition costs are kept by the circulation department.

Magazines with controlled circulation have accounts for establishing these lists and verifying that readers request the magazine.

Single-Copy Sales Expenses

- Salaries, including payroll taxes and fringe benefits
  - Executive
  - Field
  - Clerical
- Travel and entertainment
- Newsstand
  - Promotion
  - Retail display allowance
  - Other
- Direct Sales
  - Promotion
  - Other
- Other

General and Administrative Costs

- Salaries including payroll taxes and fringe benefits
  - Executive
  - Accounting
  - Office
  - Clerical
- Travel and entertainment
- Occupancy (rent, electricity, etc., or, if the property is owned or rented on a net lease, the costs of operation and maintenance)
- Telephone
- Stationery, office supplies
- Computer
- Office equipment rental
- Depreciation
- Professional fees
- Insurance
- State and local taxes
- Pension plan
- Profit-sharing plan
- Other

CHAPTER 55

Planning

WE'RE GOING TO be talking about budgeting. After all, a budget is nothing more or less than a plan, an organized one to be sure, but still just a plan.

Budgets are usually made for a year, and maybe a little longer. When we go farther, we might call it long-range planning.

Budgets cover all the income, expense, and profit items involved in a business. They are usually expressed in dollars because that is the unit that we use to quantify just about everything we do in business, but a budget can also be expressed through statistics, or in a narrative form.

While a well-designed budget results in a plan for future operations, its development and monitoring really is a planning system that accomplishes a great deal more:

1. Forces key people to think through their activities
2. Coordinates the activities in various areas
3. Examines alternative strategies and tactics
4. Involves key people in decisions
5. Gets key people involved with each other
6. Evaluates performance
7. Helps control operations
8. Ensures that the key people understand the overall plan and their place in making it work

Types of Budgets

Budgets are made for any kind of human activity, from running a family's finances to those of the largest companies.

In a business, at the very least, there will be an operating budget, a cash-flow budget, and a balance sheet budget. (Sometimes they are called by less threatening names such as projections or pro formas.) In a capital-intensive business, there will be a capital budget. In a people-intensive business, there will be a people or payroll budget. Often there are project budgets.

In magazine publishing, we have advertising page, subscription, and single-copy sales budgets, among others.

Some companies go with just one budget, while others have several, such as high, low, and expected. When conditions call for it, "disaster" budgets are prepared so that action can be taken quickly if sales decline precipitously.

Budget Periods

Budgeting periods coincide with the accounting periods so that comparisons can easily be made with actual results. In the magazine business, these would normally be on a monthly basis or whatever other periods are used in developing accounting results.

Who Is Involved in Budgeting?

Just about everybody!

The most effective budgeting process is "ground up." Everyone who has responsibility for anything gets into the process as it involves the area for which he is responsible.

The overall budget is developed by putting all the pieces together in an organized way. Thus, the Washington editor budgets for his or her department and the chief editor puts this together with other aspects to develop the overall editorial budget.

Why do it this way?

1. No one believes in a dictated budget as much as he does one that he helped develop.
2. You want to get the opinions and wisdom of everyone you can.
3. The more people who are involved, and who feel that they are part of the team, the better the budget will be—and the better they will do their jobs.
4. The closer you are to the actual activity, the more detailed knowledge you have of the function and how it really operates.

Steps in Preparing a Budget

When done correctly, the budgeting process takes a long time. Planning has to be done on many levels. Individual budgets have to be fitted together to yield a coherent and viable whole. This calls for lots of give and take, plus studies of various alternatives and, usually, compromises.

Several months before the end of a company's fiscal year, the financial people set the process in motion by giving each of those involved some background material to help in developing the coming year's budget. The treasurer, controller, or someone else in the financial end of the business is then generally in charge of pulling the budget together and of monitoring it.

To get the most out of the process, the publisher should set the tone of what is expected by pointing out his feelings about the state of the economy, state of the field served, and his profit expectations. Then all the others involved have a feeling for the overall direction they should point toward.

The type of information given each department varies, but would include:

- Figures for prior periods
- This year's budget plus actual figures so far, and projections for the rest of the year
- Statistics for these periods
- Competitive information
- Industry norms

Each department head passes his first budget try to the level above, where it is discussed and revised as needed. Eventually all the pieces are merged into one document for the whole company. The boss reviews the entire budget, consults with others as necessary, and sends the material back down the line with suggestions that will result in an overall budget that will be satisfactory. This up-and-back process continues until agreement is reached on the best plan. This can take many meetings and the study of lots of major and minor alternatives. Eventually the final budget is adopted as the plan for the year.

Using the Budget to Help Control Operations

A budget is not just developed and put on the shelf. It is a working document that is used throughout the year.

At the end of each accounting period the controller issues reports showing actuals versus the budget. These go to everyone who prepared a budget covering his or her area. Where there are deviations of any significance, either better or worse, the controller investigates the causes and indicates what they are. It is then up to each of those involved—and eventually the boss—to judge the real significance of each, to determine whether a trend is appearing, and to take whatever action might be helpful. With a good budgeting procedure, there should never be any surprises.

Rebudgeting

Remember that a business budget is just a plan and is not fixed in concrete. If major changes take place during the year, rebudgeting must be done. In doing this, however, the original budget should not be lost or forgotten—or it will always appear that you are always right on budget, no matter what changes are made. It is always good to compare the original budget, in addition to the latest one, with the actual results.

Some companies rebudget automatically every quarter or twice a year. Others run a revolving budget, planning 12 months ahead every quarter. I would not advise this because it can become very time-consuming—and it can easily lead to a mere updating rather than a real in-depth review once a year.

Why Budget Systems Do Not Accomplish All They Should

1. The boss isn't really behind it—either because he doesn't understand it or because he doesn't really want it.

2. People think the boss isn't behind it, even if he supports it.

3. Inexperience in the process.

4. Too many people with an innate fear of numbers—a holdgover from failure in the third grade.

5. Planning is harder work than most want—or know how—to do.

6. Interdepartmental rivalries make intelligent planning impossible.

7. The budget is developed by the boss and imposed on everyone else.

8. The accountants have taken over and use jargon no one else understands.

9. Departments are charged with expenses over which they have no control.

10. Lack of realization that budgeting is a process, not a static thing.

11. The budgeting process is poorly planned and organized.

12. A governmental budget complex—the budget is hard, fast, and unchangeable.

13. No matter what happens, we will spend the money allotted—no less, no more.

14. Key people are not given enough data or enough help to do a good job.

15. Actual figures are developed so late that they are meaningless (see chapter 52, "Keeping Track of What's Going On").

16. The boss is secretive about some key figures.

17. Budgets are developed simply by updating the prior year's figures.

18. There is no corrective follow-up of differences between the budget and actual.

Ways to Make the Budgeting Process Work Better

1. Run a school to explain the entire process.

2. Make sure the budget figures are developed on the same basis as the actual accounting figures.

3. Accompany the financial budget with a written description of each phase, together with the reasoning behind it.

4. Write down the schedule and ground rules of the budget process.

5. Make sure all deadlines are strictly adhered to.

6. Hold planning sessions with key people to discuss alternatives and different approaches.

7. Get the actual figures in time to do something about them.

8. Take action fast when significant deviations are found.

9. Have the boss be in charge of the budgeting. This emphasizes his involvement and gives direction to the planning.

10. Give all those budgeting enough data to do it intelligently.

11. Make sure that everyone understands that cost control is important, but that having costs way below budget is not necessarily good.

12. Have an editor rewrite accounting and budget reports from the controller so that they can be easily understood.

13. Give all the budgeters tools to make the job easier—use of computer models, worksheets, and calculators.

14. Better yet, lend budgeters people from the accounting department to do the figure work.

15. Make sure that performance in the budgeting process is part of the evaluation of employees.

16. Be sure that budgets are coordinated with long-range plans.

17. Let all budgeters know what the broad parameters of income and costs are for the coming year before beginning the process.

18. Insist on overall compliance with the budget, but give leeway on individual items within a department—and from month to month.

19. Let *all* the key people see *all* the numbers so that they get a feeling for the overall economics of the business.

CHAPTER 56

Magazine Budgeting—A Case Study

On August 1 of Year 2, New Buyer purchased A Magazine after having reviewed its operations for the first six months of Year 1 and Year 2 (discussed in chapter 53, "Using the Figures—A Case Study"). He was convinced that greater profits could be earned if better planning and controls could be developed. As one of the first steps, he decided to install a budget system.

While each of the key people knew his or her own area of activity, New Boss found that there were no regular meetings to discuss operations and little interdepartmental exchange, other than what was absolutely essential. Aside from the controller, no one had ever seen any financial information.

New Boss felt that the installation of the budget offered a good chance for the key people to get to know each other, to understand the economics of the business, and to get more involved than before. Besides that, his investigation had indicated that strong controls were needed.

Further, New Boss decided that, despite the shortage of time, a budget system should begin operating in January of Year 3. New Boss would assume leadership of the effort, with considerable work being done by the controller and his people.

Steps in Organizing for Budgeting

In August, New Boss held a meeting with the editor, ad director, circulation director, production director, office manager, and controller. Financial data for the entire magazine for Year 1 and the first six months of Year 2 were presented and explained. Cash flow figures and balance sheets were also distributed.

A week later, another meeting of the group was held to answer questions, clarify misconceptions, and generally to get greater understanding of the numbers and of the interaction of the departments. It turned out that there had been considerable misunderstanding of how things should work—and little appreciation of the problems each department faced. A written description of the budgeting process was distributed and is shown below.

B MAGAZINE—
Description of Budgeting Process

Timetable

September 1: First budget meeting and distribution of background material.

October 1: Submission of first budget figures by department heads.

October 8: Completion of first combined figures by controller.

October 15: Individual review of each department's budget by New Boss with department heads.

October 22: Resubmission of departmental budgets.

October 25: Resubmission of second combined figures by controller.

November 1: Meeting to discuss the final version of the completed budget and to make any last-minute corrections.

No major changes are anticipated in operating methods during Year 3. Printing prices are expected to increase, in line with the labor and material escalation clauses in the contract, by 5% beginning in May. The exact amount will not be known until the union contract negotiations have been completed. Paper prices will probably rise by 4% in February, but this, too. is uncertain. Postage, as usual, is almost impossible to predict and awaits completion of the Postal Rate Commission hearings. Until then, we should plan for a 15% increase in the periodical rate, 15%t in first class, and 25% in third class in July.

There was no across-the-board salary increase last year. With continued low inflation and an improved economy, we should plan for a 5% overall increase in salaries. We must also plan for rises in other prices, although none of these is as important as the paper, printing, postage, and people costs.

These increased costs obviously call for increased income or reduced costs—or both—to remain at the break-even point. But I would really like to develop $1,500,000 cash profit for 2001, with much greater earnings in later periods.

Obviously, income is related to the state of the economy and to the trends in our market, as well as to our own efforts. As you know, the economy has turned upward, which should be of some help.

From past history it does not appear that we can expect more than a small increase in advertising pages, even with the improved economy. And I can't see a bonanza of suddenly increased circulation, although there should be some growth.

It seems that we won't be able to reach even a breakeven without some rate increases in advertising, circulation, or both.

To meet the goal of a $1,500,000 profit, then, would seem to require a reduction in expenses as well—just how much remains to be seen. Obviously, any plans for doing this, or for developing new sources of revenue, would be welcome.

Big new ideas for improving profits for the future (some of you have mentioned a Web site among other things) should be kept out of this current budgeting process, however welcome they may be later.

Good luck,

(Signed) New Boss

In the meeting at which the budgeting process was explained in general and the specifics of the system for B Magazine were outlined, the following data were given to each department head to serve as historical and background material:

1. Financial statements and statistical material for the magazine for the last three years and this year so far
2. Competitive data on advertising pages, revenue, and rates; circulation prices and circulation breakdowns by geography and demographics
3. Similar material on other magazines of about the same size in other fields
4. History of salaries, commissions, fringe benefits, and travel and entertainment expenses for each person in each manager's department
5. Monthly breakdown of income and expense items, as well as statistics, for the individual's department (An example of the material for editorial is shown below.)
6. Worksheet in the same form as the financial statements for use in making out departmental budgets for Year 3 (Note that there is considerably more detail on these worksheets than on the actual operating statement.)

In addition, step-by-step instructions for filling out the worksheets were provided, as well as the controller's assistance. Because of the added burdens he was assuming, the controller was given a magazine computer model to ease the making of needed calculations. The department heads were also told that they could submit their material in any of three ways:

1. In detailed dollars for each month as indicated on the worksheets
2. By sitting with the controller and working out the numbers together
3. By writing out the plans and letting the controller complete the worksheets

In addition to providing the numbers, each department head also submitted a written description of his plans. The editorial department's plan is shown below.

Figure 56.1. Worksheet

EDITORIAL DEPARTMENT INFORMATION

	Year 1 January	Total 6 months
Pages		
Cover and contents	3	18
Listings	8	48
Reviews	6	36
Editorial, publisher's page	2	12
Puzzles	3	18
Columns	10	60
Short stuff	5	30
Letters	3	18
Features	50	320
	90	560
Black and white	36	216
2-Color	20	120
4-Color	34	224
	90	560
Expenses		
Salaries		
Editor	$6,667	$40,000
Managing Editor	$5,000	$30,000
Art Director	$5,000	$30,000
Senior Editor (2)	$5,833	$35,000
Assistant Editor (2)	$5,000	$30,000
Copy Editor	$3,333	$20,000
Editorial Assistant	$4,167	$25,000
Editorial Researcher (2)	$3,333	$20,000
	$38,333	$230,000
Columnists	$4,500	$27,000
Art and photo	$18,000	$112,000
Manuscripts	$10,000	$60,000
Travel and entertainment	$3,000	$36,000
Editorial research	0	0
Other	$5,833	$35,000
	$79,666	$500,000
Cost per edit page	$885	$893
% of total revenue	8.20%	7.50%

Editorial Department Plan—Year 3

No major changes are anticipated in the overall editorial concept for 2001. We plan to add two pages per issue to cover movies in greater depth. This should also be helpful in obtaining more advertising dollars.

I see a major picture story covering the fascinating new artwork being developed in various art colleges such as RISD, University of Denver, and other such places. This would cost some $85,000 considering the on-location shots and interviews. We can replace some of the regular features so that it won't add any pages, but I don't expect that we will save anything in the normal art and manuscript costs.

I anticipate that total salaries will increase by 5% except that one of the assistant editors is pregnant and will have to be replaced. We may be able to save a little here, but I did not dare budget for it.

It would help the magazine a lot to switch two more pages per issue from 2 color to 4 color. The difference in prepress costs would be only about $400 per issue.

Other than that, we have a good, motivated, hard-working, and dedicated team that believes that we can improve on last year's editorial product, which, as I recall, you described as "superb."

Figure 56.2. Amended Editoral Department Budget Worksheet

	Year 2 Original per Editor
Pages	
Cover and contents	36
Listings	96
Reviews	96
Editorial, publisher's page	24
Puzzles	36
Columns	120
Short stuff	60
Letters	36
Features	600
	1104
Black and white	432
2-Color	264
4-Color	408
	1104
Expenses	
Salaries	
Editor	$84,000
Managing Editor	$63,000
Art Director	$63,000
Senior Editor (2)	$73,500
Assistant Editor (2)	$63,000
Copy Editor	$42,000
Editorial Assistant (2)	$52,500
Editorial Researcher (2)	$42,000
	$483,000
Columnists	$56,000
Art and photo	$235,000
College art piece	$85.000
Manuscripts	$126,000
Travel and entertainment	$72,000
Editorial research	0
Other	$72,000
	$1,129,000
Cost per edit page	$1,023
% of total revenue	8.7%

Preparing the Budget

During September the controller spent most of his time pushing, pulling, cajoling, explaining, and helping the department heads work out their budget worksheets.

In working with the various departments on a day-to-day basis, it soon became apparent to the controller that the goal New Boss had set would not be met—in fact, it would fall far short. New Boss merely pointed out that all budgets start that way and that there was still a long way to go.

Key points indicated in the various first-round worksheets were:

- 5% increase in ad pages
- 5% increase in ad rates
- Increase of 20,000 in subscriptions
- No change in single-copy sales
- No change in circulation prices
- Printing, paper, postage, and people costs about as much as New Boss had outlined
- A few new areas for spending, such as those in the editor's plan
- Other costs up 3% to 5%

The result showed total revenue of $13 million, up $900,000 from the prior year, with costs up about the same amount. The breakeven of the previous year was gone, and the loss of $900,000 that resulted was a long way from New Boss's desire for $1,500,000 profit.

When New Boss got the first draft of the budget, each activity and each figure was reviewed with the department head who submitted it.

The conversation with the editor was probably the most difficult one. It was apparent that the thought of reducing expenses had flown right over his head—and that he had no idea that he was running too many editorial pages. He apparently had no conception of the costs involved in additional pages or in the expense involved in four color versus black and white. New Boss impressed on the editor that the total pages and the number of four-color pages had to be reduced.

In the course of developing the budget, an advertising-to-editorial ratio of about 61% to 39% was aimed at with a minimum editorial page count of 55 pages and a maximum of 75. A schedule was constructed to make the editorial page count almost automatic for each issue, depending on the number of advertising pages and the capabilities of the printer's equipment. A sample of this:

Ad Pages	Edit pages	Total pages (including cover)
100	64	164
101	63	164
102	62	164
103	61	164
104	60	164
105	67	172
106	66	172
107	65	172

The original budget prepared by the editor was changed (see chart at right):

Because there were fewer pages, cost reductions included, among other things, a reduction in the editorial staff. None of the recommended salary increases was changed.

Figure 56.3. Amended Editoral Department Budget Worksheet

	Year 2 Revised
Pages	
Cover and contents	36
Listings	72
Reviews	72
Editorial, publisher's page	12
Puzzles	24
Columns	96
Short stuff	48
Letters	24
Features	456
	840
Black and white	348
2-Color	200
4-Color	292
	840
Expenses	
Salaries	
Editor	$84,000
Managing Editor	$63,000
Art Director	$63,000
Senior Editor (2)	$73,500
Assistant Editor (2) Eliminate one	$31,500
Copy Editor	$42,000
Editorial Assistant (2) Eliminate one	$22,000
Editorial Researcher (2) Eliminate one	$21,000
	$400,000
Columnists	$48,000
Art and photo	$170,000
College art piece	0
Manuscripts	$90,000
Travel and entertainment	$54,000
Editorial research — Add	$20,000
Other	$54,000
	$836,000
Cost per edit page	$995
% of total revenue	6.4%

After each area was discussed with its department head—and agreement achieved—the second budget try resulted in these major changes:

- 7% ad rate increase rather than 5%
- $2 increase in subscription price, but no increase in the number of subscriptions

- A reduction from 55-pound paper to 50-pound
- Editorial research of $20,000 (This was added at the insistence of New Boss.)
- Major reductions in editorial pages and costs

These changes yielded a profit of $1,250,000. New Boss then went back to each department head to share some further cost reductions to reach the $1,500,000 figure.

The final budget meeting November 1 was used as a forum to discuss the entire document with everyone involved. A few minor adjustments were made, but it was essentially finished and copies distributed.

New Boss would have preferred that the group had worked up some alternative figures in addition, but because this was the first budget try and an abnormal number of hours had been spent in its preparation, he decided not to add that burden. Instead, with the assistance of the computer model, it was determined that a 15% decline in advertising would throw the magazine into a loss situation that would call for quick action. New Boss decided that for the next year the entire group would develop high, low, and most-likely figures.

The approaches to the budgeting process had varied with the different department heads. The editor sat with the controller and they did the entire worksheet together in one morning. The production and circulation managers worked up their own, which the controller reviewed. The ad director just gave the controller his written game plan and the controller actually worked up the figures, which he checked with the ad director.

In the course of preparing the budget it became apparent to New Boss that there were a number of key factors to be watched so that variations from the budget could be seen very early. While the budget was developed on a departmental basis and comparisons would eventually be shown that way, New Boss determined that other useful reports could be developed much sooner.

Publication date for B Magazine was on the 25th of the month. The final imposition was determined on the 15th, with the last ad accepted on the 10th. New Boss established the following schedule of reports that would give early warning signals each month:

- 12th—Advertising space
- 17th—Production costs
- 2nd of next month—Circulation and by-product income and expenses

With this information, some 90% of the variable income and expense figures could be determined very early. The complete accounting reports would come out on the 15th.

Actual Results

On January 12 came the first good news. Ad pages, which had been budgeted at 94, came in at 104. New Boss congratulated the ad director.

On January 17, the production report showed 78 editorial pages, 8 over the projected number. It also showed 38 4-color editorial pages, 8 over the allotment. New Boss discussed this with the editor and they agreed that the overages should be made up in the remaining issues of the year.

The production department also showed a print order of 5,000 copies above the budget. Investigation showed that the annual cleanup of the complimentary list had been bypassed because of concentration on the budget. New Boss gave orders for the list to be reduced before the next issue.

On February 2, the circulation director reported that the circulation sales report would be several days late because reports received from the fulfillment house could not be believed. He visited with the fulfillment house and another report was submitted February 9 that indicated that the higher price had no effect on either new or renewal sales. The report on by-products indicated sales about as expected.

The accounting report and statistics when they arrived contained a few surprises. Here is the report submitted by the controller:

Controller's Report: January, Year 2

Despite a 10% advertising sales increase over budget ($100,000), operations for January resulted in a loss of $30,000 versus a budgeted profit of $40,000. The major deviations from budget were:

1. Increased paper, printing, and postage costs for added advertising pages—$60,000

2. Eight excess editorial pages, eight more editorial color pages, and 5,000 more copies printed than budgeted—cost $60,000
3. Authors' alterations above budget—cost $300
4. Advertising promotion costs $13,000 over budget. This represented a brochure for selling motel advertising that had not been planned at the time of the budget
5. Increased advertising sales commissions because of added sales—cost $4,000
6. Accounting fees for assisting in setting up the budget—inadvertently omitted—cost $2,400

New Boss discussed the author's alterations with the editor, the advertising promotion costs with the ad director, and the accounting fees with the controller.

By May the actual results were pretty close to the budgeted figures—or New Boss was informed whenever there was a deviation. It had become apparent that things were coming out much better than anticipated. Advertising showed signs of being 10% above the budget. Despite higher subscription prices, circulation gave every indication of increasing by 20,000 over the previous year with no increased cost. The printing escalation was settled at 3% instead of the expected 5%, while paper was up only 2%. All this meant that profits would be nearer $2,000,000 than the original $1,500,000 forecast.

New Boss called for a rebudgeting for the year beginning with July. At the meeting, each of the key people was asked to point out additional funds he could use during the second half of Year 2 that would result in higher profits in Year 3 and subsequent years. New Boss had determined that up to $300,000 would be available, but he did not inform the group of that figure.

The same process as before was followed in rebudgeting, but much quicker and with less pain. It was agreed that the major new thrust would involve steps to increase circulation. This would then have the effect of increasing advertising rates and other sources of income in future years. The additions to the budget included:

• The college art feature	$70,000
• Newsstand promotion increase through added radio spots, point of sale material, and a contest for retailers	50,000
• Test of higher newsstand and subscription prices	50,000
• Special promotion if the art story turned out well	30,000
• Investigation of the Web	100,000

New Boss also decided that a substantial advertising rate increase could be planned for Year 3 unless unexpected difficulties developed during the next few months.

CHAPTER 57

Use of Computer Models

As I have mentioned, magazine publishing is a very unusual business because, for paid circulation magazines at least, it requires several different income streams that are interdependent—all in one product.

An additional complexity is that the amount of advertising that can be sold—and the prices that can be charged—depend not only on the number of readers who can be obtained for a magazine, but also on the quality of these readers. The acquisition of these readers is not only a science, but also a high art that requires the use of a multitude of sources, selling prices, and different methods of sale, in addition to the publication of a compelling editorial product.

This makes planning for the future very difficult—and the projection of these plans almost unbearably complex. For many years I did it in pencil on worksheets, always wishing that there were a better way.

In 1970, I developed the first computer model of a magazine that incorporated all the details of the necessary activities and made intelligent projecting not only possible, but quite feasible. Since then that model has been used in the planning for literally thousands of magazines (and would-be magazines) worldwide—and others have developed somewhat similar models.

In addition to being helpful to individual publishers, he said modestly, the model also has contributed to a better understanding of the economics of this complex business and probably saved many publishers from disasters. Today the use of these models by just about every publisher is routine.

What a Computer Model Will Do

- Develop future projections
  - For as long a time as you want
  - For whatever periods you want (daily, weekly, monthly)
  - In as much detail as you want
- Give you reports
  - Operating statements
  - Balance sheets
  - Circulation reports
  - Print order reports
  - Reports specially designed for you
- In these forms
  - On the accrual basis
  - On the cash basis
- For magazines published
  - Daily
  - Weekly
  - Monthly
  - Changing from one frequency to another

Some magazines connect their models with their subscription fulfillment houses so that the most current data is being used in their calculations. The model also acts as a checklist of all the income and expense items needed in publishing a magazine.

What a Computer Model Won't Do

Think for you. All it does is add, subtract, multiply, and divide. You must supply it with all the assumptions. It is just a tool and doesn't do anything you couldn't do by hand if you had all the time in the world.

WARNING

Don't try to develop your own model by trying to make a spreadsheet program into a magazine model. The business is much too complex for that. You are sure to leave some things out and waste an awful lot of time.

Don't try to use a generalized model. Use one that has been specifically designed for magazines. They have been tried and tested by many publishers, so you know they work and have not left out any features.

WARNING

Reports come out of computers all neat and official looking. There is a danger that you will accept them even when they are very wrong. When you use computers, seemingly minor errors can often have enormous effects in areas that you had not considered.

Question every assumption—be sure it has been entered correctly. And review all results for reasonableness.

The frequency with which models are used—and the way they are used—seems to vary within companies, usually depending on the familiarity and confidence they have with their use. Lots of companies use models on almost a daily basis—doing all their planning and budgeting on them. Others use models only when making broad projections. They play "what if" games to plan their future moves. Others confine their use to the circulation aspects of the publication because that is where the most detailed calculations take place. In those cases the model is usually operated only by the circulation department. Still others only use them when some unusual event such as a postal increase is imminent.

Other companies have their models tied right into their daily transactions and actually have figures inputted from their subscription fulfillment houses so that the data is always up to date.

Even if you do not use models on a continuous basis, their use is vital when making major decisions such as:

- Starting a new magazine
- Purchasing a magazine
- Selling a magazine
- Moving a magazine from one stage of its life cycle to another
- Merging two magazines
- Killing a magazine
- Contemplating price changes of any kind
- Analyzing major cost increases
- Resurrecting a magazine
- Making any other kind of major change

Hints in Using Models

While estimates of income and cost figures are usable, it is best to rely on detailed actual numbers wherever possible to be sure that you have not overlooked something. Be sure to examine results for reasonableness. It is very easy to mistype, to enter extra zeros, or to put things in the wrong columns, after which instantaneous computations may lead to very erroneous results.

Don't hesitate to try out what may seem to be very wild assumptions. The results may surprise you in a very happy way, and if they don't, you can erase them with a keystroke.

You may find that this is the ultimate computer game because playing with the assumptions becomes hypnotic. If you play with them enough, what works—and what doesn't work—in this very unusual business will become very clear.

Modeling for a New Magazine

A model is an indispensable tool when you are starting a new magazine. You are, of course, making up a whole business out of your head, with no real proof of how either readers or advertisers will respond. You do, however, have good knowledge of the cost factors for various items—and you have the experience of many other magazines about what will happen using different assumptions that can be used in modeling. Usually there are other magazines, either competitive or with somewhat similar characteristics in terms of the type of readers and advertisers, that we can start with.

Sensitivity Analysis

When starting a magazine, one of our first steps is to get some idea of:

- The amount of the investment that might be needed
- Time before profits will be earned
- The short-term profits (five years or so) that might be earned, to give an idea of what the magazine might be worth at that point

The first step in this is to put together a five-year projection based on our first thoughts. We normally call this the First Try.

Then, to get an idea of what will make the magazine more—or less—feasible, we do what I call a sensitivity analysis. This changes each of the major assumptions one at a time to see what effect each change will have. This is not just a simple task of changing one item at a time. For instance, if you increase the response rate from mailings, you will change the number of subscriptions. This will force you to increase the number of subscriptions you expect from insert cards and from gift mailings. All this will change the circulation for advertising, which will change the ad rate. This, in turn, will change the commissions the salespeople get.

An example of the first sensitivity analysis I did for a new magazine a few years ago is shown in Figure 57.1. You will note that each of the changes is in a positive direction, but, of course, changes downward would have about the same effect in a negative direction. This serves to give the entrepreneurs a pretty good idea of what is most important, as well as introducing them to the economics of the business.

Over the next few months, as planning for the new magazine proceeds, and ideas change, many more iterations are made using the model. Sometimes these will indicate a completely new direction (different frequency, size, pricing, etc.). In the case of the magazine in this example, the projections and basic assumptions that were put in the final business plan are shown in Figures 20.1 and 20.2 in chapter 20, "The Business Plan."

Figure 57.1. Sensitivity Analysis (000)

	Start-up	Year One	Year Two	Year Three	Year Four	Year Five
First try						
Average circulation		262.5	441.9	559.2	599.2	616.9
Cash flow	$(521.3)	$(657.9)	$ 587.3	$1,753.1	$2,183.5	$2,282.0
1. Increase mailings 20%						
Average circulation		297.7	498.1	633.8	681.6	702.7
Cash flow	$(521.3)	$(512.2)	$1,444.9	$3,734.4	$4,980.3	$5,875.8
2. Increase response rate 20%						
Average circulation		297.7	498.1	633.8	681.6	702.7
Cash flow	$(521.3)	$(31.6)	$1,964.7	$4,214.4	$5,493.6	$6,355.8
3. Reduce bad debt 20%						
Average circulation		286.7	483.5	619.2	670.4	695.1
Cash flow	$(516.3)	$(62.3)	$1,906.7	$4,161.6	$5,481.4	$6,372.1
4. Increase subscription price $2						
Cash flow	$(516.5)	$(67.1)	$1323.1	$2,529.4	$2,968.5	$3,045.4
5. Increase newstand draw 20%						
Average circulation		277.2	465.2	593.3	639.1	661.6
Cash flow	$(521.3)	$(649.3)	$1,255.6	$3,424.7	$4,755.4	$5,686.6
6. Increase newsstand % of sale 20%. Same as 5.						
7. Increase renewal rates 20%						
Average circulation		262.6	458.3	604.3	674.3	717.9
Cash flow	$(521.3)	$(590.1)	$1,347.3	$3,886.0	$5,489.3	$6,633.4
8. Increase newsstand price 20%						
Cash flow	$(521.3)	$(592.3)	$ 850.2	$2,182.0	$2,706.2	$2,856.9
9. Increase advertising rates 20%						
Cash flow	$(521.3)	$(594.2)	$1,196.0	$2,727.5	$3,410.7	$3,726.9
10. Increase advertising pages 20%						
Cash flow	$(521.3)	$(583.0)	$1,229.9	$2,772.6	$3,465.4	$3,791.2

CHAPTER 58

The Internet

THE NET IS with us, whether we like it or not. It will have effects, but, since it is still developing, we cannot be sure just what—or how major—those effects will be.

If you are starting a new magazine, however, you must keep the Internet in mind. And I am afraid that I must discuss it. The best I can do, however, is describe what I think we know about it at the time of this writing—and warn you that there will undoubtedly be changes that I have not expected in the future.

Increase in the Magazine Business As a Whole

The Net has already exhibited the same effects on the magazine business that every new technological development produces. We most recently experienced these effects starting in about 1980 when the computer field exploded, followed by a later contraction to its present state—still very healthy, but much smaller than it was at the height of its growth. As far as the Net is concerned we have already experienced:

1. The start-up of a whole raft of new business magazines (*Click, Interactive, Darwin, Profit B to B, Eweek* among them). I found 46 in the August 2000 issue of SRDS, with a total circulation of over 5 million, and there are probably others not listed there. I am sure, too, that the circulation of many of the existing magazines serving the computer and allied fields have increased—and probably in retail and other fields as well.

2. The start-up of a bunch of new consumer magazines. There were nine in that issue of SRDS, with circulation of several million (including *eBay, Web Guide, Yahoo!,* etc). Again, there were probably others not listed.

3. News and other editorial material about the Web in every kind of media.

4. An overwhelming amount of e-advertising in every type of media, but particularly on TV and in general business magazines. During 2000, technology advertising became the leading category for consumer magazines, exceeding even automotive.

5. The inevitable contraction of advertising and just about everything else with what *Fortune* called "The Collapse of the E Universe" (with appropriate graphics) in 2001. As of this writing, a number of magazines have passed away and we are bound to see a further loss of magazines in both the consumer and business areas.

In the end, however, the Net will produce a long-term increase in the number of magazines, number of readers, and amount of advertising.

WHAT ELSE WE HAVE LEARNED

We are a long way from knowing everything about the Net, but we can be pretty sure, based on the evidence to date, that:

1. It will not completely revolutionize the world we live in.

2. The new media will not kill magazines. It is a new method of delivery, not a new business.

3. Strictly Net magazines don't work. Turner tried *Spiv,* AOL tried *Global Network Navigator,* CMP tried *Net Guide Alive. American Cybercast, Happy Puppy, Web Review, Out, Adcom, Shade,* and others could not make it. E-zines have been a failure.

4. So far at least, you cannot make money on editorial content if you keep giving it away, and few Net users are willing to pay for it. *Consumer Reports* and *Wall Street Interactive* are exceptions to this, so perhaps it will not prove to be an eternal truth.

5. Its use as an advertising medium will be limited unless better methods of presentation can be developed.

6. There may be a place in the world for business magazines to develop highly profitable B2B transactional businesses, but the road is not obvious now—and will certainly not be easy.

7. The Postal Service will be irrevocably injured and publishers must come to grips with this problem and possible alternatives.

8. There are a number of ways the Net can be helpful to magazines. These are discussed in chapter 65, "Brand Extensions—The Internet."

Part IV: Making the Most of a Magazine's Strong Brand

CHAPTER 59

Brand Extensions—Integrated Marketing

TODAY JUST ABOUT every publisher is doing lots of things in addition to publishing a magazine. It wasn't always that way. Until relatively recently, few publishers realized that a magazine is a very powerful brand that can produce profits in many ways. Almost all magazines used to sell reprints, T-shirts, and coffee mugs. They rented their lists through list brokers and gained some income from the sale of microfiche copies of their issues to libraries.

Some of the women's consumer magazines published special interest publications in specific areas such as kitchens or gardening, primarily sold on the newsstand. A few other magazines established foreign editions. *Golf Digest* conducted golf schools. And then there were special issues on anniversaries and other important dates.

Business publishers produced a book or two; put out daily publications during their industry conventions; issued product directories once a year; and sold such things as slide rules, films, or videotapes that might be useful to their readers in their specialized fields.

Most publishers hired a "scrounger" to handle these offshoots with some kind of incentive compensation—and happily enjoyed whatever relatively minor profits were earned.

Intent on serving readers with excellent editorial and selling advertising pages, publishers forgot that communications with those readers could be successfully carried on in a great many other ways.

A Good Magazine Is a Marketable Brand

- It earns the loyalty, friendship, and confidence of its readers as it speaks to them one-on-one about a subject they are very interested in.
- It reinforces this through periodic publication.
- It establishes a marketplace between its readers and advertisers.
- The editors either are the leading authorities in the field or are well acquainted with them.
- The publisher knows who the magazine's readers are and has data on their demographics and other characteristics. He knows what subjects most interest them.
- The magazine's advertisers are those companies most interested in selling to those readers.
- It has access to its readers through its pages, its lists, and sometimes in other ways.

All this makes the extension of a magazine's brand relatively simple because the aura of the magazine rubs off on everything it sponsors.

While most publishers did not recognize the value of their brands, a handful have moved very aggressively in developing highly lucrative book and, in some cases, other operations—Time-Life, Reader's Digest, Rodale, Sunset, and a few others. Playboy went into areas such as clubs and films.

With the growth of cable TV, the advent of the PC, and the development of such things as CD-ROMs, fax machines, and other communications devices, publishers slowly realized that by doing nothing but publishing their magazines, they (1) may have been missing opportunities, (2) were not completely serving their customers, and (3) were allowing competitors to invade their territory.

In recent years, in trying to take advantage of this challenge, they found themselves faced with:

- A sudden technological overload that is very difficult to keep track of
- Not knowing how to do things in the new areas
- The need for substantial investments in R & D for themselves, often for the first time
- The management of costs with which they were not familiar, and that always seem to overrun all estimates
- Conquering their fear of the unknown

The explosion of the Internet in recent years has forced publishers to deal with this situation if they haven't before. Today every publisher is thinking about, or working on, ways to exploit the aura of his magazine.

Types of Brand Extensions

Lists of most of the traditional brand extensions consumer and business publishers have engaged in are in chapters 60, "Consumer Magazines" and 61, "Business Magazines". In addition, there are separate chapters for those areas that require further exploration:

- "Database Marketing," chapter 62. How lists have become more than just lists.
- "International," chapter 63. It's just one world now.
- "Books," chapter 64. Books have always seemed to be the most obvious area for expansion. This chapter has been included to give an idea of how different the book field is from magazine publishing, and to indicate the kinds of difficulties a publisher faces in making major efforts to extend the magazine's brand in other areas that may be even farther afield.
- "The Internet," chapter 65.
- "Custom Publishing," chapter 66. A completely different approach to publishing.

Steps in Extending a Magazine's Brand

There is no magic formula for determining whether, when, and how to extend a magazine's brand, it is just like starting anything else new—including a new magazine:

1. Identify and investigate the opportunity.
2. Formulate a mission statement.
3. Evaluate the field, its opportunities, competition, and market environment.
4. Evaluate your present financial and other capabilities to carry out the project.
5. Evaluate vendors and other outsiders who could be helpful. Don't forget the possibility of partnering with other organizations with expertise in the field.
6. Develop a business plan together with projections, and don't forget downside projections.
7. Test the project.
8. Make a decision to go or not.

Possible Problems of a Brand Extension

1. Most important—how does it change the relationship you have with your readers? Has your editorial integrity been compromised through a blurring of the line between editorial and advertising? This can easily happen in developing such projects as custom publishing, advertorials, sponsorships, and a number of the other opportunities. If this happens, of course, you may have killed the golden goose.
2. Will it threaten your relationship with some of your advertisers?
3. Will the new projects detract too much time, attention, and money from the basic publishing business?
4. Does your company culture inhibit the start-up of any meaningful new venture, including one where you partner with another firm? If so, is it something you can overcome?
5. Do you have the financial capability of carrying out the project?
6. Will it cannibalize your revenue from other sources?
7. If is does not succeed, will it bring down the rest of the house with it?

CHAPTER 60

Brand Extensions for Consumer Magazines

THESE ARE SOME examples of brand extensions that some consumer magazines are already exploiting. (See also the chapters on "Database Marketing," "International," "Books," "The Internet," and "Custom Publishing.")

SPECIAL INTEREST PUBLICATIONS (SIPs)

These are publications covering specific aspects of interest to the readers of the basic magazines such as *Better Homes and Gardens Bedroom and Bath, Building Ideas, Christmas Ideas,* and the like. They are issued annually or more frequently depending on the readers' reactions and are sold primarily on the newsstand. Most are concerned with the fashion, women's, or home service magazines, but others are published by automotive, gun, and some other types of magazines.

- SPECIAL ISSUES
  - *Sports Illustrated* Swimsuit Issue
  - *Forbes 400* List.
- SPIN-OFF MAGAZINES
  - *National Geographic Traveler, National Geographic Adventures*
  - *Martha Stewart Living Weddings*
  - *Parents Baby, Parents Expecting*
  - *Sports Illustrated for Kids, Sports Illustrated for Women*
  - *Forbes FYI*
- BUSINESS MAGAZINES IN THEIR FIELDS
  - *Golf World Business* by *Golf Digest*
  - *Pet Product News* by Fancy Publications
  - *Scholastic Coach & Athlete*
- DIRECTORIES AND OTHER ANNUALS
  - *Automobile* magazine's *Guide to Buying and Leasing*
  - *Sailboat Buyer's Guide* by *Sail* magazine
  - *Cats USA* by *Cats* magazine
- EVENTS
  - Wizard's World Convention by various comic magazines
  - Builder Show House by *Southern Living* and *Builder*
  - American Woodworker convention for amateur craftsmen
- TV AND CABLE PROGRAMS
  - Golf Magazine TV
  - In Style Wedding program
  - Martha Stewart's many programs
  - Playboy's cable channel
  - Mother Jones and PBS
- LICENSING THE MAGAZINE'S NAME FOR OTHER PRODUCTS
  - Better Homes and Gardens garden hoses
  - Popular Mechanics hand tools
  - Forbes office products
- DIRECT MAIL SALES OF OTHER PRODUCTS
  - Reader's Digest sells vitamins, health information products, financial services, music, TV films, condensed books
  - Time-Life sells books, music, videotapes
  - Hot Rod sells collectibles, apparel, car batteries
- ANTHOLOGIES
  - National Geographic and The Nation sell CD-ROM copies of all their issues from the inception of the magazines over a hundred years ago.
- OTHER EXTENSIONS USED BY SOME MAGAZINES INCLUDE:
  - Affinity credit cards
  - Technical manuals and training courses
  - Seminars and conferences

CHAPTER 61

Brand Extensions for Business Magazines

THESE ARE SOME examples of brand extensions that business magazines are already exploiting. But don't miss the chapters on "Database Marketing," "International," "Books," "The Internet," and "Custom Publishing."

Business magazines, with their smaller and relatively self-contained audiences of readers and advertisers, have long surrounded their fields with related materials.

Trade Shows, Seminars, and Conferences

I recall years ago when Andy Haire thought up the idea of starting associations in two of the fields in which he was publishing magazines—*Corset & Underwear Review* and *Toys & Novelties*. The idea, of course, was that this made more of a field out of them than they had been before—and it also gave him a chance to run a trade show in each area once a year. Both of these industries were centered in New York, so this was not very hard to do.

With the current booming economy and the ease of travel, of course, the trade show has become more and more important for publishers. In many industries they overshadow the magazines themselves. Profits can be very large and publishing companies buy and sell shows, often taking them over from the associations in the covered fields.

The basic benefits are:

- Strengthen the community the publisher is serving
- Introduce advertisers to an ever-increasing spectrum of new marketing opportunities
- Build stronger relationships—and value—for the publication
- Opportunity for the magazine's advertisers to meet the readers—who are the actual buyers, decision makers, and purchasing influencers
- The publishers learn from the professionals at the meetings, spot industry trends, and build alliances
- The seminars provide education and training sessions for participants, which cannot be done in the publications
- Get closer to the communities served
- Revenues from preshow, at-show, and postshow issues, as well as from special advertising inserts
- The publications provide the shows with access to readers through the availability of subscriber lists and generate sales leads though their prospect lists
- The cost for an advertiser per visitor to his booth is far less than any call he might have to make in person
- Can be highly profitable

Product Directories (Buyers' Guides)

Directories of suppliers in a field are, of course, naturals for business magazines. These have varied in format:

- Listings and classified ads in the back of each issue (a la *Folio* magazine)

- Special issues devoted to complete directories, which might also contain editorial material (*Folio* here, too)
- Separate directories covering different parts of the field (*Billboard*)
- Complete sets of books (*Thomas Register* is probably the largest in this line)
- Product literature reviews (catalogs—or portions thereof—bound together), also in CD-ROM form for ease of updating and use

There are also efforts in some fields to enhance their printed directories with more details and put them on the Web.

These buyers' guides are obviously compatible with the subject matter of the magazines, they fulfill a real need, and readers use them time and again. The publisher's job, of course, is to make sure that they are geared to the needs of the users and are easy to use. Selling an ad in a directory is also a good way to get new advertisers to try the magazine.

Directories can be quite profitable because they do not have to be surrounded with as much editorial material as the normal magazine. In many cases, additional copies can be sold as well.

Newsletters

Business magazine publishers also often offer newsletters on a more frequent basis than the magazine, sometimes by fax or on the Net. Subscriptions are paid, which may not be true of the magazine itself.

These newsletters may be geared to the entire audience of a magazine or specialized for particular segments of readers. They normally contain inside information that is not available elsewhere, up-to-the-minute news, and opinions and judgments that readers know they can trust versus such material published by others. They save reading time, and the reaction of potential subscribers is relatively easy to test before publication. They can be highly profitable and can carry a certain amount of advertising as well (which not all publishers realize).

Consumer Magazines

The growth of the computer and the Net has led some business publishers to expand their magazines' circulation to include a great many nonbusiness readers—*Computer Shopper, PC Magazine, PC World,* and *Yahoo! Internet Life.*

Special Issues

Mentioned above are special issues devoted to trade shows and buyers' guides. Others include those devoted to anniversaries of the magazine; those that note major events in an industry's history, such as important research; and others limited only by the publisher's imagination and knowledge of the field. *Ad Age* runs special sections on the anniversaries of the major advertising agencies.

Other Areas

- Postcard Decks. While many of us detest these, they seem to be useful for some publications.
- Special Research Reports. These are either sponsored by the magazine or in conjunction with others that are important for the field.
- Continuing Education Programs. Penton runs about eight Career Centers in some of the fields its many magazines cover.
- Aids specific to the field served. Such things as slide rules, video or audio instruction tapes, computer programs, and other items helpful to field representatives.

CHAPTER 62

Brand Extensions—Database Marketing

DON'T LET THEM kid you—a database is nothing more than a list, enhanced by more information than usual. The whole idea is that you can take a list of subscribers—or any other list for that matter—and, because of all the capabilities of the computer, add a lot more data until you really have a pretty good picture of the readers' interests, behavior, credit, location, etc., until you know so much about them that you can market things to them that they should like, as well as market to them more intelligently.

This was not a very exciting area when all we had to work with was the history of how subscribers behaved for one magazine. We then used the lists:

- For list rental
- To improve circulation activities:
  - Identify your most likely prospects
  - Develop more effective promotions
  - Resolve the problems of individual subscribers
  - Track distribution flaws
- To address readers better editorially by:
  - Creating columns or inserts addressed to certain subjects
  - Creating multiple editions through selective binding
- Creating new niche magazines
- To target subgroups so that advertisers could use them for:
  - Mailings
  - Inserts
  - Selective binding
  - Advertiser reader-response postcards
  - Single sponsor magazines
  - Custom publishing ventures
  - Polybag advertiser catalogs with the magazine
- For ancillary products
  - Develop and market books, videos, newsletters, conferences, seminars, and other products

Enhancing the List

The basic idea is very simple—add other information a magazine may have about subscribers and their history. Presumably you already have on file information about the original source of the subscriptions, the price paid, renewal history, and all the other normal data. To this you add information about ancillary products readers may have bought, reader service card history, sweepstakes history, and other such material.

You can then overlay this list with information available from outside firms that describes the demographics of virtually every street in the country. This gives you a good indication of the type of person on the list—and points you toward areas where further subscription acquisition efforts might be useful.

To this you add some more:

1. Information about other magazines you publish. If you are a multimagazine publisher, you merge the file for each customer with the data you have for each of the magazines. If you are Primedia, for instance, with all its magazines appealing to men—automo-

tive, gun, hunting, surfing, etc.—you may be able to add a lot to the overall picture of each customer.

2. Demographic information that can be obtained from companies that compile data on changes of address, U. S. Census, driver's licenses, and credit applications.

The resulting database is useful in obtaining circulation, list rental, and research, and in advertiser programs.

But even more can be done!

On top of all this, in recent years a number of mailers have joined in cooperative list programs operated by outside organizations such as Centrobe (EDS), Experian, and Acxiom. Here publishers and others contribute anonymously to develop huge bases of information about millions of direct-marketing buyers. More than a hundred magazines as well as many catalogs contribute data to the packages. The type of things that are of interest are:

- Past purchase activity
- Responses to psychographic or lifestyle surveys
- Demographic data
- Credit history
- Geographic data
- Mobility data

The basic idea is that the more you know about your customers, the better you can develop new products and spin-offs for them and decide in which form they should be published—and the type of marketing message. It also helps in becoming more efficient in mailing for new business, renewals, gifts, and just about everything else.

Helping Advertisers with Their Lists

Some publishers have found that by upgrading their lists, they have developed another benefit for their advertisers. They may exchange information with advertisers or in some cases actually take over the maintenance of advertisers' lists of prospects. The lists then can be used to identify potential customers for the advertisers, as well as potential new subscribers for the magazines. In some cases, the advertisers use the lists on a time-sharing basis. The databases have been used for:

- Research
- Telemarketing
- Profiling
- Customer cloning—finding new prospects with a similar profile
- List selection, according to a composite of demographic, lifestyle, or behavioral selects
- Geodemographic mapping—targeting at the ZIP or household level for retailing or marketing activities

Costs and Benefits of Enhancing Databases

As with any brand extension, a careful analysis is needed before undertaking real list enhancement. As might be expected, while the costs may be relatively easy to estimate, many of the benefits do not lend themselves to precise measurement. The enhancement of a list will not be accomplished quickly and it is probable that only the largest publishers will be able to do it well in-house. It will probably take at least a year to build a really sound database, and the help of outside experts will be needed by most companies.

Benefits will include:

- Increased list rental, perhaps at higher rates.
- Reduction in subscription marketing efforts and costs through use of in-house versus outside lists, reduction in costs for promotion, postage, bad pay.
- Improvement in subscription marketing and renewal results.
- Improvement in the sale of other brand extensions.
- Income from the advertisers whose lists are handled.
- Ability to develop further brand extensions because of the increased knowledge gained about customers.
- *Perhaps most of all,* an increase in advertising sales because of the greater available knowledge of customers. This is obviously impossible to measure.

WARNING

The extreme enhancement of lists, particularly when including the cooperatives with other companies, gets very close to the type of invasion of privacy about which governmental bodies have become interested. There is a likelihood that this type of enhancement will come under the same umbrella and become the subject of future legislation.

CHAPTER 63

Brand Extensions—International

IT ISN'T NEWS that the world has gotten smaller and smaller. People's interests everywhere are becoming the same, led by easy communications, the Net, movies, and television, and the same businesses are carried on wherever the economies can support them, often using English as the universal language.

If you hadn't realized it, consider how many of the major U.S. magazine publishers are owned internationally. Each of these companies has purchased at least one of the larger American publishers in recent years and, in some cases, has purchased some smaller operations as well.

In the consumer area:

- Hachette (French) purchased *Car & Driver, Road & Track, Flying, Woman's Day, Popular Photography,* and the other CBS (before that Ziff-Davis) magazines, and later added others.
- Gruner & Jahr (German) purchased *Parents* and other magazines from the founding company, *Family Circle* from the *New York Times,* and later added others.
- Softbank (Japanese) purchased Ziff-Davis computer games and other magazines and later added others.

In the business area:

- Reed-Elsevier (British and Dutch) purchased Cahners and later added others.
- United News (British) purchased Miller Freeman and later added others.
- Softbank (Japanese)—purchased Ziff-Davis computer magazines and later added others.
- VNU (Dutch) purchased BPI and Bill and later added others.
- Emap (British), News Corp (Australian), and Bonniers (Swedish) previously owned American publishers but have sold them.

A number of European companies have also exported editions of their magazines to this country:

- *Economist*
- *Elle*
- *First for Women*
- *Maxim*—and planning several more
- *Time Out*

Overall there seems to be more activity of other countries getting into the United States than the other way around. This is not surprising considering the prosperity we have had—and the fact that the American market is the largest by far for just about anything.

American publishers have also addressed the international situation by extending circulation of their basic U.S. magazines to other countries and by publishing separate editions in other countries.

Consumer Magazines

Extending Circulation

Not all American consumer magazines are of interest to people in other countries where their customs and mores are different. Excluding regional magazines, of course, only one in five U.S. consumer magazines has more than a token amount of circulation outside the United States and Canada—and these token amounts probably consist principally of Americans living abroad.

Normally lists are not as good abroad, delivery is expensive, and subscription prices are substantially higher than those for domestic magazines. (There are, fortunately, a number of organizations that help publishers obtain and deliver subscriptions in other countries.) In most other countries, newsstands play a much bigger part in the sale of copies than subscriptions.

Inhibiting the sale of copies abroad in many fields is the question of the value of this additional circulation to the U.S. advertisers. They may not be willing to pay higher rates for these readers.

In only a few fields have publishers made real efforts to expand their foreign circulation for their U.S. editions, primarily aviation, boating, brides, music, science, and some types of sports.

Foreign Editions

A number of the larger publishers have editions in foreign countries or international editions serving all areas outside the United States. Included are Time-Warner, Newsweek, Conde Nast, Playboy, Rodale, Reader's Digest, Hearst, and possibly a few others.

Exporting a title is not easy or inexpensive, although when it works, it can produce substantial profits. In analyzing the possibility of developing international editions, a publisher should consider:

- Is the subject matter exportable?
- How must the editorial material be adapted for a local audience?
- Will the design have to be changed—in fact, will the name of the magazine even be the same? (*Reader's Digest* is called *Selecciones* in some areas)
- Will the existing advertising relationships be helpful?
- Will the corporate brand be helpful?

There is general agreement that, because of the differences in doing business in other countries, local people should be in charge of the local editions. This often requires a partnership of some kind.

WARNING

An example of the difficulties of adapting a magazine to another country (in this case, in reverse) was the introduction of the French magazine *Oui* to American audiences many years ago.

The concept was simple—girls are the same worldwide, so they would simply take the French edition and use its graphics with captions and other editorial matter translated into English.

They were about to go to press when someone at the printer's noticed that French girls don't shave their legs. The entire edition had to be reshot before it could be published for an American audience.

Business Magazines

Extending Circulation

While the categories of business magazines are the same throughout the world, only about 20% of U.S. business magazines have more than token amounts of circulation abroad. Since most circulation is designed to reach buying influences for the advertisers in the field (and a great deal is controlled), many business magazines do not have any foreign subscriptions at all. In most business fields, there are local magazines in each discipline that cover the local markets.

The fields where there is substantial foreign circulation include amusements, appliances, automotive, aviation, computers, cosmetics, electrical, electronic, and financial.

Foreign Editions

Another 10% or so of U.S. business magazines have established editions for international audiences. More than half of these are published in the United States, with the rest published in various other countries where the publishers have established offices. Most of these cover the same fields listed above that display the most foreign circulation for other U.S. magazines. Apparently those are the fields where American know-how is most dominant.

CHAPTER 64

Brand Extensions—Books

I THOUGHT IT would be helpful to review the situation of magazines and the book field because it explains the kinds of problems you might face in trying to extend your brand in any different field. Books have been around a long time, and many publishers have made efforts to get into the field.

As you will see, it is not nearly as simple as you might expect. It involves moving into a completely different type of endeavor.

Undoubtedly, just about every magazine publisher, its editors, and/or its contributors have developed one or two books that might be of interest to its readers—and had them published in one way or another. But only a handful of magazine publishers have developed substantial—and profitable—book operations. And fewer than one in ten has gone as far as setting up separate operations for the publication of books.

Yet this may be the most obvious brand extension of them all. Let's discuss the thinking that has to be done before getting into this area.

Positive Aspects of Books for Magazine Publishers

1. They are like magazines in that they are transmitting ideas, knowledge, and/or entertainment in print.

2. Their existence, like magazines', depends on the interests of people.

3. The audience for the magazine has already displayed an interest in the subject—in many cases an interest strong enough to pay for the magazine.

4. The aura of the magazine rubs off on any product it sponsors.

5. Publishers know who their readers are, their demographics and psychographics. They also know what subjects interest them most.

6. The magazine has access to the market through its pages, its lists, and sometimes in other ways.

7. The editors either are—or know—the leading authorities in the field.

8. It is a relatively easy field to enter.

9. Books can, in turn, help the magazine itself by (a) making it appear to be more of an authority in the field, (b) helping it attract and hold editors and authors, and (c) in some cases being used as premiums to help sell subscriptions.

Negative Aspects of Books for Magazine Publishers

1. Although the magazine's customers are readers, they may not be book readers.

2. The readers may enjoy the magazine but not be interested in the depth of information given in a book.

3. It may be difficult to find enough good titles to publish.

4. It may be detrimental to the magazine if it takes key editors from their primary duties.

5. You and your editors may be great in the magazine business but fail to choose good subjects for books.

6. While it is easy for publishers to get into the book business, it is also easy for others to do the same thing. Competition can develop very quickly either from existing publishers or from new ones.

7. Publishing of just one title can take a long lead time. Establishing a whole business is very long term. It can also be quite expensive.

It Is Really a Different Business

Most important of all, while the fields may appear to be quite similar, publishing books is really quite a different business from publishing magazines. Consider these factors:

1. Each book title is one of a kind. It is a new product and must be developed and marketed on its own merits. Each issue of a magazine, on the other hand, is also a new product, but is the exemplification of a publishing formula that has previously been developed. The reader knows what to expect with each issue.

2. There is no repeat sale of a book. Magazines, of course, depend on repeat sales of both circulation and advertising. (This difference is not completely true—some authors' books are purchased on their names alone; some other types of books—westerns, mysteries, romances, for example—sell just because of their genre; and book clubs and continuity series depend on repeat sales.)

3. Books depend on different marketing channels. While some of the methods used to market magazines are also used for books, there are also many other different ones. Similar techniques are used for direct marketing and for selling mass-market paperbacks as for magazines, but books are also sold through bookstores and other outlets not often used by magazines, to schools and colleges, through book wholesalers, and in a host of other ways. Many of these methods depend on field salespeople—foreign to magazine publishing.

4. Magazines and books both are sold for many different prices to their readers. In the book field, there is a bewildering array of prices and discounts for any one title. Bookstores are given about 40% off, depending on the volume of purchases. Wholesalers have other discounts, and textbooks work on completely different schedules. The same title may be offered at one price by bookstores and at very different amounts by mail order, through book clubs, or on the Web. Often hardbound and paperbound versions of the same title are marketed at the same time for different prices.

5. While we may think that there are an awful lot of magazines, the number pales when you consider that some 50,000 book titles are published every year—and that the number of books in print at any one time is approaching a million. Even though many of these are highly specialized, there is still an enormous array of products for a buyer to choose from, if he can discover all those that exist.

6. There is no advertising revenue contributing to the profit stream, although at one time efforts were made to include some advertising in mass market paperbacks.

7. Each book title presents a problem in pricing, even though some groupings can be made. Pricing of books is a function of a number of factors: physical size, number of pages, anticipated sale, the author, royalty paid, amount of promotion, subject matter, competitive titles, discount structure, and on and on.

8. The book business involves the purchase of a whole raft of products not used in magazines. This means dealing with a new group of suppliers. While many of the items may seem to be the same as in magazines, you will find that you are dealing with different kinds of paper, different printers, different designers.

9. Relationships with authors are different. Instead of simply paying an author a flat amount for a manuscript, much more complex deals must be made. These involve advances and royalties as a percentage of sales (depending on the method of sale, the division of subsidiary rights income, and the deferral of royalty payments to save the author tax problems). Your dealings may have to be through the author's agent.

10. In many cases the publisher must also negotiate the sale of subsidiary rights including interna-

tional, mail order, book club, mass-market paperback, TV, and movie rights. This rarely exists in magazine publishing, and magazine articles rarely become movies.

11. The book publisher has an up-front investment, unlike magazines, which are, to a great extent, in a cash business. Substantial amounts are needed for paper and book inventories, accounts receivable, and authors' advances.

12. Book publishing requires the warehousing of copies plus a substantial shipping operation. Both are foreign to magazines.

13. Detailed record keeping, very different from that of magazines, is needed—inventories, inventory write-offs, sales, returns, back orders, accounts receivable, and royalties. Accounting involves a cost-of-goods-sold concept that is not required for magazines.

14. What makes for a profitable book business is very different from magazines. The book business is capital-intensive and normally requires the sale of a substantial amount of product. Balance sheet items are quite different. Interpretation of results requires different approaches.

WARNING

None of the above is meant to discourage magazine publishers from getting into the book business, but you must recognize that it is a completely different business from magazines even though we both put print on paper (for the foreseeable future).

You should consider going into the book business only if you can commit large amounts of time, energy, and forethought, as well as capital.

Among those magazine publishers that have been successful as book publishers are:

- Rodale, which piggybacked a line of semireference books covering the subjects of their magazines through very successful mailings.
- Time-Life, which sells series to their subscribers through the mail and actually had larger profits than the magazines for a while. They haven't done as well in the bookstore markets.
- Reader's Digest Condensed Books, although smaller now than it once was, is still a very successful business. These, too, depend primarily on subscriber lists.

EVEN MORE WARNING

If the book business is so different, be aware that any other businesses will be at least as different, and probably more so. Be sure you understand the business before you jump in.

CHAPTER 65

Brand Extensions—The Internet

FROM THE BEGINNING it seemed very logical that magazine publishers were best equipped to deal with the Net since:

1. They are the natural "content providers," using their existing editorial material and know-how.
2. They are comfortable with digital operations.
3. They have rich archives of information.
4. They know how to talk to readers one-on-one.
5. They have extensive direct response expertise.
6. They tend to create deep personal relationships with their readers.
7. The interactivity of the Net can be useful in solidifying the bond of reader and editor.

But there were also problems:

1. It was very new and very different.
2. No one had any idea of what would work and what wouldn't.
3. A great deal of technical know-how was involved—and publishers were gun-shy because in recent years many had spent much more than they had anticipated in developing in-house desk-top, direct-to-plate, and other digital capabilities.
4. It had been developed by technical people who thought of it as their turf, had their own language, and thought of editors only as "content providers."
5. Fear of the unknown.

Most publishers admitted the Net's existence but did little about it. A few developed their own sites and experimented with putting some of their editorial material on them. Some had rather elaborate setups, such as Time with its Pathfinder operation (which it later abandoned). Most of those involved soon decided not to "keep throwing money at it." Few have been willing to give details about their efforts—or to admit to how much they may have lost with their experiments.

So far, however, there haven't been any successful breakthrough concepts that would revolutionize the publishing world. The Net seems to be just one more direct marketing channel for reaching customers.

Convergence Is the Byword in the Field—Taking Advantage of the Capabilities of Both the Magazine and the Net

Here are the types of things magazines *have* been able to do through the Net:

- Replace or enhance present activities by providing supplementary material with reader-involvement activities through e-mail
  - Offer timely, up-to-the-minute information
  - Offer in-depth information
  - Post career opportunities
  - Make available newsletters for segments of the audience
  - Provide on-line calculators (financial impact of mortgages and college tuition)
- Communicate with readers through e-mail—less costly, faster, more personal:
  - Sell and renew subscriptions
  - Sell ancillary products such as books, conferences, and trade shows
  - Handle reader service
  - Do other reader-involvement activities
  - Test covers, do other reader research

Enhance Databases

Through all the efforts above, not only are e-mail addresses obtained, but often further information about readers and their subinterests can be captured. This is helpful, not only in subscription marketing, but also in business development, editorial improvement, new products, and in many other ways. (See chapter 62, "Brand Extensions—Database Marketing.")

Develop Spin-off Publishing Products

Newsletters for smaller groups of readers with specialized interests, on-line city guides, personal finance guides, access to stock data, and the like. Because of the self-selection of readers with these interests, premium ad rates can be charged. For example, Meredith has started a quarterly magazine, *Shop Online 123*. Penton and Forbes have collaborated in presenting a supplement. Hanley-Wood has magazinelets devoted to home plans and an electronic guide to building products. *Vogue* presents fashion shows on its Web site.

Content Redistribution

Third-party organizations such as Screaming Media, Magazine Content, and iSyndicate act much in the way that newspaper syndicates such as King Features have operated for many years by offering editorial content to other Web sites and other media. Some publishers do this on their own or set up strategic alliances with other groups to do the same thing. This brings in fees and also enhances the reputation of the magazine.

Develop Joint Product Sales Operations

An arrangement between Conde-Nast's *Epicurious* and Williams-Sonoma gives viewers a way to shop for kitchen products. *ItsStyle* does the same in the fashion area. Hearst has *Brandwise,* which rates products for consumers, partnering with Whirlpool and other manufacturers. Hachette has a site for auto accessories (*Road & Track*) and another for fashion and beauty (*Elle*).

Possible Problems of These Web-Enhanced Opportunities

Editorial Integrity

The word "commerce" is mentioned frequently with regard to the opportunities in communicating on the Web. Several practices can make editorial integrity difficult to maintain:

- It is often difficult to differentiate between advertising and editorial on the Web. Barriers to entry have been so low that many sites contain unsubstantiated, but enticing, content.
- There are ethical questions with such marketing operations as *Brandwise* and *Epicurious.*
- Interstitial ads can easily lead to corruption of the editorial matter.
- Webcasting (advertorials) need careful labeling.
- Operation of auctions and other commercial marketing devices can lead to obvious problems.

This editorial integrity problem has been duly noted, but specifics of how it should be addressed will take time to work out.

Net May Cannibalize the Basic Magazine

This was an early fear that many publishers had—putting editorial and ads on the Net might make the printed magazine unnecessary.

This does not seem to have come to pass. The different methods of addressing the audience seem to be complementary rather than antagonistic. It is probably similar to the problem the book business had a great many years ago when it feared that the publication of paperbacks or the sale of copies through book clubs would ruin the sale of hardcover books. It has long since become obvious that the sale of a copy of a book by any means simply increases the interest in a title and results in more sales of all kinds.

Privacy

This may become the biggest bugaboo for the Web. The amount and kinds of information now collected about each of us is frightening (although as a direct marketer, I can see how useful it could be if properly controlled).

The DMA for years has been able to calm legislative fears in connection with direct mail through its Mail Preference activities, but this new area is liable to blow wide open on the Web where so much more personal data are being accumulated, often using subversive methods.

CHAPTER 66

Custom Publishing

THIS BOOK IS primarily concerned with the publication of magazines that are either purchased by readers or sent to people who have made some sort of overt move to receive them.

All sorts of other publications of various kinds are distributed to people in one way or another by organizations of all kinds, whether they ask for them or not. Most of these publications are produced by the organizations themselves. When they are developed by outsiders, those who produce them are called custom publishers.

For many years a number of custom publishers have developed publications for groups where communications were desirable, mostly confined to those addressed to captive audiences such as:

- Airline in-flight magazines
- Doctors' and other waiting rooms
- Hospital patients
- Theater and concert attendees
- Patients (and their families) suffering from specific diseases
- Customers of banks, insurance companies, and hospitals
- Members of organizations such as unions, professional societies, fraternal organizations, clubs, and alumni groups

The publishers involved devoted themselves primarily to producing these kinds of publications. Included were such firms as American Airlines Publishing, C-E Publishing, Diablo Custom Publishing, McMurry Publishing, and Pace Communications.

In recent years, regular magazine publishers have realized that this is a fruitful field and such companies as Advertising Age, American Express, CMP, Gruner & Jahr, Hachette, Hearst, Meredith, Rodale, Time, and others have established custom publishing operations.

In recognition of this, in 1997, the MPA established a Custom Publishers Council for members (1) having either revenue of $2 million per year or at least 50% of their total revenue through custom publishing, and (2) who are responsible for securing or directly providing at least four of these services: editorial, design, advertising sales, production, and distribution. It conducted a survey that indicated that custom publishing accounted for $1 billion in sales per year plus another $700 million in the sale of advertising to third parties in such publications—and that this type of activity was expected to grow by 5% to 10% per year. The total corporate spending of this kind is estimated to be about $20 billion.

While the principal activity is the publication of magazines, the custom publisher normally fields a multimedia operation that produces special issues, advertorials, newsletters, brochures, videos, audios, CD-ROMs, Web sites, e-mail, conferences, and road shows.

The principal new customers for custom publishing are corporations that want to communicate one-on-one with their customers, current or potential. The basic purposes of the publications are (1) to retain present customers, and (2) to gain new customers. Custom publishers are used rather than handling the work in-house because the companies gain access to top publishing talent and can reduce expenses. The publishers also help the sponsor define audiences, target promotion, and enhance databases so that very small groups can be targeted.

Publishers like the business because it produces steady and known percentages of profits and gives them an opportunity to utilize the skills they have available. They also are able to tap into promotion budgets of the sponsoring companies that normally are not available for advertising.

The key to successful custom publishing is the development of long-term relationships. To ensure this, publishers must find ways to quantify results by using sophisticated research tools to learn about things that are not easily proven, such as:

- Increased sales for existing customers
- Increased market share
- Creation of brand awareness
- Changing the perception of a company
- Enhancing trade relations

WARNING

The prospect of developing a new source of revenue with virtually assured profits is certainly attractive, but:

- It takes months and sometimes years to develop a custom publishing relationship.
- A relationship can end very abruptly if the promotion director or CEO is changed.
- It may be difficult to prove the benefits to the sponsor.
- You may antagonize many advertisers by working with one of their competitors.
- You may divert the attention of some of your key advertising, promotion, and editorial people from their primary duties.
- You can easily call into question the editorial independence of your basic business. The very basis of the custom magazine editorial content is advocacy journalism. In some cases, the identity of the sponsoring organization is not even revealed (tobacco companies, for example).

Existing magazine publishers normally set up separate departments for custom publishing, but this cannot completely overcome all these problems.

Appendices: Facts about the Business and Sources of Information

APPENDIX A

Recent History of Magazines

Chapter 1, "The Wonderful World of Magazines" gives a taste of the recent trends in the magazine business. What follows is an amplification of this material, but is by no means an exhaustive study of the subject.

Because magazines are based on the interests people have—and want communication about—they act as a mirror of our society and the changes that take place in it over the years.

I don't believe anyone knows just how many magazines are being published at any moment. Aside from the fact that there is no real definition of just what a magazine is, there are so many comings and goings that it would be impossible to get a good figure.

The most recent National Directory of Magazines and Standard Periodical Directory have listings of many thousands of titles. These include both consumer and business publications as well as many that are issued less frequently than quarterly, some Canadian magazines, and lots of incomplete entries that seem to indicate that they may not currently be published. They also include some categories that I do not consider to be true magazines, such as comics, crossword puzzles, alumni communications, house organs, etc.

Because of this, I have based the statistical figures about magazines and their trends over the years on the data that has been published in the Consumer and Business Publication monthly of Standard Rate and Data. While these may be incomplete to an extent that I cannot quantify, they are the best sources available and contain information on the vast majority, but not all, of the meaningful magazines. They are also comparable between periods.

Based on the listings in the directories and those in SRDS, I estimate the total number of magazines published at the end of 2001 to be:

Consumer	6,200 (about 1/3 listed in SRDS)
Business	10,700 (about 1/2 listed in SRDS)

The increase in number of magazines published each year:

Consumer	50-100
Business	150-200

Because of the churn of comings and goings of titles, however, the number of new magazines started each year is substantially higher:

Consumer	250-500
Business	500-1,000

Consumer Magazines

Jack Tebbel and Mary Ellen Zuckerman in their book, *The Magazine in America, 1741–1990,* point out that the first Golden Age of magazines was the period 1825 to 1850 and was followed by a number of others, including the Golden Age of magazine illustration in 1900 to 1910.

Many of us who were around in the early post–WWII years were sure that this was the real Golden Age for magazines. That, of course, was before all those "competitors" really became important—TV, cable, the Internet.

But take a look at what has happened to our industry since:

	2000	1988	1980	1973	1963
Magazines	2,072	1,275	921	652	445
Issues	26,258	15,545	12,236	10,158	6,748
Circulation (000)	670,700	466,200	382,100	308,800	217,100
Copies (millions)	8,672,000	7,609,000	7,073,000	5,708,000	4,396,000

There has been growth in the number of magazines of all circulation sizes, with the greatest increases in those with smaller circulation because of the trend toward special interest and regional magazines, although there are still some mass circulation publications.

The number of publications with circulation:

Circulation	*2000*	*1988*	*1980*	*1973*	*1963*
Under 100,000	1147	661	438	288	215
100,000 to 500,000	672	414	318	220	142
500,000 to 1,000,000	126	100	81	64	38
Over 1,000,000	127	100	84	80	50
Averages per Publication					
Issues	12.7	12.2	13.3	15.6	15.2
Circulation (000)	324	366	415	474	488
Copies (millions)	4.2	6.0	7.7	8.8	9.9

You can see that the competing media certainly had an effect, along with all the other changes that have taken place in our lives. The effect was, of course, to increase our desire for magazines.

You may wonder why I picked those particular years. Actually, the years from 1963 to 1988 were used a few years ago when I took several looks at the field for some *Folio* pieces. There is no magic or real significance to those years. Some others would have yielded the same patterns.

You might also wonder why I discuss only circulation and not advertising. This goes back to my feeling that readers' interests are the key to the magazine business and that advertising will follow circulation in those fields where it is useful. Some overall data on advertising is shown in chapter 1, "The Wonderful World of Magazines."

CONTINUED GROWTH

If you want to start a new consumer magazine, don't be scared off because there are a lot already covering the field you are interested in. I made another study of the number of magazines covering different subjects for the periods 1981, 1991, and 2000.

Number of magazines listed in	2000	2,072
	1991	1,436
	1981	886

There has been growth in the number of publications in just about all the SRDS categories. 13 new categories were added that accounted for 281 of the titles added since 1991. The major ones were:

Parenthood	65
Alternative newsweeklies	61
Teen	39
Black/African-American	23
Lifestyle	20
Affluence	20

Others with small numbers of titles included adventure, disabilities, ethnic, home office, opinion, popular culture, and special interest.

At the same time, almost every previously existing category had an increased number of titles. The largest increases were:

Sports	135
Metropolitan	103
Automotive and motorcycle	94
Crafts	73
Home service	49
Women's	40

But even such older fields as fishing and hunting (47) and boating (29) showed good growth in titles.

CHANGE IS THE BYWORD

This is hardly a static industry. The comings and goings are huge. Look at these statistics for consumer magazines during that almost 20-year period:

Listed in 1981	886
Still listed in 2000	482
No longer listed	404
Listed in years between 1981 and 2000, but no longer published	2,197
Total listed at any time during the entire period	4,910

In other words, of the magazines published during this almost 20-year period, only about 40% are still in existence—but still the total now being published has increased substantially. A list of the number of titles in each category during these periods follows this section.

Effects of Recent History

One would, naturally, wonder what effect the Recession of 2000 and he terrorism of 9-11 have had on the consumer magazine field. here has been considerable publicity about the passing of a number of well-known titles—*Talk, Mademoiselle, Teen, George, Family Money, Mature Outlook, Walking, eCompany Now, Industry Standard, Family PC,* and some others.

The evidence overall has been that there has been no overall fall-out for the industry as a whole—rather, the normal growth from year-to-year has not taken place. The total number of consumer magazines listed SRDS in January 2002 published quarterly or more times a year has remained startlingly constant, with some 2069 versus 2065 in 2000.

There have been small declines where you would expect them in affluence, airline, computers, and science—and others where you might not expect them—youth, women's, mature, fitness, and some other. On the other hand, there have been increases in ethnic, health, metropolitan, parenthood, photography, religions, and some other areas. None of this seems abnormal

History of Some Fields

I thought it would be of interest to see the changes that have taken place in some of the areas.

General Interest

Perhaps the best known and most public of the areas.

	2000	*1988*	*1981*	*1973*	*1963*
Magazines	62	52	36	26	22
Issues	912	736	589	510	494
Circulation (000)	56,800	60,500	55,300	40,200	31,300
Copies (millions)	1,750,000	2,143,000	1,094,000	747,000	1,083,000
Averages per publication					
Issues	14.7	14.2	16.4	19.6	24.7
Circulation (000)	916,000	1,163	1,536	1,546	1,566

Life and the *Saturday Evening Post*, both weeklies, and *Look*, a biweekly, were at their peaks in 1963. Of the 22 magazines in 1963, only nine remain: *Atlantic, Ebony, Harpers, National Geographic, New Yorker, Reader's Digest, Town & Country, Yankee,* and *Natural History*. You may recall some of those that passed away: *Grit, National Observer, New Times, Realites, Book Digest, Coronet, Quest,* and *Saturday Review*.

Since then we have not seen many new large circulation publications that appeal to the public in general, much as few all-pervasive radio and TV shows still exist. Instead, we have the likes of *Biography, Guideposts, Money, National Enquirer,* and *Smithsonian,* plus many other smaller circulation magazines.

The story of changes in titles within the category for the past twenty years has been pretty typical of the industry as a whole:

Listed in 1981	36
Still listed in 2000	21
No longer listed	15
Listed in 2000	62
Listed in years between 1981 and 2000, but no longer published	94
Total listed at any time during the entire period	187

Two new titles had been added by 2002, whitle two older ones have been dropped.

Computers (consumer magazines only)

This category shows how quickly things have changed in this rapidly evolving area. This field, which has been referred to often in this book, hardly existed much before 1981. About that time, the forerunners of the PC arrived. We saw a rash of new magazines—some of you may recall such titles as *A+, Ahoy, Amiga, Antic, Commodore, Hot Coco, K Power,* and *Nibble.* But almost all of those died along with the computers they talked about, and we have ended up with this scenario:

Listed in 1981	6
Still listed in 2000	None
No longer listed	6
Listed in 2000	20
Listed in years between 1981 and 2000, but no longer published	120
Total listed at any time during the entire period	177

One new title had been added by 2002, whitle five older ones have been dropped.

Sports

This category has the most entries, but may be the most treacherous of all for magazines.

	2000	*1988*	*1981*	*1973*	*1963*
Magazines	207	100	72	48	34
Issues	2,224	1,112	830	607	498
Circulation (000)	29,600	14,000	13,000	7,300	2,300
Averages per publication					
Issues	10.7	11.1	11.5	12.6	14.6
Circulation (000)	110	140	181	152	68

Table A.1 Number of Consumer Magazines Listed in Standard Rate & Data

CATEGORY		September 2000	April 1991	December 1981	In and Out between periods	1981-2000 Total different mags listed
O	Adventure & Outdoor Recreation	18	0	0	3	21
OA	Affluence	20	0	0	16	36
1	Airline Inflight/Train Enroute	30	30	25	61	109
2	Art&Antiques	28	24	19	31	69
3	Automotive	93	68	29	60	171
4	Aviation	18	11	11	9	32
5	Babies	8	6	4	35	45
5A	Black/African American	23	6	0	16	39
6	Boating & Yachting	49	35	20	25	82
7	Bridal	12	4	2	23	35
8	Busines s& Finance	32	23	21	51	95
8A	Camping, Campers, RVs, etc.	7	12	13	20	33
9	Children's	3	2 In Youth		5	9
9A	Civic	3	3 In Fraternal		0	4
10A	Computers	20	12	6	120	177
11	Crafts, Games, Hobbies, Models	102	68	29	83	204
12	Dancing	4	1	2	0	5
12A	Disabilities	7	0	0	2	9
13	Dogs & Pets	20	14	10	23	48
14	Dressmaking & Needlework	5	5	3	2	10
17A	Entertainment & Performing Arts	29	12	12	39	76
18	Epicurean	21	15	8	25	54
18A	Ethnic	4	0	0	1	5
18B	Fashion, Beauty & Grooming	5	6	8	20	29
19	Fishing & Hunting	96	79	49	44	175
19A	Fitness	17	6	12	8	29
20	Fraternal, Professional Other Assns.	16	16	20	7	34
20A	Gaming	7	5	0	8	17
21	Gardening (Home)	19	11	9	11	37
21A	Gay & Lesbian Publications	12	3	2	7	20
22	General Editorial	65	63	36	94	187
23	Health	50	30 In Fitness		64	132
23A	History	12	11 In Literature		2	15
23B	Home Office/Small Business	3	0	0	5	8
24	Home Service & Home	99	69	50	112	237
25	Horses, Riding & Breeding	30	35	30	26	72
25A	Hotel Inroom	5	5 In Airline		20	24
27A	Lifestyle	20	0	4	3	23
28	Literary, Book Reviews, Writing	9	5	27	11	20
28A	Mature Market	31	17	8	24	61
30	Men's	28	17	11	37	72
30A	Metropolitan/Regional/State	199	160	96	232	518
31	Military & Naval	15	13	12	9	29
31A	Motorcycle	30	14 In Auto		22	58
33	Music	55	45	30	62	140
34	Mystery, Adventure, Sci-Fi	9	5 In Literature		7	21
35	Nature & Ecology	12	12 In Science		12	29
36A	News-Weeklies	11	12	14	9	22
36C	Newsweeklies (Alternative)	61	24	0	8	69
38A	Opinion, Thought, Commentary	6	0	0	0	6
38B	Parenthood	65	19	0	36	101
39	Photography	11	11	10	4	26
41	Political & Social Topics	20	15	16	13	42
41A	Popular Culture	11	0	0	7	18
42	Religious & Denominational	27	28	30	27	66
43	Science/Technology	14	12	29	27	47
44A	Special Interest	4	0	0	0	4
45	Sports	207	181	72	267	539
45A	Teen	39	0	0	19	58
46	Travel	65	49	30	109	201
47	TV and Radio	18	15	11	40	73
49	Women's	74	52	34	80	182
51	Youth	32	40	22	54	101
		2065	1436	886	2197	4910

NOTES: Includes those published at least quarterly. A few magazines have been moved from one category to another during the period. Omitted categories—Almanacs, College, Comics, Education, Entertainment Guides, Labor Mechanics, Media/Personalities, Metro/Entertainment, News-Biweeklies, Newspaper Distributed

This is a wild area. I counted magazines devoted to 73 different sports in 2000, including such popular ones as go-karting, rodeos, and ballooning. *Sports Illustrated*, with over 3 million circulation, does not choose to be listed here, but is included with the newsweeklies.

Golf is the only sport that really seems able to support a number of magazines (although it looks as if there may be too many right now). I have divided the field into two categories—golf and all others. Here are the results for the number of magazines during the period 1981 to 2000:

	Golf	*Other*	*Total*
Listed in 1981	14	58	72
Still listed in 2000	7	31	38
No longer listed	7	27	34
Listed in 2000	40	167	207
Listed in years between 1981 and 2000 , but no longer	28	239	267
Total listed at any time during the entire period	74	465	539

Sports are wonderful, but not necessarily in the magazine business. The average life of magazines in this field must be very short. Seven new titles were added by 2002 (four in gold), while six have been dropped

Boating

Typical of the growth that has taken place in an old established field.

	2000	*1988*	*1981*	*1973*	*1963*
Magazines	49	37	20	23	9
Issues	538	433	292	318	100
Circulation (000)	4,000	2,500	1,500	1,400	600
Average per publication					
Issues	11.0	11.7	14.6	13.8	11.1
Circulation (000)	82	68	75	61	67

Despite the huge size of the boating population, the magazines have always had relatively small circulations. A number are regional an there is the division between power and sailboats. *Yachting* and *Motor Boating & Sailing* are the venerable titles started early in the century. They have been joined by many new magazines covering traditional boating and, more recently, by those covering those strange things that are called "personal watercraft."

Compared with most fields, this one has been quite stable in the magazine field since 1981, but we still see lots of churn:

Listed in 1981	20
Still listed in 2000	16
No longer listed	4
Listed in 2000	49
Listed in years between 1981 and 2000 but no longer listed	25
Total listed at any time during the entire period	82

There has been no change in titles listed by 2002.

Business Magazines

In chapter 8, "The Life Cycle of a Magazine" are analyses of the situation in three business fields for 2000, 1991, and 1981. Information on the amount of circulation for each was not included because this is not as important a factor in the business magazines as in the consumer area.

An analysis of the business magazines follows. It includes data on the number of magazines in each category for 2000, 1991, and 1981. It does not, however, include information on those magazines published only in the in-between years that would show considerable churn, as in the other areas of the magazine field.

Effect of Recent Evens

The Recession of 2000 and the terrorism of 9-11 have had only a minor effect of the business magazine field, reducing he number of titles listed in SRDS published quarterly or more frequently in January 2002 declining from 3,954 to 3,909. The major declines were felt, not surprisingly in the computer and telecommunications areas with others suffering including building, chemical, motor trucks, petroleum, and retail travel. Increases were registered in the general areas of business, financial, and legal, while professional fitness and restaurants also gained entries.

Al.l areas in the healthcare sector held their own except for the major segment, medical and surgical, which registered a decline of more than 100 titles, the reason for which I have not analyzed

Farm Magazines

The farm field has seen a sea change as far as magazines are concerned.

Years ago when family farms held sway throughout most of the country, there were some very large magazines that served farmers and their families—*Farm Journal*, *Progressive Farmer*, *Capper's,* and *Successful Farmer.* They covered much more than farming—they really were general magazines covering all aspects of farm life. In the same way, the state farm papers in the major farming states served as regional lifestyle magazines.

Table A.2 Number of Business Magazines Listed in Standard Rate & Data

Category		December 2000	January 1990	January 1980
1	Advertising & Marketing	99	100	79
2	Air Conditioning, Heating, Plumbing, etc.	40	43	39
3	Amusements & Gaming Management	16	10	5
3A	Appliances	4	4	9
4	Architecture	27	25	17
5	Arts	3	3	4
6	Automotive	95	78	69
7	Aviation & Aerospace	41	41	22
9	Baking	9	9	8
10	Banking	59	56	41
11	Barbers	0	0	1
12	Beauty & Hairdressing	16	7	8
14	Boating	7	12	9
15	Books & Book Trade	9	7	6
16	Brewing, Distilling, Bottling & Beverage	51	74	65
17	Brick,Tile, Building Materials	1	4	2
18	Brushes, Brooms & Mops	1	1	1
19	Building	59	54	46
19A	Building Management & Real Estate	82	78	22
19B	Building Products Retailing	10	7	0
20	Business	126	90	35
20A	Business-Metro, State & Regional	193	138	39
21A	Campgrounds, Recreational	3	1	2
21B	Camps	4	2	2
25	Cemetery & Monuments	4	7	6
26	Ceramics	4	4	4
27	Chain Stores	3	4	7
28	Chemical & Chemical Process Industries	45	35	28
28A	China & Dinnerware	0	2	2
31	Clothing & Furnishing Goods (Men's)	4	3	9
32	Clothing & Furnishing Goods (Women's)	10	17	11
32A	Coal Merchandising	0	0	2
32B	Coin-Operated & Vending Machines	6	2	3
32C	Computers	215	156	26
33	Confectionery	7	9	9
34	Control & Instrument Systems	22	11	9
34A	Corsets	0	5	5
34B	Cosmetics	8	9	6
34C	Dairy Products	6	7	8
35A	Department & Specialty Stores	6	10	10
35B	Discount Merchandising	3	3	4
35C	Display	2	2	0
35D	Draperies & Curtains	3	2	2
38	Educational	146	117	90
38A	Educational, Adult Training, etc.	5	4	3
39	Electrical	31	26	25
40	Electronic Engineering	96	86	67
40A	Electronic Imaging	1	0	0
40B	Employment Opportunities & Recruitment	33	28	7
40C	Energy Application & Management	7	5	7
41	Engineering & Construction	111	92	87
44	Farm Implements (General)	3	6	6
44A	Farm Supplies	1	1	4
44B	Fashion Accessories	1	0	2
44C	Feed, Grain & Milling	14	14	15
45	Fertilizer & Agricultural Chemicals	6	9	8
46	Financial	88	50	28
47	Fire Protection	15	12	7
48	Fishing, Commercial	8	9	5
48A	Fitness Professional	14	0	0
48B	Floor Coverings/Insulation	8	10	9
49	Florists & Floriculture	17	14	6
49A	Fluid Power Systems	0	0	0
50	Food—Processing & Distribution	33	23	26
51	Fundraising/Philanthropy	4	0	0
52	Funeral Directors	11	6	7
53	Fur Farming	2	2	2
54	Furniture & Upholstery	25	21	18
55	Gas	10	9	11
57	Giftware/Art/Decorative Accessories/Greeting Cards	23	17	13
57A	Glass	16	12	11
59	Golf	19	8	7
60	Government & Public Works	65	47	32
60A	Graphic Design	9	0	0
61	Grocery	49	59	55
62	Hardware	5	5	8
63A	Home Economics	0	3	3
63B	Home Furnishings	7	2	7
64	Horse & Rider Supplies/Apparel/ Equipment	4	4	5
66	Hotels, Motels, Clubs & Resorts	22	16	12
67	Housewares	2	3	3
68	Human Resources	21	0	0
69	Industrial	15	17	12
69A	Industrial Automation	11	4	0
69B	Industrial Design	0	0	1
70	Industrial Distribution	3	4	3
70A	Industrial Purchasing	9	11	14
70B	Industry Purch Directories & Catalogs	46	28	14
70C	Infants, Children's & Teen Age Goods	4	6	5
71	Institutions	0	0	1
72	Insurance	60	53	39
73	Interior Design/Furnishings/ Space Planning	18	29	12
73B	International Trade	9	11	8
73C	Intimate Apparel	4	0	0
74	Jewelry & Watchmaking	13	14	13
75	Journalism & Publishing	17	25	14
77	Landscape, Garden Supplies	24	23	14
78	Laundry & Drycleaning	9	12	12
79	Leather, Boots & Shoes	8	7	10
80	Legal	90	46	11
81	Lighting & Lighting Fixtures	6	4	3
81A	Linens & Domestics	0	3	4
82	Logging, Forest Management/Prod Mfg	32	26	24
83	Luggage & Leather Goods	2	4	4
83A	Maintenance/Cleaning	18	13	7
83B	Mfg./Industries, Equip, Repair, Oper	27	12	11
84	Maritime, Marine, Shipbldg, Repair & Oper	23	12	11
85	Materials	1	6	2
85A	Materials Handling & Distribution	13	5	5
86	Meats & Provisions	5	4	6
88	Metal, Metalworking & Machinery	71	62	75
90	Military & Naval (Active & Inactive)	20	24	21
93	Mining (Coal, Metal & Non-Metallic)	12	15	18
95	Motion, Talk, Sound Commercial Pictures	26	17	17
96	Motor Trucks & Accessories	52	56	58
97	Motorcycle & Bicycle	6	9	7
97A	Moving, Storage	3	3	0
99	Music & Music Trades	37	26	23
101A	Nuclear Science & Engineering	1	1	2
102A	Nut Culture	0	1	1
102B	Ocean Science & Engineering	2	2	2
103	Office Equipment & Stationery	5	18	15
103A	Office Methods & Management	4	8	8
104	Oils (Vegetable)	1	1	2
107	Packaging Mfgrs (Including Paperboard, Flexible)	12	9	4
107A	Packaging (Users)	8	7	6
108	Paint & Wallcovering, Painting, Decorating	14	15	14

Table A.2 Number of Business Magazines Listed in Standard Rate & Data (contiinued)

Category		December 2000	January 1990	January 1980
109	Paper	18	25	25
110	Parks, Public	3	3	2
111	Petroleum & Oil	43	61	47
112	Pets	5	7	5
113	Photographic	15	20	15
113A	Physical Distribution	1	1	4
113B	Plant/Engineering, Maintenance, Repair & Oper	14	10	14
114	Plastics & Composition Products	19	19	11
115A	Police, Law Enforcement & Penology	20	12	7
115B	Pollution Control (Air & Water)	22	24	12
115C	Ports	0	1	3
116	Poultry & Poultry Products	6	11	8
117	Power & Power Plants	13	8	13
118	Printing & Printing Processes	42	39	30
119	Produce (Fruits & Vegetables)	8	3	2
120	Product Design Engineering	22	18	15
120A	Product Engineering	0	1	1
120B	Professional Association	6	6	5
121	Public Transportation & Mass Transit	10	4	5
121A	Quality Assurance	5	0	0
122	Radio, TV & Video	58	82	51
124	Railroad	6	6	7
125	Refrigeration	0	0	1
126	Religious	9	6	6
126A	Rental & Leasing Equipment	11	7	5
126B	Reproduction—Inplant & Commercial	2	2	4
127	Restaurants & Food Service	56	47	25
128	Robotics	2	2	0
129	Roofing	8	11	3
130	Rubber	5	6	6
131	Safety, Accident Prevention	12	8	7
131A	Sales Management	4	2	2
132	School Administration	32	19	13
132A	Science, Research & Development	107	80	48
132B	Security	15	12	9
133	Seed & Nursery Trade	11	11	7
134	Selling & Salesmanship	1	2	5
135	Shopping Centers	9	7	4
137	Sporting Goods	36	32	28
139	Stone Products, etc.	6	7	4
140	Sugar & Sugar Crops	3	2	3
140A	Swimming Pools	7	9	7
141	Tea, Coffee, Spices	3	2	2
142	Telecommunications Technology	67	47	6
143	Textiles & Knit Goods	16	26	23
145	Tobacco	5	5	6
147	Toys, Hobbies & Novelties	15	14	11
147A	Trailers	4	3	5
148	Transportation, Logistics & Distribution	31	41	24
149A	Travel, Business Conventions & Meetings	59	38	12
149B	Travel, Retail	38	67	41
152	Veterinary	24	24	17
154	Waste Management	14	0	0
155	Water Supply & Sewage Disposal	19	21	22
156	Welding	5	5	5
158	Wire & Wire Products	4	4	4
159	Woodworking	2	3	5
		3954	3438	2463
Healthcare				
H1	Biological Sciences	22	13	0
H2	Dental	53	45	36
H3	Drugs, Pharmaceutics	56	40	32
H4	Healthcare	108	29	0
H5	Hospital Administration	28	22	22
H6	Medical & Surgical	970	538	314
H7	Nursing & Health	112	70	40
H8	Ophthalmology, Optical & Optometry	27	13	17
		1376	770	461
		5330	4208	2924

As corporate farming has developed, the publications have become business magazines primarily devoted to the how-to of farming. This trend started shortly after WW II. You can track the results in the circulation figures covering the field during the past 30 years or so.

	2000	*1980*	*1972*
Total circulation (000)			
4 Large magazines	1,645	3,033	4,890
(Capper's existed only in 1972)			
24 state farm magazines	493	1,584	2,182
(Reduced to 21 in 2000)			

Farm Journal has been particularly interesting during this period. In trying to serve its changing audience and their regional needs, it has led the way in developing hundreds of combinations of pages—and has come close to designing an individual magazine for each reader.

In other respects, the magazines show much the same pattern as business magazines. Of the 172 magazines published in 1980, only 99 are still published. One hundred twenty-two of those published in 2000 are new. In addition, there have been many others started that do not appear at either the beginning or the end of that period. Three more titles are listed in 2002.

Table A.3 Number of Farm Magazines Listed in SRD

Category	April 2001	January 1981
1 Advisory/Crops, Chemical, Livestock	3	0
1A Dairy & Dairy Products	15	15
2 Diversified Farming & Farm Home	100	60
3 Farm Education & Vocations	1	0
4 Farm Electrification	0	4
5 Farm Organizations & Cooperatives	9	15
6 Field Crops & Soil Management	19	13
7 Fruits, Nuts, Vegetables & Special Products	35	21
9 Land Use, Irrigation & Conservation	2	2
9 Livestock & Breed	35	41
11 Poultry	1	1
	220	172

(The large and state magazines discussed above are included on this list with those in Category 2—Diversified.)

APPENDIX B

Sources of Information

I HAVE MENTIONED many times that magazine publishing is one of the most public of all businesses. You can read the editorial content of the magazines, count the advertising pages, find out how many people read them, and easily obtain data about who those readers are.

And even when it comes to the how-to of publishing magazines, there are very few real secrets—and those in the business are usually quite willing to discuss just about any aspect.

In the following chapters are lists of organizations and publications where you might find more information, as well as some data on postal rates.

Below are some of the most helpful sources:

MPA and ABM

The field is blessed with two of the most professionally operated and useful associations you will find anywhere—the Magazine Publishers of America, primarily serving consumer magazines, and the American Business Media, addressed to business magazines. In addition to servicing the specific needs of their members, they frequently operate jointly in such areas as printing, paper, postal, privacy, intellectual property, and editorial independence. They also often join in sponsoring various events for their members and customers.

The types of things both pursue very actively are:

- Information services of various kinds, including listings of suppliers and consultants
- Development of intern programs for their members
- Awards programs for editorial and advertising excellence
- Special conferences on specific subjects
- Educational seminars and white papers
- Information about the new media and custom publishing
- Cost and other reports where members can compare their operations with those of other publishers
- Marketing campaigns among advertisers and agencies
- Job fairs and other career activities
- Development of industry advertising page and dollar volume statistics
- Many other similar activities

USEFUL PUBLISHED MATERIAL

Folio and *Circulation Management*

Since *Folio* magazine was launched in 1970, its focus, as well as that of its sister publication, *Circulation Management,* which started in 1986, has been primarily on publishing articles on the how-to of publishing magazines, in addition to covering various newsworthy events.

There are articles in every issue dealing with today's news, problems, and solutions. And the back issues hold a veritable encyclopedia of useful material covering the specifics of just about every aspect of operating in the magazine business.

Many of their how-to pieces have been published in several handbooks of magazine publishing. They covered such subjects as:

- *Coping with Advertising Rate Pressure without Shooting Yourself in the Foot* by David Orlow
- *Gearing Up for Gift Subscriptions* by Eliot Schein
- *The Economics of Cover Pricing* by Ron Scott
- *How Much Should an Editorial Page Cost?* by John Fry
- *Selecting the Right Paper for Your Magazine* by Alex Brown
- *Investing in Sales Training* by Hershel Sarbin
- As well as a bunch that I wrote.

There are literally hundreds of these articles available. I have suggested that they gather together the most useful of these and offer them again to the publishing world. I hope they will.

Capell's Circulation Report

Dan Capell's newsletter is published twenty times a year, covering primarily consumer magazines. It contains analyses of circulation statistics, changes in ABC and BPA rules, and other such events, as well as suggestions of what these mean—and how to react to them.

Standard Rate & Data—Consumer and Business

As you have seen elsewhere in this book, the material covered in these monthly volumes is very useful in analyzing trends, in studying the position of different magazines versus their competitors, and in many other ways.

ABC and BPA

The periodic reports published by these (and other) circulation audit organizations are, of course, most useful to advertisers and agencies—and can also help publishers compare their situation versus their competitors.'

ABC also publishes an annual Magazine Trend Report that shows five-year statistics of the sources of circulation and prices of both advertising and circulation for the leading consumer magazines in various fields.

Advertising Data

Monthly statistics of advertising pages and dollars are published by Publishers Information Bureau (PIB) for the major consumer magazines, and by Business Information Network (BIN) for the major business magazines.

Several magazines and newsletters, including *Advertising Age, Adweek,* and *min,* also publish information on advertising pages and dollars on a regular basis.

Salary Studies

In addition to the surveys of compensation made from time by MPA and ABP, *Folio* publishes annual surveys of salaries of key positions in various departments for both consumer and business magazines.

Predictions

Predictions of future events are, of course, made by lots of people at just about any time.

Those that are most eagerly awaited are the McCann-Ericson annual predictions of advertising spending in all kinds of media—and those made by Veronis, Suhler of the future of media in its broadest sense, including entertainment as well as magazines, TV, newspapers, etc.

Books

Over the years, a number of books have been published that would be useful today, but most are out of print. I particularly recall *The Secrets of Successful Direct Mail* by Dick Benson, *Magazine Layout* by Cortland Smith, and *Renewal$ by Eliot Schein,* but there are lots of others that might be worthy of republishing. The principal not-for-profit organizations serving the magazine and allied fields with which you may have contact include the following. In most cases their name explains their purpose and who their members are.

APPENDIX C

Organizations Serving the Field

Advertising Council (Ad Council)—Nonprofit organization that approves and helps to conduct national public service advertising campaigns for nonprofit organizations. 261 Madison Avenue, New York, NY 10016. 212-922-1500. adcouncil.org.

Advertising Research Foundation (ARF)—Conducts research and publishes the *Journal of Advertising Research.* 641 Lexington Avenue, New York, NY 10022. 212-751-5656. thearf.org.

American Advertising Federation (AAF)—National association of major advertisers. 1101 Vermont Avenue NW, Washington DC 20005. 202-898-0098. aaf.org.

American Association of Advertising Agencies (4 As)—National association of ad agencies. 405 Lexington Avenue, New York, NY 10174. 212-682-2500. aaaa.org.

American Booksellers Association (ABA)—National booksellers' association. 828 S. Broadway, Tarrytown, NY 10591. 914-591-2665. bookweb.org.

American Business Media (ABM)—National association of business magazines and other business media. 675 Third Avenue, New York, NY 10017. 212-661-6360. abmmail.com.

American Institute of Graphic Arts (AIGA)—Art directors, graphic designers, printers, and others in graphic arts. 164 Fifth Avenue, New York, NY 10010. 212-807-1990. aiga.org.

American Marketing Association (AMA)—Individuals in marketing and market research. 311 S. Wacker Drive, Chicago, IL 60606. 312-542-9000. marketingpower.com..

American Society of Association Executives (ASAE)—Publishes *Association Management.* 1575 I Street NW, Washington, DC 20005. 202-626-2723. asaenet.org.

American Society of Magazine Editors (ASME)—Top editors of major magazines. Operates in conjunction with MPA. 919 Third Avenue, New York, NY 10022. 212-872-3700. asme@magazines.org.

American Society of Media Photographers (ASMP)—150 N. Second Street, Philadelphia, PA 19106. 215-451-2767. asmp.org.

American Society of Newspaper Editors (ASNE)—11690B Sunrise Valley Drive, Reston, VA 20191-1409. 703-453-1122. asne.org.

Art Directors Club. 106 West 29th Street, New York, NY 10001. 212-643-1440. adcny.org.

Associated Business Writers of America—3140 S. Peoria Street, Aurora, CO 80014. 303-841-0246. nationalwriters.com.

Association of American Publishers (AAP)—National association of book publishers. 71 Fifth Avenue, New York, NY 10003. 212-255-0200. e-publishers.org.

Association of American University Presses (AAUP)—71 West 23rd Street, New York, NY 10010. 212-989-1010. aaupnet.org.

Association of National Advertisers (ANA)—Major advertisers. 708 Third Avenue, New York, NY 10017. 212-697-5950. ana.net.

Audit Bureau of Circulations (ABC)—Independent nonprofit organization of advertisers, agencies, and publishers that provides verified audits of circulation. 900 N. Meacham Street, Schaumburg, IL 60173. 847-605-0909. accessabc.com.

Authors Guild—Writers and editors. 330 W. 42nd Street, New York, NY 10036. 212-564-5363. authorsguild.org.

Business Marketing Association (BMA)—National association of major business advertisers. 400 N. Michigan Avenue, Chicago, IL 60611. 312-409-4262. marketing.org.

BPA International—Independent nonprofit organization of advertisers, agencies, and publishers that provides verified audits of circulation. 270 Madison Ave., New York, NY 10016. 212-779-3200. bpa.com..

Certified Audit of Circulations (CAC)—Independent circulation audit organization. 155 Willowbrook Boulevard, Wayne, NY 07470. 973-785-3000. cacaudit.com.

City & Regional Magazine Association—5820 Wilshire Boulevard, Los Angeles, CA 90036. 323-937-5514. citymag.org.

Direct Marketing Association (DMA)—An outgrowth of the former Direct Mail Marketing Association, members are now from all direct marketing media. 1120 Avenue of the Americas, New York, NY 10036. 212-768-7277. the-dma.org

Editorial Freelancers Association (EFA)—71 W. 23rd Street, New York, NY 10010. 212-929-5400. the-efa.org.

Fulfillment Management Association, Inc. (FMA)—60 East 42nd Street, New York, NY 10165. 815-734-5821. fmanational.org.

Magazine Publishers of America (MPA)—National association of consumer magazines. 919 Third Avenue, New York, NY 10022. 212-872-3600. magazine.org.

National Association of Publishers' Representatives—Independent advertising reps. P.O. Box 3139, New York, NY 10163. 212-685-3254. naprassoc@aol.com..

Newspaper Association of America (NAA)—Mainly publishers of daily papers. 1921 Gallows Road, Vienna, VA 22182. 703-902-1600. naa.org.

Newspaper Guild—AFL-CIO union primarily in newspapers, but also in a few magazines. 501 Third Street NW, Washington, DC 20001. 202-434-7177. newsguild.org.

Overseas Press Club of America (OPC)—40 West 54th Street, New York, NY 10036. 212-626-9220. opcofamerica.org.

Periodical and Book Association of America, Inc. (PBAA)—Newsstand publishers. 475 Park Avenue South, New York, NY 10066. 212-689-4952. pbaa.net.

Printing Industries of America (PIA)—100 Daingerfield Road, Alexandria, VA 22314. 703-519-8100.

Public Relations Society of America (PRSA)—33 Irving Place, New York, NY 10003. 212-995-2230. prsa.org.

Publishers Information Bureau (PIA)—Part of MPA.

Society of Illustrators (SI)—128 E. 63rd Street, New York, NY 10021. 212-838-2560. societyillustrators.org.

Society of National Association Publications (SNAP)—National association of association magazines. Tyson's Corner, 1595 Spring Hill Road, Vienna, VA 22182. 703-506-3285. snaponline.org.

Society of Professional Journalists (SPJ)—Eugene S. Pulliam National Journalism Center, 3903 N. Meridian Street, Indianapolis, IN 46208. spj.org.

Verified Audit Circulation Corporation (VAC)—Independent circulation audit organization. 517 Jacoby Street, San Rafael, CA 94901. 415-457-3871. verifiedaudit.com.

APPENDIX D

Publications Serving the Field

ONLY A FEW publications are devoted primarily to serving the people running magazines. Because of the importance of advertising, circulation, editorial, and production activities to publishers, however, publications in various other disciplines are often of interest to those in the magazine field. Some of those that you might find useful include:

Primarily for Magazine Publishers

Folio: The Magazine for Magazine Management—Monthly magazine for the entire publishing team. Intertech Publishing, a Primedia Company—11 River Bend Drive South, Stamford, CT 06907. 203-358-9900. foliomag.com.

Folio First Day—Twice weekly fax or e-mail newsletter.

Min—PBI Media, 305 Madison Avenue, New York, NY 10165. 212-983-5144. minonline.com.

min—Media Industry Newsletter—Weekly newsletter primarily about consumer magazines.

min's b2b—Weekly newsletter about business magazines.

min's New Media Report—Newsletter covering new media.

min Magazine—Semiannual magazine.

Association Publishing—Bimonthly magazine for associations. Society of National Association Publications, 1595 Spring Hill Road, Vienna, VA 22182. 703-506-3285. snaponline.org.

Advertising and Marketing

Advertising Age—Weekly magazine covering the entire world of advertising and marketing. Crain Communications, Inc., 711 Third Avenue, New York, NY 10017. 212-210-0100. crain.com.

Adweek Magazines—Adweek Magazines, 770 Broadway, New York, NY 10003. 646-654-5125. adweek.com.

Adweek—Newsweekly for the advertising business.

Mediaweek—Weekly magazine covering all media.

Brandweek—Weekly magazine for brand marketing executives.

Agri Marketing—Magazine ten times a year for those selling to the farm market. Doane Agricultural Services Co., 11701 Borman Drive, Sta. 100, St. Louis, MO 63146. 314-569-1083. agrimarketing.com.

American Demographics—Monthly magazine of consumer trend and behavior information. Intertec Publishing, a Primedia Company. Address as in *Folio* above. demographics.com.

B to B—Biweekly magazine for business to business marketing. Address as in *Advertising Age* above.

Bill Communications, Inc.

potentials—Monthly magazine of new marketing ideas. 50 South Ninth Street, Minneapolis MN 55402. 612-333-0471. potentialsmag.com.

Sales & Marketing Management—Monthly magazine for those managing sales and marketing functions. 770 Broadway, New York, NY 10003. salesandmarketing.com.

Standard Rate & Data Service (SRDS)—1700 Higgins Road, Des Plaines, IL 60018. 847-375-5000. srds.com.

Business Publication Advertising Source—Monthly service of advertising rates.

Circulation 2001—Annual tabulation of newspaper and magazine circulation by areas.

Consumer Magazine Advertising Source—Monthly service of advertising rates.

Print Media Production Source—Quarterly service for production professionals.

Direct Marketing List Source—Bimonthly service.

Circulation

Capell's Circulation Report—The Newsletter of Magazine Circulation. 20 times a year.Capell Associates, 375 Bedford Road, Ridgewood NJ 07450. 201-652-1283.

Circulation Management—Monthly magazine for circulation professionals. Intertech Publishing, a Primedia Company. Address as in *Folio* above. circman.com.

Direct—Magazine 16 times a year for direct marketing professionals. Intertech Publishing, a Primedia Company. Address as in *Folio* above. intertec.com.

Direct Marketing—Monthly magazine covering this discipline. Hoke Communications, Inc., 224 Seventh Street, Garden City, NY. 11530. 516-746-6700. 71410-2423@compuserve.com.

DM News—The newspaper of direct marketing—Magazine 48 times a year. Mill Hollow Corporation, 100 Avenue of the Americas, New York, NY 10013. 212-925-8752. dmnews.com.

emarketing—Monthly magazine for B2B and B2C marketers. Professional Marketing Group, 488 Main Avenue, Norwalk, CT 06851. 203-847-7200. emarketingmag.com.

iMarketing News—Magazine 48 times a year for on-line marketers. Mill Hollow Corporation, address as in *DM News* above.

Target Marketing—Monthly magazine for users and producers of direct marketing. North American Publishing Co., 401 N. Broad St., Philadelphia, PA 19108. 215-238-5300. targetonline.com.

Newsstand Marketing

Magazine & Bookseller—Bimonthly magazine for retailers. North American Publishing Co., address as in *Target Marketing* above. magazinebookseller.com.

Magazine Retailer—Quarterly magazine. MetaMedia, 124 West 24th Street, New York, NY 10011. 212-989-6978. magretail@aol.com.

Production

Printmedia—Monthly magazine for production managers. North American Publishing Co., address as in *Target Marketing* above. napco.com.

Newspapers and News Magazines

Because of the nature of the industries in their cities, the *New York Times* and *Chicago Tribune* devote considerable attention to the advertising and media businesses. The *Wall Street Journal* and *USA Today,* too, exhibit more than a casual interest in this area. Other newspapers also cover the field from time to time, as do the general and business news magazines.

APPENDIX E

Postal Classifications and Rates

FEW BUSINESSES ARE as dependent on the Postal Service as magazines. In addition to mailing virtually all the subscription copies of the magazines, the vast majority of correspondence with subscribers is carried on through the mail, including efforts to sell subscriptions, collection efforts, renewal efforts, complaints and their resolution, and just about everything else.

The history of the Postal Service and its record of unifying the country in its early days is fascinating. To its credit, it is world renowned as the best service of its kind the world has ever known—and its costs are considerably lower than those in any other country.

Elsewhere in this book, I have noted the difficulty the Postal Service is now having because of its quasi-governmental nature and the inroads e-mail and other delivery services have made in its basic business. The rates quoted below are those in effect as this is written and are inevitably scheduled to rise considerably in the near future.

Because of the great variety of different types of mail—and efforts to reward mailers for any steps they may take to reduce the Postal Service costs—the classifications and rates charged have become a very complex mixture of basic rates less incentives offered when mail is prepared and delivered to the service in certain specified ways.

The information below gives a bird's-eye view of the classifications and rates that are most important for magazines. Further information can be obtained from the many guides the Postal Service has prepared for mailers, or from the Postal Service web site, usps.com.

First Class Mail

All matter wholly or partly in writing or typewriting, all actual and personal correspondence, all bills and statements of account, and all matter sealed or otherwise closed against inspection. Any mailable matter may be sent as First Class Mail.

	Prices as of June 30, 2002	
	Letters, Flats, and Parcels—Weight not over 1 ounce	*Postcards*
Nonautomation	$0.37	$0.23
Presorted	.352	.212
Automation		
Letter Size		
Basic	.309	.194
3-Digit	.292	.183
5-Digit	.278	.176
Carrier Route	.275	.170
Flat Size		
Basic	.341	
3-Digit	.322	
5-Digit	.302	

There are physical standards for all items that must be met, and all reduced-rate mail must be prepared in specific ways for inclusion. There are higher rates for each additional ounce. Presorted applies to mailings of at least 500 pieces. Automation applies to mailings of at least 500 pieces that must be compatible with automated handling. They must be 100% bar-coded.

Periodicals (Formerly Called Second Class)

Designed for newspapers, magazines, and other periodical publications whose primary purpose is transmitting information to an established list of subscribers or requesters. (Requester, of course, refers to the controlled circulation used by business magazines.) They must be published regularly at a stated frequency (at least four times a year) from a known office of publication and formed of printed sheets. They must be authorized to be mailed under one of these categories:

- General
- Requester
- Institutions and Societies
- Foreign
- State Departments of Agriculture.

The rates for periodicals consist of four parts:

1. Non-advertising portion based on pounds.
2. Advertising portion based on pounds and depending on the Postal zone to which the piece is sent.
3. Rate for each piece with discounts for presorting and automation.
4. Discounts from the piece rate depending on
   a. An adjustment of $.00067 for each 1% of non-advertising content.
   b. Delivery unit discount of $.017 for each piece eligible ($.005 for In-County).
   c. SCF (Sectional Center Facility) discount of $.008 for each piece eligible.

There are two subclasses—Outside County and Within County. The latter are distributed within the county of publication. Nonprofit or Classroom, except requester periodicals, receive a 5% discount from the Outside County rates, except for the rate for advertising poundage. Science of Agriculture periodicals have different rates, except for the rate for advertising poundage.

The rates, as you can see, are terribly complex and must be calculated separately for each magazine. They are the result of many years of changes and adjustments agreed to by the Postal Rate Commission after extensive hearings at which the Postal Service made proposals and the various mailing groups presented their thoughts.

Periodical Prices as of June 30, 2002

1.0 Outside-county—excluding science-of-agriculture

1.1 Pound Rates (Per pound or fraction):
   a. For the nonadvertising portion: $.193.
   b. For the advertising portion:

Zone:	DDU	DSCF	DADC	1&2	3	4	5	6	7	8
Rate:	$.158	.203	.223	.248	.267	.315	.389	.466	.559	.638

1.2 Piece Rates (Per addressed piece):

		Automation*	
Presort Level	Nonautomation	Letter-size	Flat-size
Basic	$.373	.281	.325
3-Digit	$.324	.249	.283
5-Digit	$.256	.195	.226
Carrier Route			
Basic	$.163		
High Density	$.131		
Saturation	$.112		

*Lower maximum weight limits apply: letter-size at 3 ounces (or 3.3 ounces for heavy letters); flat-size at 16 ounces (FSM 881) and 6 pounds (FSM 1000).

1.3 Discounts (Discounts for each addressed piece):
   a. Nonadvertising content, for each 1% of nonadvertising: $.00074.
   b. Destination delivery unit: $.018.
   c. Destination SCF: $.008.
   d. Destination ADC: $.002.
   e. Destination entry pallet: .015.
   f. Pallet (for other than 1.3e): $.005.

1.4 Nonprofit—Authorized nonprofit mailers receive a discount of 5% off the total Outside-County postage excluding the postage for advertising pounds. The 5% discount does not apply to commingled nonsubscriber copies in excess of the 10% allowance provided under E215.

1.5 Classroom—Authorized Classroom mailers receive a discount of 5% off the total Outside-County postage excluding the postage for advertising pounds. The 5% discount does not apply to commingled nonsubscriber copies in excess of the 10% allowance provided under E215.

Standard Mail (formerly called Third Class)

Standard Mail is mail matter not requiring expedited or First-Class service and is neither required to be mailed as that class or as Periodicals. Non-profit rates require specific authorization. This is the classification that Direct Mail, including subscription offers, uses.

These rates, too, are the result of considerable negotiation by the parties involved.

DBMC—Destination Bulk Mail Center
DCSF—Destination Sectional Center Facility
DDU—Destination Delivery Unit

Business Reply Mail

Business reply mail, of course, includes the response cards and envelopes used in the sales of subscription.

Standard Mail Prices as of June 30, 2002

1.1 Letters—For pieces 3.3 ounces (0.2063 pound) or less:

	Presorted*		Automation**			
Entry Discount	Basic	3/5	Mixed AADC	AADC	3-Digit	5-Digit
None	$.268	.248	.219	.212	.203	.190
DBMC	$.247	.227	.198	.191	.182	.169
DSCF	$.242	.222	—	.186	.177	.164

* Nonmachinable letters are subject to a $0.04 nonmachinable surcharge.
** See 1.3 for automation letters weighing over 3.3 ounces.

1.2 Nonletters—For pieces 3.3 ounces (0.2063 pound) or less:

	Presorted*		Automation	
Entry Discount	Basic	3/5	Basic	3/5
None	$.344	.288	.300	.261
DBMC	$.323	.267	.279	.240
DSCF	$.318	.262	.274	.235

* The residual shape surcharge of $0.23 per piece applies to items that are prepared as a parcel or are not letter-size or flat-size. Machinable parcels for which the residual shape surcharge is paid may be eligible for the barcoded discount of $0.03 per piece (see E620).

1.3 Letters and Nonletters—For pieces more than 3.3 ounces (0.2063 pound). Each piece is subject to both a piece rate and a pound rate.

	Presorted*		Automation**	
Piece/lb. Rate	Basic	3/5	Basic	3/5
Per Piece	$.198	.142	.154	.115
PLUS per lb.	PLUS	PLUS	PLUS	PLUS
None	$.708	.708	.708	.708
DBMC	$.608	.608	.608	.608
DSCF	$.583	.583	.583	.583

* Residual shape surcharge of $0.23 per piece applies to items that are prepared as a parcel or are not letter-size or flat-size. Machinable parcels for which the residual shape surcharge is paid may be eligible for the barcoded discount of $0.03 per piece (see E620).
** Automation letters weighing up to 3.5 ounces (inclusive) receive a discount that equals the applicable nonletter piece rate (3.3 oz. or less) minus the applicable letter piece rate (3.3 oz. or less).

Standard Mail Prices as of June 30, 2002

ENHANCED CARRIER ROUTE STANDARD MAIL

2.1 Letters—For pieces 3.3 ounces (0.2063 pound) or less:

Entry Discount	Basic	High Density*	Saturation*	Automation Basic**
None	$.194	.164	.152	.171
DBMC	$.173	.143	.131	.150
DSCF	$.168	.138	.126	.145
DDU	$.162	.132	.120	.139

* See 2.3 for letters weighing over 3.3 ounces.
** Pieces weighing up to 3.5 ounces (inclusive) are charged basic piece/pound postage (see 2.3) minus a discount that equals the basic nonletter piece rate (3.3 oz. or less) minus the automation basic letter piece rate (3.3 oz. or less).

2.2 Nonletters—For pieces 3.3 ounces (0.2063 pound) or less. Residual shape surcharge of $0.20 per piece applies to items that are prepared as a parcel or are not letter-size or flat-size.

Entry Discount	Basic	High Density	Saturation
None	$.194	.169	.160
DBMC	$.173	.148	.139
DSCF	$.168	.143	.134
DDU	$.162	.137	.128

2.3 Letters and Nonletters—For pieces more than 3.3 ounces (0.2063 pound). Each piece is subject to both a piece rate and a pound rate. Residual shape surcharge of $0.20 per piece applies to items that are prepared as a parcel or are not letter-size or flat-size.

Piece/lb. Rate	Basic	High Density*	Saturation*
Per Piece	$.068	.043	.034
PLUS per lb.	PLUS	PLUS	PLUS
None	$.610	.610	.610
DBMC	$.510	.510	.510
DSCF	$.485	.485	.485
DDU	$.453	.453	.453

* Letter-rate pieces weighing up to 3.5 ounces (inclusive) receive a discount that equals the applicable nonletter piece rate (3.3 oz. or less) minus the applicable letter piece rate (3.3 oz. or less).

APPENDIX F

Major Suppliers and Consultants

I HAD HOPED to include a list of the major suppliers and consultants of the many kinds that serve the magazine field, but have been unable to discover one that is available and all-inclusive—and one that omits any of the leading sources might be worse than useless.

Folio and *Circulation Management* magazines' Annual Publisher's Resource and Suppliers Guides have a good number, but many of the leading suppliers and consultants have not chosen to be listed there. You might be able to supplement this with other names from those exhibiting at the annual Folio show, possibly with those who conduct seminars or write articles for the various magazines in the field, or with data the MPA and ABM have, but I don't believe that even then the list would be complete.

Once again, networking is probably the answer.

Glossary

This is a glossary of the terms used in this book that may not be familiar to you, plus a number of other terms used in magazine publishing and direct marketing. It is not all-inclusive. It also discusses the definitions only as they are used in these businesses, which is not always the way the terms may be used in other contexts.

absolute rate—actual dollar price of a page of advertising. Different from the cost per thousand circulation. Sometimes a magazine can attract advertising because the absolute rate is lower than its competitors', even though the cost per thousand circulation is much higher.

a-b split—research technique in which different ads for the same product or service appear in alternate copies of a magazine

accidental sampling—research technique that relies on chance, such as interviewing passersby at a mall.

account executive—in an advertising agency and many other businesses, one who maintains contact and nurtures a client.

accrual basis—one of the basic methods of doing accounting. Income and expenses are recorded when the event takes place rather than when the money changes hands.

accumulated audience—total number of individuals reached over a period by ads.

actives—subscribers whose subscriptions have not expired.

added value—extras offered an advertiser to induce the purchase of space in a magazine in place of a price reduction.

Address Change Service—automated process for change of address provided by the Postal Service.

address correction—correction of a subscriber's address in the fulfillment system.

Adobe—one of the manufacturers of computer software used in magazine composition.

ad retention—research measurement that indicates the percentage of readers of a publication who remember the advertising in the current issue.

advance renewal—subscription that is renewed far in advance of its expiration. Often promoted by pointing out that the price will go up soon. Sometimes used to raise cash. Some believe it increases the total renewals.

advertiser—company that buys space or time in media.

advertising—use of media to sell products or services.

advertising agency—company that prepares and places ads for advertisers. A commission is usually paid by the media at 15% of the price of the space or time, although the agency's real clients are the advertisers.

advertising budget—annual budget developed by advertisers. It is finalized for most companies in the fall.

advertising clutter—too much advertising in a small space in a magazine or in a short time on television, etc.

advertising director—head of the advertising sales effort for a magazine.

advertising-driven—magazine with more than half its revenue from advertising.

advertising position—where an ad is placed in a magazine. There are extra charges for covers and other special spots. Some advertisers want to be next to editorial matter. Many routinely ask for a right-hand page, far forward, although much research has shown that position is not important for readership.

advertising promotion—promotion done by publishers to acquaint advertisers and agencies with their magazines.
advertising rate base—circulation on which a magazine's rates are based. Not necessarily a guarantee.
advertising rates—rates charged for advertising space.
advertising representative—independent person or group selling advertising for more than one publisher, usually on a commission basis.
advertising salespeople—publisher's employees who sell space.
advertorial—advertisement in editorial style. Can compromise the editorial independence of a magazine.
agency commission—commission paid to ad agencies by the media. Usually 15%.
agency-sold subs—paid subscriptions sold by outside, commissionable sources.
aided recall—in research, a technique for determining how well a test respondent, who has been aided by prompting, remembers an ad.
airline in-flight—magazine published by or for airlines and put on their planes for the passengers.
alternate delivery—delivery of subscription copies of magazines through organizations other than the Postal Service. Often threatened by publishers as a way of developing quicker and less expensive delivery during postal rate hearings, but so far never achieved.
alternate source—any subscription source other than direct mail.
alternative press—nontraditional publications, mostly weekly regional papers.
analysts—those in financial firms who analyze companies for investors. They usually specialize in different industries. Because there are not many public magazine companies, few analysts specialize here.
ancillary products—products that publishers sell in addition to their magazines. Nowadays called brand extensions.
angel—investor in a business.
A piece of the action—part ownership of a company, something devoutly desired, but rarely achieved by most managers.
arrears—continuing the service of a subscription after it expires. The circulation auditing organizations include these for a certain period as paid circulation.
art director—in charge of the layout, artwork, photos, etc. of a magazine.
article—short, complete piece of nonfiction writing.
artwork and photos—those used in the editorial content.
assumptions—used when making projections for a magazine.
attached mail—first-class mail accompanying other mail. As long as the attached mail is incidental, the postage rate is that of the host piece.
audit—normal financial audits. Also those of the circulation of magazines.
audited publication—magazine whose circulation has been verified by an independent auditing service.
authorization—needed in chain stores for display of single copies.
authors alterations—changes made in editorial material after it has been set.
automatic renewal—agreement where subscriber allows the publisher to automatically renew the publication using the subscriber's credit card, until subscriber terminates it. Used in continuous service.
automation discount—postage rate reduction offered for bar-coding and other address helps that can be used by automated equipment.
average net paid circulation—average paid circulation copies during the preceding six-month period.
back copies—those served to a new subscriber that are older than the current issue.
back-of-book—material at the end of a magazine.
bad debts—as in any business. Often discussed in publishing in connection with the sale of subscriptions. Shorthand in the industry refers to cancellations as bad debts even though subscribers are specifically told they can write "cancel" on a bill and will not have to pay.
balance sheet—in accounting, the financial situation of a company at any moment in time. Usually developed at the end of each month.
bangtail—in direct marketing, a remittance envelope with a merchandise offer or other advertising printed on the reverse side.
bar code—machine-readable bars printed on the covers of single copies of magazines to expedite their sale in retail outlets. Also bars on various types of mail to expedite operations, usually with some kind of discount from normal postal rates.
barter advertising—where goods or services instead of cash are used to pay for ads.
basic rate—one-time black-and-white full-page ad rate. Also the standard published subscription price.
basis weight—weight of a ream (500 sheets) of paper 25" x 38". If it weighs 70 pounds, for instance, the paper is called 70 pound paper.
bellwether—in advertising, the leading companies in any field. Getting them to advertise makes it easier to sell others.
bids—in buying printing and other outside services, offers of prices.

billing—of advertising, subscriptions, and other services sold. Particularly important in the sale and renewal of subscriptions where a billing series can run to a dozen pieces.

binding—joining the pages of a magazine with adhesive, staples or in other ways.

bind-ins—insert cards bound in a magazine. Used in soliciting subscriptions of various kinds, selling ancillary items, and for reader service (bingo cards)

bingo cards—cards enabling readers to order products, brochures, etc. from advertisers and/or the publisher.

black-and-white—pages printed without color.

bleed—an illustration or advertisement reaching over the edge of the page. Sometimes charged extra for ads.

blow-in—cards blown between the pages of a magazine, but not attached. Annoying for the recipient, but good for obtaining subscriptions.

blurb—summary or excerpt from an article placed before, after, or within the article in a different typeface to induce readership.

body—main part of an article or publication.

body stock—paper used for the main part of a magazine.

body type—typeface used for the major portion of the text as differentiated from the headlines.

bogey—in ad sales, provides that a commission comes into play only after sales of so many dollars or pages have been achieved.

bold—text set in boldface.

bonus circulation—that in excess of the minimum guaranteed to advertisers.

book—in the field, a magazine is often referred to as "the book."

booklet—small book or pamphlet, generally with paper covers. Not a magazine.

bounceback—card to order merchandise inserted with a direct response mailing or magazine.

box—item in an article enclosed within borders. Good for breaking up text or calling attention.

brand—specific product identified by a mark or name. In marketing any product, including a magazine, it is important to establish a well-known brand.

brand extension—use of a well-known brand to sell other products.

BRC and BRE—business reply card and envelope.

breakeven—point where revenue less expenses equals zero.

brochure—pamphlet or booklet generally stapled. Not a magazine.

brokers—intermediaries who serve in the sale of magazines, advertising, printing, and many other goods and services.

b-to-b—business to business magazines, sometimes written b2b.

budget—any plan for the future, usually in connection with financial futures.

bulk—thickness of paper, not necessarily related to weight.

bulking stock—paper that is thicker than that normally used in the magazine. It is often less expensive than coated paper, can provide a change of pace for the reader, and adds to the heft of the magazine.

bulk mail—3rd and 4th class mail delivered to the Postal Service in bundles organized by destination.

bulk mail center (BMC)—highly mechanized processing plant for Standard mail.

bulk subscriptions—subscriptions purchased by an organization and delivered to members, or others that the sponsor is trying to reach. Usually reported separately on circulation audit statements. Sometimes bulk single copies are used in the same way.

business magazine—for business-to-business communication.

business manager—sometimes used to describe someone who is in charge of all business operations of a magazine as opposed to editorial.

business to business advertising—to a business audience, sometimes called industrial advertising, as differentiated from consumer advertising.

business plan—plan for any business, but particularly for a new magazine or other new venture, a plan developed to explain the planned operations—essential in raising capital.

business press—publications addressed to a business rather than a consumer audience.

buyer's guide—issue of a magazine listing suppliers and other information about the field.

buyout—purchase of manuscripts, photographs and the like.

byline—identification of an author.

by-products—products developed to take advantage of the aura of the magazine— also called ancillary products or brand extensions.

calendared paper—paper that has been made smooth and glossy, generally by being pressed between smooth rollers—not necessarily coated.

call-out—words taken from an article and included in a larger type face to induce reading. A blurb.

call report—record of a salesperson's meetings or phone calls with agencies or advertisers. Essential in running a good sales organization.

caption—description of the content or subject of a photograph or artwork that appears adjacent to it.

card deck—collection of ads, usually printed as business-reply cards, sent as a package.

card rate—official printed ad rate without discounts.

carrier route—stops in the sequence of an individual letter carrier in the Postal Service. Mail sorted in this way receives a discount.

carryover—portion of text carried over from one page to another.

cash basis—accounting method which records items as payment is received or made.

cash discount—price reduction for prompt payment, generally 2% within ten days. Not often offered for ads these days.

cash field agent—independent subscription agent who sells for cash, usually door-to- door or on the telephone.

cash flow—cash income and outgo—important to watch in addition to regular accounting records.

catalog—publication containing many items for sale, often with illustrations.

catalog agent—subscription agency that sells many magazines through a catalog, usually to libraries.

CD-ROM—compact disc, read-only memory—with considerable memory for text, graphics, video and sound that can be used on a computer screen.

cell—in market research, and in testing direct mail, a small homogeneous group within a larger sample.

charter advertising rate—lower ad rate normally offered by new magazines during their startup periods. These may give three pages for the price of two, and the like.

charter issue—first issue of a new magazine.

charter subscription rate—lower rates often offered during a startup. Sometimes charter subscribers are offered lower rates forever.

checkerboard—magazine layout in which quarter—or half-page ads are placed diagonally on the same or facing pages with editorial material between them. Good for advertiser, but makes text hard to follow.

check-out—in retail stores, the place where the customer pays. This is the most desirable area for the display of magazines and they often pay extra to be placed there.

checkups—in single copy sales, the process of trying to determine how many copies were displayed, and the number that were sold.

Cheshire—machine for affixing printed address labels.

circulation—number of copies of a magazine sold and/or distributed free.

circulation-controlled—distribution of copies with a preconceived pattern of the recipients' eligibility. Can be paid or free.

circulation director—person in charge of circulation.

circulation-driven—magazine with little or no advertising with the majority of its revenue from circulation.

circulation guarantee—major consumer magazines sometimes guarantee the average circulation for a period. If they fall short, they either make a refund to advertisers, offer them free space, or make up the difference in other ways. A Rate Base is not necessarily a guarantee.

circulation, non-paid—circulation that meets the requirements of qualified circulation and is sent free to the recipients in the field served.

circulation, paid—paid for, not for resale, and sent to the field served.

circulation price—price at which magazines are sold. This includes the single copy price as well as the subscription prices. Most magazines sell subscriptions at various different prices depending on the method of sale, timing, number of issues sold, and other reasons.

circulation promotion—all the activities involved in selling circulation including single copy costs, subscription mailings, agent commissions, etc.

circulation, qualified—paid or non-paid, sent to the field served and verified by auditable documentary evidence dated within 36 months.

city magazine—consumer publication whose subject matter revolves around its area.

class magazine—publication for upscale readers as opposed to mass.

classified advertising—help wanted, positions wanted, and other categories usually with special rates and in uniform type of a single size.

classroom magazines—those sold to kids in classrooms, such as Scholastic.

closing date—last possible time by which material must be received for publication.

clubbing—sale of ads in a group of publications at a combined lower rate

coated paper—smooth paper of various kinds which reproduces colors well. Most magazines are printed on coated paper.

coffee table book—a highly visual, decorative publication.

cold type—versus the old metal type—about the only kind used nowadays.

collection series—a series of mailings to subscribers who purchased on credit. These can run up to a dozen efforts.

color pages—printed in color rather than simple black-and-white. Sometimes people only refer to four-color when they use the term.

color separation—negative made from color art from which a color print can be produced, using the three primary colors and black. Seldom used with today's printing processes.

columns—vertical divisions of a page of type.

combination rate—special advertising rate for multiple ads placed in two or more publications of the same or affiliated companies.

combination sale—subscriptions to two or more publications sold at a special price.

coming attractions—a page, box, or other space devoted to telling about editorial material in future issues.

commercial printer—one who handles all types of printing jobs. Normally not the best for printing magazines because of their special requirements.

commission—percentage of the revenue paid ad sales people for space sold.

communication—transmission or exchange of information, messages, or data by any means.

company culture—the style and identity of a company; an amalgam of beliefs, mythology, values and rituals that characterizes the general way a company appears and acts.

comparability—publishers, advertisers and ad agencies in a market define terminology for use in the market, coverage, and recipients of magazines.

competition—primary consists of other magazines serving the same field of readers and advertisers. Secondary can be from magazines in fields closely related. Other competition consists of all other media, promotion devices, public relations, etc.

compiled list—in direct marketing, a list that is compiled, such as all lawyers. Normally does not pull very well for magazines.

complaint mail—in subscription fulfillment terminology, any mail received from a subscriber other than an order or a payment. This includes such innocuous messages as changes of address, as well as complaints.

composition—the setting of type, almost always now done by computer.

computer graphics—any diagrams, drawings, and other non-text material that is computer generated.

computer letter—in direct mail, a letter generated by a computer with the recipient's name and other fill-ins in one or more places.

computer models—models of businesses that have been developed for doing projections. A number have been developed specifically for the magazine business.

computer personalization—using a computer to mass-produce individualized items, from letters to publications, with the name of the recipient and other individual fill-ins.

computer-to-plate (CTP)—edit or ad material developed on the computer and converted to printing plates without any intermediate step.

confidence level—in research, a measure of the assurance that samples or test results are accurate, expressed as a percentage, such as 95%.

confidentiality agreement—any agreement where a concept may not be passed along without approval. Often asked for by those starting new magazines.

confirmation mailing—in direct mail, after a test has been made, a remailing of part or all of the test to other names to confirm the original results.

consecutive page discount—one of the many types of ad discounts devised to increase the amount of space an advertiser uses.

consignment—merchandise sold to a retailer which, if he cannot sell it, may be returned for full or partial refund. Normal method for selling single copies of magazines, except that the copies usually are not returned, but are shredded and sold as paper waste.

consolidated tax return—corporation with subsidiary companies can file tax returns that include the results of its subsidiaries (if owned 80%). Often used when starting, or investing in, new magazines so that the losses can be applied against profits from other operations.

consultants—those with specialized knowledge or talents who help companies improve their operations. There are a number of consultants in just about every area of magazine publishing.

consumer magazines—addressed to members of the general public, rather than to those in specific businesses. Sometimes the dividing line is a little hazy, as in magazines devoted to computers.

content provider—term used in the computing field for those providing the editorial or other content shown on a computer or on the Internet. An editor.

contents—usually the editorial matter of a magazine.

contents pages—page, or pages describing the contents of a magazine.

continuity series—a series or books sold by direct mail, usually covering a specific subject. The number of volumes is often not known at the start. As long as there is good response, volumes can be added.

continuous service—term used for automatic renewal of subscriptions, replaces older term—till forbid.

contributing editor—writer who is not on the staff of a magazine, but who is listed on the masthead.

contribution to overhead & profit—accounting method sometimes used in determining the profitability of a magazine. Overhead is not included because the publisher of the magazine cannot control the amount of overhead applied. Leads to lower expectations of profit.

control package—in direct mail, the package containing the price, offer and copy against which all other packages are tested. Similar concept used in market research.

controlled circulation—normally sent free to the

readers. Called controlled because it is directed specifically to people (or job titles) that the publisher thinks advertisers will want to reach. Mostly used by business magazines, although some consumer magazines also use it.

controlled sampling—any method of selecting a research sample proportional to the parts of a population being studied

controller—usually the person in charge of the accounting records. Sometimes different titles are used.

convergence—recognizing the similarities among different media so that they can work together for the benefit of customers and/or advertisers.

conversion—first renewal of a new subscription.

conversion rate—percentage of conversions, usually measured by each subscription source. A key figure in the subscription business.

convertible debentures—debentures (loans) that are convertible into stock, warrants, etc. signifying part ownership of a company.

cooperative advertising—sharing of the cost of an advertising campaign between a manufacturer and retailers.

cooperative mailing—where a number of different products, sometimes including magazines, are advertised.

copy allocation—allocation of single copies to various retail outlets.

copyright—exclusive legal right to reproduce, publish, and sell the matter and form of a literary, musical, artistic, or other work.

copywriter—one who writes advertising or other publicity material.

correspondent—reporter who is a full or part-time employee of a magazine based other than at its headquarters. Differentiated from stringers or freelancers.

cost center—department to which costs are allocated. If revenue is also allocated, it might become a profit center.

cost per impression—cost of an ad reaching an individual in any media.

cost per inquiry—in direct marketing, the cost of a campaign divided by the number of responses.

cost per order—similar, based on actual orders.

cost per thousand (CPM)—advertising cost per thousand circulation of a magazine.

costing—accounting process of determining the costs of various factors. In some cases this can be a very complex and difficult process.

counter card—advertising card or point-of-sale display on a store counter.

cover—outer pages of a magazine. The front cover is the introduction and is usually designed to lure readers inside. Some magazines put a Kraft or other cover over the real one to avoid harm to the magazine during mailing, a questionable practice because it hides the actual cover. The other cover pages are prime space for advertisers and carry a higher rate than other pages.

cover date—on the magazine, usually a date later than the actual date the issue is published.

cover lines—copy on the front cover that is carefully written to promote various features inside. Important for all magazines, but particularly for those on the newsstand.

cover price—price of a single copy. Helpful to have a price even on magazines that are distributed free since it is an indication of value.

creative—referring to people in the business. Usually reserved for editorial, those writing ads, copy for direct mail, and the like.

credit subscription—order to purchase future issues of a publication that is not accompanied by full payment. Offering credit usually increases response, but the pay-up of these can vary considerably, and it is not a real subscription until it is paid.

crystallize the editorial—probably the most important thing to do in publishing a magazine. If you don't know what you are trying to do editorially, it usually results in disaster. See chapter 18, "If You Can't Say It in Ten Words."

CTP—computer to plate—digitized workflow without film.

cushions—in doing projections, the practice of adding to the cost of each item of expense to be "conservative." Liable to kill the project.

custom publishing—publishing magazines for others for distribution to the public, employees, or others.

database—collection of related information, a list.

database marketing—selection, analysis and use of customer lists and other computerized data in direct mail and other marketing. By using multi-product purchasing history and other data, cross-selling and upselling can be done. See Chapter 62—*Database Marketing.*

deck—secondary line in a multiline headline.

deferred subscription income—in accounting, the remaining amount of the subscription price to be served in a paid magazine subscription. Appears as a liability on the balance sheet although it may be the most important asset a magazine has. An accounting fiction.

demographics—external characteristics of the readers of a magazine, such as age, sex, income, education, etc. Helpful in obtaining advertising. Statistics usually are developed by outside research organizations.

demographic edition—edition of a magazine targeted for a specific demographic group, such as those of certain ages, income levels, education, etc.

depth interview—a research technique consisting of a relatively long, detailed, and, to some extent, unstructured interview.

design—usually of a magazine, although it can also apply to promotion pieces, etc.

designer—one who designs a magazine. The design of a magazine is quite different from the design of other printed material because a magazine has to hold together from a design standpoint from cover to cover.

desktop publishing—popular term for doing the composition, layout and all other features of a magazine on a computer.

Dick strip—mailing label on a magazine, named long ago for machines made by A.B. Dick.

die cut—hole intentionally cut from a printed page as part of the design.

digest—either a magazine of digest size—or one whose content is made up of material from other sources.

digest-size—that of the Reader's Digest or similar magazines. Ads have to be specially prepared for this size.

digital printing—using digital data to produce images without the use of plates.

direct distribution—in single copy sales, an alternative to the System, bypassing the wholesaler and the national distributor. Retailers often receive a larger discount. It is used with major bookstores, discount chains and specialty stores, but does not cover major magazine outlets.

direct mail—direct marketing to the ultimate consumer through the mail.

direct mail agents—American Family Publication (AFP), Publishers Clearing House (PCH) and other agents selling subscriptions through the mail. These have traditionally used stamp-sheets and sweepstakes. Recent problems in this area have greatly reduced the production of these agents.

direct marketing—sale of products directly to the ultimate consumer through any medium—mail, radio, TV, the Web, telephone, fax, etc.

direct response advertising—direct mail, newspaper, Web, or other ads with coupons or other response devices offering products or services directly to consumers.

direct single copy—see direct distribution.

direct to plate (DTP)—edit or ad material which goes directly from the computer to a printing plate.

direct to the publisher—subscriptions that are obtained through a publisher's efforts rather than through an agent.

directory—publication with listings and ads, such as a classified telephone directory.

directory source—controlled circulation where the qualified individuals' names come from directories. Not as good as request.

discount—reduction from the full or regular price for any of many reasons.

display—advertising other than classified.

distribution—the entire process of getting a magazine to the reader.

dog—an unattractive person, product, or performance. Sometimes used by printers about some of their magazine customers.

dollar volume discount—one of the many types of ad discounts devised by publishers to increase the amount an advertiser spends.

donee and donor—involved in gift subscriptions.

door opener—anything that gets you in the door, such as a good business plan for a new magazine.

dot-com—anything having to do with the companies active on the Web.

down-side projections—those that show what will happen if the anticipated results are missed by a substantial amount. Essential to have available when talking to potential investors.

draw—the number of copies placed on the newsstand. Also, an advance to a salesperson from anticipated commissions.

drop ship—distribution of copies to a local point from where they may be entered in the Postal Service or distributed by other methods.

dry run—rehearsal, sometimes used in producing a copy of a magazine that will never be sent to readers in order to get the staff organized.

dry test—direct mail or other campaign to solicit subscriptions for a magazine that has not yet been published to determine the likelihood of success.

dummy—preliminary layout, mock up or set of blank pages to show the size, shape, form and general style of a magazine.

dump-bin—container with an assortment of items, seemingly casually put in, to attract attention in a retail store.

dupe elimination—in direct mail, eliminating names from rented lists which are duplicates of existing subscribers.

Dutch door—ad space involving half-page gatefolds.

earned rate—ad cost based on actual usage of space in a magazine.

e-commerce—that carried on through e-mail on the Web.
economical forms—in printing, developing the most economical way of laying out pages.
edit—to alter, correct, or revise a manuscript or other work.
edition—copies of a publication printed from a single typesetting, often used in discussing regional or demographic editions of a magazine.
editor—person responsible for the editorial content of a magazine.
editorial—opinion piece written by the editors.
editorial calendar—list of the major upcoming articles of a magazine. Useful for advertisers to know which issues might be most helpful for their products. A good editor will have the calendar organized at least twelve months ahead.
editorial content—material that goes on the editorial pages.
editorial independence—state of mind that divorces the editors from pressure from advertisers. Often used as a shield by editors to insulate themselves from the business side of the magazine.
editorializing—insertion of an opinion. If it occurs in news articles, readers may become skeptical of the publication's objectivity.
editorial piece—any material run in the magazine.
editorial plan—detailed plan for each issue of the magazine.
editorial rationale—why the magazine exists—essential if you are to have a good magazine.
editorial well—central section of a magazine that contains longer articles with little or no interruption by ads.
effort—any individual promotion to a subscriber or prospect.
electronic data exchange—method of exchanging data on the Web.
electronic publishing—production of text and illustrations using media other than paper.
Eliot—old-fashioned plate-oriented method of addressing magazines. Not now used.
e-mail—that forwarded on the Web as opposed to the Postal Service and other means.
engravings—metal plates formerly used in printing.
enhanced list—list which has added information about the person or company in addition to his name and address.
entering subscriptions—the process of recording subscriptions on the fulfillment files.
entrepreneur—as in any business—in publishing, the person who originally had an idea for a new magazine and is trying to launch it.
entry points—in the Postal Service, periodical mail costs more the further it travels. Large publishers reduce this cost by trucking copies to various locations and entering them in post offices closer to the ultimate recipient.
escalation—in printing and some other contracts, the increase in prices agreed to based on increases in various factors such as union agreements, costs of outside purchases, etc.
ethnic media—magazines and other media addressed to specific races, nationalities, etc.
evaluation dates—in launching a magazine, the dates when actual results are compared with projections to determine whether the project should be continued.
events—sporting, entertainment, or other events sponsored by magazines or their advertisers.
exchange advertising—frequently done with competing magazines in obtaining subscriptions.
executive compensation—a term used to describe the many methods of rewarding the key people in a company, often using tax gimmicks, stock options, etc.
executive recruiter—some one (head-hunter) who assists in recruiting key executives. Usually paid a percentage of the first year's salary, often as high as 35%.
executive summary—popular method of introducing a new project to potential investors through a very short summary. Unnecessary if the business plan is properly written.
exercycle—stationary bicycle purchased on which a person can exercise. Rarely used after purchase.
exit strategy—way an investor can eventually realize profits from his investment.
expense account—art form through which various employees account to their managements for their business expenses.
expire—subscription (or group of subscriptions) that runs out on a certain date.
expire list—list of former subscribers, among the best prospects for new offers.
extensible markup language (XML)—one in which people using computers can easily converse with each other. Needed because of the many different systems and languages used in the computer world.
extension—continuance of a subscription by the publisher beyond its original expiration date.
external publication—a magazine or other matter directed to customers or others outside an organization. These days often prepared by the custom publishing arms of magazine companies.
facing text—ads opposite edit matter, frequently asked for, sometimes with more specific location requests such as facing the first edit page.

facsimile (fax)—method of transmitting hard data over the telephone.

fair use—amount of copyrighted material that may be quoted without permission.

FAQ—frequently asked questions—used in the Web world because it is often very difficult to know how to get from one place to another.

farm publication—for farmers and their families.

feature article—a major article.

field force—for magazines that depend on newsstand, representatives of a publisher or national distributor who obtain retail authorizations and check on draw and sale at various outlets.

50% rule—postal rule previously followed by the circulation audit bureaus to define paid circulation (sold at 50% of the basic price).

film—used in transmitting copy and illustrations in the printing process. Becoming obsolete.

financial plan—in the business plan for a new magazine, the anticipated financial results and the assumptions on which they are based.

financial projections—efforts to see the effect of various assumptions in starting or publishing a magazine. Essential to make many of these to get the best results.

financial statements—showing the results and current position of a magazine or publisher.

finder—someone who claims to be able to find money for entrepreneurs. I have yet to meet a successful one in the magazine field.

first bound copy—first batch of copies printed, often sent to advertisers.

fFirst class—in the Postal Service, the fastest non-premium service.

first law of publishing—the less you give them, the more you charge.

first try—the first attempt to do projections, a take-off point for further calculations

flat-bed press—a moving flat horizontal surface holds the printing plates while an impression cylinder applies pressure.

flats—newsstand display where the magazine is displayed face-up. Very desirable.

flipchart—series of sheets on an easel used in presentations.

flyer—small advertising circular.

focus group—research technique used to determine the subjective opinion of a particular public. Very helpful in judging the future of a proposed magazine.

Fog index—method of evaluating the readability of a sentence based on the average length and percentage of difficult, or foggy, words.

folio—number of pages in a magazine or a page number. Also a magazine for magazine publishers.

font—typeface of a particular size and design.

form—number of pages printed in one pass through the press, generally in multiples of 8 (and as many as 128) and then folded. Careful use of page placement is important in controlling costs.

foundation—not-for-profit organization that sometimes publishes or invests in magazines.

four-color—printing reproduction in full color through the use of black and the three primary colors.

fourth class postage—packages.

free circulation—magazine provided at no charge to readers.

freelancer—self-employed writer, artist, etc.

free standing insert—unbound advertising section used by advertisers in newspapers.

frequency—number of issues of a magazine per year. Most are in relation to the calendar, but many have other frequencies (5, 7, 11, etc.). Also the number of insertions by an advertiser.

fringe benefits—what employees receive in addition to their salaries, such as pensions, profit-sharing, medical plans, etc.

fringe publication—those of secondary importance to an advertiser or audience.

front of book—first pages of a magazine, considered desirable by advertisers.

fulfillment—processing of subscriptions including everything that entails.

full cover display—on the newsstand, where the entire cover can be seen. Very desirable.

full run—ad in every edition of a magazine.

galley—typeset proof of a manuscript prior to being set in page form.

gang-print—printing a number of pages together to achieve economies, such as covers for four issues at one time as one 16-page form.

gatefold—page in a magazine larger than the other pages, folded to fit.

general interest magazine—designed for the general public rather than for a specific segment.

generic advertising—ads that complement the editorial content of the magazine.

gift subscriptions—sent by donors to others. Inexpensive to obtain, and renew very well. Some magazines have been able to develop substantial gift circulation.

go-no go point—in doing projections, point at which decisions to continue or stop a project are made. Be sure to include several of them.

gracing—subscriptions extended beyond their expiration which can be included as paid. Also called arrears.

graphics—everything that contributes to the look of the publication.
gravure—printing process where the printing surface is depressed, used for long-run printing.
gray matter—block or page of type in a magazines which is large and uninviting.
Greek type—garbled type sometimes used in pilot issues—a poor practice because it doesn't look real.
grid—system for laying out the various features on a page.
grossing up the figures—including as revenue all the amounts a customer pays before commissions, etc. to others. Makes a small business look much larger.
gross response—total prospects ordering a subscription (but not necessarily paying).
groundwood—paper, usually used in newspapers, that is not chemically processed.
group commission—in advertising sales, when a group shares in some sales commissions.
group discount—lower ad rate for advertising in more than one publication.
group subscriptions—sold in quantity to companies or other organizations.
guaranteed circulation—minimum amount of circulation guaranteed to advertisers. Rebates are given if the circulation is not attained.
gutter—blank space between facing pages in a magazine.
half-life—in direct marketing, the time it takes for half the total of responses to be received. Conventional wisdom is that this is two weeks after the mailing went out, but don't bet on it.
halftone—in printing, screening process which turns images into dots.
hard copy—text or an ad on a piece of paper.
hard offer—in direct marketing, a subscription offer that asks for payment in cash or with a credit card.
headline—title of an article.
heft—physical feel of a magazine. One without enough heft will seem skimpy.
high negative cash flow—in projections, the largest amount of cash loss anticipated before profits are achieved.
high tech—where most venture firms like to invest rather than in magazines.
horizontal publication—business magazine that has a broad orientation, vs a vertical publication covering a portion of a field.
horsey—artwork or type that is too large or poorly proportioned.
hotline lists—in direct mail, those including people who have recently purchased. Generally give a better response than a general list.
house account—one reserved to the company with no commission paid to an ad salesperson.
house ad—one for the publication or its owner.
households—common way of expressing population figures for research and ad purposes.
house organ—controlled circulation publication published by a company for its employees, customers, or others. Many are published by custom publishers.
idiot marks—put on a promotion or other piece to show the printer how to set it up.
imposition—arranging pages in a form so that, when printed and folded, they will fall in the proper numerical sequence.
independent contractor—someone who does work but is not an employee. Payroll taxes do not have to be withheld and he may be able to reduce his income taxes by taking some home and other expenses as a deduction. Be careful—The IRS is after those who do not fit their description of an independent contractor.
independent sales representative—person or group that sells ads for more than one magazine.
indicia—page containing name, date, frequency, serial number, publication office, subscription price and notice of entry. Supposed to appear within the first five pages of each issue—often doesn't.
in-flight agents—those who make arrangements for placing magazines on airplanes.
infomercial—audio or video segment that combines ads with information, sold as a commercial. Similar to an advertorial in a magazine.
inkjet printing—non-impact computerized printing process in which a coded tape controls laser-activated nozzles that spray ink on paper. Used in personalizing items, including magazines.
insert—card or section inserted in the magazine for circulation or advertising purposes. If an ad, priced differently than normal pages.
insert cards—those which are bound in or blown into a magazine to obtain response for the publisher or an advertiser.
insertion order—printed form or other authorization from an advertiser or agency to publish ads.
installment billing—as in any other business, subscribers are sometimes given the opportunity to pay in installments.
institutional advertising—to create goodwill rather than sell goods or services directly.
intangible assets—those which a company owns that are not tangible, such as mailing lists, editorial inventory, goodwill, etc.
intangible business—one dealing in intangibles, such as magazines.
intercept interview—in market research, a person picked at random such as at a shopping mall or on the street.

interstitial—on the Web, ad that pops up while viewing a site. Terribly annoying.

involved reader—the best kind.

IPO (initial public offering)—the first shares of a company to be offered for sale to the public, as described in a prospectus.

island position—ad surrounded by edit matter.

issue—all the copies of a magazine published on a given date, including all its editions.

issue plans—editorial plans for future issues.

jet printing—high speed process in which charged ink particles are emitted from a nozzle onto paper.

journal—publication issued by a legal, medical or other professional organization.

jump—to continue an article from one page to another.

junk mail—direct mail ads and other unsolicited material, generally sent by third class. Most consumers actually like to receive it.

justify—type set so that all margins are aligned.

key—code number of each subscription promotion.

kill fee—payment to a freelancer for an article not used.

label—in magazines, the mailing label for subscription copies.

late copy—copy which is late in getting to the printer. Can be very expensive. Usually the sign of a disorganized edit department.

launch—introduction of a new product or service. Here, a magazine.

launch scenario—outline of the steps involved in launching a magazine or other product showing the steps, time schedule and estimated costs of each step.

laundry list—when composition was done with metal type, the billing for composition with each item listed. Not important in today's computerized world.

layout—drawing, sketch or plan of an ad, brochure, magazine, or whatever. Preliminary stage is called a rough; more carefully, a comprehensive; finally, a finished layout.

lead investor—when raising money from individuals or venture firms, it is almost always necessary to find one. He monitors progress for the others who would rather be followers.

lead time—time before the start of something, used in terms of edit material and ad copy.

legibility—ability of one or more characters to be read easily. Differs from readability, which is the degree of comprehension. Sans-serif type may be more legible, but is usually not as readable.

letterpress—printing in which the area to be printed is raised.

letter-shop—mailing house that offers printing and other services, usually for direct mail.

life cycle—stage in the life of a person or other entity. Magazines all have them.

lifestyle—the way a person lives—purchasing habits, dress, and other expressions of personality and values.

lift factor—in direct marketing, a factor added to actual results because of its timing, content, price, offer, etc. Dangerous.

lift letter—in direct mail, a small memo accompanying the primary sales letter. Designed to lift the response.

limited liability corporation—a corporation with some of the characteristics of a limited partnership from a tax standpoint.

limited partner—partner in a limited partnership whose liability for losses is limited to the amount he has invested. If he becomes active, may become a general partner.

limited partnership—one made up of one or more general and one or more limited partners.

Linotype—keyboard operated machine for setting letterpress type in which a whole line of type is produced as a single slug. Hard to find now.

list—a group of names and addresses.

list broker—one who arranges the rental of mailing lists compiled by others.

list compiler—organization that puts together special lists for sale or rental.

list manager—person in a publishing house in charge of renting its lists.

list rental—rental of another's list for direct marketing.

lithography—printing from a flat surface with no ridges or depressions. Called offset.

local rate—reduced ad price offered to local advertisers.

lockbox—locked container, such as a post office box. Used for cash receipts.

logo—unique trademark, name, symbol, signature, or device to identify a company or other organization. A magazine's logo is its nameplate.

long-range plan—for 5 or more years—essential in starting a magazine.

Ludlow—machine used in letterpress where handset type was cast in slugs, primarily used for headlines and statistics. Hard to find now.

Madison Avenue—street in New York. A euphemism for the advertising business.

magalog—mail order catalog containing editorial matter in addition to merchandise offered.

magazine—periodical containing miscellaneous pieces, usually illustrated. See chapter 2, "Just What Is a Magazine?"

magazine model—computer program specifically designed for calculating the results of various operating patterns of a magazine.

magazine supplement—section of a newspaper in magazine format.
magic 97s—in direct marketing, ending a price with $.97 frequently increases response.
mail—matter conveyed by the Postal Service in the US and other such services in other countries. Divided into various classes with different prices and delivery standards. Now sometimes called snail mail.
mailing date—in direct mail, the date mail is dropped. Important because response rates vary with times of the year.
mailing house—see letter-shop.
mailing lists—lists of names and addresses used in direct mail.
mailing list service—service from the Postal Service that corrects names and address lists, occupant lists, or sorts mailing lists on cards by 5-digit ZIP code.
mail order catalog—catalog delivered through the mail. One of the major retail selling methods.
mail preference service—provided by the Direct Marketing Assn for consumers who request that their names be removed from mailing lists.
mainfile (or masterfile)—all of a magazine's subscriber lists giving their history.
mainline—in single copy sales, the main magazine display area. Not as desirable as checkout.
major financing—money raised for a new magazine as opposed to seed money.
major investors—who contribute the major financing.
major mailing—large drop as opposed to a test mailing.
make-good—ad space provided free to replace ads printed improperly.
make-ready—in printing, all the preparation prior to the final printing.
makeup—arrangement of type and art of a page, or of the entire magazine.
mall intercept—survey research in which consumers are stopped at random at a mall.
manuscript—text of an article as prepared by the author prior to publishing.
market, the—securities, commodities and other public investment markets.
market penetration—degree of usage of a product or service among current users.
market potential—maximum sales (ads or circulation) that can be obtained by all magazines serving an area, industry or product category.
market research—study of the demands or desires of consumers (or other publics) in relation to actual or potential products or services.
market share—portion of sales in a category obtained by one product.
marketing—all the functions involved in moving goods from producer to customer. Includes advertising, public relations, distribution, pricing, sales, credit, warehousing, market research and other functions.
mass communications—delivery of information to large audiences via print and electronic media.
mass magazine—intended for a general audience vs a class or special interest magazine.
masthead—area in a magazine containing personnel, motto, statement of policy, etc.
matte finish—paper with a dull finish without luster, generally textured.
mechanical—assembled type, artwork and other material ready to be reproduced.
mechanical requirements—specifications about ad sizes, etc. shown on the rate card.
media—categories of communications vehicles.
media buyer—those in ad agencies who buy time and space. Currently there is a feeling that this task has been turned over to young and inexperienced people who put too much emphasis on numbers rather than the intangible aspects of individual magazines.
media kit—packet of materials for advertisers about a specific publication.
media plan—specifications of media to be used in an ad campaign.
merchandising—marketing functions related to presenting and selling of products and services, including advertising, display, promotion and public relations.
merchandising service—service offered by magazines to increase the effectiveness of advertising, such as direct mail, point of sale displays, etc.
merge-purge—in direct mail, combining lists to eliminate duplications and unwanted names to reduce mailing costs.
MESBIC—Minority Enterprise Small Business Investment Company—an SBIC set up to finance minority enterprises.
mission statement—the basic reason for the existence of a company or a magazine.
model—mathematical simulation for forecasting.
most difficult—each item in starting a magazine is the most difficult thing to do.
multi-buyer list—names found on several lists, a byproduct of merge-purge. Best names.
national distributor—handles distribution of magazines and paperback books in the single copy system.
natural circulation level—amount of circulation that is relatively easy for a magazine to maintain. More than this becomes terribly expensive.
natural classifications—in accounting, expenses in categories depending on what they include, no mat-

ter where in the organization, such as salaries, insurance, telephone, etc.

NCOA (National Change of Address) System—address correction system the Postal Service provides to mailers.

negative aspects of magazines for investors—See chapter 28, "Raising Money."

negative cash flow—losses on a cash basis—actual or projected.

net paid—circulation as defined by the audit bureaus.

net response—total subscription orders from a promotion that are paid for.

networking—contacting people, often for the exchange of information, raising money, job searching, and the like.

new business—new subscriptions as opposed to renewals.

new media—electronic communications media—Web, broadcast e-mail, Webcasting.

new product tabloid—in business magazines, one devoted editorially to showing new products in a field.

newsletter—informational publication, generally without ads and for a special group. Hard to differentiate from a magazine in some cases.

newspaper—publication issued daily, weekly or at frequent intervals, containing news, features and advertising. Hard to differentiate from a magazine in some cases.

newspaper distributed magazines—those distributed along with the newspaper.

newsprint—paper on which newspapers are printed, generally 30 pound and with poorer reproductive qualities than paper for magazines.

newsstand—retail outlet at which newspapers and magazines are sold. Few strictly newsstands still exist and sales are primarily in supermarkets, drugstores, convenience stores, and other retail outlets, collectively now called newsstands.

newsstand draw—the number of copies of a magazine provided to a newsstand.

Nielsen A, B, C, D counties—classification of counties by amount of population.

nixie—mail that is undeliverable and returned, usually because of an incorrect, illegible or insufficient address.

non-machinable—in mail, a piece that cannot be sorted on processing equipment.

non-qualified distribution—that doesn't conform to the definition of a qualified recipient.

not-for-profit—organization formed for charitable, governmental or other purposes which do as not have profit-making as its primary goal.

offer—in direct marketing, the offer, which differs from the price, made to the recipient. A hard offer asks for cash or a credit card. Other offers are various degrees softer.

official organ—periodical owned by an association which is its appointed mouthpiece.

off-line—in subscription fulfillment, sending copies of a magazine or other material without going through the normal steps. A good idea is to send the first issue quickly to a new subscriber off-line.

off-sale date—date single copies of a magazine are no longer on sale.

offset—printing method in which the ink image is transferred from the printing plate to a rubber blanket or roller and then to the paper. Most magazines are printed this way.

one-shot—publication produced only one time.

one-time rate—charge for a single ad insertion (open rate).

on-sale date—when single copies of an issue are put on sale.

opacity—in paper, the degree of being opaque (without show-through).

operating statement—in accounting, one that shows the revenue and expenses of an operation on the accrual basis over a period of time.

opportunity bonus—arbitrary bonus give on the spot to an employee who has done something particularly helpful. Not often used, but can be a great morale builder if done right.

optical character reader (OCR)—in mail, machine that interprets address and sprays ZIP code on the piece.

opt-in and opt-out lists—opt-in means you have agreed to get mail; opt-out, that you have not specifically asked to be removed.

options—for employees to purchase stock and get a piece of the action.

order regulation—in single copy sales, the 200 or so major titles where detailed records used to be kept about draw, sales, etc.

organization chart—diagram showing the personnel or parts of a company and their reporting relationships. Very difficult to keep up to date—or to reflect how things actually operate.

outlets—retail stores where magazines and other items are sold.

outsert—advertising material outside the covers of a publication. Wraparound.

overhead—costs not specifically associated with basic production, editing, etc. of a magazine, such as rent.

overlay—superimposition in graphics. Also in subscriptions, overlaying direct mail results with other information to improve results.

override—commission to a sales manager or other supervisor based on the sales of the those who report to him.

overrun—copies printed above the number specified.

ownership statement—every publication with periodical mailing privileges must print this once a year, giving ownership information and the number of copies printed and sold. It is the only public source of newsstand returns.

package—elements in a mailing,

page makeup—assembly of all the elements on a page.

page proof—exact copy of a page as it will look when printed.

page rate—cost of a full page black and white ad one time.

paid circulation—circulation which is paid through single copy sales or subscriptions.

paid during service (PDS)—subscription agents who sell subscriptions of many publishers either door-to-door or by telephone, collecting on the installment basis, usually during the first few months.

paid on scan (POS)—in retail sales of single copies, determining the amount of sales and payment for them based on scanning at the check-out. Not yet often used.

pallet—portable platforms for storing or moving objects. Publishers use them in printing and in delivering copies to the Postal Service to reduce costs.

pamphlet—an unbound booklet or other printed work. Not a magazine.

paper merchants—brokers between paper manufacturers and buyers.

partnership marketing—a relatively new approach in obtaining circulation in conjunction with outside organizations wanting to reach readers.

pass-along—readership of magazines beyond the initial buyer. Some (in flight) have lots; others, very little. Helps in selling ads.

pasted-up dummy—one way the look of a proposed magazine can be presented. Does not look or feel like a magazine. There are better ways.

pay-up—percentage of credit subscribers who pay. Very important because a good gross response is not meaningful until you know how many paid.

PDF (Portable Document Format)—software making it simple to duplicate the fonts, etc. of a printed piece.

perfect binding—affixing the pages to the spine with glue rather than staples.

perfecting press—one that prints both sides of the paper at the same time.

performance units—units used in some incentive programs to measure the amount of the incentive.

periodical—class of mail consisting of newspapers, magazines and other publications. Formerly known as Second Class.

per inquiry (p.i.)—payment for advertising based on the number of inquiries the advertiser receives.

per order (PO)—payment for advertising based on the number of orders the advertiser receives.

per-pocket fees—in single copy sales, an extra fee paid for checkout display.

personalized—the practice of personalizing direct mail through the use of computers.

phantom stock—used in incentive programs, phantom stock, with all the characteristics of real stock, but without actual ownership, is given.

pica—typographical unit of measure, expressed in points. One pica is 12 points; one-sixth of an inch.

picture editor—finds and chooses pictures for editorial.

piece—article, essay or other literary or artistic work.

pilot issue—printed issue developed before actually going into business for use in raising money and in other ways.

pink sheet—un-audited circulation figures provided by magazines to the audit companies and widely distributed..

point of purchase advertising (POP)—displays, signs and other materials to identify and promote products at the retail point of sale.

point of purchase scanning—electronically reading data imprinted on products using the Universal Product Code.

Pollard-Alling—a method of keeping mailing lists on stencils before the advent of the computer. Very picturesque because the stencils were connected like a chain and flew all around the circulation department.

poly-bag—polyethelene bag containing a magazine and outserts.

pooled shipments—shipping copies of different magazines together from a printer to various postal entry points to take advantage of lower postal rates

portable document format (PDF)—one of the new methods of transmitting material to the printer.

position—location in the magazine asked for by advertisers. Some prime positions, such as covers, cost more.

positioning—creation of a distinct identity, image or concept for a magazine. See chapter 35, "Positioning."

positive aspects of magazines—see chapter 28, "Raising Money."

Postal Service—an independent agency of the Federal government which delivers the mail.

pound mark—#, which designates the weight of paper.

preferred position—choice ad location subject to an extra price.

prematures—in single copy sales, copies of magazines delivered to retail stores and returned without ever being put on the newsstand for sale.

premium—in direct marketing, something in addition to the magazine offered for subscribing, or for paying for a subscription. They vary from reprints from the magazine to pens, calendars, and other items with no connection.

pre-print—printing an ad before publication for earlier publicity.

presort—preparing mail by ZIP or other ways to bypass some postal operations. Reduces postal rate.

press run—total copies of a magazine printed.

price—in direct marketing, the price of a subscription as opposed to the offer.

price-earnings multiple—multiple the price of a public stock is of its earnings.

price elasticity—extent to which the price of a product or service can be changed in relation to its sales. (price sensitivity)

primary audience—readers in a household to which a magazine is sent.

printer—firm involved in printing. There are many of varying sizes and types.

printing broker—intermediary between the printer and the publisher. Most publishers do not use them, but in some cases they can be helpful.

printing forms—the way a magazine is laid out for the most economical printing.

print media—newspapers, magazines and other printed media. Note that there is nothing that dictates that these can only be transmitted in this way. If some other method will serve as well, a magazine will still be a magazine.

print order—number of copies of an issue ordered. A good printing contract will allow the printer an over-run of a certain percentage, but never an under-run.

private placement memorandum—legal document used in raising money. Usually includes all the reasons one should not invest along with a description of the situation.

production—the actual making of the magazine.

production director—in charge of production.

profit center—operation expected to be profitable. Each magazine is a profit center, while the accounting department is not.

profits—the excess of income over expenses on the accrual basis.

profit sharing—a method of sharing profits with employees, often made more attractive by the income tax laws.

program related investments—a method by which a foundation is able to invest in ventures that may become profit-making. Little known, even in the foundation world.

projection—forecast of the expected results for any operation.

promotion—furtherance of sales through advertising, public relations, and the like.

promotion allowance—subsidy provided by a producer to a seller to promote or advertise the sale of a product or service.

promotion copies—those sent to prospective advertisers and their agencies.

promotion director—advertising—in charge of promotion to help the sale of advertising.

promotion director—circulation—same for circulation.

proof—an inked impression of material to be printed to check accuracy and quality.

psychographics—study of social class, lifestyle, and personality characteristics of individuals and groups vs demographics. Often accurate in predicting behavior. Used by magazines in selling ads.

public companies—those whose stock is traded publicly.

public relations—activities intended to analyze, adjust to, influence, and direct the opinion of any group.

public service advertising—provided at no charge to not-for-profit organizations.

publicity—public relations technique in which information from an outside source is used by the media.

publisher—person or company whose business is publishing. Also the chief executive at a magazine. Sometimes the title is bestowed on the advertising director although he may not be the CEO.

publisher's page—often used to explain the contents of the issue, or telling something about the authors. Possibly a wasted page.

publisher's statement—circulation statistics filed twice a year with the audit bureaus (pink sheets). Sometimes can also publish other interim statements.

publishing economics—what makes for a profitable magazine. Not always understood because of the three interdependent revenue streams.

pulp magazine—printed on groundwood or other cheap paper and designed for a less sophisticated audience.

push money—incentive to salespeople for selling certain products. Spiff money.

qualification form—used to qualify a controlled circulation subscriber.

qualified distribution—to those who meet certain requirements, usually in business magazines. Can be paid or free.

qualitative research—subjective research, such as focus groups.

quantitative research—based on statistical differences, such as polling and sampling.

quantity discount—price allowance for volume of advertising in a limited period.

Quark—one of the leading desktop publishing programs.

questionnaires—often used in market research.

quota—sales assignment or goal, usually in selling ads.

rack—in retail stores, usually by the check-out, containing magazines. The magazines involved often pay for the racks.

ragged—unjustified margin where type is not flush with or extended to the full width of the line. Can be ragged right or left or both. Often jarring for the reader.

raising money—really the most difficult part of starting a magazine.

random sampling—in research, where each unit has an equal chance of inclusion.

rate base—average circulation a magazine expects over a period. Not necessarily a guarantee.

rate card—list of the prices for various size, frequency, and positions of ads, along with any conditions the magazine may have. Some get very complicated. In recent periods the rates are seldom strictly adhered to.

reach and frequency—things advertisers want. Reach concerns the size of the audience; frequency, how often published.

readability—capable of being understood easily.

reader service cards—placed in magazines making it easy to contact advertisers. (bingo cards)

readership—facts about the number who read an issue, amount of time spent, and which pages are read.

readership research—highly sophisticated research used by editors and to attract ads.

rebate—refund of ad payment when less space is used than originally charged for. Also for reduced circulation.

recall testing—method of judging effectiveness of ads by determining what is recalled at some period after it was read.

recycled paper—waste paper that has been reprocessed, usually called that if the paper contains a certain percentage of recycled paper. In demand, but more expensive and not universally available.

red tag publication—those identified with a red tag to expedite mail delivery, usually dailies or weeklies.

regional edition—distributed only to a certain area. For advertisers who want to reach only certain audiences, who want to test results of different ads, or who do not want to pay for the entire issue.

registration—in printing, the process of combining images and exactly matching their position. In color printing, the exact imposition of successive colors.

regression analysis—in statistics, an estimation technique.

regular rate—periodicals that pay the regular postal rather than the non-profit rate.

remit rate—percentage of the price of a subscription remitted to the publisher by agents.

remnant space—unsold ad space, usually in regional or demographic editions, sold at a reduced price.

renewal—any subscription that has been renewed. Usually used only for those after the first one, called a conversion.

renewal at birth (RAB)—asking subscribers to extend their subs when they first subscribe. Helps cash flow.

renewal rates—important to develop for each source of subs.

renewal series—series of letters to subscribers asking them to renew. Can run to a dozen pieces, but usually is 5 to 7.

reprints—of articles or ads. Sometimes an additional revenue source.

requested—Periodical Rate postage is only available to periodicals which are 50% paid or requested by the recipient.

research—careful study into reader attributes and attitudes. The magazine business is probably the most researched business in the world. Best if conducted by well-known independent outside firms.

response rate—percentage of returns from a mailing for subscriptions or research.

retail display allowance (RDA)—in single copy sales, an amount, usually 10% of the cover price, paid a retailer for giving a magazine good display. Not that simple—see chapter 47, "Single Copy Sales."

retailer—one who sells single copies and other goods to the final consumer.

retreat—group withdrawal for study. Originally for religious groups. Now often used in business for rethinking problems, renewing enthusiasm, and creating teamwork. Good thing to do every so often.

return on investment—method of measuring what an investor will get back. Various ways of calculating are used, so be sure you and the investor understand each other.

return postage—in subscriptions, the cost of having business reply cards or envelopes returned by the Postal Service. The more the better.

return privilege—in direct marketing, customers often have the opportunity of returning the merchandise at no cost.

returns—in single copy sales, the number of copies sent to retailers which were not sold. Rarely are the copies actually returned to the publisher, although this can be done (expensive). The wholesalers shred them and sell the waste paper.

revenue stream—activity that produces revenue for the publisher. Magazines are different from most businesses because they have three or more in one product. Makes planning difficult, but more chances for profits.

reverse type—usually the text is printed on the paper. In reverse type the paper shows through as the text and the rest is in black or some color. Very hard to read.

rigged lists—in list rental, the unethical practice of supplying particularly responsive portions of a list for a test with the hope that the entire list will be used later.

rights—legal claim or title for the use of copyrighted material.

risk/reward ratio—shows an investor what his investment will be worth if the project succeeds. Usually expressed as so many times his investment.

rollout—movement of a product into new markets after testing. Used in both single copy sales and subscriptions.

rotary press—with a rotating cylinder to which curved plates are attached over which a continuous roll of paper passes at very fast speeds.

rotating controlled—controlled circulation magazines, in an effort to obtain enough people requesting subscriptions, might send three issues to one group, then three to another, etc.

rotogravure—See *gravure.*

run-around—type area fitting around a picture or other design element.

run of book (ROB)—ad position anywhere within a magazine, not a preferred position.

run-over—piece continued on another column or page.

S corporation—special class of corporation that has the tax characteristics of a partnership. See Chapter 27—Raising Money. Has restrictions on stockholding.

saddle stitch—fastening of signatures with wire through their center folds.

sales compensation plan—that used to compensate ad sales people. See chapter 38, "Compensating Salespeople."

sampling—statistical procedure for selecting a representative group of people for testing or other market research. Also attempt to recruit new subscribers by offering one or more free issues.

sandlot TV—referring to the fact that there is no inexpensive TV because of the production costs involved.

sans serif—typeface without the fine lines or decorative cross-lines at the ends of the main strokes of a letter. Harder to read, probably because we are used to serifs.

schizophrenia—disease from which magazines can suffer when the ad and circulation people are selling a magazine which differs from the one the editors are producing.

school plan agents—sell subscriptions through kids and classrooms.

scratch and sniff—ads conveying a scent released by scratching the paper. Not always appreciated by readers.

second class—class of Postal Service for periodicals, now called Periodical Class.

sectional center facility—mail processing hub of the Postal Service servicing the area of the first three digits of the ZIP code.

seed—in direct marketing, the insertion of decoy names in a mailing list to see how they are handled.

seed money—in raising capital, the money needed to get a project started and to test its viability. It is the money at the highest risk

see-through—visibility of printed matter from one side of a sheet to the other.

selective binding—magazine with material bound in for specific groups of readers.

self-cover—cover using the same paper as the inside.

self-mailer—direct mail with no need for a return envelope, such as a double postcard.

sensitivity analysis—systematic approach to making projections whereby each major assumption is changed one at a time. See chapter 57, "Use of Computer Models".

serial rights—permission to publish copyrighted material in a periodical.

serif—type with a short thin line projecting above and below the main strokes of letters—the kind we were taught to read in school.

service standard—delivery standards of the Postal Service for different classes of mail. Sometimes not met.

Seven Sisters—The seven big circulation women's service magazines—*Better Homes, Family Circle, Good Housekeeping, Ladies Home Journal, McCall's, Redbook,* and *Woman's Day*. No longer as important as they once were.

share-of-market—percentage of any category in ad pages and dollars.

sheet fed—printing on separate sheets of paper rather than rolls.

shelf extender—tray-like extension in a retail store. Can put magazines in them.

shelf life—sales life of a retail product. Because of their on and off sale dates, magazines have a very short shelf life.

shopper—a penny-saver or free-circulation newspaper, mostly ads.

short rate—additional cost of ad program that did not meet its anticipated discount.

short-term subscription—less than a year.

shotgun—a scattered or dispersed sales campaign versus a targeted rifle shot. Magazines offer the latter.

shrinkage—loss of items due to natural causes or pilfering. Happens with popular magazines in single copy sales.

sidebar—item inserted within, adjacent to or following a related article.

side-stitch—binding on the side near the spine. Makes a spread hard to read.

signature—section of a magazine printed from a large folded sheet of paper.

single copy system—system which has evolved for selling single copies of magazines. See chapter 47, "Single Copies."

single copy sales—sales of magazines at newsstands and other retail outlets.

single subject issue—one devoted to just one subject. May be useful at times, but not as a steady diet because it violates the basic idea of a magazine—to give a reader variety.

skimming—in single copy sales, the practice of wholesalers of not sending copies of a magazine to retailers, but simply shredding them.

slack time—when a company is not busy. In dealing with a printer you might get better service and prices by using his slack time rather than when he is busy.

Small Business Administration (SBA)—arm of the Federal government that was set up to provide capital to smaller businesses.

Small Business Investment Company (SBIC)—venture capital company set up to take advantage of funds that it can obtain from the Small Business Administration in addition to those it invests itself.

soft offer—in selling subscriptions, one that requires very little commitment from the subscriber. The softest might be one which offers to send twelve issues of a magazine before billing and gives the subscriber the option of writing cancel on the bill and owing nothing.

source—channel of sale that produced a subscription.

source evaluation—study of subscriptions, their conversions and renewals by source. See chapter 47, "The Confusing Single Copy Sales Situation."

spam—in e-mail, unsolicited advertising mail.

special-interest publication—magazine with a particular theme or appeal as opposed to a general interest magazine. The vast majority of magazines are special interest.

speedbar—an editorial call-out luring readers into reading an article.

Speedomat—stencil plate system used for subscription fulfillment before the computer age.

spine—backbone of a magazine.

spin-off—magazine or other venture based to some extent on an existing magazine.

split commission—in advertising, when the commission for the sale of a page is split between two or more people. For instance, when the advertiser is in one location and its agency in another.

split fountain—in printing, a method by which different colors can be put on different pages without the expense of having to run 4-color throughout the form.

split run—ad in different incarnations in various copies. Used for testing purposes.

split the territory—done when a salesperson is not able to service all the advertisers in a territory. Must be done delicately.

sponsored subscriptions—obtained through not-for-profit organizations with the publisher donating a portion of the price to the organization.

spread—text or an ad carried on two facing pages.

stacked ads—arrangement of small ads on the page, such as restaurants.

staff-written—magazine, or article written in house rather than by an outside author.

Standard Industrial Classification (SIC)—numerical code often used by business magazines in classifying recipients.

standby space—ad space available at a reduced rate, but with no commitment about when or where an ad will appear.

standard mail—advertising mail formerly known as third class.

standard size—for a magazine, about 8" x 10 1/2" or slightly smaller.

startup—a new magazine.

standing ad—one that runs in several successive issues.

statement stuffer—subscription offer in a customer's bill.

stochastic screening—technique to improve color quality, particularly with more than four primary colors, in which the distance between the centers of the halftone dots varies.

stock—paper used in a magazine. Also evidence of ownership in a corporation.

stock options—options to buy stock in a company in the future when it may be valuable.

stop the press—command to be avoided, but sometimes needed because of late information or detection of errors. Very expensive.

straight commission—compensating ad salespeople simply with a commission.

straight salary—compensating ad salespeople simply with a salary.

stringer—correspondent not on the staff, often used in foreign or other geographic areas.

structuring the deal—designing a deal in a startup, purchase, or sale of a business taking advantage of all the legal and tax maneuvers to reach the optimum result.

stuffer—advertising piece inserted in newspapers, merchandise packages, billing envelopes or other material. Often used in selling subscriptions.

subhead—secondary headline below the main headline.

subject matter—what an editorial piece or a magazine is all about.

subscriber—one who has contracted with a publisher for the purchase and delivery of copies of a magazine.

subscription—purchase of a magazine for a specified period.

subscription agent—independent organization selling subscriptions for magazines.

subscription fulfillment—all the activities having to do with receiving, keeping track of, collecting for, and sending copies of a magazine to a subscriber.

subscription price—price a subscription is sold for. There is usually a published price which is heavily discounted, often in many different ways.

subscription promotion—any of many devices used to sell subscriptions.

subscription source—method by which a subscription is sold by a publisher.

Sunday supplement—special section included with a Sunday newspaper.

super-calendared—paper that is highly smoothed and polished, but not coated.

supplier—independent organization supplying materials or services to a publisher.

supply train management—current management fad to provide just in time inventory.

sweepstakes—lottery in which winners are randomly selected. Until recently extensively used in selling magazine subscriptions.

SWOP color standards—in printing, standards which have been adopted by the industry.

syndicated research—survey sold to several media customers giving advertisers comparative data for various magazines or other media.

synergism—in mergers, etc. where 2 + 2 = 5. Eternally desired, very rarely achieved.

tabloid—magazine larger than standard size, smaller than standard newspaper size, usually 14 1/4" x 10 1/4".

takeaway—subscription blank removed from a pad in a car card or point of purchase display (take-ones).

tax shelter—method by which an investor can reduce the cost of his investment through the use of provisions of the Internal Revenue Code. Not as good now as they once were for magazines.

tear-sheet—page from a magazine. Often used as proof of printing of an ad.

telemarketing—selling via the telephone. Used in selling ads—and often in selling renewals of subscriptions.

tell-all copy—giving all information needed for making a purchase decision, usually used by business magazines.

territory—in ad sales, geographic areas or categories of advertisers assigned to a specific salesperson.

test mailing—mailing to test the response of potential subscribers to different copy approaches, prices, offers, and lists.

test mailing grid—description, in the form of a table, of the parts of a test mailing.

text—editorial material, as differentiated from ads or artwork.

third class mail—printed matter and merchandise under a pound, including most of the bulk direct mail. Now known as Standard Mail.

thought transference—communications without the use of any media.

till forbid—instruction to continue a subscription or other order until notified to the contrary. Until recently not very often used for subscriptions, but now very popular, but under the better title of "continuous service."

time discount—given for ad frequency or regularity vs quantity discount.

tint block—block of color used to highlight part of an article. Often overdone and renders the text unreadable.

tip-in—item glued to a printed piece, sometimes within a magazine's pages.

token—in direct marketing, a stamp, tear-off piece, or other device the customer places on an order card. Often helps response.

tonnage—a very big audience—makes advertisers happy.

trade advertising—to those in a particular trade or business.

trade out—exchange of ad space and/or time. Barter.

trade press—publications that deal with specific industries; the business press.

trade show—commercial exhibition in a specific industry. Many are operated by business magazines.

trademark—symbol, logo, word, etc. legally registered for exclusive use.

the trades—business publications in a specific field.

traffic—production activities that keep work moving on schedule. Also the activities having to do with the movement of copies of the magazine to the proper places at the proper times.

trim size—dimensions of a magazine after trimming.

twin lists—in direct marketing, those so alike that the response will be about the same.

typeface—design of the type being used.

typeset—to set in type.

umbrella magazine—one covering an entire industry. There often are others devoted to specific parts of large industries.

unaided recall—in research, ability of a reader to remember the name of an advertiser without prompting.

undercapitalized—without enough money to carry on.

unearned discount—taken by an advertiser who has not met the terms of the publisher.

unit audit—for business magazines, audit of number of plants, units, establishments, etc. served by a magazine.

Universal Product Code (UPC)—bar code on products used by retailers.

universe—entire potential market for a magazine. Also total population from which a sample is drawn for research.

unpaid copies—free circulation or distribution that is inadequate to qualify as paid.

unpaid distribution—term used by audit bureaus for rotated, show, promotion, etc. copies.

updating cycle—in subscription fulfillment, the periods when the file is updated. Some are continuous, but most are weekly or biweekly.

value—fair market value, in this case usually of a magazine or company.

value added—currently popular in denoting things besides ad space offered to advertisers without cost, such as editorial support, research, merchandising, etc.

venture—speculative business enterprise.

venture firms—those specifically organized to invest in new ventures.

vertical publication—those within an industry, as differentiated from horizontal, covering all of an industry.

waiting room agents—selling subscriptions to doctor and other waiting room areas.

warrant—instrument issued by a corporation giving the holder the right to purchase stock at a stated price prior to a stipulated date, or at any future time.

web offset—process using the offset method of printing and a web press. Most magazines today are printed with these presses.

web press—with continuous paper rather than sheets.

white mail—subscriptions where people use their own envelopes and the promotion source is unknown. Named this way because it is presumed Aunt Emma sent them in without using the publisher's usual forms.

white space—unprinted area in a publication or ad.

wholesaler—in the single copy system, those which physically handle the distribution of copies to retailers. They also engage in marketing and other in-store service.

widow—less than half a typeset line. Some publishers abhor them.

windfall—unexpected or sudden gain or advantage.

work-sharing—in the postal area, efforts publishers make to ease the burden for the Postal Service. For instance, sorting mail by carrier route. In some cases discounts are offered for this.

wraparound—promotional band around a magazine.

wrapper—paper or other matter that partially or fully covers the magazine.

WYSIWYG (wizziwig)—in computers, what you see is what you get.

yellow page research—use of very obvious source for research rather than the more exotic and time-consuming methods. Can often be used with magazines because facts have been researched by other magazines.

zero-based planning—when all aspects are considered anew. Not easy.

zine—special interest magazine generally produced by amateurs on the Web.

ZIP code—you never knew it stood for Zoning Improvement Plan when introduced in 1963.

zones—in Postal terms there are eight geographic zones with different rates for some classes of mail, including the advertising portion of periodical mail.

Index